NAVIGATING THE INTERNET WITH AMERICA ONLINE

Wes Tatters

sams
net

201 West 103rd Street
Indianapolis, Indiana 46290

This book is dedicated to my Grandparents.

Copyright © 1995 by Sams.net Publishing

FIRST EDITION

International Standard Book Number: 0-672-30763-4

Library of Congress Catalog Card Number: 95-68850

98 97   4 3

Interpretation of the printing code: the rightmost double-digit number is the year of the book's printing; the rightmost single-digit, the number of the book's printing. For example, a printing code of 95-1 shows that the first printing of the book occurred in 1995.

Composed in AGaramond and MCPdigital by Macmillan Computer Publishing

Printed in the United States of America

Trademarks

President, Sams Publishing *Richard K. Swadley*

Publisher, Sams.net Publishing *George Bond*

Managing Editor *Cindy Morrow*

Marketing Manager *John Pierce*

Acquisitions Editor
Mark Taber

Development Editor
Fran Hatton

Production Editor
Johnna VanHoose

Software Specialist
Merle Newlon

Editorial and Graphics Coordinator
Bill Whitmer

Editorial Assistant
Carol Ackerman

Technical Reviewer
Glenn Fincher

Cover Designer
Tim Amrhein

Book Designer
Alyssa Yesh

Director of Production and Manufacturing
Jeff Valler

Manufacturing Coordinator
Paul Gilchrist

Production Analyst
Mary Beth Wakefield

Team Supervisor
Brad Chinn

Graphics Image Specialists
Brad Dixon, Clint Lahnen, Craig Small, Dennis Sheehan, Jason Hand, Jeff Yesh, Laura Robbins, Ryan Oldfather, Sonja Hart, Todd Wente

Production
Georgiana Briggs, Michael Brumitt, Charlotte Clapp, Bront Davis, Mike Dietsch, Tim Griffin, Kevin Laseau, Paula Lowell, Steph Mineart, Casey Price, Nancy Price, Brian-Kent Proffitt, Susan Springer, Mark Walchle, Colleen Williams

OVERVIEW

CONTENTS

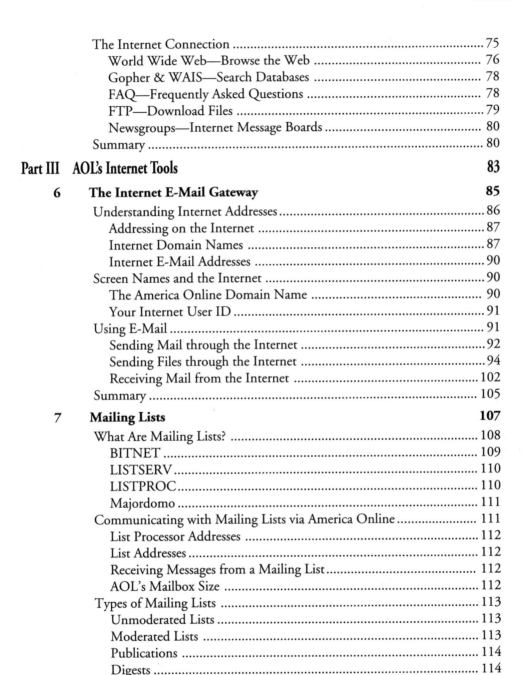

ACKNOWLEDGMENTS

Where I have directly quoted from additional sources throughout this book, you will find that I have attributed the quote to the appropriate person. However, because much of the information in this book comes from personal knowledge gained over a period of years, it has been impossible to directly attribute all sources of information.

To this end I would like to express personally my appreciation to all of the people I have corresponded with in the past few years, many of whom have provided me with valuable insights into the workings of the Internet and more recently, America Online as well. Special thanks also goes to Kathy Johnson and the staff at America Online.

For his assistance with the "History of the Internet" section by producing the H'obbes' Internet Timeline, thanks goes to Robert H'obbes' Zakon. Thanks also to author Bruce Sterling for his "Short History of the Internet," and to Bernard Aboba for his interview with Vinton Cert— "How the Internet Came to Be." In addition, thanks to the Internet Society for the graphics and data they make so readily available.

To Gene Steinberg for *Special Edition Using America Online* published by Que, and to Henry Hardy, whose Masters thesis "The History of the Net" prompted me to begin my own exploration of the Internet's history and whose writings are a valuable contribution to the historical understanding of the Internet today, I also give thanks.

I would also like to acknowledge the work of the many hundreds of people responsible for the creation and collation of the thousands of Request for Comment, For Your Information, and Standards documents maintained by InterNIC, the historical and informational articles compiled by the Internet Society, and the Frequently Asked Questions documents produced so regularly and tirelessly by people whose sole interest is in promoting and developing the Internet.

And finally, thank you to all the people who helped make this book a reality:

- My girlfriend, Cait Spreadborough, for reading and editing the original manuscript.
- Glenn T. Fincher's work in checking the many sites, services, and technical aspects of this book.
- The staff at Sams who helped guide this project to its completion, and especially Mark Taber, Fran Hatton, and Johnna VanHoose.

ABOUT THE AUTHOR

Wes Tatters has worked in the computer industry since 1984 as a computer programmer and systems designer. During this time he worked on many computer platforms using a variety of computer languages and communications tools. Currently, he operates a video production company while writing regular articles for a number of Australian computer magazines and the Internet Daily News at `http://tvp.com/`. These articles deal with a diverse range of topics including the Internet, CompuServe, Amiga Computers, Windows 95, and database technology. He is also the author of *Navigating the Internet with CompuServe*, by Sams.net, and can be reached on the Internet at `wtatters@world.net` or `taketwo@webcom.com`.

INTRODUCTION

It seems that hardly a day goes by without some mention of the Information Superhighway or the Internet in newspapers and on television. Over the past few years, the Internet has begun to permeate many aspects of day-to-day life, moving what was once a system fixed staunchly in the world of scientists and academics to the forefront of public interest and accessibility.

In response to this growth in public interest, a number of previously closed communications services have begun to open their doors to the Internet and the multitude of new capabilities it provides. Of these services, one company stands out from the rest due to the close integration of its existing services with the new features offered by the Internet. This online service is America Online.

Since beginning the implementation of Internet support in 1992, with the opening of an e-mail gateway, America Online has spent a considerable amount of effort ensuring that the Internet services it provides are as easy to use as the standard forums, channels, and message boards found on America Online itself.

For America Online members, this now means that accessing the Internet is no more difficult than using AOL, which over the years has gained so many compliments. Today you can take advantage of FTP, Usenet newsgroups, e-mail, Gopher, WAIS, and even the World Wide Web, without any of the difficulties so often associated with doing so in the past.

> The term AOL is used throughout this book when referring to the software that is used to navigate around America Online.

But America Online has not yet finished its move onto the Internet. Although AOL gives America Online users easy access to the Internet, for some users this isn't enough. As a result, in June 1995, America Online announced its intention to create a dedicated TCP/IP-based Internet service based on the same principals that have always driven its AOL developments. The end result of these plans will be an Internet service that is as easy to use as AOL and as simple to connect to as well.

The flagship for this new service is a program called GNNWorks, which was developed by America Online's newly formed Internet Services company. GNNWorks is one of the first truly integrated TCP/IP connectivity tools offering access to e-mail, Gopher, the World Wide Web, and IRC, all from a single application.

What This Book is All About

This book has been designed to guide you step by step through the various new Internet services America Online now provides. To do this, I have divided the book into six separate parts that deal with various aspects of the Internet and America Online's Internet Service:

◆ Part I—America Online and the Internet

This section takes a look at the history of the Internet and examines the path taken by America Online as it has moved from a dedicated communications service to a full Internet service provider.

◆ Part II—Getting Started on the Internet

To give you a better understanding of the new capabilities the Internet brings to America Online, this section first looks at the range of services available on the Internet. Then, in the last two chapters, you will find information dealing with the installation of AOL and its new World Wide Web browser, followed by exploration of the basic services offered by the AOL.

◆ Part III—AOL's Internet Tools

Once you have an understanding of the concepts behind the Internet, this section expands on this knowledge by examining in detail many of the popular Internet services that can now be accessed using AOL. These include e-mail, mailing lists, FTP, Usenet newsgroups, and Winsock-based client applications.

◆ Part IV—The Internet Navigators

Like AOL itself, which allows you to navigate your way around America Online, the World Wide Web and its predecessor, Gopher, provide you with the best method of navigating the Internet. In this section, you learn about the World Wide Web and Gopher services provided by America Online.

◆ Part V—Where to Now?

The Internet is not simply composed of software tools and communications services. Instead, it is best considered as an electronic world. To expand on this concept, in this section of the book you find examples of many of the different places you can visit on the Internet and a discussion of some of the ways that you can locate new information.

This section also examines some of the many ways America Online is integrating its existing services with the Internet.

◆ Part VI—The Next Step

As a special added bonus, this final section takes a look at GNNWorks and the new TCP/IP-based Internet service currently being beta tested by America Online.

Then in the final chapter, you find a brief discussion of the future of the Internet and a list of some additional places to visit.

◆ Appendixes

Appendix A–Information about the availability of alternate Internet service providers.

Appendix B–Logging on to America Online via the Internet using Telnet.

Appendix C–A short discussion of many popular Winsock client applications available for downloading from America Online and the Internet.

Appendix D–A discussion of software-based compression and encryption tools such as Wincode and PGP.

Appendix E–This appendix looks at the differences between the Macintosh and Windows versions of America Online.

AOL for Windows and AOL for the Apple Macintosh

America Online currently provides users of both the Apple Macintosh and Microsoft Windows with a version of the AOL software suitable for their separate environments.

Unfortunately, however, because the current versions of each were released some time apart, there are a few differences in the two programs that affect their operation. In Appendix E, you will find a discussion of the most significant differences between the two current versions.

Having said that, because the Windows-based version is the later of the two current releases, throughout this book you will find that this version has been used for most examples and screen shots. The reason this has been done is based on the fact that America Online will soon release an updated version for the Apple Macintosh that includes all the newer features. In addition, where a feature is not currently supported on the Macintosh version or is implemented in a different way, you will find that a note box has been included to explain the differences.

Some Windows users will also possibly notice differences between the appearance of figures shown in this book and those displayed on their screens. The reason for this is that all the Windows-based screen shots were taken on a computer running Windows 95. If you are using an earlier version of Windows, 3.11 for example, the layout of some screen elements will be slightly different.

All the screen shots displayed in this book represent the most up-to-date information available at the time of publishing. However, because both the Internet and America Online itself are in a continual state of change, occasionally you will encounter images that differ slightly from those shown in this book.

Conventions and Common Representations

Throughout this book I have adopted a few standard conventions to assist you in recognizing important pieces of information. These include special highlighting methods for information displayed by your computer and for information you need to type in yourself.

Typographical conventions used in this book.

Typeface	*Meaning*
`Computer Type`	There are a number of Internet addresses, directory paths, and World Wide Web URLs defined throughout this book that are printed in computer type to make them easier to recognize.
`Bold Computer Type`	Text printed in bold computer type represents information you need to type at your keyboard while working with the various programs discussed in this book.
Italic	When you encounter a word printed in italic, this indicates that you are about to examine a new concept and should pay close attention to what is being discussed.
Shortcut Key	Many menus and buttons associated with programs running under Windows support the use of shortcut keys, which allow you to bypass the mouse and instead select them by using a keyboard combination. Where a button or menu mentioned in this book supports the use of a shortcut key, the letter that corresponds to the key is printed in **B**old. To use this shortcut, hold down the Alt key on your keyboard and type the letter specified.

Information printed in Note boxes provides you with additional points of interest relating to the topic currently being discussed.

Tips offer additional suggestions about the use of programs and services.

Warning messages are designed to make you aware of important issues that may affect your use of America Online or the Internet in general.

Where you see a CD icon displayed in the margin next to a paragraph, this indicates that the file mentioned in this paragraph is included on the CD-ROM that accompanies this book.

The Keyword Window

Apart from the point-and-click hierarchy of navigation windows and menus provided by AOL, there is a very quick way to move from area for area on when using America Online.

Many of the forums, services, and channels available at America Online can be accessed directly using what is known as a keyword. Throughout this book you will find the following representation used to indicate these words: Keyword: **www**, where **www** indicates the actual keyword you need to use.

To jump to a service by using its keyword, hold down the Control key and type the letter "K". For Apple Macintosh users, where the Control key is mentioned (usually in the form Ctrl+[letter]) you need to use the ⌘ key instead. Regardless of which method you use, AOL opens a small window in which you can enter the keyword of the service you want to explore.

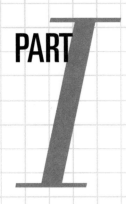

PART I

AMERICA ONLINE AND THE INTERNET

CHAPTER

1

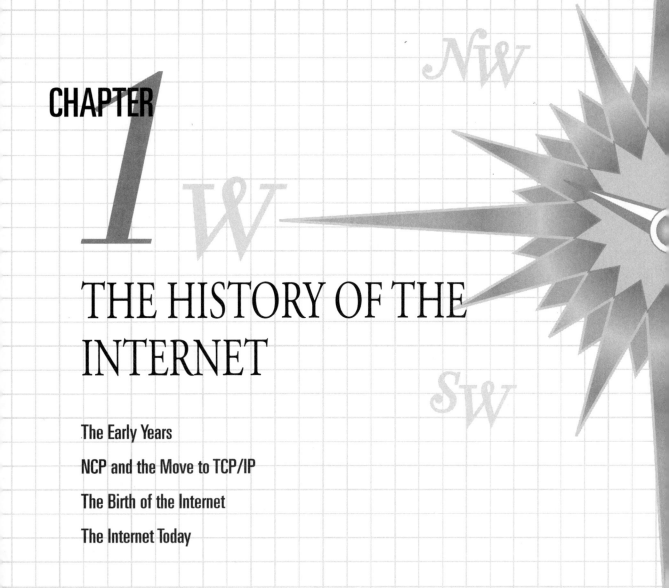

THE HISTORY OF THE INTERNET

Before looking at the powerful Internet-based services America Online now brings to its members, it is important that you first have a basic understanding of what the Internet is all about. No doubt many of you have already encountered terms like the "Information Superhighway" and descriptions of a global computer network. But what is the Internet really all about?

To begin to answer this question, this chapter provides you with a brief overview of the history of the Internet. It examines how the Internet began and how it has evolved into the global computer network it is today. This chapter examines the following topics:

◆ The early years

◆ NCP and the move to TCP/IP

◆ The birth of the Internet

◆ The Internet today

The Early Years

Not long after the first computer was invented, people began to look for ways to share the power these valuable machines offered. As the *switch panels* of early computer giants were replaced by *paper tapes* and *punched cards*, the age of computer communications dawned.

> Before the advent of keyboards or computer monitors—and their early predecessor, the teletype—the only way to communicate with a computer was by toggling banks of switches and by reading combinations of flashing lights. Later, these switches were replaced by punched cards—small cards with holes punched in them to represent the sequence of instructions a computer was to perform. For long instruction sequences, rolls of paper tape were also used. Like the punched cards, paper tapes also had holes punched in them to represent information.

Suddenly people could share information and exchange computer programs, and for a short time everything was good. Nevertheless, progress marches on, and before long, mailing punched cards and paper tapes around the country was deemed unacceptable. As teletypes began to replace punched cards, and computers grew in power, a better alternative was needed: one that could physically connect computers separated by great distances.

Modems and Telephone Lines

After much experimentation, it was decided that telephone lines offered the most viable solution. However, this still left computer developers with a problem. Computers communicate using electronic signals that represent bits of information. Telephones, on the other hand, use sounds as the basis of their communication.

To resolve this problem, the *modem* was invented. This device, an early predecessor of the equipment you probably use now to connect to America Online, converts the electronic signals sent from a computer into a series of audible tones. These tones can be easily transmitted over a telephone line to a second modem, which converts them back to a form that computers can understand.

The U.S. Government and the RAND Corporation

At around the same time that modems were in the developmental stage, the U.S. government was busying itself with its own research concerns. With the world locked in the grip of the Cold War, the government was concerned that in the event of a nuclear holocaust, America would need a command and control network that could still function despite the loss of any number of cities, states, or bases.

As author Bruce Sterling outlined in his paper titled a "Short History of the Internet," Paul Baran, an employee at the RAND Corporation—America's foremost Cold War think tank— was given the problem, and in 1964, made the RAND proposal public. In the quote that follows, Bruce Sterling explains the basics of the RAND proposal:

> *The principles were simple. The network itself would be assumed to be unreliable at all times. It would be designed from the get-go to transcend its own unreliability. All the nodes in the network would be equal in status to all other nodes, each node with its own authority to originate, pass and receive messages. The messages themselves would be divided into packets, each packet separately addressed. Each packet would begin at some specified source node, and end at some other specified destination node. Each packet would wind its way through the network on an individual basis.*
>
> —Bruce Sterling
> First Published: *The Magazine of Fantasy & Science Fiction*, Feb. 1993

By using a system such as the one described, the computer sending the message doesn't need to concern itself with the path the message needs to take to reach its destination. In fact, if the same message is transmitted twice, it could quite possibly take an entirely different route each time, depending on the condition of the network at the time it was sent.

What made this design so attractive was that regardless of the extent to which the network would be damaged by a nuclear war, while any part of the network was still operating, messages could eventually reach all surviving nodes.

Note

A copy of Bruce Sterling's "Short History of the Internet" is available online at the Internet Society Gopher site. It is well worth the read because it puts into perspective much of the hype currently surrounding the Internet. You can obtain a copy of this paper and one by Vinton Cerf—the past president of the Internet Society—by opening the Gopher service, Keyword: **gopher**, and selecting the Internet Information icon. From there select the Internet Society item, then the Internet item and finally the History item.

The Birth of the ARPANET

In 1969, as a result of numerous presentations and discussions regarding the potential of modem-based communications and RAND's proposed network technology, the U.S. Department of Defense's *Advanced Research Projects Agency (ARPA)* launched an ambitious research project to further explore the possibilities of packet-based networking and the RAND proposal.

One of the main features of this proposed network was the use of *packet switching* as the means of inter-computer communications. Packet switching is the term used to describe the communications process developed to implement the message-packeting concept proposed by the RAND Corporation.

To test the viability of packet switching, ARPA decided to connect four high-speed computers—the supercomputers of their time—using a packet-switched network. This would allow scientists to better explore and develop the emerging communications technology. At the same time, they could also take advantage of this new technology to better share the limited computer resources available at their individual campuses.

Three sites on the west coast—the University of California at Los Angeles, the Stanford Research Institute at Stanford, and the University of California at Santa Barbara—were chosen for the project, with the University of Utah completing the network. This network was named the *ARPANET* after the Advanced Research Projects Agency that sponsored it.

Over the course of the year, the computer hardware and software required to make the network a reality was gradually put into place, with all the effort finally culminating around September 1, 1969. On this day the first of the four packet-switching nodes, or *interface message processors* as they were then known, was delivered from Bolt, Beranek, and Newman, the firm contracted to design them. During the weeks that followed, as the remaining sites took delivery of their interface message processors, the ARPANET was officially born.

The Dawn of E-Mail

Following this somewhat inauspicious start, interest in ARPANET grew slowly. Nevertheless, once the network became stable, and all the bugs were ironed out of NCP—the network communication protocol software that controlled the network—other computing facilities began to take advantage of the technology offered by ARPANET. By 1971 there were 15 operational nodes on the network, connecting 23 independent host computer systems.

Ironically, as is so often the case, the force that seemed to drive the growth of ARPANET was not the opportunity to share computing resources or the availability of remote computing tools that the system's developers had predicted. Instead, the ARPANET had been turned into the world's first electronic postal service. People were using ARPANET to discuss research projects, exchange notes and documents, and eventually just to shoot the breeze. It is fair to say that e-mail took ARPANET by storm. In fact, by the end of 1972, it was accountable for more network traffic than all the other services.

In recent years the Internet has been described by many people as a state of controlled anarchy. On the Internet almost anything goes, there are relatively few controls and just about anyone can connect to it. Much of the reason for the nature of the Internet today can be traced back to the early formative days of ARPANET. While e-mail and many of the other uses people found for ARPANET were frowned upon by the establishment, it became rapidly apparent that there was very little anyone could do to stop this "creative" use of the network.

Coming Out of the Closet

While network usage was booming, ARPA was still concerned that the number of network connections continued to grow too slowly. To encourage even more involvement in ARPANET, it was decided that a public demonstration of the network should be arranged to coincide with the 1972 International Conference on Computer Communications. To stage this event, a packet switch and a terminal was installed in the basement of the Washington Hilton Hotel.

If ever there was a coming-out party for the Internet, this demonstration was it. Over a period of almost a year, plans were made and connections organized to ensure that the demonstration would be a success. Those in attendance were treated to an entirely new communications experience as they watched the terminal in the Hilton hotel connect to an impressive 40 nodes—the largest number of ARPANET connections ever.

To put it mildly, the demonstration was an outstanding success. It impressed even its most persistent skeptics, and as of that day the ARPANET was officially here to stay. Indirectly, this demonstration also opened the way for the launch in 1973 of the first international ARPANET connections with England and Norway.

NCP and the Move to TCP/IP

As the expanding network grew in popularity, ARPA became increasingly interested in the possibility of connecting other networks, including the new satellite and radio packet networks, to the existing ARPANET network. Unfortunately, the Network Control Protocol software (NCP), which until 1982 managed all network communications for ARPANET, relied heavily on the nature of the existing network, and as such was not capable of supporting the new internetworking requirements now being demanded of ARPANET.

To resolve these problems, a new network protocol was needed; one that could encompass all types of computer networks and the growing array of computer hardware that was beginning to appear.

The TCP/IP Protocol

Development of this new protocol, which was to become known as TCP/IP, started in 1973 in the lab of Vinton Cerf, then an assistant professor at Stanford.

> Vinton Cerf, the current president of the Internet Society, is regarded by many as one of the founding fathers of the Internet. If you are interested in exploring the early life of the Internet, "How the Internet Came to Be," his account as told to Bernard Aboba, makes for fascinating reading.
>
> Copies of this paper, along with the Bruce Sterling paper mentioned earlier in this chapter, are available from the Internet Societies Gopher site. Alternatively, you can also download a copy from the Society's FTP server at `ftp://ftp.isoc.org`. The files are located in the `/internet/history` directory.

The name TCP/IP is actually an acronym for two of the major components that comprised the new protocol, namely the Transmission Control Protocol (TCP) and the Internet Protocol (IP).

Unlike NCP, development of TCP/IP was to become a joint effort. Following the publication of a paper entitled, "A Protocol for Packet Network Internetworking," by Vinton Cerf and Robert Kahn, three sites began to work on the project. The first site, naturally, was located at Vinton Cerf's lab, with the second site at Bolt Beranek and Newman, where Robert Kahn had been instrumental in the development of the ARPANET's interface message processors. What made the effort truly international, though, was the third site at University College-London, which also began working on the problem.

As the project progressed, it became obvious to developers that, to ensure the success of TCP/IP as the globally adopted standard for internetwork computing, it had to be freely available. To achieve this ideal, the TCP/IP protocol was released into the public domain, giving any computer developer or operating system designer the right to include TCP/IP communications as a part of their product.

Interestingly, in many eyes, it was this decision that heralded the birth of the Internet and signaled its potential.

> A considerable amount of information dealing with the development of TCP/IP, and indeed many other aspects of the Internet, has been made available online in a collection of documents known as Request for Comments or RFCs. Copies of all these RFCs can be downloaded from `ftp://ftp.internic.net`.

The Birth of the Internet

While many dates, including September 1, 1969, have been put forward as the birthdate of the Internet, it is in fact very difficult to define how or when the Internet as we now know it actually came into being. In many ways the Internet was never born, but more truly evolved from the collection of networks that many today consider its parents.

Certainly the move to TCP/IP was the catalyst, but many other factors, including the availability of cheaper computer hardware and more reliable communications technology, have also been a controlling factor. What TCP/IP did, however, was make the complexities of computer inter-connectivity a considerably less daunting task.

Network of Networks

As TCP/IP grew in popularity and availability, an ever-increasing number of sites began to form links with ARPANET. In fact, suddenly it seemed like anyone who owned a computer system wanted to be a part of ARPANET.

Ironically, while all the new sites were embracing TCP/IP in its entirety, many of the early ARPANET sites were reluctant to make the move. After considerable prompting, it seemed the only option was to force these sites to change. As a result, in what was seen by some as an underhanded ploy, NCP was removed from the ARPANET backbone on January 1, 1983. In effect, they simply turned it off.

Finally, the network of networks had begun, and with it the first true signs of the Internet as we know it today.

Growth Beyond Imagination

With this move the role of ARPANET began to change. No longer was it just a network. Instead it had become the *backbone* of the new Internet, carrying data from machine to machine and network to network.

In communications speak, a backbone is a high-speed communications link that acts as the main connection for individual computers. Instead of wiring each computer to every other computer in a network, each computer is wired only to the backbone. All its communications with every other computer are then carried down this backbone connection.

Note

In the years following the 1983 NCP switch-off, the Internet began to grow far beyond the expectations of even its most broad-minded prophets. According to the Internet host growth data published by the Internet society (see Figure 1.1), the 560 host sites reported in 1983 had grown to include nearly 4 million connected hosts by the end of 1994.

FIGURE 1.1.

The growth of Internet host connections from 1969 to the end of 1994. (Data courtesy of the Internet Society.)

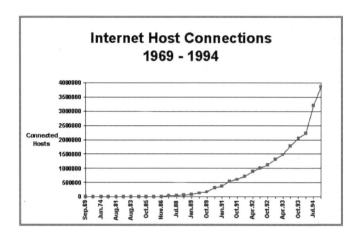

NSFNET

A large part of the Internet's growth can be attributed to the construction of several publicly accessible supercomputing centers by the National Science Foundation (NSF) in 1986.

To connect these centers and provide education and research institutions with direct computer access, the NSF initially planned to use ARPANET. However, ARPANET's minders, fearful of what this extra load would do to their network, decided not to allow ARPANET to be used. As a result, the NSF decided to construct their own backbone, which became known as NSFNET. However, in what was to become yet another irony of the Internet's development, ARPANET eventually opened network connections with NSFNET and thus the supercomputers it joined.

NSFNET brought with it a number of radical new developments that would again change the very nature of the emerging Internet. When the NSF was designing its network, they decided that instead of having individual computers connected to the main NSFNET backbone, as was the practice with ARPANET, only regional networks would be permitted to have a direct connection. Computer sites in each region were to connect to the local network, which in turn would allow them access to NSFNET.

To support this plan, the concept of *service providers* was born. The NSF, not interested in managing the local networks, began to contract these regions to interested organizations—some of whom planned to make a profit by providing access to NSFNET and the Internet, and others who were looking simply to provide network services to their particular community.

Out of this process grew the concept of Internet service providers, and thus, with the creation of NSFNET, the final foundation of the current Internet structure was laid.

The Internet Today

Not wanting to be left behind, many other government and non-government organizations also began forming their own networks.

Before long, networks such as BITNET, the LISTSERV network (see Chapter 7, "Mailing Lists"), and Usenet, the newsgroups service (see Chapter 8, "Usenet Newsgroups") were up and running. In addition, more specialized services, such as NASA's National Science Internet (NSI), the education and research network CSNET, and MILNET, the unclassified military network, which was separated from ARPANET in 1983, also began to service the needs of their communities.

At around the same time, networks were also beginning to appear in other countries, with services such as JANET in the United Kingdom, NORDUNET in Europe, and AARNET setting up an educational network in Australia.

Gateways

Before too long, however, users on many of these new networks began to encounter a problem. If two people wanted to communicate with each other, they had to make sure that they were both connected to the same network. This problem led to absurd situations in which computers in the same building could not communicate with each other because they were connected to different networks.

To alleviate this difficulty, special connections called *gateways* began to appear. These connections formed bridges between two unrelated networks. Once the individual networks were connected through one of these gateways, people on each of the networks were able to communicate as though they were connected to a single system. In fact, in many cases they didn't even need to know that the computer they were communicating with was connected to another network.

The Internet Completed

As an ever-increasing number of networks began to open gateways with each other, the Internet as we know it today was finally formed.

For NSFNET, things were rapidly changing as well. By default, it had become the main backbone of the Internet for the mainland U.S., and in effect the global backbone as well. It had even surpassed and replaced ARPANET, which died a silent death in 1989. Unlike the upset caused by the 1983 switch-off of NCP, the closure of ARPANET occurred with hardly a murmur, as most of the early ARPANET sites had long since moved to NSFNET or to one of the other interconnected networks.

Commercial Interest

As the Internet gained momentum, it did not take commercial interests long to realize the potential power of this new resource. However, because ARPANET and NSFNET both grew out of educational and research projects, they were very dubious about letting commercial users onto their network backbones.

This resulted in a rather difficult situation. Even though many of the NSFNET service providers were willing to have the new commercial networks connected to their regional networks, NSFNET forbade any commercial information from being transmitted across its primary NSFNET backbone.

This resulted in a problem similar to the pre-gateway difficulties discussed earlier. This time, however, it was people and computers on the commercial networks that were unable to communicate with each other. Obviously, this was not an acceptable alternative for commercial users, who could only sit and watch the types of communications possible between NSFNET-approved services.

Out of this impasse between the NSFNET and the commercial networks, a new commercial backbone was formed. In March of 1991, Alternet, CERFnet, and PSInet, three of the largest commercial networks at that time, announced the formation of the Commercial Internet Exchange (CIX). With the introduction of CIX, the commercial community now had the same communications flexibility as its educational and research counterpart.

Managing the Internet

While no one actually owns the Internet, it was realized in the late 1980s that some structures needed to be put in place to ensure the ongoing reliability, integrity, and stability of the network.

Of primary importance was a method of issuing and tracking the IP addresses and domain names assigned to each host computer connected to the Internet. (See Chapter 6, "The Internet E-Mail Gateway," for a full discussion of domain names.) In addition, the creation and maintenance of accurate address and user lists, not unlike the White and Yellow Pages provided by telephone companies, was also flagged for consideration.

To answer these suggestions, the NSF proposed the creation of an Internet Network Information Center (InterNIC). To manage this center, NSF issued tenders for three contracts. The first, awarded to Network Solutions, was for the creation of the Internet Registration service. The second contract, going to AT&T, was for the maintenance of Internet-related databases and directories. The third contract went to General Atomics, who provides and maintains the computer system that houses the Gopher, Web, and FTP sites that form the InterNIC service.

Like most Internet services, information about InterNIC, including the AT&T databases, can be found on the World Wide Web at http://www.internic.net/.

The Internet Society

Despite the Internet's haphazard development, expansion, and near anarchic state of existence, the Internet has flourished and continues to do so. One of the reasons for this success is the willingness, on the part of many people, to take part in working groups and other discussion forums. Over the years, many such meetings have taken place to plan, develop, and guide the Internet.

However, even with all these good intentions, the Internet needed some direction. By the end of 1991, even NSFNET was being swamped by the Internet's astounding growth in popularity. As a result, it was decided that an organization should be created to provide a forum for discussion about the operation and infrastructure of the Internet. This same body would also be responsible for facilitating evolution of the Internet as a global communications network and the promotion of new services and Internet-related developments.

In June of 1992, the Internet Society was officially chartered. At the same time, the Internet Architecture Board and its two major committees, the Internet Engineering Task Force and Internet Research Task Force, were also brought under the control of the new society. Jointly, these bodies now plan and direct the development of the Internet by coordinating the input and efforts of the millions of people who continue to work for a better Internet.

Note

> The Internet Society offers membership to all members of the Internet community. More information about membership and the activities of the society, including online registration, is available from the Internet Society World Wide Web site at `http://www.isoc.org/`. To access this site from AOL, open the Internet Organizations window, Keyword: `internet.org`, and select the ISOC item. Alternatively you can jump straight to the Internet Society WWW page using Keyword: `isoc`.

Toward the Future

With the Internet doubling in size on almost a yearly basis, its future is somewhat blurred. The one thing that is certain, however, is that with nearly every country in the world now connected to the network in one form or another (see Figure 1.2), the Internet is here to stay.

As the Internet expands its reach, it is rapidly changing the way people work, think, and even live. Banks and businesses now use it to conduct business transactions. Students are using it to share classes with children across the world, and even rock and roll bands like the Rolling Stones have fallen into its grasp.

For many people, the Internet is now a part of their everyday lives. As to exactly how it will affect your life—only time will tell.

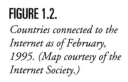

FIGURE 1.2.

Countries connected to the Internet as of February, 1995. (Map courtesy of the Internet Society.)

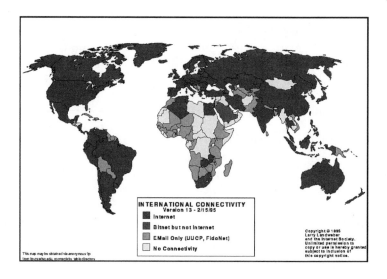

Summary

What started out as a Cold War research tool is now the basis of the most complex global communications system known to man. Even the countries that were the focus of all the Cold War rhetoric are now encompassed by its global net.

For many people, however, its power lies not in the complex interplay of communications networks and computer systems that make it function. Instead, it lies in the ability to use the Internet without the need to understand how any of this technology works.

Whether by design or accident, the Internet now reaches into nearly every aspect of computer communications. While many commercial services such as Prodigy, CompuServe, and America Online long resisted the move to connectivity with the Internet, they are now faced with a simple choice: Connect or be overrun!

The next chapter follows the path that led to the linking of America Online with the Internet. At the same time, it explores some of the key differences between the two systems and introduces the range of new services the Internet offers to America Online members.

CHAPTER 2

THE HISTORY OF AMERICA ONLINE AND ITS CONNECTION TO THE INTERNET

Unlike the Internet, whose origin is grounded firmly in the hallowed halls of education and research institutions, America Online's history is steeped in the commercial communications market. From its inception, America Online was destined to be a saleable commodity, a computer service available to anyone who wished to purchase the resources it provided. And more importantly, it was designed to be a service that anyone could afford and one which was simple to use.

Driven by this strategy, since America Online was first launched, it has grown to become America's leading online computer service. This chapter explores the development of this online service and follows the path that led to America Online's current links with the Internet.

America Online: The Early Years

While government, education, and even businesses were using online computer systems on a regular basis by the middle of the 1980s, for most home or hobby users the prospect of owning a modem was one of those fantasies that made movies like *Wargames* so exciting. For the most part, they were complex items of hardware that required considerable computer knowledge to operate and a decent-sized bank account to afford.

And then, assuming that you had managed to purchase and set up one of these beasts, there was very little that you could actually do with it. If you were lucky enough to live in a part of the country where hobbyists were operating a *bulletin board system (BBS)*, then you were set. But for many people, owning a modem was a bit like the computer equivalent of being the first person on the block to buy an Edsel.

Quantum Computer Services, Inc.

As a result, in 1985, when Quantum Computer Services, Inc. announced to the world that it was going to start up an online computer service for everyone, few people were surprised when the doors weren't knocked down by people rushing to take advantage of the service.

At that time, the only commercial online services with any sort of market acceptance were those such as CompuServe, which had made a name for itself in the business market by providing companies access to services such as Reuters news reports and share prices. But, for the most part, very few home users were actively participating in these services, due to both the costs involved and technical difficulties associated with getting connected.

When Steve Case, Jim Kimey, and Marc Seriff—the co-founders of Quantum—began to examine the potential of the online market, they realized that the general public was not being catered to by existing services. As a result, they decided to set up a service for home users. A service that was easy to use, affordable and…believe it or not, fun!

Commodore International Ltd and Q-Link

In 1985, by far the most popular home computer on the market was the Commodore 64. The IBM PC was still very much a business machine, and the recently released Apple Macintosh, with its predecessor the Apple Lisa, while offering amazing capabilities, were both very much machines that had yet to penetrate the consumer market. Commodore International was at the head of the class with their flagship computer—the C64—outselling all others.

Into this market came Quantum, and in a move unheard of at the time, they formed an alliance with Commodore International. Basically, Quantum set up a national bulletin board system called QuantumLink, or Q-Link for short, which was dedicated to Commodore 64 owners. In return, Commodore agreed to package the Q-Link software and connection information with every computer system they sold.

The Q-Link software was specially designed to make the most of the environment provided by the Commodore 64, one which its users were already comfortable with. By doing this, connecting to Q-Link became a simple exercise. There were no cryptic messages or screen loads of jumbled garbage, just a simple, easy-to-use program that allowed people to enter the world of online communications.

Over the course of the next few years the popularity of the BBS service offered by Quantum grew from strength to strength. But Quantum did not sit back and rest on its laurels either. As new markets began to appear, other alliances and deals were struck with companies such as Apple Computers, Tandy Electronics, and even IBM.

America Goes Online

By the start of 1989, there were over 80,000 people using the various online services offered by QuantumLink. But this increase in popularity was creating problems for QuantumLink. Maintaining separate services for each individual computer platform was placing a considerable load on the company's resources.

At this stage, America Online was not exactly the service offered today, but many of the concepts developed as a part of this system are still a popular part of America Online. While services such as online chat sessions were already gaining popularity, the concept of point and click graphical interfaces was still some way off. At the time, menu-driven interfaces were the best show in town.

Despite this, and in keeping with their early aims, what people got—even at this stage—was a simple to use, and affordable online communications service that suited their needs. Having said that, it did not take long for improved and enhanced interfaces to begin to appear. In 1991, America Online released a DOS-based graphical interface, followed in 1993 by Windows and Macintosh interfaces, again offering improved access and ease of use. The culmination of these developments is the online multimedia software currently available for Windows and Macintosh users as WAOL 2.5 and MacAOL 2.6, respectively.

No longer are people forced to navigate an online service by selecting from a list of text-based menus on a sterile screen. Instead, with the latest incarnation of America Online's software, you get graphics, live audio, point and click windows, and a host of visual delights.

Thanks to this popular interface—and some very aggressive marketing—America Online has gotten stronger. By the end of 1992, the year that America Online was listed as a public company, there were 219,000 members. At the end of the following year, that figure had jumped to 500,000, and on August 16, 1994, the corks began to pop at America Online head offices as the number passed the 1,000,000 mark.

America Online Today

Today, America Online provides more than 3.5 million users with regular access to online services via its computer center in Vienna, Virginia. In a single day, it has been estimated that as many as 1 million people will take advantage of the services offered by America Online, be it checking their electronic mail, chatting in an online forum, or downloading a file from the extensive online software library.

To keep this entire system operating, America Online uses a technique that you will become very familiar with as you delve further into this book—*client/server* networking. When you connect to America Online, you are not just logging on to a computer system as you would when dialing a local BBS. Instead, your computer actually becomes a part of the America Online computer network and in doing so reduces the amount of work done by America Online itself. Your computer does this by looking after details like screen display, printing, and even the play of audio samples. This frees up the America Online servers to look after the task of feeding your computer with the information it requires.

Your computer is said to be a *client* of the America Online *server*, hence the name client/server network. This method of online communications is very similar to that used by many of the Internet-based tools you encounter later in this book.

New Markets

In addition to the U.S. market, America Online is now also beginning to explore the prospects of expansion into both the European and Asian markets. By coupling the services already provided by America Online with unique local content, they plan to be one of the first services on the block to deliver truly global online multimedia and communications in a simple easy-to-use software package.

As a part of this global push, America Online is also investing heavily in the Internet and related technologies, and you, the users, are the first ones to get its benefits. In the next section, you will discover how America Online became involved with the Internet and get some idea of the services they now provide.

The Internet Gateway

At the same time that America Online was beginning to rapidly expand its membership, popularity and interest in the Internet was also on the increase.

Eventually, it was inevitable that the paths of these two services would cross, and as had often been the case in the past, the driving force behind the initial meeting was electronic mail.

The E-Mail Gateway

By the beginning of the 1990s, both America Online and the Internet had well-established electronic mail systems operating on their respective networks. The problem was that users on one system couldn't send mail to users on the other. The reasons behind this problem were twofold. First, there was no physical connection between the two services, and second, the methods each system used when addressing e-mail were not compatible.

Although connecting separate networks through TCP/IP gateways was, by this stage, a popular Internet pastime, little work had been done on linking non-TCP/IP-compatible systems to the Internet. As a result, for America Online and the Internet to be able to communicate, a new type of gateway was needed.

In addition, a number of new policies needed to be put into place by America Online to ensure that its users could both send and receive e-mail across the Internet. To make the whole system work, it was decided that each America Online user would be given an Internet address in addition to their screen name. This address was created by altering their screen name.

For example, on the Internet, `Wtatters`—my America Online screen name—becomes `wtatters@aol.com`. You don't need to be too concerned at this stage about exactly what this address means. It is discussed in greater detail in Chapter 6, "The Internet E-Mail Gateway."

In 1992, once these policies were in place and the gateway constructed, America Online and Internet users were able to send electronic mail messages from the Internet to America Online and back.

The Internet Center

As interest in the Internet began to grow, America Online decided to expand the gateway to encompass other Internet services. To manage this growth and to provide its many curious members with information about the Internet, at the end of 1993 America Online opened the Internet Center.

The Internet Center was the precursor for the Internet Connection (see Figure 2.1) channel available today on America Online. To access this channel use the Keyword: `Internet`. Alternatively, you can select the Internet Channel icon from the AOL main menu.

FIGURE 2.1.

Use the Keyword:
Internet *to access the*
Internet Connection.

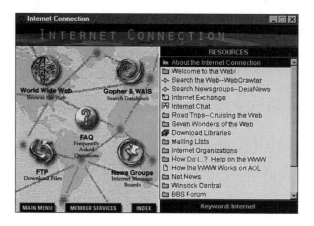

Usenet

When America Online announced the opening of the Internet Center, they also indicated that they were planning to introduce a range of Internet-related services to complement the extremely popular e-mail gateway. By this time, the e-mail gateway was already handling over 5,000,000 messages each month.

After extensive testing and experimentation, America Online opened a Usenet gateway service on March 28, 1994. In doing so, they gave America Online users access to over 10,000 discussion groups covering a wider range of topics than was physically possible on America Online alone.

Note

> Today there are over 20,000 newsgroups available on the Usenet, all of which can be accessed via America Online.

While not everyone on the Internet was happy with this influx of new people to the Usenet, for America Online users, their world was rapidly expanding. No longer were they forced to keep to the confines of their own service, now they could venture out onto the world of global communications and discussion as well. (See Chapter 8, "Usenet Newsgroups," for full coverage of America Online's Usenet services.)

Gopher and WAIS

With their Usenet gateway up and running, America Online moved rapidly to add Gopher and WAIS connectivity. While the Usenet had given America Online users the ability to communicate and conduct discussions with people on the Internet, Gopher was to give them the ability to physically leave the confines of America Online and visit other computer systems connected to the Internet. (See Chapter 11, "Gopher and WAIS" for more information.)

There was a problem, however, with thousands of computers and databases connected to the Internet: How were America Online users to locate sites they were interested in visiting? Some sort of search tool was needed that provided capabilities similar to those with which America Online users were already familiar. To this end, access to a special Internet search and indexing system called WAIS was incorporated into the new Gopher system. Using WAIS, users can search in a matter of seconds through millions of pages of text located on sites all over the Internet.

FTP

Following the opening of the Usenet gateway, which technically allows only discussions to be exchanged across the Internet, a number of users began asking for access to files stored on Internet host computers. America Online users familiar with AOL's software libraries expected not only to be able to conduct discussions with other users, but also to be able to download files and computer programs in the same way that their familiar AOL software permitted.

Unlike America Online, the Internet requires separate software to access libraries of files and computer programs. This software or *file transfer protocol* is commonly referred to as *FTP*. (See Chapter 9, "File Transfer Protocol (FTP)," for a full discussion of FTP.) To allow users' access to Internet file libraries or anonymous FTP sites as they are known, an FTP gateway was opened by America Online early in 1995.

TCP/IP Connections to America Online

While AOLnet—the telephone communications network that allows most people to connect to America Online for the cost of a local phone call—is rapidly expanding its coverage, there are still people in some areas that need to pay either long distance phone charges or a surcharge for using the 1-800 phone number provided by AOLnet.

Although America Online itself is a reasonably priced service, when you add an additional hourly connection fee to the price it can start to become a little expensive. In addition, if you happen to live outside the U.S., then the cost is even more. But there is a global communications system already in operation that should, in theory, be able to reduce these charges considerably. The system I am talking about is, of course, the Internet.

For people who already have access to an Internet connection, AOL now includes the ability to sign on to America Online without using AOLnet or any other phone service. Instead, you use your Internet connection. If you would like more information on this capability, take a look at Appendix B, "Connecting to America Online via the Internet."

America Online and the Internet Today

Trying to keep track of the latest Internet developments at America Online is a bit like trying to guess the winners of a race before you know who the contestants are. There seems to be so many things happening at once.

To help sort through the thick of it, the last section of this chapter, examines the latest breaking news.

The World Wide Web

For most America Online users the most significant announcement of 1995 was the May release of full World Wide Web access. (See Figure 2.2.)

FIGURE 2.2.

You can now explore the World Wide Web using AOL's online software.

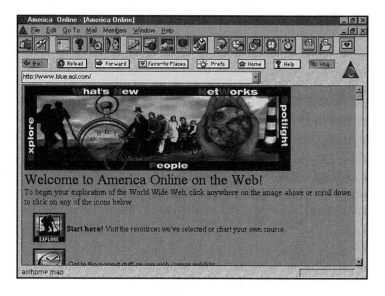

The World Wide Web is without a doubt the most talked about and hotly debated subject on the Internet today. In many ways the Web is not unlike a global version of the America Online's AOL navigator. (See Chapter 12, "The World Wide Web," and Chapter 13, "World Wide Web Productivity," for an in-depth look at the World Wide Web.)

> The World Wide Web is referred to by many terms these days. Often it is called the Web, or WWW, or even W3. For consistency, this book refers to it as WWW.

America Online did not just stop at adding WWW functionality to its AOL software. Instead, they have embarked on the comprehensive integration of the World Wide Web into their online service. Each of America Online's 14 channels have been redesigned to include links to relevant World Wide Web sites. This includes the Kids Only channel which even provides a special version of the WWW browser for America Online's younger users.

> Mac Users: While America Online offers a WWW browser for Macintosh computers, it is not as fully integrated with AOL as the Windows version.

Winsock and AOL

Despite all of the Internet services announced by America Online, it seems that some people are never happy. The moment you give them one thing, they want something else.

Of all the "want something else" requests received by America Online, one of the most persistent has come from people wanting access to remote logon or Telnet capabilities. Using Telnet you can physically log your computer onto a remote computer connected to the Internet. One of the main reasons people are interested in this sort of service is to gain access to a special type of online game called a MUD.

Other people have also expressed a need for access to a program called IRC or Internet Relay Chat. IRC is a bit like being in an online chat at America Online. The only real difference is that there are people from all over the world on IRC and there is technically no limit to the number of people that can be in a room at any one time.

To answer these requests, in August this year America Online announced the availability of *Winsock* access for people using the Windows version of AOL. By installing a file called Winsock in your c:\windows\system directory, you are automatically granted access to programs such as Telnet and IRC. The only catch is that these programs are not a part of AOL itself. They are separate tools called *clients* that can be run simultaneously with AOL. (See Chapter 10, "AOL and Winsock" for details of this new feature.)

> If you already have a `winsock.dll` file installed on your computer, make sure you make a backup copy of it before installing the AOL version. This file is usually found in the C:\WINDOWS\SYSTEM directory.

> Mac Users: At this stage, no such capabilities have been announced for Macintosh users, but it is expected that such an option will follow in the near future.

Although Chapter 10 gives you a general introduction to the concept of TCP/IP connections and the use of Winsock, a complete discussion of the subject is outside the scope of this book. However, to get you started, Appendix C, "Internet Software," discusses some of the more popular Winsock client software currently available.

There are also a number of very good books dealing specifically with TCP/IP connections to the Internet. *Teach Yourself TCP/IP* from Sams is a good book for people who are just beginning to explore the Internet, while *Using the Internet, Second Edition* from Que offers probably the best in-depth coverage of the Internet and the myriad of software programs that can be used in conjunction with it.

GNNWorks and MegaWeb

Probably the most stunning announcement for 1995, from a commercial perspective, was the announcement that America Online is planning to launch a service that provides people with a direct TCP/IP link to the Internet—as opposed to the gateway services provided by AOL.

To make this service a reality, America Online has acquired a number of prominent Internet companies and services over the past year. These include: GNN—the Global Network Navigator, WAIS Inc, WebCrawler, and NaviSoft, each of which bring to America Online vital components for what is planned to be the ultimate Internet service.

As this book goes to press, this new service—code named MegaWeb—is still being tested, along with its World Wide Web browser—GNNWorks. (See Figure 2.3). In Chapter 18, "The GNN Internet Access Service," you find an introduction to this new tool and discussion of its use. To find out more about America Online's plans in this area you should also visit the GNN area with Keyword: **GNN**.

FIGURE 2.3.

GNNWorks takes you onto the Internet without the need for AOL itself.

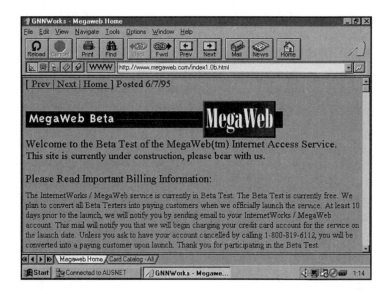

The Future of America Online

Even with the introduction of TCP/IP connectivity, the future for dedicated America Online services looks very bright. Most important among all of these plans is the continued development of AOL. With the addition of support for the World Wide Web and Winsock connectivity, it has become one of the most useful tools a person can own.

Over the past few years, AOL has grown. As it now stands, it is by far the easiest to use all-in-one Internet navigator, and at the same time it still offers full access to the AOL channels you are no doubt already familiar with.

By offering users a consistent interface and simple one-click connectivity, AOL is the tool that will finally carry many users onto the Internet and the global information superhighway.

Summary

As was so often the case with the development of the Internet, the creation of links between America Online and the Internet was driven, for the most part, by the needs of its users.

In opening up these links, America Online has brought its ability to provide highly user-friendly communications technology to the Internet. Using its existing network and familiar tools such as AOL, America Online users can now explore the Internet without needing to be concerned about the many problems and difficulties so often associated with Internet access. As a result, millions of users who, in the past, never even have considered the possibility of connecting to the Internet, now have the opportunity to find out what its all about.

This, however, brings us to an important point. With all the capabilities that America Online already provides, why would anyone want to use the Internet?

To help answer this question, the next chapter explores some of the unique services that the Internet now offers to America Online users. In addition, it also looks more closely at the types of services that comprise the Internet today.

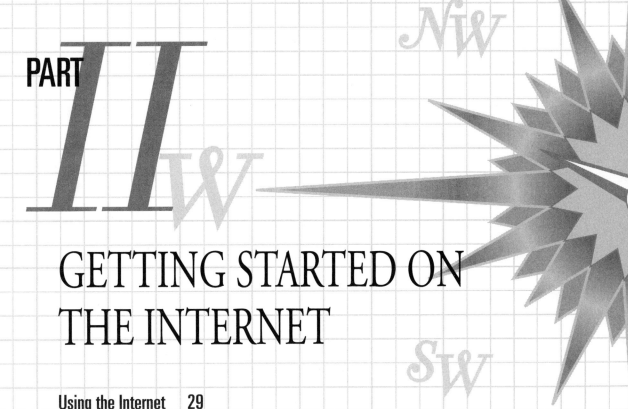

PART II

GETTING STARTED ON THE INTERNET

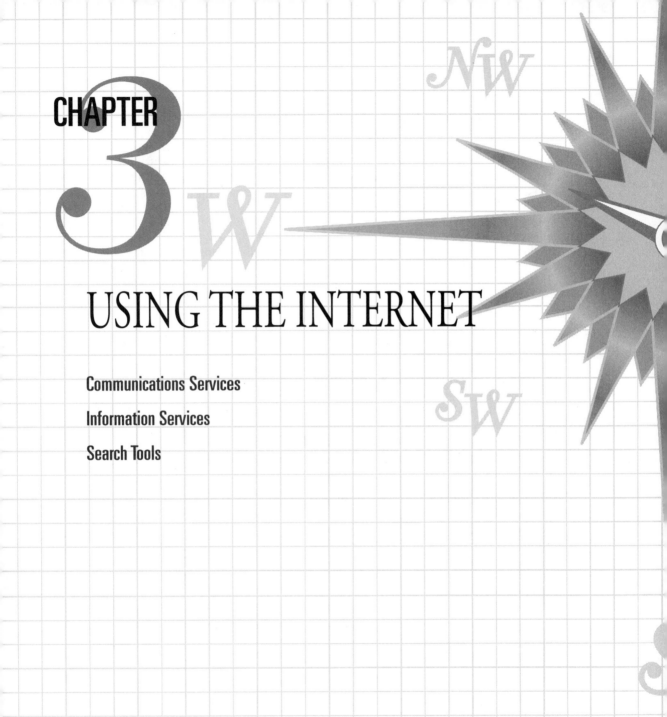

CHAPTER 3

USING THE INTERNET

Communications Services

Information Services

Search Tools

For many AOL users, the services that America Online already provides give them everything they need. This begs the question, "I'm happy with the services I have now, so why should I be concerned about using the Internet?"

On its own, this question is a hard one to answer. In much the same way that different people use America Online for different reasons, the Internet is different things to different people. As a result, the only person who can really answer this question is the person asking it.

This chapter will help you to answer this question by looking more closely at what the various Internet services mentioned in Chapter 2 offer America Online users. These services can be broken down into three main topic areas. To investigate the Internet further, this chapter deals with these topics in the following order:

◆ Communications services

◆ Information services

◆ Search tools

Communications Services

At its heart, the Internet is primarily a communications tool. No matter how you look at it, using the Internet involves the communication or exchange of information between one or more computers. Regardless of the content of this information, be it electronic mail, computer programs, images, and even live video or audio, basically you are looking at a communications system.

When the ARPANET was designed, it allowed computers to communicate and share resources. Before too long, people began to realize that if the system could allow two computers to communicate with each other, two people working on those computers should be able to communicate as well.

Electronic Mail

This realization led to the development of the service known today as *e-mail*. In essence, e-mail allows people to exchange messages using their computers. With e-mail, two people can correspond electronically in much the same way that they would write letters to each other using the postal service. (But it's much faster, of course.)

For America Online users, e-mail is probably one of the most important reasons for becoming familiar with the Internet. As the use of e-mail becomes commonplace, more and more people are obtaining electronic mailboxes on one or more of the computer networks that now span the globe. However, not all of these people have accounts with America Online.

As a result, to send e-mail messages to these people, you will need to know at least a little bit about how the Internet works. You will also need to understand the procedures you need to follow to send e-mail to these people using America Online. To ease the way, Chapter 6, "The Internet E-Mail Gateway," explores this process in detail.

Mailing Lists

One of the capabilities that became available as the first e-mail software began to appear on ARPANET was the ability to send the same e-mail message to more than one person. This was the electronic equivalent of photocopying a letter a number of times and mailing it to many different people.

Not long after this feature appeared, a few enterprising individuals realized that they could use this capability to conduct conference-like discussions. By setting themselves up as *moderators,* they could receive messages sent by people participating in a discussion. Then, using what was to become known as a *mailing list,* the moderators would forward each message to all the people or *subscribers* who subscribed to the discussion. Using this technique, there was no need for each person to have a copy of the mailing list. Instead, all they needed to do was send their messages and comment to the moderator, who would look after the distribution for them.

Although this system is suitable for small mailing lists, it soon became apparent that to manage some of the more popular mailing lists, a dedicated computer program was a better proposition. Over time, two main computer programs have emerged to manage this task. Between them, LISTSERV and Majordomo handle a large percentage of the 12,000+ mailing lists now available on the Internet. Chapter 7, "Mailing Lists," discusses how you can participate in mailing lists using America Online.

Mailing lists eventually became so popular that a dedicated network was created to maintain the distribution process. This network is known as BITNET, the "Because It's Time NETwork".

Newsgroups

Another service that grew out of the use of e-mail was the popular network known as Usenet. Usenet, like mailing lists, allows users to take part in online discussions.

However, where mailing lists use e-mail to automatically distribute a copy of each message to all participants, Usenet messages are stored on a dedicated network of interlinked computers. When a person wants to read these messages, they use a special program called a *newsgroup reader* (see Figure 3.1). This program is used to communicate with Usenet and retrieve messages or *articles* that have been posted to it.

Although the Usenet is the correct name for this service, the term newsgroup is used by many people. This name is derived from the way that messages on Usenet are categorized in separate discussion areas, these areas are called newsgroups. When you use a newsreader, all the messages in each newsgroup are displayed together. As a result, you can easily locate articles that you are interested in and at the same time ignore those you are not.

FIGURE 3.1.

AOL includes a built-in newsgroup reader, which allows you to read newsgroups articles and create new ones.

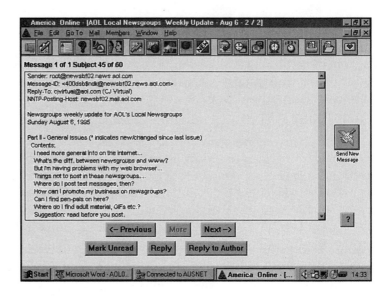

Newsgroup readers or simply newsreaders also let you post messages to Usenet newsgroups. When you post an article to a newsgroup, it is stored on the Usenet computer that your newsgroup reader is connected to. A copy of the message is then sent to every other computer on the Usenet network, using a process known as *store and forward*. This name reflects how newsgroup messages are distributed from computer to computer on the Usenet network.

Like mailing lists, there are literally thousands of newsgroups available on Usenet. To assist you in getting the most out of them, Chapter 8, "Usenet Newsgroups," explores the topic in depth.

Remote Computing

Even though the preceding discussion might seem to indicate that the only method of communicating on the Internet is by e-mail, this could not be further from the truth.

When ARPANET was first proposed, the big problem facing computer researchers was getting access to the limited number of high-powered computers that existed at the time. Naturally, people wanted to be able to use the most powerful machines available to reduce the amount of time their projects took to run. What the ARPANET team suggested was a way of sharing these computers that would allow researchers to log onto these machines from distant locations. In addition, unlike dial-up terminals which require the use of dedicated phone lines, these remote connections would take advantage of the ARPANET network.

To achieve this goal, a remote logon service was developed that eventually become known as Telnet. Today, Telnet allows people to log onto computer systems all over the world. Some of these computers are very similar to the bulletin board systems (BBS) that many of you have probably used in the past. Other systems offer access to databases, while some provide access to a wide variety of online computer gaming environments, such as MUDs, MOOs, and MUSHES.

At this stage, America Online does not provide direct access to Telnet. However, a program has recently been released which lets people using the Windows version of AOL take advantage of the popular Winsock protocol. Using Winsock, you can gain access to Telnet remote logins by running a separate Telnet client program while connected to America Online. In Chapter 10, "AOL and Winsock," you will find a discussion of Winsock along with information about Telnet and Telnet client programs. In addition, Appendix C, "Internet Software," contains a brief description of some of the more popular Winsock client programs.

Real-Time Communications

As modem speeds and the speed of the Internet backbone increase, a new form of computer communications is becoming popular. Although all the standard e-mail communications tools are extremely fast when compared to services such as couriers and mail delivery, they lack the ability to compete with real-time services such as the telephone. To redress this failing, Internet Relay Chat (IRC) was developed.

IRC is very similar to the Online Chat system provided by America Online. It uses a party-line system that allows any number of people, anywhere on the Internet, to gather in virtual rooms or *channels,* where they can communicate in real time using their computers. (See Figure 3.2.) When a person types a comment using an IRC client program, it is immediately displayed on the screen of every other person connected to the same channel. Using IRC, people can stage conferences, hold meetings, and simply spend time chatting with other people from all around the world.

FIGURE 3.2.

WSIRC, one of the more popular IRC clients, lets people all over the world take part in real-time conversations.

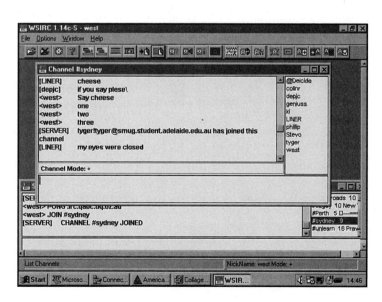

As was the case with Telnet, currently America Online does not directly support the use of IRC. Having said that, by installing the Winsock program mentioned in the previous section, you can gain access to IRC by running a separate IRC client program. Chapter 10 contains a discussion of IRC and examines two of the more popular IRC clients.

Information Services

Apart from being a communications tool, the Internet is rapidly becoming a valuable source of information. Thousands of computers connected to the Internet now contain material stored in computer files, databases, and information systems, which for the most part are publicly available to people on the Internet.

To cope with this ever-increasing amount of information, a number of services have been developed to assist people in retrieving data located on the Internet.

File Transfer Protocol

One of the first services developed for the Internet was the File Transfer Protocol (FTP). Using this tool, a person can exchange files with a remote computer system. In many ways, FTP is similar to Telnet. Both services allow you to log on to a remote computer and use it as though you were connected locally. In the case of FTP, however, instead of connecting to the remote system as a terminal, a special technique called a *client/server connection* is used.

Computer systems containing files that people can retrieve use a computer program called an *FTP server.* To obtain a file from one of these FTP servers, you need to run a program called an *FTP client* on your local computer. This program is responsible for all communications with the remote FTP server. These two programs communicate with each other and allow you to browse the directories and files located on the remote machine. When you locate a file you wish to retrieve, you tell your FTP client which one it is. The FTP client communicates this to the FTP server, which in turn sends the file back to your FTP client so that it can be stored on your local hard drive.

Not all computer systems that run FTP servers allow just anyone to access their files. To protect these sites, you must log on with a user ID and password when you connect to any FTP server. To get around this built-in FTP limitation, sites that allow free access to their files use a special user ID called anonymous. As a result, these FTP sites have become known as *anonymous FTP servers.* When you access an FTP site using the anonymous ID, you will usually be expected to enter your e-mail address as the password.

For America Online users, FTP is the ideal complement to the thousands of files already available in AOL's software libraries. Chapter 9, "File Transfer Protocol (FTP)," looks at how you can connect to FTP sites using AOL's built-in FTP client software. It also investigates some of the major FTP libraries recommended by America Online.

Gopher

FTP offers users a good method of exchanging computer files, but it is often a very difficult job to actually locate the information you want to download. To reduce this difficulty, a number of menu-based tools began to appear in the early 1990s that allowed users to move around the Internet more easily.

Of these services, the most popular is a system known as *Gopher*. Like FTP, Gopher relies on the use of client/server communications. Computer systems that allow people to access their information using Gopher menus need to operate a Gopher server. This server, like an FTP server, communicates with a Gopher client running on your local computer.

The Gopher client displays the directories and files available on the Gopher server as a list of menu items. By selecting from these menu items, you can explore the information stored on the *host computer* and download items you are interested in.

Gopher also provides its users with a feature that FTP cannot provide. As well as providing easy access to files on a Gopher system, Gopher menu items can also contain *links* to other Gopher servers. When you select one of these links, you are automatically transferred to the new Gopher server and its menu items are displayed on your Gopher client's screen. To find out more about using Gopher with AOL, see Chapter 11, "Gopher and WAIS."

World Wide Web

Unless you've just returned from the dark side of the moon, you've probably seen the name World Wide Web (WWW) mentioned somewhere in the past few months. To put it mildly, this client/server offering has taken the Internet by storm.

Developed in the late 1980s by CERN, the European Laboratory for Particle Physics, the World Wide Web was designed to provide scientists and researchers with easy access to the thousands of documents and publications stored on computers throughout the Internet. At the time, many of the new users who were being introduced to the Internet quickly became confused and frustrated by the number of different tools they needed to use to achieve what were seemingly simple goals. The bold plan for the World Wide Web was to create a client/server tool that allowed people to move around on the Internet without needing to learn anything other than how to use a WWW client program.

> The acronym CERN comes from the French title for the project, "Conseil European pour la Recherche Nucleaire."

Note

In many ways, using a WWW client is similar to using AOL's navigation software. Using a simple point-and-click interface (see Figure 3.3), a WWW client allows you to roam the Internet almost at will. There is no need to learn the complexities of Internet addressing and its related hieroglyphics; all you need to do is click on the part of the screen that represents the place you want to go and you are almost instantly transported there.

FIGURE 3.3.

When using a WWW client, clicking on any underlined text transports you to the information it describes.

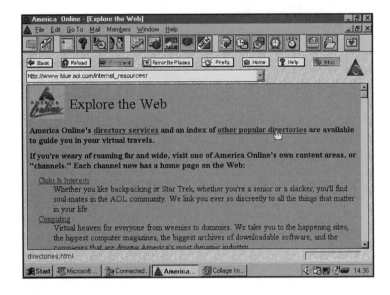

Instead of displaying menus as Gopher does, WWW clients display *documents* containing pages of information. These documents contain special links called *hypertext* links. By clicking on one of these links, a user can:

◆ Load a new WWW document

◆ Download files from an FTP site

◆ Browse the menus on a Gopher site

◆ Read newsgroup messages

◆ Open Telnet connections

◆ Listen to audio clips

◆ View pictures and digitized video clips

> WWW documents are written using a special format called the *hypertext markup language (HTML)*. This has led to WWW documents being more commonly referred to as HTML pages. Chapter 14, "WWW Publishing with AOL," looks at how you can use HTML to create your own WWW documents and publish them on the Internet.

Given all the capabilities the World Wide Web offers, it should come as no surprise that its popularity has extended beyond the walls of the research institutions that developed it. Today, organizations of all shapes and sizes are setting up World Wide Web sites, and millions of people are using the World Wide Web to explore the Internet on a daily basis.

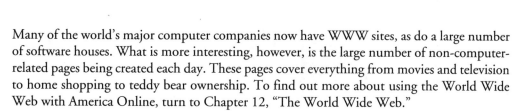

Many of the world's major computer companies now have WWW sites, as do a large number of software houses. What is more interesting, however, is the large number of non-computer-related pages being created each day. These pages cover everything from movies and television to home shopping to teddy bear ownership. To find out more about using the World Wide Web with America Online, turn to Chapter 12, "The World Wide Web."

Search Tools

With all the information now available on the Internet, finding the item you are looking for brings to mind the story of the needle in the haystack. To help lighten the load, a number of services now exist whose job it is to help you find the material you are looking for.

The InterNIC Database

As discussed in Chapter 1, when the NSF set up InterNIC, it appointed AT&T to look after the maintenance of a collection of Internet-related databases and related search tools.

Using a World Wide Web client, InterNIC can be reached at `http://www.internic.net/`. Alternatively, access to InterNIC is also available via AOL's Gopher client. To do this, open the Gopher client, Keyword: **gopher**, and click on the Internet Information icon. This opens the Internet and Network Information Gopher menu. All you need to do then is select the InterNIC: Internet Network Information Center entry from the menu of sites provided. (For more information about using Gopher see Chapter 11, "Gopher and WAIS.")

> Many of the menus displayed by Gopher are longer than one screen. If you cannot see the InterNIC: Internet Network Information Center entry listed on your screen, you may need to use the scrollbars at the side of the list to display additional entries.

Internet White Pages

With more than an estimated 35 million people now in possession of an e-mail address, one of the more popular tools provided by the InterNIC is the *Internet White Pages*. To access the Internet White Pages, go to the InterNIC gopher site, as described in the previous section and select the InterNIC Directory and Database Services (AT&T) menu item. Then on the next Gopher menu select the InterNIC Directory Services (White Pages) entry. When you do this you should see a menu similar to the one shown in Figure 3.4.

This service brings together many of the most popular Internet e-mail directories and listings. Using tools like Netfind and WHOIS or the experimental X.500 directory project, it is possible to look up a person's e-mail address and, in some cases, non-Internet related details such as phone numbers and postal addresses.

FIGURE 3.4.

Like a telephone directory, the Internet White Pages helps you locate people on the Internet.

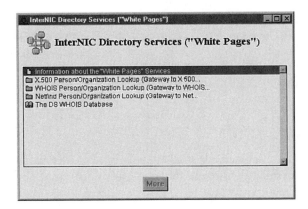

Note

Unfortunately, the White Pages project is still in its infancy, and as a result not all people with e-mail address are currently listed in the database. Over the coming years this should begin to change as the X.500 project expands. The ultimate goal is to eventually list all e-mail users who wish their address to be known.

Directory of Directories

Along with locating people, locating specific computers and services is also a regular Internet pastime. When you are trying to find a specific site, there is probably no better place to start than the InterNIC Directory of Directories. This directory contains lists of nearly every machine known to be connected to the Internet. To assist you further, they are categorized into services such as those shown in Figure 3.5.

FIGURE 3.5.

The Internet Directory of Directories.

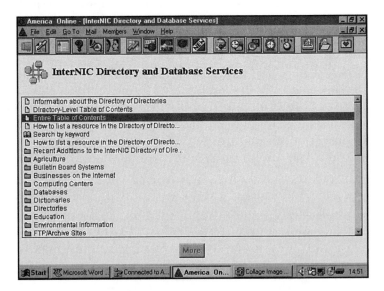

You can access the Directory of Directories, either by selecting the InterNIC Directory of Directories menu entry shown on the InterNIC Directory and Database Services (AT&T) menu or by choosing the using the InterNIC Directory and Database Services menu item displayed in the main Internet and Network Information menu discussed previously.

RFCs and FYIs

As mentioned in previous chapters, the InterNIC also maintains a full listing of all Requests for Comment (RFCs), For Your Information (FYI) and many other documents published by the Internet Engineering Task Force (IETF). These documents contain a wide variety of valuable information dealing with all aspects of the Internet, including its operation, policies, and practices. If you're looking for information about the Internet, these documents are a good place to start.

In addition, not content with just storing these documents, the InterNIC Gopher also provides you with search tools that let you sift through the contents of RFCs and many of the other databases maintained by InterNIC. For example, to access the search tool for the Directory of Directories, all you need to do is select the Search by Keyword menu item shown in Figure 3.5.

Archie

The InterNIC Directory of Directories may be of great assistance when you need to find a specific FTP site, but in many cases you may not actually know the location of a file you are trying to find. When this happens, you need to turn your attention to a different type of information database.

Archie was developed for the specific purpose of collecting the names of files and directories on every FTP site on the Internet and storing them in a publicly accessible database. When given a filename or the name of a related directory, Archie conducts a search of all FTP sites. When finished, it provides you with a list of every site that contains files or directories with names similar to the one you are looking for.

In Figure 3.6, an Archie client was asked to provide a list of all FTP sites containing Winsock files. On the left side of the screen it has listed all the FTP sites containing Winsock files. In the middle section it lists the directories for each site and where they can be found. For more information on Archie, be sure you read the "Archie" topic in Chapter 10.

You can also gain access to Archie search tools using the World Wide Web. Figure 3.7 shows the ArchiePlex search form located at `http://cuiwww.unige.ch/./archieplexform.html`. To find out more information about ArchiePlex take a look at Chapter 13, "World Wide Web Productivity."

FIGURE 3.6.

Using Archie you can easily locate files stored at FTP sites.

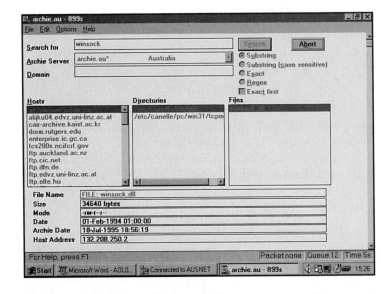

FIGURE 3.7.

ArchiePlex lets you use the World Wide Web to locate files stored at FTP sites.

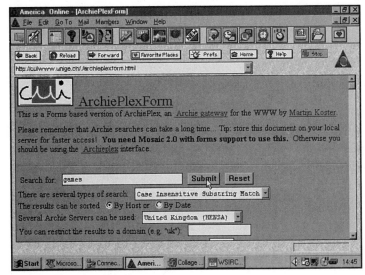

WAIS

Of all the search tools developed for the Internet, the Wide Area Information Service (WAIS) is one of the most amazing. Where most other Internet tools contain databases of files or Internet addresses, WAIS contains databases that index the documents themselves.

When the Thinking Machines Corporation decided to test the capabilities of its Connection Machine computer system, they decided to develop an environment capable of bringing the library to the user's desktop.

The Connection Machine was a radically new type of computer system that worked on the principle that the best way to get a job done fast was to share the task between many computers. Instead of wiring these computers together using a network, the Connection Machine was designed in such a way that it consisted of many computer processors in a single box. As a result, this machine was capable of performing many tasks at the same time, or in parallel, which led to the Connection Machine being called a massively paralleled supercomputer.

To test this system, they combined the power of this machine with an extensive global library of documents, papers, and in some cases entire electronic books. The result was WAIS, a document indexing system capable of searching through the contents of hundreds of thousands of documents in a matter of seconds.

Using WAIS, it is possible to locate any mention of a specific word or phrase in documents as diverse as *Australian Aboriginal Studies*, *Tantric News*, the phone and fax numbers of members of the U.S. Congress, papers on mathematical studies at MIT, and *The CIA World Fact Book*. Not satisfied with doing just this, they added a technique called *relevance feedback*. Using relevance feedback, WAIS can take a document you have retrieved and use it as the basis for additional searches of WAIS databases. In other words, the search says, "Now find anything that looks like anything in this document."

Like most Internet tools, you can access WAIS using Telnet, Gopher, the World Wide Web, or a dedicated WAIS client. In Chapter 11, "Gopher and WAIS," you will find a discussion of the WAIS client built into AOL. For those of you that prefer to use the World Wide Web, WAISgate, a WWW page operated by WAIS Inc.—now a subsidiary of America Online—is discussed in Chapter 13.

WWW Search Tools

With the number of pages on the World Wide Web now past the 6 million mark, finding your way around by pointing and clicking could take quite some time. To cope with this astonishing growth, a number of dedicated WWW search tools are appearing.

Using tools such as Lycos, InfoSeek, WebCrawler, or CUSI, it is possible to quickly and efficiently search the World Wide Web and locate pages of information you are interested in. For many people, this is the best way to move around the World Wide Web, but others prefer to *surf the Web* using lists such as Yahoo. (See Figure 3.8.) Unlike WWW search tools, these lists provide a categorized index of hot pages and cool Web sites.

To find out more information about the World Wide Web search tools and directories be sure to take a look at Chapter 13. It looks at both types of World Wide Web tools, and also discusses how you can publish your own WWW pages.

FIGURE 3.8.

Yahoo helps people surf the Net in comfort.

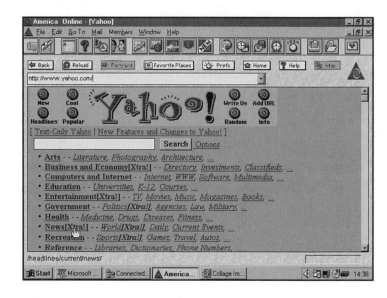

Summary

Since its inception, the Internet has been a service whose development is driven by its users. As a result, it can truly be said that the Internet contains something for everyone.

Like most areas of the computer world, the Internet is no longer the domain of scientists and researchers. Instead, it now offers just about anyone the ability to communicate, explore, shop, play, and even be entertained. Services like America Online have been providing these sorts of capabilities for some time, but as the World Wide Web grows in size and popularity, many people are finding the incentive they need to make their first tentative steps onto the Internet.

To meet this demand, America Online now offers access to Internet-based services through the gateways and tools outlined in Chapter 2 and expanded upon in this chapter.

Now that you have an understanding of how the Internet works, and some background information on the Internet services offered by AOL, it is time to get your hands dirty so to speak. In the next chapter you learn how to install AOL on your computer, and more importantly, how to install the Internet components such as the World Wide Web navigator.

CHAPTER 4

GETTING CONNECTED
TO AMERICA ONLINE

Installing AOL

Registering as an America Online User

Other Installation Issues

Before you can take advantage of any of the services discussed in this book, you will need to obtain a copy of a program called AOL. AOL is the navigation software for America Online. Currently there are two versions of AOL available, one for the Macintosh and the other for Microsoft Windows.

This chapter looks at the various ways that you can obtain a copy of this software and install it on your computer. Also, it discusses the steps involved in upgrading your existing AOL software to the latest version.

> If you are currently using a version of AOL prior to 2.5 for Windows or 2.6 for the Macintosh, you will need to upgrade your software so that you can access all the new Internet services.

Once you have installed AOL, you need to register yourself as an America Online member and select a screen name and password for your online sessions. You will also find a discussion of this subject later in this chapter.

Installing AOL

Historically, one of the biggest complaints leveled at online service providers and indeed the Internet as well, is the difficulty involved in setting up your computer before you ever get online.

Apart from the wide variety of software packages, all claiming to offer you the solution to your online needs, many service providers compound this problem with complex connection procedures and registration processes. Then, assuming that you manage to get online and registered, in many cases you are faced with a barrage of software options and add-ons that need to be installed before you can take advantage of often the most basic features.

And now, with the rapid growth in popularity of Internet connections, this situation has reached an all-time high, with literally hundreds of Internet-based computer programs flooding the market. To make things worse, each one works a little bit different from all the others and needs to be specially set up before it will operate correctly.

The developers of America Online, fully aware of the difficulties associated with other online services, decided that what was needed was a simple yet efficient program that replaced all the complicated terminal and communications programs, while at the same time providing you with access to all the online tools and services you could possibly need.

When they developed AOL, they created an online navigation program that is easy to install, includes a simple step-by-step online registration system, and a wide variety of features in one easy-to-operate program.

Obtaining the Software

There are a number of different ways to obtain a copy of AOL. These include:

The CD-ROM	You will find a copy of the latest version of both the Windows and Macintosh versions of AOL on the CD-ROM that accompanies this book. For information about installing this version of AOL, be sure to read the information printed on the page accompanying the CD-ROM.
Magazine Disks	If you have purchased any magazines or periodicals in recent months that include a cover disk, chances are that you may already have a copy of AOL on disk. America Online is continually promoting its services through magazines and also occasionally offers special subscriber deals for new members who use one of these cover disks.
Downloading an Upgrade	If you are already a member of America Online, you can download a copy of the latest version of AOL using the Keyword: **upgrade**. When you use this keyword, AOL determines which version of AOL you require and places you in the appropriate service area.

As an added bonus, you are not charged for your online time while downloading AOL upgrades.

FTPing a copy	If you have access to the Internet via another Internet service provider, you can download a copy of AOL using FTP from: `ftp://ftp.aol.com/`. (See Chapter 9, "File Transfer Protocol (FTP)," for more information about FTP.)

Windows Installation

Once you have obtained a copy of AOL, the next thing you need to do is install it on your computer system. To make the process of transferring the AOL software easier, America Online has created a special compressed archive file that contains all the individual files needed to run AOL on your computer.

To extract the files contained in this archive file you need to follow these steps:

1. Using the Windows File Manager, or Windows Explorer for Windows 95 users, locate the compressed file discussed in the previous section. The name of this file is SETUP.EXE.

   If you downloaded the file as an upgrade, it will most likely be stored in the C:\AOL20\DOWNLOAD or C:\AOL25\DOWNLOAD directory. On the other hand, if you have a copy on floppy disk, select the appropriate drive.

   To install AOL using the CD-ROM that accompanies this book, read the information printed on the page opposite the CD-ROM—the very last page of this book.

2. To run SETUP.EXE and install AOL, double-click on the file.

3. The setup program first examines the type of modem you have connected to your computer system. If you want to ignore this step, click on the Skip button.

Tip

Make sure your modem is turned on before starting the AOL installation, otherwise you will need to manually configure your modem at a later stage.

---

4. After determining the type of modem you are using, you are given the option of installing AOL, or upgrading an existing version. (See Figure 4.1.) Choose which options suit your needs.

FIGURE 4.1.

Select Install to load AOL, or select Review to alter the directory and upgrade options.

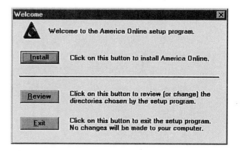

5. The SETUP program then proceeds to install all the required files in a new directory on your hard drive. The default name for this directory is C:\AOL25.

If you are upgrading an existing copy of AOL, SETUP creates a separate directory for the new version. If you want SETUP to overwrite the existing version, you can alter the default directory by clicking on the Review button. However, doing this wipes out all your previous settings and screen names.

6. During the installation process, SETUP.EXE adds a new folder to your Program Manager desktop, which includes an icon for America Online. To start AOL for the first time, double-click on this icon.

Windows 95 users will find that a new entry has been added to the Program submenu, accessed by clicking on the Start button. Therefore, to run AOL all you need to do is select the America Online 2.5 Double-Click to Start entry from the Start menu.

Macintosh Installation

Like the Windows version of AOL, the Macintosh version is also stored in a compressed archive. To install this version on your Macintosh computer, follow these steps:

1. Locate the America Online icon on either the CD-ROM, floppy disk, or in your AOL Download folder.

   To install AOL using the CD-ROM that accompanies this book, read the information printed on the page opposite the CD-ROM—the very last page of this book.

2. Double-click on this icon to start the installation process.

3. When you do this, the install program opens and displays a message advising you that you are about to load AOL. Click on the Continue button to confirm that you want the installation to take place.

4. You are then asked to select the folder in which the new AOL software is to be installed. (See Figure 4.2.) You can either accept the default location offered or select a location of your own.

FIGURE 4.2.

Select the folder to which the AOL software is to be stored.

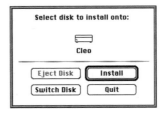

5. The new AOL software is then installed and a new application icon is created representing AOL. Double-click on this icon to start AOL for the first time.

Registering as an America Online User

Once your AOL software is installed, you will need to register yourself as a member of America Online before you can take advantage of the services they provide. To guide you through this process, the first time you start AOL you are taken step by step through the online registration system.

> If you are simply upgrading an existing version of AOL, as a rule you will not need to re-register, because the installation process will have copied all your current settings across to the new version.

To register yourself as a member of AOL, you need to follow the steps outlined. The figures in the section have all been taken from the Windows version of AOL; however, apart from some minor visual and layout differences, the same process applies for the Macintosh version as well.

1. The first time you start AOL, you are presented with a message window similar to the one shown in Figure 4.3. AOL provides you with the option of doing an express registration or a custom one. If, like most people, you meet the requirements listed in this message window, click Yes to begin the registration process, otherwise click No, so that you can alter the settings for such options as modem type and speed before registering.

FIGURE 4.3.

Select the folder in which you want the AOL software to be stored.

2. Assume for the moment that you have selected Yes. When you do this, AOL dials America Online's 1-800 number (see Figure 4.4) and begins the registration process. To let you know what is going on, the window shown in Figure 4.4 displays a series of messages as AOL negotiates a connection with the Online Registration system, culminating with Figure 4.5.

FIGURE 4.4.

AOL first dials the America Online toll-free number.

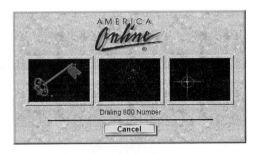

FIGURE 4.5.

When all three boxes contain a graphic, AOL is finally connected to the Online Registration.

3. The first piece of information you are asked to supply is the area code for your phone number. (See Figure 4.6.) Although you can connect to America Online from anywhere in the mainland United States using the toll-free number, you are charged an additional fee by America Online for doing so. As a result, where possible you are better off dialing a local phone number.

   By entering your area code, AOL is able to locate a list of phone numbers that you can call locally.

FIGURE 4.6.

Enter the area code of your phone number in the space provided.

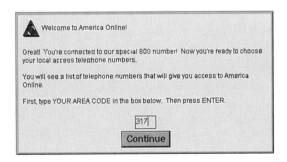

4. After a few seconds AOL displays a list of all the possible phone numbers in your local area. (See Figure 4.7.) Take a look at this list and highlight a local phone number that operates at the same speed as your modem. When you have done this, click on the Select Phone Number button.

If there are no local numbers listed for your area, click on the Can't Find a Local Number button to default AOL back to the 1-800 number.

FIGURE 4.7.

Select a phone number in your local area that matches your modem speed.

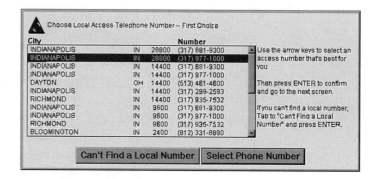

5. Once you have selected your primary phone number, AOL asks you to select a second number. On certain occasions you may find that AOL encounters difficulties connecting to your primary phone number. When this happens AOL attempts to connect using a secondary phone number.

   To choose this secondary number, again highlight a number in your local area and then click on the Select Phone Number button.

6. After you have selected your primary and secondary numbers, AOL displays both of them again in another window to give you the option of removing area codes. As a rule, all you should need to do is click on the Continue button.

7. You are now ready to register yourself with America Online.

   To do this, you first need to enter the Certificate Number and Certificate Password that accompanied your AOL software.

   For information about the Certificate number for the AOL software included on the CD-ROM, you need to read the instructions on the page opposite the CD-ROM itself.

Note

If you are already a member of America Online, enter your screen name and password instead of the Certificate information.

8. After displaying a few "housekeeping" screens, AOL asks you to provide some personal details about yourself for billing and registration purposes. This includes your name, address, and both your daytime and nighttime phone numbers. Once you have entered this information, click on the Continue button to proceed.

FIGURE 4.8.

If you are already registered, enter your screen name and password; otherwise enter the certificate number that accompanied your AOL disk or CD-ROM.

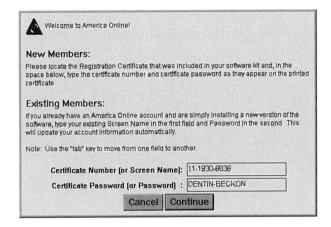

You must complete all the information required by America Online before you are permitted to proceed any further with the registration process.

9. Once you complete the registration information, AOL displays a description (see Figure 4.9) of any special connection offers associated with the Registration Certificate number you entered previously. This usually includes a trial connection period to give you the chance to explore AOL at America Online's expense.

    If at this stage you to decide not to accept the offer made by America Online, you can click on the Cancel button to stop the Online Registration process. Otherwise, click on the Continue button to complete the final details.

FIGURE 4.9.

If you decide that you don't want to continue the registration process, you can click on the Cancel button at any time.

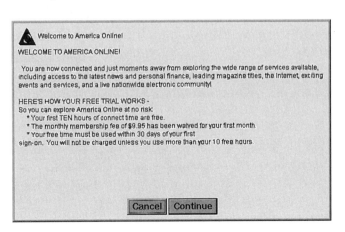

10. If you choose to accept the trial offer made by America Online, you then need to enter your billing details. The Billing Options window shown in Figure 4.10 provides you with a list of possible payment methods. Select the one that is appropriate to your needs.

AOL then asks you to enter all your credit card details, including credit card number, expiration date, billing address, and bank branch.

> For those of you who prefer not to use credit cards, America Online offers a direct debit facility via the More Billing Options button. However, there are some additional charges associated with using this service.

FIGURE 4.10.

If you decide that you don't want to continue the registration process, you can click on the Cancel button at any time.

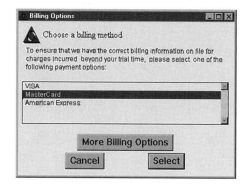

11. With the billing details out of the way, you are almost finished. Before you proceed any further, however, America Online requires that you read and agree to the Membership Conditions displayed in Figure 4.11.

FIGURE 4.11.

Make sure you read all the Membership Conditions before you agree to accept them.

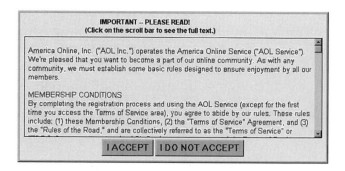

> By accepting the Membership Conditions and completing the Online Registration process you are entering into a binding contact with America Online. Therefore it is vitally important that you read and understand exactly what you are signing up for.

Warning

12. The final step in the registration process requires you to select a screen name for yourself. (See Figure 4.12.) Your screen name is your user ID at America Online. It is used whenever you sign on and when people address messages to you. In addition, it is also used to create your Internet e-mail address. (See Chapter 6, "The Internet E-mail Gateway," for more details.)

    Many people use their name, for example: Wtatters, Westatters, WesT, Wes. While other people choose names that represent hobbies, interests, or sometimes just nicknames.

    There are a few rules that control what you can use as a screen name, these are:

    ◆ It must be at least 3 characters and no more than 10 characters in length.

    ◆ It must begin with a letter.

    ◆ It may contain letters, spaces, and numbers, but no punctuation marks.

    ◆ It cannot already be in use by another member.

FIGURE 4.12.

Your screen name can be just about anything you choose.

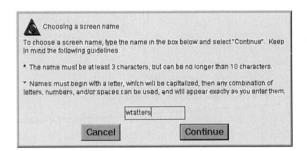

> If you select a screen name that is already in use, AOL asks you to select another one.

Note

13. In addition to your screen name, you also need to choose a secret password as shown in Figure 4.13. This password is used to protect your account from misuse by other people.

14. Once you have selected a password, you are ready to sign on to America Online.

    To do this, enter your new screen name and password into the fields provided on the Welcome window (see Figure 4.14), and click on the Sign On button.

FIGURE 4.13.

You must always keep your password a secret to protect your account from misuse.

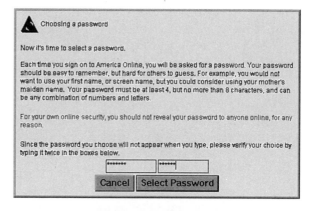

FIGURE 4.14.

Click on the Sign On button to start your first America Online session.

Other Installation Issues

As you begin to explore the services offered by America Online, you will occasionally come across areas that ask you to update certain parts of AOL before you can use them.

Graphics Updates

One of the most constantly changing aspects of America Online is the visual appearance and layout of windows and forums. As areas of America Online are enhanced, you will sometimes be informed that the graphics for an area have been upgraded.

If only a few images need to be updated, AOL automatically downloads them and then includes the new images on the appropriate window or screen. However, when major changes occur, America Online has decided that expecting members to pay for online time while 15 minutes' worth of graphics are downloaded is simply not acceptable.

Under these circumstances, you will find that AOL displays a message similar to the one shown in Figure 4.15. When you select the Get Artwork Now button, AOL takes you to a Free Area and downloads all the graphics without charging you for any online time while it does so.

FIGURE 4.15.

AOL downloads all the new images free of charge.

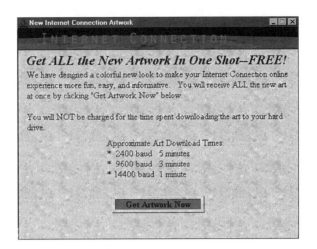

When you enter a Free Area, all online chat sessions, background file downloads, and forum areas are deactivated. As a result, you will not be able to do anything else online while the graphics download proceeds. All the activities that were deactivated will be automatically restarted when you exit the Free Area.

The World Wide Web

Because the World Wide Web service provided by America Online is still undergoing changes, you will occasionally be told that you need to update your WWW software before you can access a WWW site. (See Figure 4.16.)

FIGURE 4.16.

Clicking on the Update button tells AOL to update your WWW browser software without charging you for online time while the download occurs.

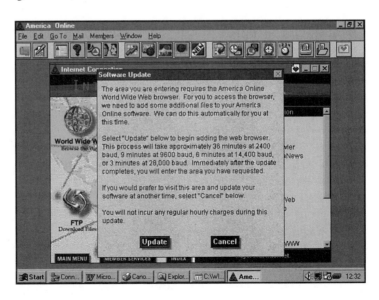

When this occurs, AOL allows you to update your software automatically and does so without billing you for online time while it downloads the new software.

> Macintosh users should also check the update area (Keyword: **Update**) for information regarding the latest version of the WWW browser for their system.

Summary

As you have seen in this chapter, America Online has developed a program that is easy to use and install and that gets you online with a minimum of fuss and none of the difficulties so often associated with online services.

Once you have installed AOL and registered as a new user, you will no doubt be anxious to explore America Online for yourself. To get you started, the next chapter gives you a quick course on the basics of AOL and also introduces you to the Internet services that take up the remainder of this book.

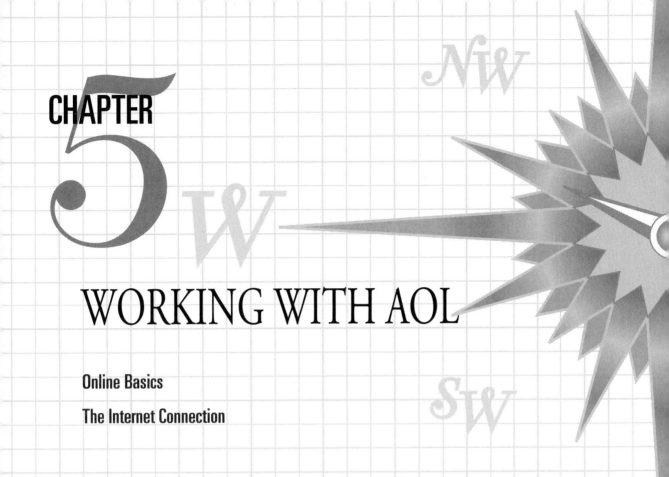

WORKING WITH AOL

Online Basics

The Internet Connection

Once you have made your initial connection to America Online and signed on for the first time, you will naturally want to begin to explore the many services provided by America Online.

To help you get started, this chapter provides you with a brief overview of the features provided by America Online and its AOL navigator software. However, if you want to learn more about using AOL itself, you should consider obtaining a copy of *Special Edition Using America Online*, published by Que. This book discusses in detail the use of AOL and examines each of America Online's 14 departments, or channels, in detail.

This chapter does, however, provide you with all the information you need to get up to speed, so that you will be able to use the Internet services discussed in later chapters. It does this by exploring the following subjects:

◆ The AOL Main Menu

◆ The Toolbar

◆ The Menus

◆ FlashSessions

◆ The Personal Filing Cabinet

◆ The Internet Connection

Online Basics

Once you have signed on to America Online, the AOL software provides you with all the tools you need to access the services provided by America Online. There is no need to load additional programs to access services like electronic mail or even read the daily news. AOL does everything for you in one combined package.

When people first hear statements like this there is often a tendency to think that such a program must be very difficult to operate if it provides so many options in the one package. However, with AOL nothing could be further from the truth.

By taking advantage of the latest graphical user interfaces provided by computers like the Apple Macintosh and PCs running under Windows, using AOL becomes a point and click operation. As a result, all the popular services on America Online are represented by what are known as *icons* or *click boxes,* which, when clicked on, start the service they represent.

Technically, icons are the small square pictures or images that represent graphically an option available to you, while a click box or clickable area is any part of the screen that can be clicked on to start a service or option. However, for simplicity's sake, throughout this book the term icon will be used to describe any type of clickable area, be it a true icon or a click box.

The AOL Main Menu

To make life easy for you, America Online uses a hierarchical system of menus that group all the major services into 14 main areas. These areas are referred to as either departments, channels, or forums, depending on who you talk to.

When you sign on to America Online, the Main Menu window shown in Figure 5.1 is displayed by default. This menu provides you with the means to directly open any one of the 14 main channels by simply clicking on the box that represents it. Table 5.1 lists each of the 14 main channels and describes briefly the services they contain.

FIGURE 5.1.

Clicking on any of the icons causes AOL to load the appropriate service.

Table 5.1. America Online's 14 main channels.

Channel Name	Description
Today's News	As the name implies, this channel provides you with up-to-the-minute news and information. You can read the news as it happens and in some cases also view photos of the event, as well. There are also sections dealing with sports, business, entertainment, and world news, plus as an added bonus, you can check both local and global weather reports that include full weather maps.
Newsstand	Sections of many of the most popular magazines available today can now be read online at the Newsstand. This includes articles, and often pictures, from current and past editions of magazines like *Wired, Time, Elle,* and *Omni.* Newspapers such

continues

Table 5.1. continued

Channel Name	Description
	as the *New York Times* and the *Chicago Tribune* also publish the highlights and features of each edition online.
Personal Finance	If you want to keep track of your stock portfolio, catch up on all the latest business news, or maybe get online tax assistance, then this is the area for you.
Entertainment	This forum brings you all the latest gossip, information, and news from the entertainment world. There are TV networks online like NBC, ABC, and E! along with Warner Brothers and MTV. Or, if the movies are more to your liking, check out Hollywood Online and catch all the latest movie reviews.
Clubs & Interests	There is something for everyone in this part of America Online. This is an area you really need to visit to get some idea of its scope. But, to give you some ideas of the topics covered, here are just a few examples: Religion, Cooking, Genealogy, Pets, The Environment, Health, and even Baby Boomers.
Education	Visit the Smithsonian or search the contents of the Library of Congress all from the comfort of your own home. Or maybe you need to look up an encyclopedia, no problem, the Compton's Encyclopedia is available online.
Computing	Enough said? Basically, every possible PC- and Mac-related computing issue, be it software or hardware is covered online.
Reference Desk	The Reference Desk provides you with the means of accessing a wide variety of online databases covering subjects as diverse as the Bible, Online Cookbooks, and Scientific research. Using AOL you can search any of these databases and print out copies of the results for future reference.
Travel	If you're thinking of planning a vacation and want to know where the best places to visit are, then check out the Travel Forum. One of the main features of this forum is the EAAsy Sabre online travel system that allows you to book airline tickets, make hotel reservations, and even organize a rental car all while online.
Internet Connection	The Internet tools and services discussed in this book can all be accessed from the Internet Connection area of America Online. (This area is discussed in more detail later in this chapter.)

Channel Name	Description
Marketplace	America Online, like most online services, provides you with access to the world of online shopping. The Marketplace forum is the electronic equivalent of your local shopping mall.
Sports	Whether you play sports or just like to watch, then the America Online Sports channel should be at the top of your list of favorite places. You can catch up on all the latest stats for your favorite team, run your own sports team in the Fantasy & Simulation leagues, or catch all the play-by-play action live, courtesy of ABC Sports.
People Connection	One of the most popular features of America Online is the ability to chat with other people while online. When you click on the People Connection icon you are transported to one of the many online chat lobbies. From there, you can either join in the conversation or explore any of the other online chat rooms.
Kids Only	This area is specially designed for America Online's younger users. You will find services such as Kids News and Sports, the Disney Adventure Magazine, special games, and Kids Only competitions in this channel.

The Toolbar

Across the top of the screen on the Windows version of AOL there is an area known as a Toolbar. (See Figure 5.2.) This toolbar contains a set of icons that provide you with another method of accessing some of the channels discussed in the previous section. In addition, many of the other services provided by AOL that you will find yourself using on a regular basis, are also represented as icons on this toolbar.

FIGURE 5.2.

AOL's Toolbar provides Windows users with the most direct method of accessing America Online's most popular tools and services.

The Toolbar is the most direct way to access many of the features provided by AOL because it is always displayed. Clicking on any of the icons displayed in this toolbar instantly transports you to the activity it represents. To give you some idea of what each icon does, Table 5.2 discusses each of the icons on the toolbar, working from left to right, followed by a short discussion of their functions.

Table 5.2. The AOL Toolbar.

Icon	*Icon Name*	*Description*
	Check Mail	When AOL detects unread messages in your mailbox, the New Mail icon activates. When you click on this icon, a list of all your unread mail is displayed on the screen.
	Compose Mail	Click on this icon to create a new e-mail message and send it to another person. (See Chapter 6, "The Internet E-Mail Gateway," for more information.)
	Go to Main Menu	If the AOL Main Menu window is not currently open, clicking on this icon displays it.
	Online Help	Clicking on this icon causes AOL to display the main window of the online help system.
	Directory of Services	AOL's directory of services provides you with a list of all the services and areas available online. You can search the directory using keywords, or you can explore lists including the Best Of AOL Services and *New* Features & Services.
	Go to People Connection	This is the equivalent of selecting the People Connection area on the AOL Main Menu.
	Quotes and Portfolios	If you click on this icon, the Quotes and Portfolios window of the Personal Finance channel is opened. Here you can check current share and stock quotes or keep track of your own portfolio.
	Go to Top News	This is the equivalent of selecting the Top News channel on the AOL Main Menu.

Icon	Icon Name	Description
	Go to Center Stage	When you click on this icon you are transported to the America Online Center Stage. This is an online conference area where special guests are invited to chat with AOL users.
	Go to Internet Connection	This is the equivalent of selecting the Internet Connection channel on the AOL Main Menu.
	New Features and Services	Clicking on this icon opens America Online's New Features and Services window. To keep up to date with all the latest AOL developments, you should visit this area on a regular basis.
	Keyword	As discussed previously, many of the services on America Online can be accessed directly using a keyword. This lets you jump straight to a service without having to click your way to it. When you click on the Keyword icon, AOL opens a small window where you can enter a keyword. This is the equivalent of using the Ctrl+K (⌘+K for Macintosh users) shortcut key combination.
	Download Manager	Click on this icon to open the AOL Download Manager window. The Download Manager lets you download files in the background while you explore America Online.
	Software Search	To locate files that you want to download, click on this icon to open the Software Search window. (See Chapter 9, "File Transfer Protocol (FTP)," for a discussion of the Software Search tool.)
	Online Clock	Click on this icon to find out how long you have been connected to America Online during the current session.
	Personal Choices	Alter your personal choices and preferences by clicking on this icon. You can

continues

Table 5.2. continued

Icon	Icon Name	Description
		control how AOL operates, how and what it displays, and set passwords or define screen names. Using this option, each of your five possible screen names can be assigned separate preferences.
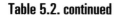	Print	Whenever there is a picture or some text displayed in any AOL windows, clicking on this icon generates a hard copy printout of it for you.
	Save As	Whenever there is a picture or some text displayed in any AOL windows, clicking on this icon saves copy of it as a file on your local hard drive.
	Favorite Places	Clicking on this icon opens the AOL Favorite Places menu. This is a user-defined menu where you can add those services that you visit on a regular basis.

The Menus

Both the Macintosh and Windows versions of AOL provide you with a set of drop-down menus that allow you to access all of the most used features of America Online. Of these menus the four you will access most often are:

◆ File

◆ Go To

◆ Mail

◆ Members

> Because the latest release of the Macintosh version of AOL is somewhat older than the Windows version, you will occasionally encounter options mentioned in this book that are, as yet, not fully support by the Mac version. (See Appendix E for a comparison of the two current versions.) All these functions should, however, be included in the next Macintosh release.

The File Menu

The File menu (see Figure 5.3) provides you with access to all the functions that allow you to read, save, print, and manage the downloading of files from America Online. Table 5.3 describes each of the entries on this menu. Many of these entries can also be accessed by using special key combinations called *hotkeys*, instead of selecting them from the menu itself. For example, the Ctrl+P hotkey for Windows users automatically prints out a copy of the text or image currently displayed in the active AOL window. In Table 5.3, all hotkeys are referred to using the Ctrl key; however, for Macintosh users, instead of using the Ctrl key, you use the ⌘ key.

FIGURE 5.3.

The File menu.

Table 5.3. Functions available on the File menu.

Menu Item	Hotkey	Description
New	Ctrl+N	Starts the built-in AOL text editor and creates a new text file.
Open...	Ctrl+O	Starts the AOL Open a File dialog box. You can view pictures, play AVI movies, display HTML WWW pages, and listen to audio files.
Save	Ctrl+S	Saves a copy of text or images displayed in an AOL window.
S**a**ve As...		Saves a copy of a text file or image file using a new name.
Print...	Ctrl+P	Prints out a hardcopy of any text or images displayed in an AOL window.
Print Setup...		Alters your printer default settings.
Download Manager...	Ctrl+T	The Download Manager lets you download files in the background while you explore America Online.

continues

Table 5.3. continued

Menu Item	Hotkey	Description
Logging…		Instructs AOL to record copies of your conversations in online chat areas or keep a record of your actions while online.
Stop Incoming Text	Esc	Used if you select a page containing a large amount of text; it can take some time for all the information to be downloaded to your computer. (To stop such a download you can also click on the Escape key.)
Exit		Select this entry to sign off from America Online and close AOL.

The Go To Menu

The Go To menu(see Figure 5.4) closely replicates many of the areas available via the Windows Toolbar. Using this menu you can quickly jump to many of the most popular areas on AOL, and as a special bonus you can also include 10 of your own favorite areas as a part of the menu. In Table 5.4 the purpose for each entry on this menu is examined, with hotkeys also listed for any menu items that support them.

FIGURE 5.4.

The Go To menu.

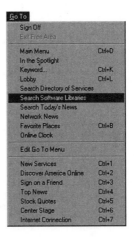

Table 5.4. Functions available on the Go To menu.

Menu Item	Hotkey	Description
Sign Off		Signs off from America Online, but keeps AOL running. When you are offline, the name of the entry changes to Setup &

Menu Item	Hotkey	Description
		Sign On. If you select it in this state, the AOL Welcome and Sign On window are opened.
Exit Free Area		A few special areas are designated by America Online as free of connection charges. When you enter one of these areas all other online activities are halted until you leave the free area. Select this menu item to do just that.
Main Menu	Ctrl+D	If the AOL Main Menu window is not displayed on the screen, selecting this menu item or corresponding hotkey opens it for you.
In the Spotlight		By default, the In the Spotlight window is displayed as soon as you sign onto AOL. It lets you know if you have any new mail, and also provides you with links to the latest news and special, highlighted services. This entry redisplays the In the Spotlight window.
Keyword...	Ctrl+K	Opens the Keyword window.
Lobby	Ctrl+L	Visits the online chat lobby.
Search Directory of Services		Opens the Directory of Services search window.
Search Software Libraries		Opens the Software Search window.
Search Today's News		Opens the Today's News window.
Network News		Use this entry to open the Network News window. This window contains any messages that have been broadcast to everyone online by America Online itself.
Favorite Places	Ctrl+B	Opens your Favorite Places window.
Online Clock		Find out how long you have been online by selecting this item.
Edit Go To Menu		AOL lets you add a list of your 10 personal favorite areas to the bottom of the Go To menu. To select the entries you want included, select this menu item.

continues

Table 5.4. continued

Menu Item	Hotkey	Description
New Services	Ctrl+1	Each of the favorite places you select are displayed in the bottom section of the Go To window. For example, New Services is currently defined as my first personal favorite. It should also be noted that each of the 10 entries is assigned the hotkeys, Ctrl+1 through Ctrl+0, respectively. For Mac users: ⌘+1 through ⌘+0.

The Mail Menu

One of the most popular features of America Online is the ability to exchange electronic mail, or e-mail, messages with other people, both on America Online and the Internet as well. (See Chapter 6 for more information.)

Because this is such an important area for so many people, America Online has devoted a separate menu to all the possible electronic mail services they provide. In Table 5.5 all the options listed on the Mail menu shown in Figure 5.5 are discussed.

FIGURE 5.5.
The Mail menu.

Table 5.5. Functions available via the Mail menu.

Menu Item	Hotkey	Description
Post Office		Opens the AOL Post Office window.
Compose Mail	Ctrl+C	Select this entry to open the Compose Mail window. From there you can send an e-mail message to other users both on AOL and the Internet.
Read **N**ew Mail	Ctrl+R	Requests a list of any unread messages currently stored in your mailbox.

Menu Item	Hotkey	Description
Check Mail You've **R**ead		America Online now maintains an online archive of the most recent messages you have received and read. Messages are kept on file for a period of about 7 days. To look at any of these messages again select this menu entry.
Check Mail You've **S**ent		To complement the receive messages archive, there is now also a sent mail archive as well. To read any of the messages you have composed in the past 7 days, select this menu item.
Edit **A**ddress Book...		To edit your personal address book, select this item.
FlashSessions...		Select this option to configure FlashSessions. (See the "FlashSessions" section later in this book for more information.)
Activate FlashSession Now		Start a FlashSession immediately by selecting this menu item.
Read Incoming Mail		Read any of the messages retrieved by your last FlashSession.
Read Outgoing Mail		Read any of the messages that are waiting in your Outgoing mail box for transmission during the next FlashSession.
Personal Filing Cabinet		Opens your personal filing cabinet. You can store copies of Mail, newsgroup articles, records of files you have downloaded, and your personal list of favorite sites and WWW pages in the filing cabinet.
Mail Gateway		Visit the America Online Mail Gateway information window by selecting this entry.
Fax/Paper Mail		To find out how you can send a person a fax or printed letter via America online, select this menu item.

The Members Menu

The Members menu (see Figure 5.6) is devoted to tools that let you control information such as your system preferences, user profile, parental controls, and passwords. In addition, it also contains entries that allow you to locate other people who use America Online and even send them messages if they are online at the same time that you are.

Table 5.6 explains the use of each entry on the Members menu and lists the hotkeys for any menu items that support them.

FIGURE 5.6.

The Members menu.

Table 5.6. Functions available on the Members menu.

Menu Item	Hotkey	Description
Member Services		America Online provides a special online area where you can update your billing information, search the online help system, and read documents such as the Terms of Service. Select the Member Services entry to visit this area. (This is a Free Area.)
Member Directory		To search through the directory of America Online users, select this entry.
Send an Instant Message	Ctrl+I	You can send a message instantly to any other person who is currently online by selecting this option.
Get a Members Profile	Ctrl+G	To find out who a user is, you can use his or her screen name to retrieve a copy of his or her Membership Profile.
Locate a Member Online	Ctrl+F	Use this option to search America Online and locate members who are currently online.
Personal Choices		Select the personal choices item to configure your personal online preferences. This includes areas such as Multimedia Support, Parental Controls, and Marketing preferences. These choices all relate to the screen name you are currently using. Each of your five possible screen names can be assigned different preferences.

Menu Item	Hotkey	Description
Parental Control		You can access the Parental Control setting directly by selecting this option.
Set Preferences	Ctrl+=	Unlike most of the other preference options on this menu, you can alter the setting in this area while offline. Some, but not all, of the settings available through this option are duplicated in the other areas.
Edit Stored Passwords		Alters the passwords stored on AOL. These are the passwords AOL automatically sends when you logon. If you want to protect your system from misuse, you should consider disabling this feature and entering your password manually each time you connect.
Edit Your Online Profile		Select this entry to alter your Online Profile. This is the public information about yourself that other America Online members can read.
Edit Screen Names		Add additional screen names to your account or edit existing ones by selecting this option. Each America Online account can have up to five separate screen names associated with it.

FlashSessions

One of the most recent additions to AOL is the ability to have AOL automatically sign on to America Online and retrieve new e-mail messages, send messages stored in your Outgoing folder, download files, and even retrieve copies of newsgroup articles from selected newsgroups, and when it's done, sign off for you as well.

Using this feature, which is known as FlashSessions, you can reduce considerably the amount of time you spend online doing simple tasks like sending and reading e-mail. To set up your computer to use FlashSessions, choose the FlashSession option discussed previously in the Mail Menu topic. When you do this, a window similar to the one shown in Figure 5.7 is displayed on the screen.

To configure a FlashSession, all you need to do is follow these steps:

1. If you want to obtain unread mail during a FlashSession select the Retrieve unread mail entry.

2. You can also decide whether AOL will automatically download files that people have e-mailed you by selecting or deselecting the …and attached files option.

FIGURE 5.7.

The FlashSessions window lets you configure your FlashSession options.

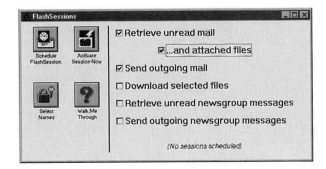

3. To send mail composed using the Send Later option, select the Send outgoing mail option.

4. If you want to automatically download any files currently listed in the Download Manager window, you should select the Download selected files option.

5. To retrieve copies of newsgroup articles during a FlashSession, select the Retrieve unread newsgroup messages option. This instructs AOL to retrieve a copy of all the messages in any of the newsgroups that you have selected for offline use. (For information about newsgroups and selecting ones that you want to read offline, see Chapter 8, "Usenet Newsgroups.")

6. Once your have read your newsgroup articles offline, you will no doubt want to make your own comments. To ensure that these comments are forwarded back to the right location select the Send outgoing newsgroup messages option.

Note

If you have more than one screen name defined on your system, you can use Select Names button to select which screen name or names will be used for the FlashSession. In this way, e-mail for all of your screen names can be collected at the same time.

7. After you have finished defining your FlashSession options, you can either activate a FlashSession immediately by clicking on the Activate Session Now button, or you can set up a schedule that tells AOL when you want sessions to be run.

   To set up a FlashSession schedule, click on the Schedule FlashSession button. When you do this, a dialog box like the one shown in Figure 5.8 is displayed.

8. Select the days on which you want FlashSessions to run and select the frequency. FlashSession can be configured to run every half hour, hourly, every two hours, every four hours, every eight hours, or once a day.

   You also need to select the time of day that the first session of the day will be run. When setting the time you can set the start time to 13 minutes past the hour or 43 minutes past the hour.

9. Finally, once you have set up your schedule, select the Enable Scheduler option at the top of the dialog box to turn regular FlashSessions on.

FIGURE 5.8.

Select the days and frequency of FlashSessions in the Schedule.

To ensure that your FlashSessions run on time, your AOL software must be running at the time scheduled for the start of the FlashSession.

Tip

Personal Filing Cabinet

When AOL runs a FlashSession, the results are stored in your Personal Filing Cabinet. (See Figure 5.9.) This is a special area on your hard drive that AOL sets aside for each of your separate screen names. Whenever you sign on using a different screen name, AOL automatically switches to the Personal Filing Cabinet associated with it.

FIGURE 5.9.

Your Personal Filing Cabinet.

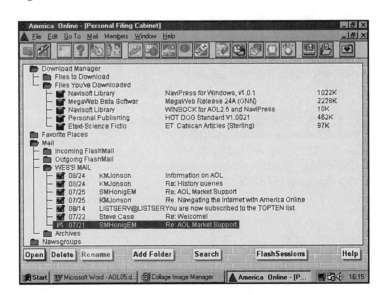

In your Personal Filing Cabinet, you will find a number of folders containing files, messages, and newsgroup articles that AOL has retrieved while online. To help you understand the purpose of each folder, in the following section each of the information categories that can be stored in your Personal Filing Cabinet are discussed.

> Mac Users: Currently, the Personal Filing Cabinet and Offline Newsgroup features are only available in the Windows version of AOL.

Download Manager

The first folder at the top of the Personal Filing Cabinet belongs to the Download Manager. The subfolders appearing below the main Download Manager folder contain a list of all the files you have either queued for download or have downloaded already.

Favorite Places

The Favorite Places folder contains all the links to World Wide Web pages and AOL departments or areas that appear when you open the Favorite Places window. This list should not, however, be confused with the list of Favorite Places listed on the Go To menu, which is a separate list entirely.

In Figure 5.9, the contents of this folder are currently hidden, as opposed to the Files You've Downloaded folder which is currently open. If you look at the icon appearing next to these two folders you will see that the Files You've Downloaded folder is depicted as open and the Favorite Places folder is depicted as closed. To open a closed folder, double-click on it using your mouse.

If the Favorite Places folder were open, you could double-click on any of the entries it contained to instruct AOL to automatically open the WWW page or America Online area it represented.

> Any window or area of America Online that can be added to your Favorite Places menu has a small heart-shaped icon located in the message bar at the top of the window. If you double-click on this icon, the window is automatically added to your Favorite Places list.

Mail

The Mail folder contains a number of subfolders that hold all your e-mail correspondence. The Incoming FlashMail folder contains any mail retrieved during a FlashSession. The Outgoing FlashMail folder contains any mail composed using the Send Later option which has not yet been sent to America Online.

To read any of these messages, open the folder you are interested in and double-click on the message concerned. AOL opens a standard message window where you can read the message, compose a reply, forward a copy to someone else, or delete the message from the filing cabinet.

The next folder in the list is a special one that I have set up to keep copies of important messages. You can create a new folder by clicking on the Add Folder button located at the bottom of the screen.

The Archive folder listed below the WES'S MAIL folder is where AOL stores a copy of messages once you have read them, and it also contains a copy of each message you have sent as well. Because such a feature can consume a considerable amount of disk space, you can enable or disable this option via the Set Preferences menu time on the Members menu.

Newsgroups

If you choose to take advantage of the Newsgroups feature of FlashSessions, a separate folder is created under the Newsgroups folder for each newsgroup you want to read offline.

In these folders, copies of every article posted to the newsgroup is stored so that you can read them once AOL has signed off. Because reading articles can be a very time-consuming process, being able to read them without the AOL usage meter running will save you a considerable amount of money.

You can also compose new articles and reply to existing ones while offline as well. Any of these articles can then be posted back to the appropriate newsgroups by AOL during the next FlashSession.

The Internet Connection

Being one of America Online's 14 main channels, the Internet Connection area acts as the main access point for all the Internet-related services provided by America Online.

As you have already discovered in this chapter, there are a number of ways you can access this area. You can select the Internet Connection icon on the AOL Main Menu, click on the toolbar icon—if you are a Windows user—or define it as a favorite place in the Go To menu.

Alternatively you can access the Internet Connection, by using its Keyword: **Internet**. To do this, open the Keyword window, shown in Figure 5.10, using the Ctrl+K or ⌘+K key combination. Then, in the field provided, enter the word **Internet** and click on the Go button.

Regardless of which option you choose, eventually the Internet Connection window shown in Figure 5.11 is displayed. This window is broken down into two main areas. On the left side of the screen there are five icons that take you to the main Internet services provided by America Online. The other side of the screen contains a list of additional services and special interest areas dealing with specific aspects of the Internet, or that contain features such as message boards, that and online discussions dealing with Internet-related topics.

FIGURE 5.10.

Enter **Internet** *as the keyword to open the Internet Connection window.*

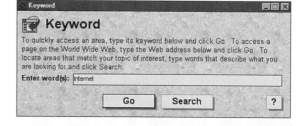

FIGURE 5.11.

The Internet Connection window gives you access to all the Internet services provided by America Online.

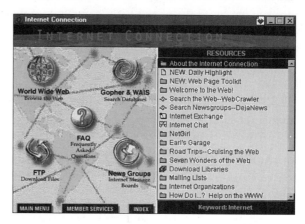

In the closing pages of this chapter, each of the major Internet services provided by America Online are explored briefly to give you a better idea of the range of services available.

World Wide Web—Browse the Web

To access each of the major Internet services provided by America Online, click on the icon associated with each one in the Internet Connection window.

Clicking on the World Wide Web icon causes AOL to start its World Wide Web browser and display the home page of America Online's World Wide Web site. (See Figure 5.12.) Alternatively, using the Keyword: **www** achieves the same result.

If you are using the Windows version of AOL, the World Wide Web browser opens as a part of AOL itself. On the other hand, if you are using the Macintosh version, then the World Wide Web browser is a separate application. (See Figure 5.13.)

In Chapter 12, "The World Wide Web," you'll find a detailed discussion of the World Wide Web and the use of AOL's World Wide Web browsers.

FIGURE 5.12.

Exploring the World Wide Web with AOL for Windows.

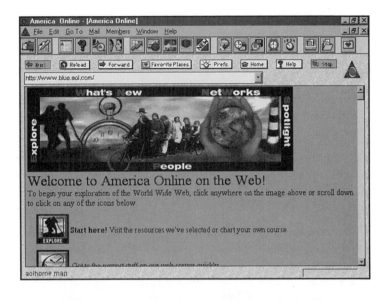

FIGURE 5.13.

The Macintosh version of AOL uses a separate application for browsing the World Wide Web.

Mac Users: Depending on how your computer is configured, you may need to manually start the WWW browser before starting AOL. (See the "Troubleshooting Tips for the Mac WWW Browser" section in Chapter 12, for more information about the Mac WWW browser.)

Tip

Gopher & WAIS—Search Databases

One of the big problems facing many people when they first begin to explore the Internet is coming to grips with the immense size. There are literally millions of different places you can visit, all of which might contain something you are interested in. However, because the Internet is actually nothing more than a set of connections between these millions of locations, you will need to use a very good road map to help you find your way around.

One of the best road maps, or Internet navigators, is based on a service known as Gopher. Gopher is a menu-based system containing links to information stored on thousands of major computer systems connected to the Internet. As a result, by using Gopher you can move around the Internet and visit different sites without needing to understand many of the complexities such a task would involve.

When America Online decided to introduce a Gopher service (see Figure 5.14) they did not stop at just creating a standard Gopher client. Instead, they built an enhanced system that also incorporates a powerful database search system known as a Wide Area Information Service or WAIS for short. By doing this, finding your way around the Internet was made even easier.

FIGURE 5.14.

America Online provides you with a customized Gopher and WAIS service that integrates AOL with the Internet.

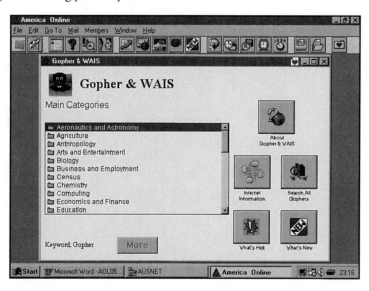

To learn about Gopher and WAIS turn to Chapter 11, "Gopher and WAIS."

FAQ—Frequently Asked Questions

One of the features that has become a regular part of the Internet is a set of documents known collectively as *Frequently Asked Questions* or *FAQs*. Most newsgroups, many Internet services, and some WWW pages contain a Frequently Asked Questions document that contains a list of questions and answers covering issues related to their particular service.

In keeping with this tradition, America Online has compiled its own set of FAQs covering all the Internet-related features and services that can be accessed using AOL. To read any of these documents click on the FAQ icon located in the Internet Connection window. When you do, AOL displays a window like the one shown in Figure 5.15. All the major subject categories are listed on this window. Select the one you are interested in to obtain a list of all the documents covering this subject.

FIGURE 5.15.

If you have a question about the Internet, then the Internet FAQ is a good place to start.

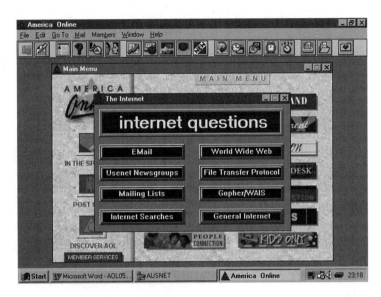

The Internet FAQ area is one of America Online's free areas.

Note

FTP—Download Files

If you are unable to locate a file in America Online's Software Library, maybe you need to take a look at the many file archives available via the Internet. To do this, click on the FTP icon in the Internet Connection window.

When you click on this icon, AOL displays the File Transfer Protocol—FTP window, shown in Figure 5.16. Along with a list of information files and a Frequently Asked Questions document, this window provides you with four icons that give you access to the various FTP services offered by America Online.

Chapter 9, "File Transfer Protocol (FTP)," explains in detail the FTP client software provided by America Online and looks at the types of files you are likely to find on some of the more popular FTP servers that America Online recommends.

Note

FIGURE 5.16.

*Download files from the
Internet using FTP.*

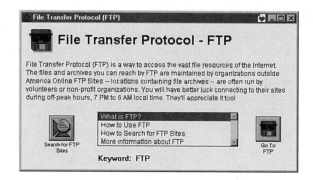

Newsgroups—Internet Message Boards

When you click on the Newsgroups icon, AOL opens the main Newsgroups window shown in Figure 5.17. This window gives you access to AOL's Usenet newsreader and the 20,000+ Internet-based discussion groups it provides. In many ways, newsgroups are like America Online's message boards.

As has already been discussed in this chapter, you can read articles posted to Internet newsgroups either while online or while offline by using FlashSessions.

FIGURE 5.17.

*When you click on the
Newsgroups icon, AOL
starts its newsgroup reader.*

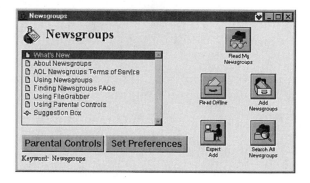

In Chapter 8, "Usenet Newsgroups," you'll find a detailed discussion of newsgroups and AOL.

Summary

Now that you have some understanding of the features offered by America Online, it is time to begin in earnest your exploration of the Internet.

In Part III of this book, "AOL's Internet Tools," each of the main Internet gateways offered by America Online is explained one chapter at a time, beginning with a discussion in the next chapter which covers techniques you need to learn to exchange e-mail with others on the Internet.

Then in Part IV, "The Internet Navigators," you will examine the ways that you can access the World Wide Web and other Internet navigation tools like Gopher, through the services offered by America Online.

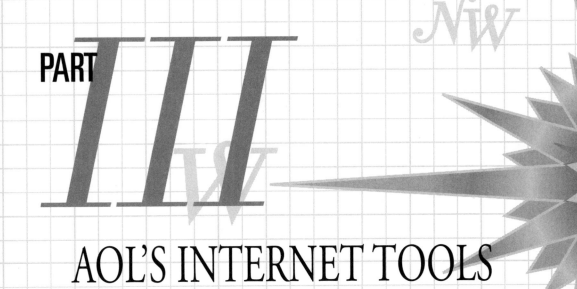

PART III

AOL'S INTERNET TOOLS

THE INTERNET E-MAIL GATEWAY

Understanding Internet Addresses

Screen Names and the Internet

Using E-Mail

Electronic mail, or e-mail, as discussed in previous chapters, has long been the driving force behind the widespread growth of the Internet.

Even though the original developers of ARPANET may not have foreseen the popularity of e-mail or even imagined its potential, for many people it is the main reason that they have an Internet connection. So, why is it so popular?

E-mail is fast! Unlike traditional communication methods, such as courier and postal services, e-mail can be sent and received almost instantly. There is no need to make trips to a mailbox or to wait for a postal worker to deliver an important letter. In addition, the same e-mail message can be sent around the corner, across the country, or even to the other side of the world, all in a matter of minutes and sometimes seconds.

E-mail can be sent and received at any time of day and from just about any location—provided, of course, that you have access to a computer and a phone line. For people who travel regularly, e-mail has become an invaluable tool. Using e-mail, they can keep in almost constant contact with company offices, their families, and their friends while on the road.

This chapter looks at how America Online users can exchange messages with people on the Internet. To do this it explores the following topics:

◆ IP addresses and Internet domain names

◆ Internet e-mail addresses

◆ Your America Online Internet address

◆ Sending e-mail to the Internet

◆ Sending files using e-mail

◆ Receiving e-mail from the Internet

Understanding Internet Addresses

Before looking at the steps required to send an e-mail message through the Internet using AOL, it is important that you understand the addressing system used by the Internet.

When you send e-mail to a person on the Internet, you need to consider the fact that they could actually be connected to any one of the thousands of separate networks that make up the Internet. In addition, most of these networks are entirely independent and have no relationship with any other network, apart from the fact that they are connected to the Internet. As a result, in many cases the same user ID or username is assigned to different people on different networks. Simply addressing a message with just a username or screen name, as is the case on AOL, would result in the message never reaching its desired destination.

To resolve this problem, the Internet uses an addressing system. This system gives each computer on the Internet a unique address, not unlike the street or city address you use when sending someone a message through the mail.

Addressing on the Internet

When TCP/IP was developed, it was realized that there needed to be a method of uniquely representing every computer connected to the network. To do this, a special numbering system was developed that assigned each machine a unique value known as an *IP address.*

This value consists of four separate parts, each containing a number between 1 and 255. When combined, these four values form what is known as a *dotted quad* or IP address. The reason for the term "dotted quad" relates to the way the address is written. The four numbers are written one at a time with a dot separating them. For example, the Internet site that maintains my Internet e-mail mailbox is represented as `190.192.215.5`.

> The actual process of assigning IP addresses to new computer systems is not a simple matter of picking the next number in the queue. However, because a full discussion of the procedures involved in determining an IP address is outside the scope of this book, you should take a look at the InterNIC Gopher site or the Internet Society WWW site for additional information.

Internet Domain Names

Even though IP addresses gave each machine a unique identifier, it wasn't long before people began to dislike them. As the number of computers connected to the Internet continued to grow, remembering all these somewhat confusing numbers became an increasingly difficult task.

After much discussion, a new addressing system was proposed. Instead of representing each site as a number, it was suggested that each site could be represented by a unique name. From a user's standpoint, this seemed like a wonderful idea. On the technical front, however, changing the way the entire Internet operated was deemed to be impractical.

A compromise was needed. Internally, TCP/IP needed to use the IP addressing system, while externally, users wanted to use a simpler naming method. To achieve this compromise, a system similar to that used by telephone companies was developed. A phonebook-like database was put in place that allowed people to use system names while TCP/IP retained the use of IP addresses.

When a system name (or *domain name,* as it has become known) is used where an IP address was expected, the computer in question contacts a special machine called a *domain name server.* The domain name server contains a list of IP addresses and domain names that it can cross reference. After conducting a search of its records, the domain name server tells the calling computer the IP address that corresponds to the domain name it was given. This allows the computer to continue its use of IP addressing, while at the same time freeing end users from the need to remember complex numbering systems.

This process is helped even further by the way domain names are formed. Much of the reasoning behind the term "domain name" comes from the fact that the name is used to describe not only the computer, but also the type of network it is connected to. In addition, in some cases, it also describes the geographical location of the network as well.

As Figure 6.1 shows, the domain name is broken into four parts. Not all parts are needed to create a valid domain name. However, regardless of which parts are used, the end result must be a name that is unique throughout the entire Internet.

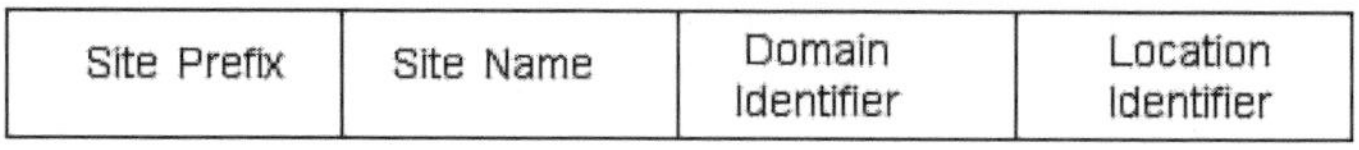

FIGURE 6.1.
Internet domain name structure.

Site Prefix	Site Name	Domain Identifier	Location Identifier

The two most common parts of a domain name are the *site name* and the *domain identifier*. Of these two, the domain identifier defines the type of network or organization that owns the site, and the site name usually represents the actual name of the organization.

While the site name can be just about anything an organization wishes to use, the domain identifier is expected to be one of a group of common names listed in Table 6.1. These identifiers are assigned by Network Solutions Inc. as a part of the InterNIC service set up by the National Science Foundation. The InterNic is also responsible for the approval and administration of domain names.

Table 6.1. Common domain identifiers.

Identifier	Description
.com	Commercial companies
.edu	Educational institutions
.gov	Government bodies
.mil	Military networks
.net	Internet-related network hosts
.org	Any organization that fails to fit into any of the other categories

Like the domain identifier, the *location identifier* is used to describe a site in greater detail, and in some cases actually replaces the domain identifier. While the domain identifier describes the type of organization, the location identifier defines the geographical location of the system. For example, Microsoft uses the domain name `microsoft.com`, which tells people that it is a commercial operation. In this case example there is no location identifier, due mainly to the fact that Microsoft is a U.S.-based company. As a rule, only non-U.S.-based computer systems use location identifiers.

However, if Microsoft decided to set up its own Internet site in the United Kingdom, it would most likely use a domain name such as `microsoft.com.uk`, which would describe both its ac-

> In a perfect world, such a system should result in unique names for every host. Unfortunately, there are sometimes clashes that prevent organizations from being granted the domain names they desire. In addition, with InterNIC already overloaded, there is little time to consider copyright and trademark issues when authorizing domain names. As a result, if the National Biscuit Company registers the name `nbc.com` before the popular broadcaster with the same initials, the domain name will be owned by the Biscuit company and there is very little that the broadcaster NBC can do about it.

With organizations increasing the number of machines connected to the Internet, the use of *site prefixes* has also become a common occurrence. When an organization decides to connect a new computer to the Internet, they usually want to give it a domain name similar to the one they are currently using. To do this, they add site prefixes to the front of their existing domain name. For example, if Microsoft were to set up a special computer dedicated to, say, Windows 95, they would probably give it a domain name such as `windows95.microsoft.com`.

The other reason for using site prefixes is to indicate the type of activities a particular computer can handle. When Microsoft decided to open a World Wide Web site, it set up a new machine with the address `www.microsoft.com`. In this case, the site prefix 'www' was used to describe the type of service the machine provides to the Internet. Table 6.2 provides a list of some of the more common site prefixes.

Table 6.2. Common site prefixes.

Prefix	Description
ftp	File Transfer Protocol servers
gopher	Gopher servers
news	Usenet news servers
wais	Wide Area Informationservers
www	World Wide Web servers

> Throughout this book you will often find domain names described using a special type of address called a Uniform Resource Locator or URL. Such an address adds an additional prefix to a domain name that describes its purpose. For example: `ftp://ftp.aol.com/` indicates that the domain name shown is associated with an FTP server, while `http://www.blue.aol.com/` indicates the address of a World Wide Web server. (For more information about URLs, see Chapter 12, "The World Wide Web.")

Internet E-Mail Addresses

The concept of domain names is of vital importance to your understanding of Internet e-mail. Because there are so many different computer systems and networks co-existing on the Internet, when you send e-mail to someone on the Internet, you need to address the message not only to their user ID or username, but also to the computer where their e-mail messages are stored.

To make this system work, most computers on the Internet use a special program known as an *e-mail server*. These programs, which are a lot like electronic post offices, handle the distribution of e-mail messages between all the different computers and interconnected networks on the Internet. In addition, they also collect and hold messages for users who have *accounts* with an e-mail server. These messages are stored in the electronic equivalent of a *mailbox*.

Each person who has an e-mail account on one of these servers is given a username similar to your AOL screen name. They use this username to access their mailbox. In addition, it is this username that, when combined with the domain name of their e-mail server, represents their e-mail address. For example, the domain name of my e-mail server or Internet mailbox is `world.net`, and my username on that system is `wtatters`. Therefore, to form my Internet e-mail address, you take these two pieces of information and join them together with the @ symbol.

My resulting e-mail address is `wtatters@world.net`.

It is interesting to note that you can also use a site's IP address instead of its domain name when forming an e-mail address. In that case, if you were sending an e-mail message to me, you could also write my e-mail address as `wtatters@192.190.215.5`

Screen Names and the Internet

As discussed in Chapter 2, "The History of America Online and Its Connection to the Internet," it was inevitable that AOL users and Internet users would eventually want to be able to exchange electronic mail messages with each other.

To make such a connection possible, there were two hurdles that needed to be crossed. The first was a purely technical issue which involved the construction of a physical connection between AOL and the Internet, while the second was an issue of aesthetics, and concerned the way that AOL users were to be addressed by people sending them e-mail from the Internet.

The America Online Domain Name

The first part of the problem was relatively easy to fix. As is the case for every computer that opens a link with Internet, when America Online opened its gateway to the Internet, it needed to obtain a domain name and an IP address. The domain name that AOL selected was naturally `aol.com`. If a person on the Internet wants to send you an e-mail message, this is the domain name they need to use.

You may also encounter another domain name for AOL called `AmericaOnline.aol.com`. If you want to log onto AOL via the Internet instead of the usual dial-up telephone number, this is the domain name you need to use. For more information about connecting to AOL in this manner, see Appendix B, "Connecting to America Online via the Internet."

America Online also has a special domain name for its WWW server which is `www.blue.aol.com`. This is the domain name you use when exploring the World Wide Web site operated by America Online. Finally, to round out the set, there is an FTP domain name called `ftp.aol.com` where you can download various AOL-related files.

Your Internet User ID

The second part of the problem was not quite as easily solved. Unlike Internet usernames, which consist solely of alphabetic names or codes, AOL screen names can and often do contain spaces. Although the characters and numbers in a screen name themselves do not pose any problems, spaces in a username are not permitted by the Internet.

To make screen names compatible with the Internet, it was decided that spaces in screen names would need to be removed when they were used in an Internet user ID. In addition, in most cases the Internet doesn't care about capitalization of names. As a result, all screen names should always be converted to lowercase.

You now have the two pieces of information needed to form an Internet e-mail address—a valid screen name and the AOL domain name. As a result, if you take your screen name—mine is `WTatters`—and append AOL's domain name to it, separating them with an '@' symbol, you get your AOL Internet e-mail address.

If you do this with my AOL screen name the resulting e-mail address is `wtatters@aol.com`. It is important to note again, that it is the domain name that determines the destination of an e-mail message. Even though my username at `world.net` is also `wtatters` like my AOL screen name, the Internet knows that America Online is the destination for any e-mail message addressed to me at `aol.com`.

Using E-Mail

Now that you understand the principles behind the Internet's e-mail addressing system, you are ready to look at how messages are exchanged between America Online and the Internet.

In the following section you learn how to send an e-mail message to the Internet, how to send both text files and binary files using e-mail, and also how to read messages and receive files sent to you by someone on the Internet.

Sending Mail through the Internet

The procedure for sending e-mail messages to the Internet is a relatively simple one. If you have ever sent a message to another person on AOL, you are well on the way to sending your first Internet e-mail message.

For the sake of this example, let's look at the steps involved in sending a message to my Internet mailbox. The e-mail address you will be using is `wtatters@world.net`:

1. On the AOL main screen, open the **M**ail menu and choose the **C**ompose Mail option, as shown in Figure 6.2.

FIGURE 6.2.

Select Compose Mail to create a new e-mail message.

You can also open the Compose Mail window by clicking on the Compose Mail icon located in the toolbar—it's the second icon from the left. Alternatively, holding down the Control key and the 'M' key (⌘+M on a Macintosh) when using the Windows version of AOL achieves the same result.

In addition, clicking on the Post Office icon located on the left-hand side of the Main Menu window displays the AOL Post Office window. There is also a Compose Mail icon in this window.

2. The Compose Mail window shown in Figure 6.3 should now be displayed on the screen. In the To: box of this window, type the e-mail address of the person you want to send the message to. In this case, enter **wtatters@world.net**.

Note

You can send the same message to more than one person by entering additional e-mail addresses in the To: box, and you can also send the same message to another AOL user by entering their screen name instead of an Internet e-mail address. The only rule you need to follow is that each e-mail address and screen name must be separated by a comma. For example: "wtatters@world.net, WTatters, taketwo@webcom.com" would send the same message to my Internet address, my AOL mail box, and my World Wide Web site.

FIGURE 6.3.

*Create messages you want
to send to people on the
Internet in the Compose
Mail window.*

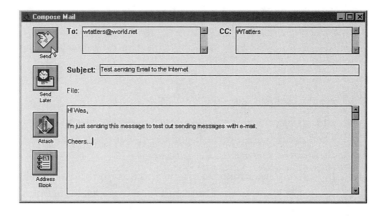

3. You can also tell AOL to send a copy of the message to people using what is known as a blind carbon copy. When you include a list of multiple people in the To: box, each person receiving a copy of the message is told the e-mail address or screen name of everyone else who received a copy of the message. By entering e-mail addresses or screen names in the CC: box instead of the To: box, these recipients will not be told the e-mail address or screen name of anyone else.

   In this example, enter your screen name in the CC: box to send yourself a copy of this message. I entered `WTatters`, but you should change this to reflect you own screen name.

Use the AOL Address Book to store commonly used Internet addresses. The only change you need to make from a regular AOL address is to put the person's Internet address in the field that says Screen Name.

4. Once you have finished addressing your message, use the Tab key to move to the Subject: field. In this field enter a brief description of the purpose and contents of the message.

It is considered bad form to send someone an e-mail message without a subject line. To ensure that the messages you send are read by their recipients, make sure you include something in the subject line. If you don't include a subject, it is highly unlikely that your message will ever be read.

5. Once all the paperwork is out of the way, type your message in the body of the Compose Mail window. There is no need to worry greatly about the length of each message, but you should keep in mind that the size of each message you send is limited to 27k, or around 27,500 characters.

Note

> Mac Users: Although the Macintosh version of AOL allows you to add different fonts and styles to text in your messages, these fonts and styles will not be displayed in any messages sent to the Internet.

6. Once you have entered your message and checked to make sure that the subject and address information are correct, click on the Send button located at the top left of the Compose Mail window. If you are currently online, doing this immediately sends a copy of the message to the Internet.

   If, however, you are not currently signed on to AOL, click on the Send Later button located below the Send button. Doing this places the message in your Outgoing Mail box. The next time you sign on to AOL you will need to run a FlashSession to get AOL to send the message for you. (See the "FlashSessions" topic in Chapter 5, "Working with AOL," for more information.)

If you've been following along through all these steps, congratulations! You have just sent your first e-mail message to someone on the Internet.

Sending Files through the Internet

Sometimes sending a typed message to a person is just not good enough. Maybe you want to send someone a copy of a spreadsheet, a picture, or a wordprocessing document. To answer this need, AOL provides you with a button that allows you to send copies of files stored on your computer to another person.

Clicking on the Attach button opens a File Attachment dialog box (see Figure 6.4). This dialog allows you to attach to a message almost any file stored on your computer. When you mail the message, a copy of the file is sent along with it.

FIGURE 6.4.

The Attach File dialog box allows you to attach a file to an AOL message.

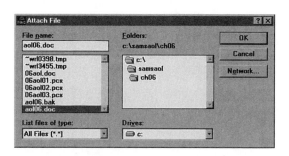

Unfortunately, due to the way that Internet mail works, you will need to check with people you want to send files to before sending them attached files. Not all Internet mail readers are capable of separating attached files properly.

Files attached to Internet messages can contain only *ASCII text*, unlike files attached to messages sent to other people on AOL, which can be what are known as *binary files*. A binary file can be a file such as a spreadsheet, a computer program, or even a wordprocessing document; basically, any file you use on your computer, apart from those that you can edit with a *text editor*.

> Computers store information as numbers. This is great for doing mathematical calculations, but it is of little use if you need to use a computer to store written information. To get around this problem, a table was developed called the ASCII table, which assigned each letter of the alphabet to a number. Using this table, a computer stores text as a long list of numbers. As a result, text files are often referred to as ASCII files or 8-bit ASCII text files.

To get around the fact that you can only send text files across the Internet, America Online now includes a special feature that automatically converts any file you attach to a message into what is called a MIME-encoded ASCII file. (See the "MIME" topic in the following section for more information about MIME encoding.)

If the person you are communicating with uses an e-mail program that can also encode and decode files using MIME, then you will be able to use the Attach button to send them messages. If not, you will need to use the techniques discussed later this chapter, in the "Encoding Files under Windows" and "Encoding Files on a Macintosh" topics.

Luckily, this problem is not unique to America Online. The same problem has existed throughout the Internet since the use of e-mail first began. To get around this weakness, a number of programs have been developed that can convert a binary file into a special type of ASCII text file.

To give you a better understanding of the options available, the following section of this book discusses the two major ASCII encoding methods currently available.

UUENCODE and UUDECODE

The most popular method of converting binary files to encoded ASCII files involves the use of a program made popular by theUNIX operating system. This program, called UUENCODE, when given the name of a binary file, converts the file into a special type of ASCII text file that is created in such a way that it uses only the letters listed in what is called the 7-bit ASCII table.

> The 7-bit ASCII table is a special version of the ASCII table containing the 128 most-used characters, as opposed to the 8-bit table mentioned earlier that includes 256 characters.

Once created, this file can be easily transmitted as a part of an e-mail message. When the message arrives at its destination, all the receiver needs to do is run UUDECODE—UUENCODE's sister program—to convert the ASCII text file back into a binary file.

However, as the effects of the 1990s multimedia explosion have begun to work their way into the Internet, a number of UUENCODE's weaknesses have started to become apparent. Specifically, some types of binary files cannot be properly encoded using UUENCODE, resulting in garbaged binary files when the encoded file is decoded. Files such as some audio and compressed video files fall into this category.

MIME

Because people obviously want to be able to send all types of files using e-mail, a new encoding standard was developed. Although specially targeted at the multimedia market, it also provides a number of benefits for all encoding purposes.

The Multipurpose Internet Mail Extension format, or MIME, can properly encode and decode numerous types of binary files, including:

◆ Images and pictures

◆ MPEG and full motion video

◆ Sampled and computer-generated sound files

◆ Executable computer programs

◆ Compressed files created by PKZIP and other utilities

In addition, the process used by MIME when it encodes a binary file generates an encoded file that is often noticeably smaller than a file created using UUENCODE.

> Files created by UUENCODE and MIME are much larger than the original files they are generated from due to how they are created. This increased size should be taken into consideration when you send files using e-mail, as not all e-mail systems can handle large e-mail messages. To get around the problem of large messages, most UUENCODE and MIME utilities offer a feature that allows you to split a large file into a set of smaller files.

Encoding Files Under Windows

If you want to send a binary file to a person who does not have the ability to decode MIME encoded messages, you will need to encode the file manually using a program that can handle the UUENCODE message format.

Even though UUENCODE is a UNIX program, users of other operation systems have also been well provided for. On computers running Windows, the most popular program available is called Wincode. A copy of Wincode is included on the CD-ROM that came with this book.

Alternatively, to locate a copy of the latest version of Wincode, a good place to start is the Macmillan World Wide Web server Software Library. This site contains a wide variety of computing-related files, including many programs specific to the Internet. The URL for the software library main directory is `http://www.mcp.com/softlib/` and for the page that contains a copy of Wincode, `http://www.mcp.com/softlib/windows-utilities/wapps.html`.

> Appendix D, "Compression and Encryption Software," provides an in-depth look at many of the options and functions offered by Wincode.

While there are a number of different encoding utilities available for Windows, the area that sets Wincode apart is its ability to encode and decode both UUENCODE and MIME format files. In addition, it can also oversee the process of splitting large files into small segments suitable for use on e-mail systems that can't handle large files.

As a result, by using Wincode in combination with AOL, you can very easily attach binary files to a message destined for an Internet e-mail address. To send a file as a part of an Internet e-mail message follow these steps:

1. Assuming you have installed a copy of Wincode, start it and select the **E**ncode option from the **F**ile menu. You can also start the Encode module by clicking on the Encode icon located on the Wincode toolbar, as indicated by the mouse pointer in Figure 6.5.

FIGURE 6.5.

Clicking on the Encode button starts Wincode's encode module.

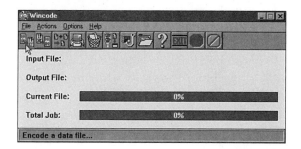

2. Once the File to Encode dialog box (see Figure 6.6) opens, click on the **O**ptions button located at the bottom right hand side of the dialog box.

3. By default, when Wincode encodes a file, it saves the encoded version as a single file. However, because messages sent using AOL are limited to 27k, or 27,684 characters in length, you need to tell Wincode to limit the size of the encoded files it creates to this size. When you do this Wincode automatically creates a set of files instead of a single one.

   To tell Wincode to do this, make sure the Single File checkbox is turned off. Then, in the Bytes per File box, type **27000.**

   In this example, I have also changed the Encoded File Directory so that encoded files are stored in a separate directory. This is a matter of taste, but if you use Wincode on a regular basis it is a good practice to adopt.

FIGURE 6.6.

The File to Encode dialog allows you to select the file you want to encode.

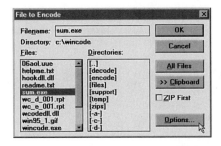

FIGURE 6.7.

The Encode Options dialog lets you tailor the way Wincode works to suit your needs.

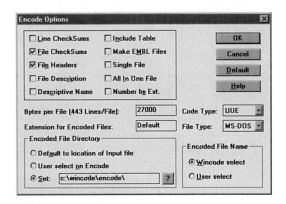

4. Once you set the required options, click on the OK button to return to the File to Encode dialog box. At this stage select the file you wish to encode and then hit the Enter key or click on the OK button.

5. A UUENCODE version of the file you selected is saved in the c:\wincode\encode directory with a .UUE file extension. For example, the SUM.EXE file in Figure 6.6 was saved as SUM.UUE.

Note

Because SUM.EXE was a small file (less than 27k when encoded), Wincode only needed to create one file. If the file was larger that 27k when encoded, Wincode would have created a series of files, such as SUM01.UUE, SUM02.UUE, SUM03.UUE and so forth.

6. Now that your file is encoded, open AOL and select **C**ompose Mail using one of the options discussed previously.

   In the TO: box type the Internet e-mail address of the person you want to send the file to, and in the Subject: field type a description of the contents of the file.

The contents of the Subject field are even more important if you need to send a large file—one with multiple sections. This is because each section must be sent as separate message.

As a result, to let people know whether there is more than one section for a file, it is standard practice to append something like (1 of 1) or (1-1) to the end of the Subject: field, even for single section files. Naturally, for multiple section files, you would change the Subject: for each, for example: LARGE.EXE (1-3), LARGE.EXE (2-3), LARGE.EXE (3-3).

7. You now need to add the encoded file to the message.

   Because the Attach option does not yet work with Internet e-mail, you need to take a slightly different path. Select the File menu at the top of the screen and choose the Open option.

   This will open the Open a file dialog box shown in Figure 6.8. Using this dialog box, locate and select the file you encoded previously and then click on the OK button. In this example, SUM.UUE was selected.

FIGURE 6.8.

The Open a file dialog box allows you to open a wide variety of files while using AOL.

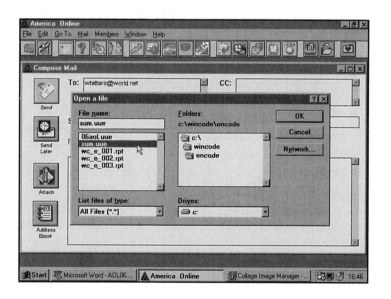

8. AOL has a built-in tool that allows it to display a wide variety of files. In this case, AOL detected that the file was a text file and has displayed it using an appropriate viewer. (See Figure 6.9.)

FIGURE 6.9.

The contents of SUM.UUE *are automatically displayed using AOL's built-in text viewer.*

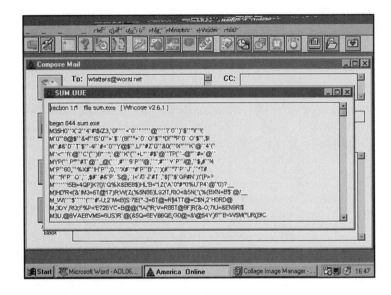

You can also use AOL to display graphics files. If AOL detects that you have selected a image, it automatically displays the contents of the file as a picture.

9. With the contents of SUM.UUE displayed on the screen, open the **E**dit menu and choose the **S**elect All option to highlight the contents of the text viewer. Ctrl+A (⌘+A on a Macintosh) performs the same action. Then, open the **E**dit menu again and choose the **C**opy option to copy the text onto the Windows clipboard. Ctrl+C (⌘+C on a Macintosh) performs the same action.

   Once you have copied the text, close the text viewer.

10. In the Compose Mail window, click in the message area and then open the **E**dit menu and choose the **P**aste option. (Ctrl+V performs the same action as selecting the **P**aste option.)

   If you have been following these steps, your screen should now look something like the one shown in Figure 6.10.

11. After checking that your address and subject are correct, click on the Send button or the Send Later button to transmit the file to the Internet.

FIGURE 6.10.

Click on the Send Later button to delay the sending of this message until you run your next FlashSession.

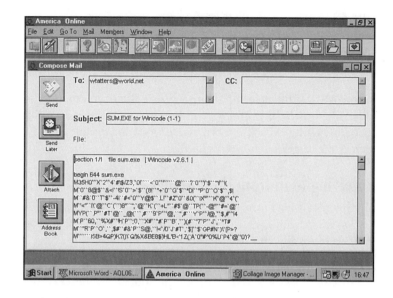

Encoding Files on a Macintosh

The actual process of sending a file using the Macintosh version of AOL is the same as for the Windows version. Where the difference obviously lies, however, is in the encoding software.

One of the best places to find copies of Macintosh software is at the University of Texas WWW site located at: `http://wwwhost.ots.utexas.edu/mac/main.html`. This site contains copies of all the most popular Macintosh shareware programs and related files. More specifically, it also contains many compression and encoding programs. These files can be found at `http://wwwhost.ots.utexas.edu/mac/pub-mac-compression.html`.

Of all the utilities available at this site there are two that are a must for any serious Internet users.

UUlite

Probably the most well-known program currently available is the one developed by Jeff Strobel called UUlite. Using this program you can encode and decode UUENCODED files.

You can choose from Smart Encode and decode options or perform the conversions manually. There is also support for automatic mapping of UNIX file extensions to Macintosh type/creator codes, and the ability to manually adjust type/creator settings. UUlite also includes a feature that allows you to convert UNIX style text files into ones which are compatible with the Macintosh.

The only limiting factor with UUlite is the lack of MIME encoding support. There is, however, a solution to that problem in another program called MPack.

MPack

MPack version 1.5 was developed by John Myers and ported to the Macintosh by Chris Newman. While a copy is available at the University of Texas site, you can also obtain a copy from the MPack host site at `ftp://ftp.andrew.cmu.edu/pub/mpack`.

Where MPack differs from UUlite is that it allows you to work with MIME-encoded files. It fully supports the BASE64 standard which is the basic encoding standard used for MIME encoding. Using MPack you can both encode and decode MIME files and control parameters such as the length of encoded/split files.

Receiving Mail from the Internet

Any Internet e-mail messages sent to you at AOL are stored in your private mailbox until you wish to read them. Each time you connect to America Online, your AOL software checks to see if there are any unread messages in your mailbox.

If there are new messages, the Letter Box icon is activated in the toolbar and a YOU HAVE MAIL message is displayed on the In the Spotlight window. (See Figure 6.11.) In addition, if at any time while you are online AOL detects that new mail has arrived, the Letter Box icon is activated automatically.

FIGURE 6.11.

The Letter Box icon in the toolbar is activated when you have new mail in your mailbox.

Letter Box icon

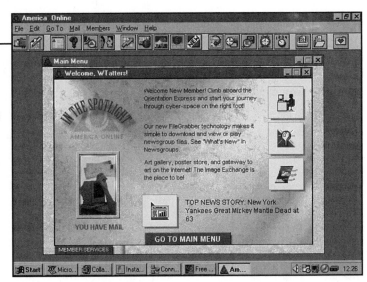

Reading New Messages

To read any new messages, all you need to do is follow these steps:

1. Click on the Letter Box icon in the toolbar—it is the first icon from the left. This opens the New Mail window shown in Figure 6.12.

The New Mail window displays an itemized list of all your new messages, showing the date the message arrived, who it was sent by, and the subject of the message.

> AOL does not differentiate between messages you receive from different services. As a result, messages from the Internet, AOL, and other services, are all listed together. In fact, the only way that you are able to tell the source of most messages is by the address of the sender.

2. To read the contents of a message, select it and then click on the Read button.

   When you do this a message window opens that displays the message contents. Figure 6.13 shows the third message listed in the New Mail window from Figure 6.12.

FIGURE 6.12.

The New Mail window lists all new messages you have received from both AOL and the Internet.

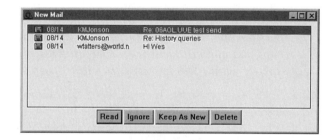

FIGURE 6.13.

The AOL message window.

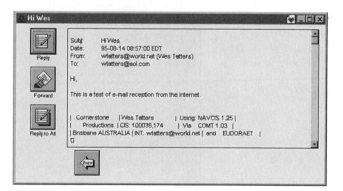

3. After reading the message, you can send a reply to its sender by clicking on the Reply button. In addition, if you highlight any part of the original message before you click on the Reply button, the highlighted section is automatically copied into the body of the new message and surrounded by '>>' '<<' symbols. These are known as quote symbols.

   If there are multiple recipients listed in the header section of the message, clicking on the Reply to All button sends a copy of your reply message to each person listed.

   Finally, you can also send a copy of the message to another person by clicking on the Forward button.

4. The message window also contains navigation buttons that allow you to move to the next new message or the a previous new message, depending on where you are in the list.

In Figure 6.13, because this is the last message in the list, only the Prev button is available. If you click on this button, the message prior to this one is displayed.

Receiving Files from the Internet

Obviously, if it is possible for you to include an encoded file in a message you send to the Internet, it should also be possible for someone on the Internet to send attached files back to you.

As was the case when sending files to the Internet, you have two options depending on the capabilities of the person sending you a message. If they send you a file encoded in the MIME format, AOL looks after the coding for you and then lets you download the decoded file directly to your hard drive.

However, if they can only send files in UUENCODE format or their mail systems force them to send you large files split in a number of small messages, you will need to use a program like Wincode to decode the file and convert it back into binary format.

If you receive a message from the Internet that AOL can not automatically decode, the message will look something like Figure 6.14. On the Internet, the attachment process physically includes the file as ASCII text in the body of the message. The jumble of letters near the bottom of the message area in Figure 6.14 is, in fact, the start of the encoded file.

FIGURE 6.14.

An e-mail message containing an encoded file.

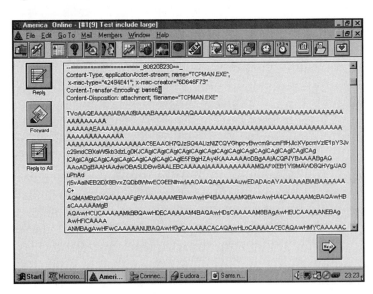

To decode this file manually you will need to follow these steps:

1. Retrieve the message as discussed in the previous section using the New Mail window.

2. Once the e-mail message is displayed in a message window, select the Save **A**s option from the **F**ile menu. This opens a Save As dialog box similar to the one shown in Figure 6.15.

FIGURE 6.15.

The Save Text As dialog allows you to store a copy of the message in a format suitable for decoding.

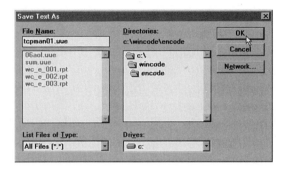

3. You need to give the message a filename. In this case I used TCPMAN01.UUE. The UUE file extension is the default expected by Wincode and the 01 because this was, in fact, a part of a set of multiple messages. You also need to set the directory to `C:\WINCODE\ENCODE` or some other appropriate location on your hard drive. When all the information is correct, click on the OK button to save the message.

4. The message can now be read by Wincode or any other appropriate conversion/encoding utility and converted back into a binary format. See Appendix D for more information on encoding and decoding files.

If you are having trouble decoding a message, it may be because it has been encoded using a format other than UUENCODE or MIME. In this case, you will need to talk to the person that sent you the message to find out how the message was encoded.

Summary

Over the course of the last 25 years, e-mail has opened communications doors that, in the past, people would never have thought possible. The capability of conducting written exchanges using e-mail is changing the way people communicate. It is expanding their horizons, changing the way they do business, and making global communications as commonplace as a chat over the back fence with your neighbor.

For America Online users, access to Internet e-mail opens up a wide range of new possibilities, not least of which is the ability to join any of the thousands of mailing lists currently running on the Internet.

Chapter 7, "Mailing Lists," takes a look at how you go about joining one of these lists and also explores the benefits of doing so.

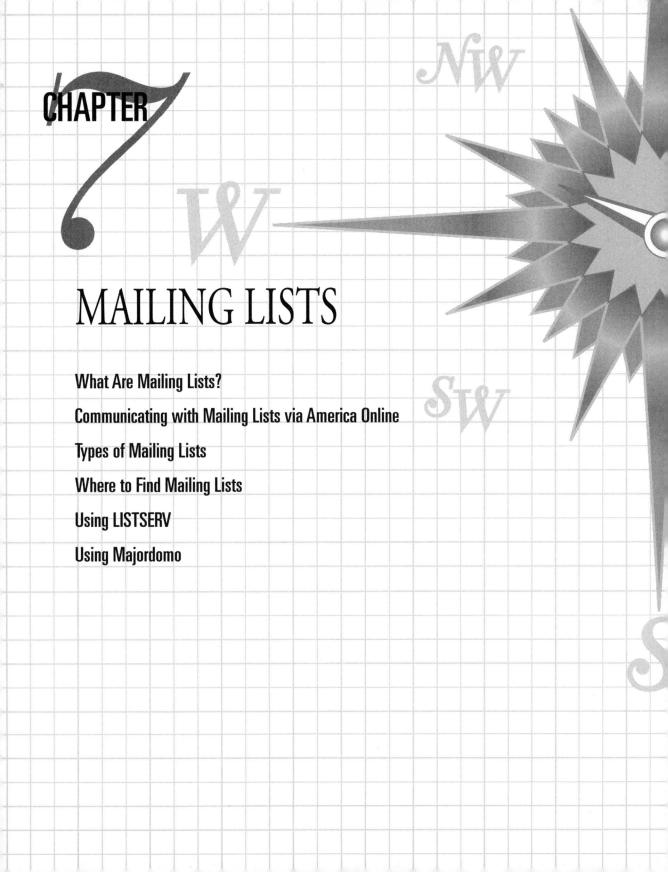

CHAPTER 7

MAILING LISTS

With the advent of e-mail, suddenly people were able to communicate more freely and effectively than they had ever thought possible.

As they became more familiar with the capabilities e-mail offered, the idea of using e-mail to conduct discussions and share ideas with groups of people dawned. This realization eventually led to the development of mailing lists.

Today mailing lists are used for a variety of reasons. Some allow people to discuss topics of mutual interest, while others are more like magazines or periodicals—delivering the equivalent of electronic newspapers to their subscribers.

This chapter looks at how America Online users can participate in mailing lists by discussing the following topics:

◆ What are mailing lists?
◆ Communicating with mailing lists using AOL
◆ The different types of mailing lists
◆ Using LISTSERV
◆ Using Majordomo

What Are Mailing Lists?

Essentially, a mailing list is a register of people who have requested or *subscribed* to a special e-mail service. This e-mail service is used to forward copies of each message it receives to every person on the mailing list. In this way, electronic messages can easily be shared by many people.

In practical terms, this capability provides a mechanism that allows general discussions, software support, conferences, and even electronic debates to be conducted using e-mail. It does this by ensuring that every participant is mailed a copy of each e-mail message sent to the mailing list.

Today there are mailing lists covering thousands of topics, hosted by computer systems all over the Internet. Many of these mailing lists discuss educational topics, while others deal with practical issues such as food and nutrition or computer software and hardware. Some, on the other hand, deal with less conventional subjects, such as David Letterman's nightly Top Ten List. To give you an idea of the wide variety of topics available, Table 7.1 lists 10 of the most popular mailing lists on LISTSERV—one of the major mailing list services.

Table 7.1. The LISTSERV Top 10.

List Name	*Subscribers*	*Description*
TOPTEN	66,184	David Letterman's Top 10
MINI-AIR	23,173	The Mini-Annals of Improbable Research
TIDBITS	19,253	A newsletter for Mac users

List Name	Subscribers	Description
ROADMAP	17,180	Roadmap workshop subscription list
NEW-LIST	14,760	New list announcements
OMRI-L	10,630	Open Media Research Institute Daily Digest (SUNY)
INDIA-D	10,373	The India News & Discussion Network at BGSU
CCMAN-L	9,794	Chinese Magazine Network
LOOKING	9,327	The Personals India Network at BGSU
CHINA-ND	8,773	China News Digest (US News)

Although some of the smaller mailing lists are managed by hand, this is not a practical option when you begin to deal with lists that have tens of thousands of subscribers. To cope with these large lists, a special type of computer program known as a *list processor* was developed. Using such a program, it is possible to manage both the registration of names on a mailing list and the distribution of messages to each member of the list with little or no human intervention.

BITNET

For the researchers and scientists who began to use mailing lists in the early 1970s, they were like a dream come true. They made possible a whole new level of interaction and flexibility of discussion. Previously, the only way to communicate findings and engage in scientific discussions with your peers around the world was to attend conferences and meetings. Unfortunately, for many people these were held far too infrequently to be of much practical day-to-day use. Mailing lists replaced all this with daily correspondence and rapid feedback.

During the 1970s, however, only research and government institutions were permitted to connect to ARPANET. This left a large number of people in the education community out in the cold, so to speak. Many of them were beginning to hear about e-mail and mailing lists from their acquaintances, but because they did not have access to ARPANET, they were unable to participate. Eventually, some of these people decided to create their own network, and as a result, in 1981 BITNET was born.

By connecting to BITNET, any education or research body could offer e-mail and mailing list communications to all members of its campus community. Due to this more open connection policy, BITNET soon became a popular network, with nodes rapidly springing up across the country and eventually around the world.

Unlike ARPANET, which was built for the purpose of remote computing, BITNET was designed from the ground up as an e-mail and mailing list service. Instead of using packet network connections such as those operated by ARPANET, BITNET was built around a *store and forward* communications system based on a popular IBM protocol. Using this system, it was possible for even small organizations to use BITNET without the costs associated with the permanent connections required of ARPANET. Today BITNET is managed by the Corporation for Research and Education Network (CREN), which represents over 1,000 academic and research centers in 50 countries worldwide.

While BITNET was initially a separate network to that of ARPANET, when the ARPANET was eventually replaced by NSFNET and the connectivity limitations decreased, gateways were opened to the emerging Internet. This permitted BITNET and the Internet to exchange e-mail. As an added bonus, these gateways also gave Internet users the ability to participate in any of the 5,000+ public BITNET mailing lists.

LISTSERV

LISTSERV—a computer program written for VAX/VMS computers—is the list processor responsible for the distribution of all mailing lists operated by computers connected to BITNET.

In addition to managing the distribution process, LISTSERV also maintains subscription requests and other user related activities. You communicate with LISTSERV by sending it e-mail messages containing a set of simple commands or instructions. Using these commands, you can

◆ Subscribe to a mailing list

◆ Cancel a current subscription

◆ Request catalogs of available mailing lists

◆ Retrieve files stored on BITNET computers

The section titled "Using LISTSERV" later in this chapter looks at the commands used to perform these actions and discusses how you use AOL to send them to LISTSERV.

Note

> Today, LISTSERV is available on platforms other than the original VMS. For more information on LISTSERV, you may like to visit the L-Soft International WWW site at: http://www.lsoft.com/.

LISTPROC

In recent years, CREN has begun to promote the use of a replacement for LISTSERV called LISTPROC. This software, unlike LISTSERV, runs on computer systems based on UNIX—the popular system of choice for Internet servers.

From a user's standpoint, LISTPROC operates in much the same way as LISTSERV and supports the same basic set of commands. At this stage, there are only a relatively small number of mailing lists using LISTPROC, but over the coming years, it is likely that more and more lists based on this program will begin to appear.

A full discussion of the capabilities offered by LISTPROC is available from the CREN WWW server at `http://www.cren.net/`. This site also contains information about BITNET, BITNET II and many of the new services CREN currently has under development.

Majordomo

Although LISTSERV is a very popular tool for mailing list management, it is suitable only for use on computers connected to BITNET. Computers connected to the Internet that want to operate mailing lists need to use a program that can take advantage of Internet-based e-mail services. To meet this need a number of different programs have been developed, but by far the most popular is the list processor known as Majordomo.

Majordomo is not a computer program in the true sense of the word. Instead, it is a collection of script files written in a computer scripting language called PERL. By using PERL, it's possible for Majordomo to operate on a variety of computer platforms and operating systems. Because of this portability, Majordomo has become the most popular mailing list processor available on the Internet.

Like LISTSERV, Majordomo uses e-mail messages to control its operations. However, some of the commands and capabilities offered by Majordomo differ from those supported by LISTSERV. The section titled "Using Majordomo" later in this chapter will discuss the differences between LISTSERV and Majordomo and look at how you communicate with Majordomo using AOL.

The developers of Majordomo operate a WWW server at `http://www.greatcircle.com`. This site also contains a number of discussion papers, dealing with mailing lists in general, that some of you may find of interest.

Communicating with Mailing Lists via America Online

As I mentioned in the previous section, list processors use e-mail messages to control their operations. For this to occur, each list processor needs an e-mail mailbox and a corresponding e-mail address. (See "Where to find Mailing Lists" later in this chapter for tips on locating these addresses.)

In most cases there are actually a number of e-mail addresses the list processor uses for different tasks. These e-mail addresses can be categorized into two types—list processor addresses and mailing list addresses.

List Processor Addresses

The first e-mail address you need when communicating with mailing lists is the e-mail address of the list processor. This is the address you use when you want to communicate with the list processor itself.

For a LISTSERV list processor, this will be an address such as `listserv@bitnic.cren.net`. This address is in fact the e-mail address of the list processor operated by CREN. Messages you send to this address tell the list processor what actions you require it to perform. (See "Using LISTSERV" and "Using Majordomo" later in this chapter for a full discussion of the commands available using these two services.)

As was the case when sending Internet e-mail, all you need to do to send messages to a list processor address using AOL is to enter the e-mail address in the TO: field of the Compose Mail window, instead of a screen name.

List Addresses

Each mailing list operated by a list processor will also have its own e-mail mailbox and corresponding address. This is the address that you use when you send messages that you want the list processor to distribute to the mailing list's subscribers.

It is important to understand that you should not send command messages to this e-mail address. Instead, they need to be sent to the list processor's e-mail address.

Receiving Messages from a Mailing List

As I discussed in Chapter 6, any e-mail messages you receive from the Internet are stored in your AOL mailbox until you retrieve them. Because messages distributed by mailing lists are essentially e-mail messages, America Online does not differentiate between them in any way.

When you receive new mail using AOL, any mailing-list based messages will appear in the New Mail window, along with any other messages you receive from people on America Online or the Internet.

AOL's Mailbox Size

There is one issue relating to mailing lists that you do need to be careful about. Your AOL mailbox can only hold 550 messages at any one point in time.

Now while this may sound like a lot of messages, if you happen to subscribe to some of the more popular mailing lists it would only take a couple of days for your mailbox to become full. When this occurs, any new mail that is sent to you will be returned to the sender—the mail will be *bounced* in Internet terms. Bounced mail has a tendency to get people upset and can result in your name being removed from a mailing list.

As a result you need to keep a careful check on the number of messages in your mailbox, by running regular FlashSessions. Alternatively, if you do subscribe to a very busy list, you may like to consider creating a separate screen name which you use just for that list.

> Each AOL account can have up to five separate screen names associated with it.

Types of Mailing Lists

Regardless of which list processor a mailing list is managed by, each list falls into one of the following categories:

◆ Unmoderated

◆ Moderated

◆ Publications

◆ Digests

Unmoderated Lists

Most mailing lists tend to allow a fairly free range of discussion. However, you are expected to keep the conversation in line with the mailing list's subject. These mailing lists are called *unmoderated* lists.

Basically, there are no traffic cops watching these lists to ensure that the subject is maintained. However, most people who subscribe to a list have done so for a good reason, so moving off the topic is a sure-fire way of getting your mailbox stuffed with messages from people telling you to get back to the topic.

Although these lists may sound like a free-for-all, you are still expected to play by the rules, and failing to do so can result in your removal from the list.

Moderated Lists

Moderated lists, on the other hand, have an *administrator* who views and approves each message before it is distributed. As opposed to unmoderated lists, these mailing lists tend to deal with more intellectual discussions and operate in a orderly fashion.

Unfortunately, there is one downside to participating in moderated lists. Whereas messages sent to unmoderated lists are usually distributed within minutes of being sent, messages sent to moderated lists can sometimes take days to be distributed. How long it actually takes often depends on the amount of time the administrator can give to the list, and also the number of messages that need to be approved.

Publications

Not all mailing lists are used for discussion purposes. There is a special type of list that can best be thought of as an electronic newsletter or magazine.

A number of organizations now use this type of list to keep people up to date or to communicate information. In recent months, Microsoft has started one such mailing list, which has received considerable publicity, that keeps people informed regarding the latest Windows 95 developments. Every 14 days, each WinNews subscriber receives an electronic newsletter from Microsoft in the form of an e-mail message. This e-mail message contains various tips and hints and other useful information dealing with Windows 95.

Unlike a normal mailing list, you do not send messages to these mailing lists for automatic distribution. As such, they are strictly a one-way affair from the list's administrator to its subscribers.

Note

> To subscribe to WINNEW send an e-mail message to ENEWS99@MICROSOFT.NWNET.COM with the words "SUBSCRIBE WINNEWS" in the message body.

Digests

For many people, one of the big problems with mailing lists is the large number of messages that flood into their mailbox at all hours of the day and night.

To get around this problem, *digests* were developed. Instead of each message being distributed immediately, they are collected by the list processor or by the list's administrator and compiled into one large message or digest. At a predetermined time—either once a day, once a week, or once a month—a copy of this compiled digest is mailed to all subscribers.

Instead of receiving hundreds and maybe thousands of individual messages, subscribers receive a single message that contains all the discussions since the last digest was distributed. There is one disadvantage with digests, however. Because all the messages arrive together, it is more difficult to make replies to individual participants and to follow individual conversations.

Many moderated and unmoderated lists now offer you the choice of receiving a digest or continuous messages. Also, some of the newer systems allow you to tailor the type of digest you receive to your own needs.

Where to Find Mailing Lists

With all this discussion about the thousands of mailing lists that are available, you are no doubt saying, "Great—but how do I find out which ones are best for me?"

It will probably come as no surprise to discover that you are not the first person to ask this question. As a result, over the years a number of lists have been compiled that attempt to catalog all of the mailing lists currently available. To help you locate these catalogs, this section looks at some of the popular mailing list catalogs.

The AOL Mailing List Directory

For America Online users, the best place to start is the AOL Mailing List Directory. To access this directory, you need to first open the Internet Connection window, Keyword: **Internet**. (See Figure 7.1.)

FIGURE 7.1.

The Internet Connection window gives you access to the many Internet-related services offered by AOL.

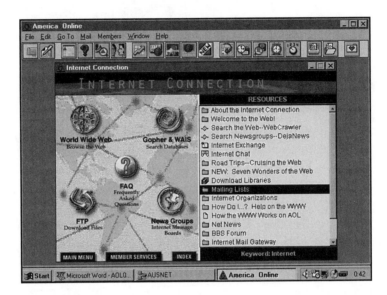

The Internet Connection window is the main gateway to all the Internet-related services offered by America Online. From this window you can easily select any of the available services by either clicking on the appropriate button or by selecting an option from the Resources list.

To open the Mailing List Directory, double click on the Mailing List entry in the Resources list. Doing this opens a window similar to the one shown in Figure 7.2.

FIGURE 7.2.

The AOL Mailing List Directory.

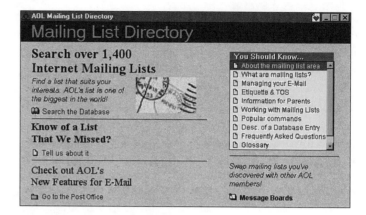

You Should Know

The first time you visit this window, it is a good idea to spend a few minutes reading though the information provided by the entries in the You Should Know list.

When you do this you should pay special attention too the Frequently Asked Questions information. Chances are that, if you have a problem with using mailing lists, someone else will most likely have asked about the difficulty before you. The Frequently Asked Questions entry contains a list on commonly asked questions and answers that may very well assist you with any difficulties you may have.

A quick review of the Etiquette & TOS entry will not go too far astray either. While most mailing list users are relatively tolerant of new users, however, there are a few things that you can do that will get just about everyone else offside in no time at all. This entry details some of these major faux pas and offers some simple suggests about keeping the peace on the Internet. (See Chapter 8, "Usenet Newsgroups," for more information on Etiquette and Netiquette.)

Search the Database

AOL maintains a cross-referenced listing of over 1400 of the most popular mailing lists currently available on the Internet. Now while there are a number of other lists available, some of which list considerably more mailing lists, where this database stands alone is in the level of detail it contains about each list.

Unlike other databases that only contain the name of each list and possibly some topic information, the AOL database is indexed by Keywords, Moderation type, List Owner, List Processor type, Language and a detailed description. As a result, when you search this list you will usually find all mailing lists relating to the topic you are interested in, and not just those that contain the topic in their name or description.

To search this database all you need to do is follow these steps:

1. On the Mailing List Directory window click on the Search the Database book icon. This will open a window similar to the one shown in Figure 7.3.

FIGURE 7.3.

Enter the topic you want to search for in the field provided.

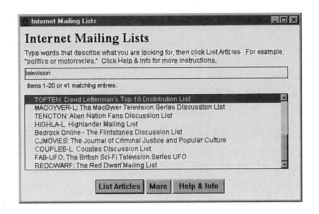

2. In the field at the top of the window enter the topic or topics you are interested in search for and then click on the List Articles button at the bottom of the Window. In this example, "television" was nominated as the topic to search for.

   After a few seconds AOL will display a list of all the mailing lists in the database that match you search request.

3. If you find a mailing list topic that interests you, double click on its entry using the mouse. When you do this AOL will open a window that displays the subscription details for the list. Figure 7.4 show the information held on the AOL Mailing List Database for the David Letterman's Top 10 list.

FIGURE 7.4.

Make a note of the information displayed by the database by printing a copy using the File Print option.

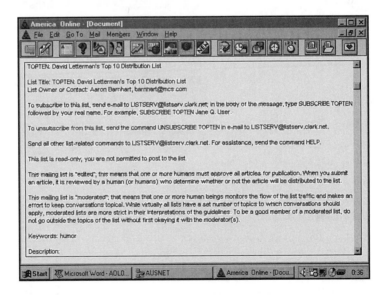

4. If this list is suitable to your needs, you should print out a copy of the information shown in figure 7.4 by opening the File menu and selecting the Print option. You will need this information later when you subscribe to the mailing list.

Message Boards

Another good source of mailing lists is AOL's Internet Message Board. This Message Board contains a range of discussion topics covering all aspects on the Internet and AOL. For example, there is a regular discussion of new and popular mailing lists which is currently called E-Mail Lists II. This discussion is a good place to start if you are trying to find new mailing lists.

To get to the Internet Message Board select the icon at the bottom left hand side of the Mailing List Directory window. When you do this a window similar to the one shown in Figure 7.5 will be displayed. From this window you can browse the various folders or subjects available (see Figure 7.6), look for new discussions and search for subjects by date.

FIGURE 7.5.

The Internet Message Board contains a variety of Internet- and AOL-related discussions.

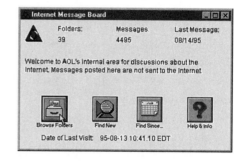

FIGURE 7.6.

Topics like E-Mail Lists II are a good source of new mailing lists.

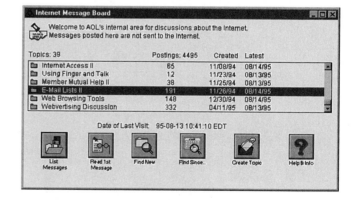

The List of Lists

Another good place to look is in the mailing list systems themselves. All the major list processors offer a facility that permits them to e-mail you a catalog of the mailing lists they maintain.

For example, if you send an e-mail message containing the word "LIST" or "LISTS" to a LISTSERV processor, you receive an e-mail message in return that details the name and description of each mailing list it manages. (See "Using LISTSERV" and "Using Majordomo" later in this chapter for a full description of commands and options offered by these services.)

> LISTSERV can also provide you with a list of all the mailing lists operated by every LISTSERV processor.

FTP Sites

An extensive list of publicly accessible mailing lists is also posted on a regular basis in a number of locations, including the `news.answers` Usenet newsgroup. A copy of this list is stored in an *archive* on the public FTP site at `ftp://rtfm.mit.edu`.

Using FTP, you can retrieve a copy of this 14-part listing from the `/pub/usenet/news.answers/mail/mailing-lists/` directory. Each part is stored in the directory as a separate file given the name `part01` through `part14`.

WWW Sites

If you prefer not to wade though pages of mailing list names looking for the one you are interested in, maybe one of the WWW pages devoted to mailing lists will be more to your liking.

InterNIC

One of the first places you should consider investigating is the InterNIC Directory of Directories mentioned in previous chapters.

Not all mailing lists are currently listed in the directory, but there are a sufficient number there to get most people started. At the very least, this list can provide you with the e-mail addresses of a good number of list processors. The other advantage of this list is that it is available using the World Wide Web or Gopher.

TILE.NET

One of the latest arrivals on the WWW scene, and at the same time one of the most useful, is the catalog service developed by the Walter Shelby Group Ltd. Called TILE.NET, this WWW server contains a list of all know LISTSERV mailing lists.

Using the sorting and search capabilities offered by TILE.NET, it is possible to locate mailing lists by name, type, popularity, and special categories such as membership policy.

> Located at `http://tile.net/`, TILE.NET also contains an extensive list of newsgroups, anonymous FTP sites, and computer vendors with a presence on the Internet.

Indiana University Support Center

There are also a number of other WWW servers that contain mailing list compilations. To find out how to locate these servers on the World Wide Web, read the "Search Tools" section in Chapter 13, "World Wide Web Productivity."

Of special note among these is the database maintained by the Indiana University Support Center for the UCS Knowledge Base. As of April, 1995, this list contained the names and locations of 11,254 mailing lists located at over 300 sites, including not only LISTSERV but also Majordomo and LISTPROC list processors.

To allow people to search this database, the university has set up a special WWW page at `http://www.ucssc.indiana.edu/mlarchive/`.

Using LISTSERV

To participate in a mailing list, the first thing you need to do is *subscribe* to it. This registers you as a member and places your name in the distribution list.

Two pieces of information are needed before you can subscribe to a list. First, you need to know the *list name* assigned to the mailing list by LISTSERV. In most cases, this name will be a single word like `TOPTEN` or a hyphenated name such as `NEW-LIST`. You also need to know the e-mail address of the LISTSERV processor that operates the mailing list. In the case of `TOPTEN`, the LISTSERV address is `listserv@listserv.clark.net`, and for `NEW-LIST` it is `listserv@vm1.nodak.edu`.

Subscribing to a LISTSERV List

With this information in hand, you are ready to subscribe to your first list. To subscribe to `TOPTEN`, you need to follow these steps:

1. Using AOL, open the Compose Mail window using and of the methods discussed in Chapter 6, "The Internet E-Mail Gateway." Clicking on the Compose Mail icon located in the tool bar is one of the easiest methods to use—it is the second icon from the left.

2. Enter the e-mail address of the LISTSERV processor into the TO: field, as shown in Figure 7.7.

FIGURE 7.7.

You must include an entry in the Subject field before AOL will send the message.

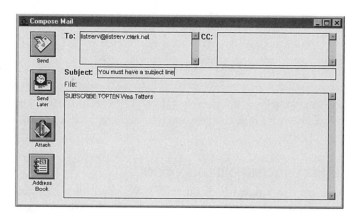

To subscribe to TOPTEN use: `listserv@listserv.clark.net`.

> Due to the fact that all LISTSERV processors are connected using BITNET, you can actually use the address of any LISTSERV when subscribing to a mailing list. If the list name is not found by the LISTSERV processor you specify, a global register of all known LISTSERV mailing lists will be searched. If the list name is located, the message will be forwarded to the correct LISTSERV address.

Note

3. Although LISTSERV ignores anything placed in the Subject: field, you need to enter something in it before AOL will allow you to send the message. I entered the message "You must have a subject line" in Figure 7.7, but any entry would have sufficed.

4. The last step you need to take to complete the subscription procedure is to tell the LISTSERV processor which mailing list you want to subscribe to and who it is that wants to subscribe. To do this, in the message area type **SUBSCRIBE TOPTEN**, followed by your full name. In this case I entered:

`SUBSCRIBE TOPTEN Wes Tatters`

5. Finally, click the Send button to mail the message.

If everything goes according to plan, within a few minutes, you will have received two messages from the LISTSERV processor. The amount of time it takes will vary greatly depending on the mailing list you are subscribing to, some, like TOPTEN, only take a few minutes to respond, while others may take days.

The first message you will receive is a housekeeping message from the LISTSERV processor. It should look something like the message in Figure 7.8, which contains a list of the instructions you sent to the LISTSERV processor and a report outlining their completion. As a rule, this message can be safely ignored if the actions you requested appear to have been carried out correctly.

In most cases the second message you receive will be a welcome message. This message contains some important information and should always be read. Probably the most important piece of information contained in the welcome message is the name of the e-mail address known as the list address.

> By selecting the Add to Favorite Places option from the Windows menu, you can save a copy of all welcome messages in your Personal Filing cabinet. This way, whenever you need to refer to one, they will all be stored in the same place. You may also want to create a separate folder in the Filing cabinet for these messages and move each one into it after saving them a favorite place.
>
> For Mac users the same effect can be achieved using the Save to Flashbox option.

Note

FIGURE 7.8.

Housekeeping messages can safely be ignored unless you seem to be encountering problems.

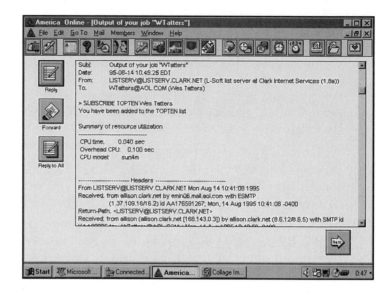

The welcome message from TOPTEN, shown in Figure 7.9, indicates that the TOPTEN list address is topten@listserv.clark.net. This is the e-mail address you use to participate in the conversations and discussions distributed by the mailing list. Usually the welcome message also provides you with instructions on how you cancel your subscription using the list processor's e-mail address.

FIGURE 7.9.

The welcome message contains details of all the e-mail addresses that relate to the mailing list.

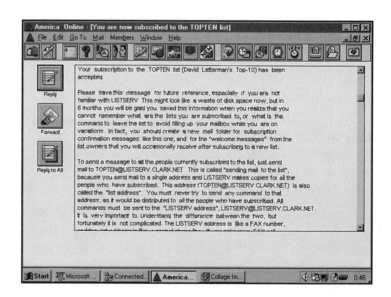

Unsubscribing from a LISTSERV List

If you decide that you no longer wish to subscribe to a particular mailing list, you need to send an e-mail message to the mailing list's LISTSERV processor.

To unsubscribe to TOPTEN, follow the steps used when you subscribed to the mailing list, making sure that you send the message to the list processor e-mail address listserv@listserv.clark.net and not to the list address. This time, however, instead of entering SUBSCRIBE TOPTEN Wes Tatters in the body of the message, enter SIGNOFF TOPTEN.

This tells LISTSERV to remove your name from the TOPTEN distribution list and cancel your subscription. You can also direct a LISTSERV processor to cancel your subscription to every mailing list it manages by sending the message SIGNOFF *.

Taking this one step further, because all LISTSERV processors are connected using BITNET, you can instruct any single LISTSERV processor to cancel your subscription to every LISTSERV mailing list on all LISTSERV processors by sending it the following command: SIGNOFF * (NETWIDE.

> This is a handy command to use if your e-mail address or AOL screen name ever changes. The last time you use your old address, e-mail the message SIGNOFF * (NETWIDE to listserv@bitnic.cren.net to ensure that you are not leaving any old mailing lists registered to an invalid address.

Finding LISTSERV Mailing Lists

As I mentioned in the section titled "Where to find Mailing Lists," each LISTSERV processor holds a list of all the mailing lists it manages.

If you send an e-mail message to a LISTSERV processor containing the word "LISTS," an e-mail message similar to the one shown in Figure 7.10 will be sent back to you. This message shows the list name of each mailing list managed by the LISTSERV processor, followed by a short description.

> Some earlier versions of LISTSERV may not recognize the LISTS command. In versions before 1.8a, you may need to use LIST instead of LISTS.

It is also possible to obtain a list of every mailing list located anywhere on BITNET. You can request a copy of this List of Lists by sending the command LISTS GLOBAL to any LISTSERV processor.

FIGURE 7.10.

A list of all the mailing lists managed by the LISTSERV processor at `listserv.clark.net`.

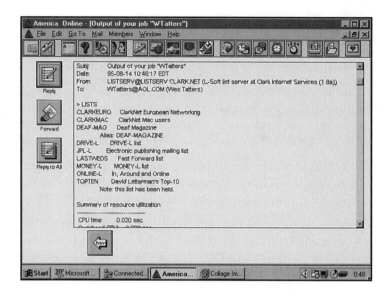

> Because this list is very large—over 600KB—it can be somewhat of a pain to receive using AOL—remember that AOL will try to split the message into 27K sections. Retrieving a copy of the list stored on the FTP server at MIT or browsing one of the WWW pages listed in the "Where to Find Mailing Lists" section probably offers you a better means of locating mailing lists.

LISTSERV also allows you to perform rudimentary searches of the List of Lists by adding a list of keywords to the `LISTS GLOBAL` command. For example, to obtain a list of mailing lists that deal with sporting activities, you could try sending an e-mail message containing the command `LISTS GLOBAL SPORT`.

When you receive a response to this request (see Figure 7.11) the name of each mailing list is listed along with the e-mail address of the site that manages it.

Other LISTSERV Commands

In addition to the standard commands already discussed, each LISTSERV processor also provides subscribers with a number of other commands. Although the exact commands available at each site may differ slightly depending on which version of LISTSERV the system is running, there are a few commands that remain constant.

FIGURE 7.11.

Global lists display the mailing list names and the site that manages it.

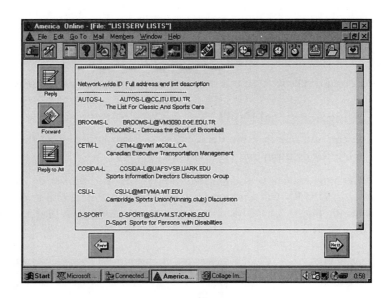

The HELP Command

Sending a message to a LISTSERV processor containing the word "HELP" results in an e-mail message outlining the most commonly used commands available on that LISTSERV. This message will contain information similar to that listed in Figure 7.12.

FIGURE 7.12.

Common LISTSERV commands.

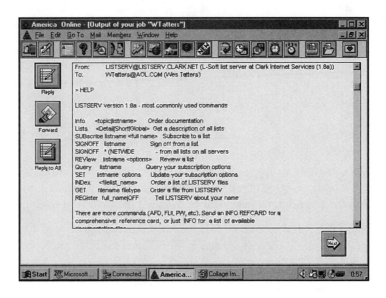

This figure also raises an interesting point. Up until now, you have been using the full name for all mailing list commands. It is possible to abbreviate many of the commands, using just the letters shown as capitals in the Command column of Figure 7.12.

As a result, SUBSCRIBE TOPTEN Wes Tatters could also be written as SUB TOPTEN Wes Tatters.

Getting Additional INFO

You can also obtain more detailed instructions covering all the commands supported by LISTSERV by using the INFO command.

This command can be used in two ways. If you send the word "INFO" to LISTSERV on its own, LISTSERV will send you back an e-mail message containing information similar to that shown in Figure 7.13. This list outlines all the information files that the LISTSERV processor can provide you with.

FIGURE 7.13.

Information files available from LISTSERV.

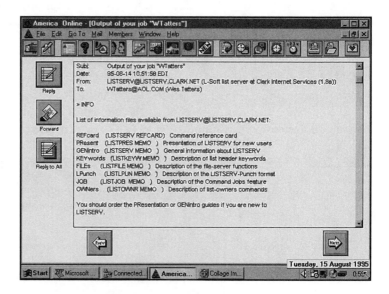

Once you have a copy of this list, you can send LISTSERV the INFO command followed by the name of the document you are interested in. For example, to request a copy of the LISTSERV Reference Card document, you would send the following command: INFO REFCARD.

New LISTSERV users should also consider requesting a copy of the "Presentation of LISTSERV for new users" document, called PRESENT, and GENINTRO, the "General Information about LISTSERV" document.

The REGISTER Command

Regular LISTSERV users often choose to register their full names with LISTSERV. By doing this, they do not need to include their names when subscribing to new LISTSERV mailing lists.

To register your name, send the command REGISTER, followed by your full name, to any LISTSERV processor. To register myself, I sent REGISTER Wes Tatters to the LISTSERV processor at listserv@bitnic.cren.net.

Now, instead of typing SUB TOPTEN Wes Tatters, all I need to type is SUB TOPTEN and LISTSERV will fill in my full name for me.

Grouping Commands

Until now, all the LISTSERV messages you've seen have been restricted to a single line. However, LISTSERV can handle any number of instructions in a single message. Provided that each command is placed on a line of its own, LISTSERV will treat each one as a separate action.

Many people use this capability, when subscribing to a new mailing list, to obtain updated information about LISTSERV and alter default settings for the mailing list. For example, when I wanted to subscribe to a blues mailing list, I sent the following messages to listserv@brownvm.brown.edu:

```
SUB BLUES-L
SET BLUES-L DIG
INFO REFCARD
```

The first line you should recognize as a subscription command that assumes that I have registered my Name with LISTSERV.

The second line, on the other hand, you probably won't recognize. The SET command allows you to alter distribution options that relate to the BLUES-L mailing list. This mailing list can deliver messages in either message by message or digest form. By issuing the command SET BLUES-L DIG, I am instructing the LISTSERV processor to send the digest version of the mailing list.

Finally, the last line simply requests a copy of the reference card for this LISTSERV processor.

Sending Messages to the Mailing List

Although you can have hours of fun exchanging messages with the LISTSERV processor itself, the real reason for subscribing to a mailing list is to communicate with other people by sending messages that they, not the list processor, will receive.

To send e-mail to the mailing list itself, you need to know its list address. In most cases, this address will consist of the list name and the domain name of the list processor that manages it. For the blues mailing list discussed in the preceding section, this means that its list address is blues-l@brownvm.brown.edu.

Occasionally, there are situations where this may not apply, in which case, the best approach is to look up the list address in the welcome message you received when you first subscribed to the mailing list.

With the list address in hand, you are now ready to send a message to the mailing list by following these steps:

1. Open the Compose Mail window by using the Ctrl-M (⌘-M on the Macintosh) short cut and enter **blues-1@brownvm.brown.edu** as the e-mail address in to TO: textbox.

2. Unlike messages you send to LISTSERV, messages sent to the mailing list are expected to have a subject. This allows people to follow the flow of conversations in the mailing list. Because this is my first message to the BLUES-L list, I used the subject line to introduce myself (see Figure 7.14).

FIGURE 7.14.

When you join a mailing list, don't forget to introduce yourself.

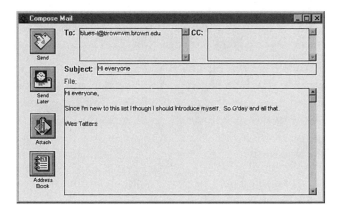

3. Finally, type your message in the body of the Compose Mail window and click the Send button to mail your message.

MAC Users: Although the Macintosh version of AOL does allow you to add different fonts and styles to text in your messages, these fonts and styles will not be displayed in any messages sent to the Internet.

If you are planning to send a number of messages to different mailing lists or simply to a number of people, click on the Send Later button instead of the Send button. This will hold all the messages you compose until you run your next FlashSession.

Using Majordomo

Like LISTSERV, Majordomo handles the maintenance and distribution of messages for mailing lists. In many ways, the two services are alike, using most of the same commands and supporting many of the same features. There are, however, a number of differences that merit a separate discussion.

These differences fall into two major categories. First, there are some common actions that require different commands on each system. In a real sense, coming to grips with these differences merely involves the learning of some additional commands.

The other major difference is not as easily dealt with and is viewed by many as a major weakness. This difference revolves around the fact that there are no interconnections between Majordomo list processors. As a result, there are no LISTS GLOBAL-like commands available on Majordomo. You must also know the correct e-mail address of a Majordomo processor before you can subscribe to any of the lists it maintains.

Subscribing to a Majordomo List

Because of the lack of LISTS GLOBAL, you will need to rely on the various catalogs and archives containing addresses of mailing lists to locate lists managed by Majordomo.

One of the first things you will notice about Majordomo mailing lists is that the list name can be almost any length, unlike LISTSERV list names, which tend to be kept quite short. By using longer names, it is a lot easier to figure out what a mailing list does. For example: `biz-marketing-consulting`. This list, which is operated by the Majordomo processor at majordomo@world.std.com, obviously discusses subjects relating to marketing and consulting in the business world.

Once you find a Majordomo list that you want to subscribe to, the steps you take to subscribe are basically the same as those for a LISTSERV mailing list:

1. Open the Compose Mail window using any of the techniques previously discussed.

2. Enter `majordomo@world.std.com` into the TO: box, as shown in Figure 7.15.

FIGURE 7.15.

You must use the address of the list processor that manages the mailing list.

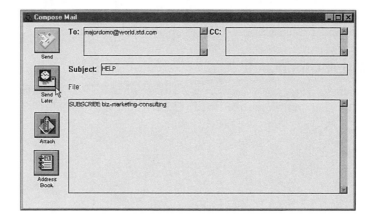

> Unlike LISTSERV, the e-mail address you use *must* be the address of the list processor that manages the mailing list you are subscribing to.

3. On most systems, Majordomo—like LISTSERV—ignores anything placed in the Subject field. However, on some systems Majordomo will attempt to process the Subject: field. For this reason I usually put a recognizable command in the Subject field when subscribing to a Majordomo list. As a rule HELP, INFO, or WHICH are suitable options.

4. Now enter **SUBSCRIBE biz-marketing-consulting** in the body of the message. You should also note that there is no need to enter your name when using a Majordomo List.

5. Finally, click the Send button or Send Later button to mail the message.

Like LISTSERV, the time frame for the receipt of a response from the mailing list will vary greatly. However, in most cases your Mail Box will usually activate within a few minutes, indicating that you have received mail.

Unsubscribing from a Majordomo List

To cancel a list, instead of using `SIGNOFF` you need to use `UNSUBSCRIBE`. Apart from this change, the process remains the same. To cancel your subscription to `biz-marketing-consulting`, send this message to `majordomo@world.std.com`:

UNSUBSCRIBE biz-marketing-consulting

Unfortunately, there are no global unsubscribe capabilities available with Majordomo. For this reason, make sure you keep a record of all the Majordomo mailing lists you subscribe to and remember to unsubscribe from them all if your screen name or e-mail address ever changes.

Other Commands

There are a few other commands available when using Majordomo that either function differently or are not supported by LISTSERV. These include:

◆ INFO
◆ LIST
◆ WHICH

Getting Mailing List Information

Of these, the `INFO` command is probably the most relevant. With Majordomo, you use the INFO command to request information about the different mailing lists a Majordomo processor maintains. If you send a message containing the words `INFO biz-marketing-consulting` to `majordomo@world.std.com`, you will receive a message similar to the one shown in Figure 7.16.

FIGURE 7.16.

The INFO command requests information about mailing lists, not the list processor itself.

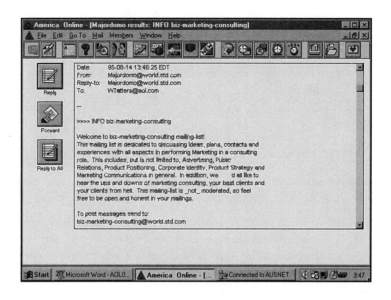

Using the LIST command

As mentioned at the beginning of this section, when using Majordomo, the LIST command does not perform all of the functions offered by LISTSERV.

That said, you can still use the command to obtain a catalog of all the mailing lists operated by any given Majordomo list processor, provided that you know its e-mail address in advance.

The WHICH Command

The one command that you may find useful that LISTSERV does not support is the WHICH command. This command requests a list of all mailing lists you subscribe to on the Majordomo list processor the e-mail message is addressed to.

Unfortunately, the WHICH command cannot tell you about mailing lists you subscribe to on other Majordomo list processors, but nevertheless it can come in handy when you're trying to track down a stray mailing list.

Communicating with the Mailing List

Like LISTSERV, each mailing list has a separate list address that you need to use when sending messages to the mailing list itself.

To find the name of the list address, use the INFO command discussed previously or look at the welcome message you received when you first subscribed to the mailing list.

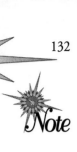

Note

Make sure you do not send Majordomo commands to the list address. As was the case with LISTSERV, they should be sent only to the list processor address. Sending them to the list address is a sure fire way to get the other people who have subscribed to the list offside.

Summary

The big advantage of using mailing lists for electronic discussions is that you do not need to use anything other than simple e-mail messages to make them work.

For many Internet users, this offers a number of advantages in terms of flexibility and ease of use. However, mailing lists are not always the best choice for discussions, due to the fact that your mailbox can rapidly become stuffed full of messages that you many not really be interested in reading. Luckily, there is an alternative discussion and conferencing system that in many cases duplicates the messages distributed by mailing lists.

Chapter 8, "Usenet Newsgroups," looks at how this service, known as Usenet, operates, and explores some of the discussions or *newsgroups* it offers. It also looks at how AOL can be used to gain access to Usenet and discusses the steps this involves.

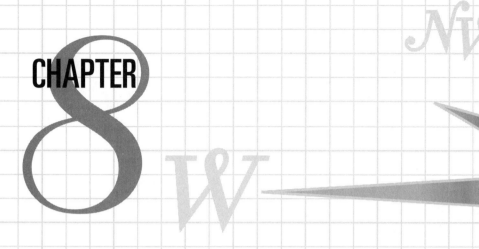

CHAPTER 8

USENET NEWSGROUPS

Until the recent arrival of the World Wide Web, access to Usenet and its newsgroups was one of the main reasons many people ever sought access to the Internet.

Newsgroups are discussion areas, not unlike AOL message boards, where people can exchange ideas and discuss just about any topic imaginable. In this sense, they are also a lot like the mailing lists discussed in the previous chapter. Unlike mailing lists, however, newsgroups do not rely on e-mail for the delivery of their messages, or more correctly, their articles.

Instead, when you send an *article* to a newsgroup, the Usenet network itself oversees the distribution, transferring a copy of the article to each of the computers (Usenet servers) connected via the Usenet. This article is then made available by each of these servers to anyone who wants to read articles stored in the newsgroup it was posted to.

At last count there were over 20,000 Usenet newsgroups discussing topics as diverse as gardening and human relationships, making Usenet one of the largest forums for free discussion in the world. There is literally a newsgroup for just about every topic imaginable, and for those subjects without a dedicated newsgroup, chances are there is a general discussion group of some description that will be only too happy to discuss the topic you are interested in.

To cover all the issues relating to Usenet and also look at how you can read newsgroups using AOL, this chapter covers the following topics:

- ◆ Introduction to Usenet
- ◆ How newsgroups differ from AOL message boards
- ◆ Newsgroup categories
- ◆ Netiquette
- ◆ Using AOL to access newsgroups
- ◆ Advanced techniques

Introduction to Usenet

The UNIX User Network, or Usenet, is an example of one of the more common distributed processing systems used by the Internet. Usenet consists of two separate components. The first component, called a *server*, monitors the day-to-day management of Usenet, the distribution of messages, and maintenance of all the newsgroups. There are thousands of Usenet servers all over the world devoted to ensuring that a copy of every article posted to a newsgroup on any server is automatically distributed to every other server.

The second component, called a *client*, is a program used to read any of the articles stored on a server. This type of client program is more commonly known as a *newsgroup reader*, which in some ways is a misnomer because the reader can be used to post new articles as well. By using a client/server approach to newsgroup management, there is no need for you to operate your own server. Instead, all you need is access to a client program and permission to access one of the many Usenet servers—host programs.

What Is Usenet?

Like so many of the services currently available on the Internet, the early history of Usenet can be traced back to a simple experiment or private tool developed by someone for their own needs. In the case of Usenet, it was a University of North Carolina graduate named Steve Bellovin who, in 1979, decided to write some simple shell scripts on his UNIX system to simplify the exchange of news and information between his campus and Duke University.

A Short History Lesson

For some time prior to the creation of these scripts, students at both Duke and North Carolina had been experimenting with a program called UUCP (UNIX-to-UNIX copy) as a means of exchanging messages between two UNIX servers. The idea for using UUCP in this way was first proposed by Jim Ellis and Tom Truscott, two graduate students at Duke. What Steve Bellovin did though, was take the process one step further by automating it.

Once people began to hear about what Steve Bellovin had done, copies of the scripts—known collectively as *News*—began to appear on a number of other UNIX computers. These computers too, then began to exchange messages with the North Carolina and Duke news servers using the News scripts, and in almost no time at all, the Usenet was born.

As News grew in popularity, Steve Bellovin and Tom Truscott eventually rewrote the scripts using the C programming language. This allowed them to include new capabilities and improved the service's performance. With the release of this News version, the idea of newsgroups came into being, as did an early version of the hierarchical structure now used by Usenet. In this version there were two main Usenet hierarchies, called `mod` and `net`. In the `mod` *hierarchy,* newsgroups could be created that were moderated by a single user, while the `net` hierarchy handled unmoderated newsgroups.

Hot on the heels of this upgraded system, which was to become known as version A, another version of News—version B—was released in 1981 by Matt Glickman and Mark Horton. This new version removed the limitation of version A that forced moderated newsgroups to be stored only in the `mod` hierarchy. In doing this, version B signaled the first restructuring of Usenet and pointed the way for its future development.

> Usenet utilizes a hierarchical layout which categorizes newsgroups by various classifications. During the development of Usenet, a number of events and subsequent releases of the Usenet programs have resulted in the reclassification of newsgroups into different areas and in some extreme cases the merger or removal of newsgroups. As a result, these restructurings have usually caused a considerable number of problems and in one case an enormous amount of heated debate.

Note

In the years following the release of version B, Usenet went through many changes, the most noticeable of which was the eventual replacement of UUCP—the communications program originally used by News to exchange articles between computers in the Usenet network. As ARPANET grew in popularity, many Usenet sites began to take advantage of its backbone for the distribution of newsgroup discussion. To achieve this, a new protocol called NNTP (Net News Transfer Protocol) was developed. NNTP allowed Usenet sites to exchange articles using TCP/IP instead of UUCP.

TCP/IP and the Great Renaming

With the move to TCP/IP, an action that added many new sites to the growing list of Usenet servers, the structure of Usenet was forced once again to adapt so that it could cater to this increased popularity.

Until 1986, there were still only three top-level hierarchies on Usenet: mod, net, and fa. Because there were relatively few newsgroups on Usenet, having just three hierarchies did not pose any real problems. But, as the number of newsgroups began to increase rapidly, many people started to suggest the need for a new structure.

This led to what has become known as the "Great Renaming" and spurred the biggest *flame war* in the history of Usenet. Although it was very easy to say, "Let's restructure Usenet," it seemed that everyone had different ideas about how it should be done. Following thousands of sometimes heated exchanges, it was decided that seven new top-level hierarchies should be created to replace the three original ones.

Note

In Internet parlance, a *flame war* is a heated discussion that rapidly grows out of all proportions. Hundreds, and sometimes thousands, of people begin to reply to comments made by other people, who in turn attempt to post replies. Within no time at all the Usenet can become flooded with literally thousands, or in the Great Flame War, hundreds of thousands of articles, all making claims, counter claims and often totally absurd comments.

Newsgroup Hierarchies

The seven top-level hierarchies created as a result of the "Great Renaming," were designed to represent equally the wide cross-section of discussion topics that Usenet was handling at the time. These seven hierarchies are listed in Table 8.1 with a brief description of the types of newsgroups each one contains.

Table 8.1. Newsgroup top-level hierarchies.

Identifier	Category
comp	Computer-related discussions
misc	Unclassified newsgroups
news	Internet/Usenet news and information

Identifier	Category
rec	Recreation, sports, and hobbies
sci	Scientific newsgroups
soc	Social newsgroups
talk	Debate-oriented newsgroups

Once the new hierarchies were decided on, the next difficulty that faced the Usenet community was working out how to implement this new structure. As a result, the Great Renaming did not happen overnight. Because the Usenet is a distributed network, each server needed to be reorganized separately. At the same time, all existing newsgroups needed to be sorted into the new hierarchies, often with lengthy debates ensuing over the exact location of some of the less generic newsgroups.

Then, to complicate matters even further, the ability to add subhierarchies to each of the top seven was also added to the Usenet specification. Doing this allowed newsgroups to be categorized by subtopics within each top-level hierarchy. For example, the `rec` hierarchy is devoted to newsgroups that discuss recreation, sports, and hobbies. Within this hierarchy, a number of subcategories have been created describing the primary areas of discussions. These include `rec.arts`, `rec.autos`, `rec.game`, and `rec.sport`, to name just a few. Below this primary subject area, you will also sometimes find additional subgroups and eventually the newsgroups themselves.

In the `rec.sport` area, for example, newsgroups are further categorized by type of sport, including `rec.sport.baseball`, `rec.sport.cricket`, and `rec.sport.football`. The end result of all this subclassification is a newsgroup name, such as `rec.sport.football.australian`, that clearly defines the newsgroup's contents.

> In most cases, newsgroups are classified by no more than three levels, but it isn't uncommon to find newsgroups with up to five classification levels as well. Naturally, there is always an exception to the rule, as one newsgroup I encountered proves:
> `alt.help.me.get.out.of.trouble.trouble.trouble-please`

Usenet Today

Since 1987, Usenet has grown from strength to strength, with thousands of newsgroups being added each year. To accompany this growth, other top-level hierarchies have also been added to cater to both location-specific and topic-specific newsgroups.

Of all these new hierarchies, by far the most popular is the `alt` hierarchy, which caters to many alternative discussion areas. This hierarchy, while being very popular, is often the cause of considerable consternation as well, due to its acceptance of newsgroups whose subject matter is often "racy," to put it politely.

Some of the `alt` newsgroups are so bad that a number of Usenet sites have chosen not to distribute them. This is in fact why the `alt` hierarchy exists at all. When people were prevented from setting up groups like `rec.sex` and `rec.drugs` in the more respectable hierarchies, they decided to create a hierarchy catering to this type of discussion. By doing this they also provide a mechanism that allowed these groups to be excluded by servers as required.

> Although AOL has chosen to allow its members access to all the `alt` newsgroups, it does provide mechanisms that allow you to lock out these areas if you so choose. This should be of special interest to parents who are concerned about the types of information available to their children.

Netiquette

Although Usenet does provide a free environment for the exchange of information and ideas, there are still a number of rules to which participants are expected to adhere. These rules, or guidelines, are designed not so much to restrict your personal space, but instead to help keep the enormous community of people who spend time on Usenet happy.

Language

The first rule of Usenet is that as a rule, any rude, insulting, or degrading comments are simply not welcome. If you feel you need to express yourself in this way, either send your comments as a private e-mail or visit some of the `alt` newsgroups that are somewhat more tolerant of such outbursts.

Racist comments and opinions will also not be tolerated on nearly all newsgroups and can result in being barred from a Usenet server, as can the use of foul language or swearing.

Usenet Grammar

There are also a few grammatical precedents that apply to newsgroups.

◆ You should only use capital letters when you need to make a point. TYPING IN CAPITAL LETTERS IS REFERRED TO AS *SHOUTING* and should be avoided wherever possible. For one thing, it makes your articles very hard to read and is considered to be very rude. In most cases, people will simply ignore articles typed in capital letters, apart from possibly firing off a message to you telling you not to shout.

◆ If you want to make a point, the placement of *asterisks* around the words you want to highlight is considered to be far more effective. Some people also use the _underline_ symbol in the same way.

◆ While a few people worry about perfect grammar and punctuation in your articles, the use of correct spelling and clear, concise ideas is a sure fire way to gain you the respect of other readers. However, most people are more interested in the content than the grammatical quality.

◆ You should also try to keep your articles as short as possible and resist the desire to write pages of flowing prose when a simple Yes or No would suffice.

Message Quoting

Having said that, you should always attempt to keep the size of your articles down to their barest minimum. When you reply to an article that you have read in a newsgroup, you should always include a copy of the relevant parts of the original article in your own posting. Sending a message that says, "Yes, I agree," serves little purpose if nobody knows what you are agreeing with.

When you quote from a previous article, all the lines that you quote in your new article should have a ">" symbol placed as the first character of the line. This tells other people that the line of text that follows was not written by you, but instead by the person you are replying to.

There is a delicate balance, however, between good and excessive quoting. Don't quote any more of the original article than is absolutely necessary, and whatever you do, don't quote the entire article. What you are trying to do is give people some background to your posting, and not simply resending or restating someone else's comments.

Flame Wars

A *flame* is a sarcastic or rude message sent to someone in response to a comment or article the reader did not appreciate. Although the sending of flames is not regarded as accepted behavior, such messages are usually tolerated and sometimes even admired, especially when the contents of the flame are particularly well thought out.

If you are in the habit of making stupid comments, you can expect to be flamed, although sometimes even the most well-written article can attract a flame if one of its readers disagrees with your particular point of view. When you receive a flame, there are two ways that you can treat it. You can ignore it and accept it as a simple fact of life, or you can respond to the sender. However, if you do choose to respond, be prepared for yet another response.

By responding to a flame, you can also ignite what is known as a *flame war*. Often other people in the newsgroup decide to make their own comments about the flame or one of its ensuing replies and counter-flames. It is not uncommon on such occasions for the conversation on a newsgroup to degenerate into a flame war, replacing for a short time all other conversations on the newsgroup.

Smileys, Emoticons, and Abbreviations

To help keep your articles to a readable length, a number of abbreviations and other symbols have become a common part of the Usenet language.

For example, you can replace the commonly used "by the way" with <BTW>. Some of the more common abbreviations are shown in Table 8.2.

Table 8.2. Commonly used abbreviations.

Abbreviation	Description
<IMHO>	In my humble opinion
<PMFJI>	Pardon me for jumping in
<ROTFL>	Rolling on the floor laughing
<GD&RFC>	Grinning ducking and running for cover
<G>	A grin
<BG>	A big grin
<VBG>	A very big grin
<OTOH>	On the other hand
<BFN>	Bye for now
<FWIW>	For what it's worth

Another popular form of abbreviation is known as a *smiley* or *emoticon*. This form of abbreviation is used not so much to replace words, but instead to express the writer's state of mind. These symbols are often used to express complex emotions and feelings not otherwise apparent in a normal message. The most well-known smiley is : -) or :)—the happy face. You can also use a similar symbol to express sadness : - (or surprise : -0. The number of possible combinations is extensive, with some of the more unique combinations including a happy person wearing glasses 8 -) and a person winking ; -).

Tip

> Even though the use of abbreviations and emoticons can seem like a good idea at first, you should use them sparingly. They should be used to enhance what you are writing, not to overwhelm it.

Signature Lines

Another popular part of many Usenet articles is the *signature*. This usually consists of one or two lines of information that your newsgroup reader automatically appends to every article you send.

On these lines, people often include messages and quotes along with their name and e-mail address. Unlike AOL, where simple signatures or none at all are the norm, a complex or clever signature is regarded by many a sign of prestige in a newsgroup. These messages also serve as your calling card on the Usenet, and people often look to the signature line in an article to find out something about the author.

> Although a clever signature line is appreciated by most people, you should make sure you keep the length down to no more than four or five lines. There is nothing worse than loading a 20- or 30-line article only to find that it contains a 2-line message and a 28-line signature.

Using AOL to Access Newsgroups

America Online has been providing its members with access to Usenet for some time, via the Internet gateway it originally opened to permit the exchange of e-mail with people on the Internet. Using a simple graphical interface, provided as a part of your AOL software, you can subscribe to any of the thousands of newsgroups currently available and both send and receive articles.

To gain access to the Usenet forum area, select the Internet Connection icon on the AOL Main Menu window. Alternatively, you can jump to it using the Keyword window (Ctrl+K or ⌘+K). The keyword for Internet Connection is, Keyword: `Internet`. There is also a third option you may like to use for opening the Internet Connection main window. By clicking on the Internet Connection icon located in the toolbar, you also achieve the same objective. (See Chapter 5, "Working with AOL," for a full discussion of the icons available in the toolbar.)

Regardless of which option you choose, the end result is the opening of the Internet Connection window shown in Figure 8.1.

FIGURE 8.1.

The Internet Connection window gives you access to AOL's Usenet services.

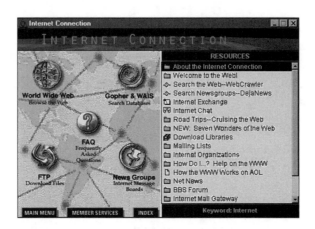

The Internet Connection window is the base window for all the Internet services provided by America Online. From here you can access any of the Internet-related message boards and forums or obtain information about AOL's Internet gateway and access all the currently supported Internet utilities.

In this case, you want to access the Usenet services. To do this, click on the News Groups icon located in the middle of the Internet Connection window. This instructs AOL to open the Newsgroups window, shown in Figure 8.2.

FIGURE 8.2.

The AOL Newsgroups window.

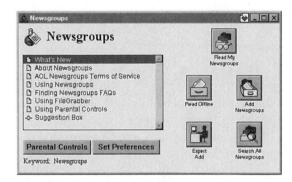

FIGURE 8.3.

Enter **Newsgroups** *in the Keyword dialog box.*

Note

> You can also jump directly to the Newsgroups window by entering the word **Newsgroups** in the Keyword dialog box (see Figure 8.3).

The Newsgroups window is split into three main areas, each of which are dealt with separately in the pages that follow. These areas are:

- ◆ The Information Menu
- ◆ Newsgroup Navigation Buttons
- ◆ Parental Controls and Preferences Buttons

The Information Menu

The Information Menu contains a number of text files that provide you with a wealth of information about AOL's Usenet services. Before you begin to experiment with Usenet, take a few minutes to read through these entries to familiarize yourself with the latest information.

Of these items, you should pay particular attention to the What's New entry. This item contains any late-breaking information and brings you up to date on important new developments.

You should also read the AOL Newsgroups Terms of Service document to find out how the use of Usenet differs from the standard AOL Terms of Service.

Most of the remaining documents in this list discuss the use of Usenet and related services. These include Using Newsgroups, Using FileGrabber, Using Parental Controls, and tips on locating newsgroup related FAQs.

Finally, there is also a Suggestion box option on the menu for sending queries and suggestions to AOL's support staff. Usually you'll receive an answer to any queries within 24 hours, depending on the query's complexity and the number of questions currently being handled.

Newsgroup Navigation Buttons

Down the right-hand side of the Newsgroups window there are five buttons. You use these buttons to access the various newsgroup-related services provided by AOL. In the sections that follow you learn how the options provided by each of these buttons assist you as you explore the Usenet. They will be discussed in the following order:

◆ Add Newsgroups
◆ Search All Newsgroups
◆ Expert Add
◆ Read My Newsgroups
◆ Read Offline

Add Newsgroups

Before you can read any newsgroup articles, you need to tell AOL which newsgroups you are interested in reading. To do this, you need to subscribe to these newsgroups by following these steps:

1. Click on the Add Newsgroups button. This will display a window similar to the one shown in Figure 8.4.

2. This window displays a list of all the top-level hierarchies carried by AOL on its Usenet server. To look at any of the newsgroups in these hierarchies, double-click on the one you are interested in or highlight it and click on the List Topics button. For now, double-click on the Computers and Computer Science Newsgroups (comp.*) hierarchy.

3. You should now see a dialog box like the one shown in Figure 8.5. This window lists all the newsgroup topics currently available in the hierarchy you selected. It also lists the number of newsgroups available for each topic. To select a topic from the ones displayed either double-click on it or highlight it then click on the List Newsgroups button.

   In Figure 8.5, the Computer Specific, Binary-Only Newsgroups (comp.bin) topic was selected.

FIGURE 8.4.

The Add Newsgroups - Categories window displays a list of all the top-level hierarchies available via AOL's Usenet gateway.

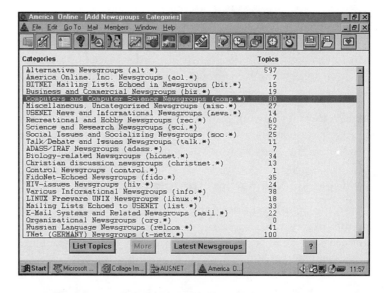

FIGURE 8.5.

*Topics available under the Computers and Computer Science Newsgroups (comp. *) hierarchy.*

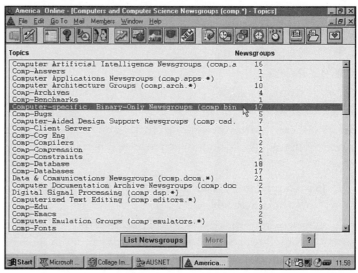

4. A list of all the newsgroups that fall under the selected topic is then displayed in a window similar to the one shown in Figure 8.6.

Note

By default, AOL displays an English language description for each newsgroup, not the physical name of the newsgroup. To find out the physical name of each newsgroup, click on the Internet Names button.

FIGURE 8.6.

Select a newsgroup you want to subscribe to and click on the Add button.

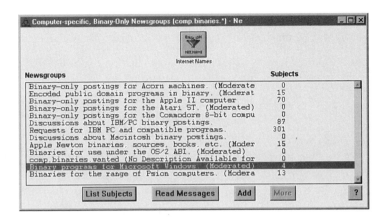

5. To subscribe to any of the newsgroups listed in this window, highlight the one you are interested in and the click on the Add button. If AOL is able to subscribe you to the selected group, you get a message similar to the one shown in Figure 8.7, otherwise a message is displayed explaining why the request failed.

FIGURE 8.7.

When you subscribe to a newsgroup, AOL sends you a message to let you know that the request was successful.

6. There are also a few other options available on this window that are designed to assist you in deciding which newsgroups you want to subscribe to:

    If you click on the Internet Name button located just above the newsgroups list, a popup window opens that lists all the Usenet names for those newsgroups currently being displayed.

    Clicking on the List Subjects button displays a list of all the current message topics in the selected newsgroup.

    By clicking on the Read Messages button you can preview the types of messages posted to a newsgroup before you subscribe to it.

7. Once you have subscribed to all the newsgroups you are interested in, click on the Close box and return to the main Newsgroups window.

Search All Newsgroups

While the hierarchical structure of Usenet does make it easier to locate newsgroups, sometimes they aren't always placed where you would expect them to be. This is especially relevant to the `alt` hierarchy which contains newsgroups whose topics often cross over into areas covered by other hierarchies.

As a result, a mechanism was devised by AOL that allows you to search for newsgroups by keywords. To make use of this feature you need to follow these steps:

1. On the Newsgroups main window click on the Search All Newsgroups button. This opens the dialog box shown in Figure 8.8.

FIGURE 8.8.

The Search Newsgroup Titles dialog helps you locate newsgroups you are interested in reading.

2. Enter a list of keywords to search for. In Figure 8.8, the words **mac and comp** were entered. This tells AOL to search for any newsgroup with the words 'mac' and 'comp' in its name. The reason for doing this, instead of just typing **mac** on its own, is to prevent newsgroups with names like street.machines being displayed.

3. When you click on the Search button, AOL uses the keywords you enter to search its list of available newsgroups and display the results in a window like the one shown in Figure 8.9.

FIGURE 8.9.

Highlight the newsgroup you want to subscribe to and click on the Add button.

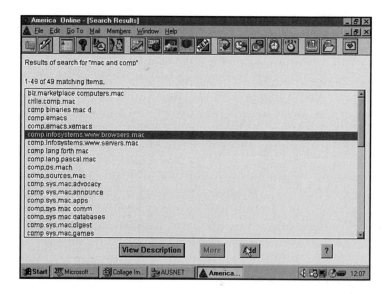

4. Now, select a newsgroup that you want to subscribe to and click on the Add button.

> To obtain a brief description of any newsgroup you are interested in highlight it and click on the View Description button.

5. After you have subscribed to any newsgroups that you are interested in, click on the Close icon and return to the Newsgroups main window.

Expert Add

There is one final option available when you already know the name of the newsgroup you are interested in subscribing to. You can enter the name of the newsgroup directly, without having to navigate your way though Search dialogs and Topic Lists.

You can subscribe to a newsgroup using this method by doing the following:

1. At the Newsgroup main window, click on the Expert Add button. This opens a small window where you can enter a newsgroup name. (See Figure 8.10.)

FIGURE 8.10.

To take advantage of the Expert Add option, you must already know the full name of the newsgroup you are interested in.

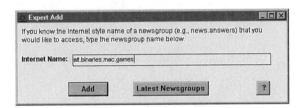

2. In the field provided, type the full name of the newsgroup to which you want to subscribe. In Figure 8.10, `alt.binaries.mac.games` was entered. When you have typed in the name of the newsgroup, click on the Add button.

   If the action is successful, AOL advises you of this. On the other hand, if you have entered an invalid newsgroup or you have set the Parental Controls option to disallow access to certain areas, an appropriate message is displayed.

> Because some of the newsgroups on the Usenet and particularly those in the `alt` hierarchy contain material that is less than savory in its content, you can disable access to the Expert Add option using the Parental Controls dialog discussed later in this chapter. Alternatively, you can leave Expert Add active and disable individual newsgroups or categories of groups.

Read My Newsgroups

Once you have nominated the newsgroups you are interested in, the next logical step in the process is actually reading the articles that have been posted to them.

To do this, return to the Newsgroups main window and click on the Read My Newsgroups button. After a few seconds, a window like the one shown in Figure 8.11 opens, showing a list detailing all the newsgroups you have subscribed to.

FIGURE 8.11.

The Read My Newsgroups window lets you manage all the newsgroups you have subscribed to.

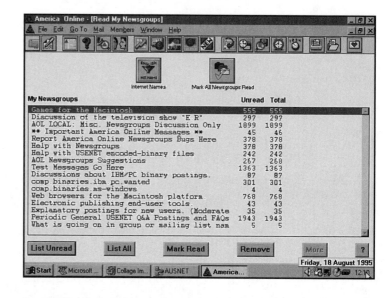

The first time you open the Read My Newsgroups window you may find a number of newsgroups that you don't recall subscribing to. This is because, there are a number of AOL related newsgroups that you are automatically subscribed to. If you don't want to keep them, you can remove them from the list.

Working with Newsgroups

There are a number of buttons on the Read My Newsgroups window that assist you in managing all the newsgroups you have subscribed to. Table 8.4 lists each of these buttons and explains what actions they perform.

Table 8.4. Options available via the Read My Newsgroups window.

Button	Action
Internet Names	When you click on this button, a window displaying the Internet Names of each newsgroup you have subscribed to is displayed.

Button	Action
Mark All Newsgroups Read	AOL keeps track of which articles you have and have not read. If you click on this button, all the articles in each newsgroup you subscribe to are marked as read.
List Unread	Before you click on this button, select a newsgroup you want to look at. Then, when you do click on this button, a window opens listing all the articles in that newsgroup that you have not yet read.
List All	If you use this button, all articles in the currently selected newsgroup are displayed, including those you have read previously.
Mark Read	When you click on this button, all the articles in the currently selected newsgroups are marked as read.
Remove	Clicking on this button removes the selected newsgroup from the list of those that you subscribe to.
More	If you subscribe to more newsgroups than will fit on one screen, clicking on this button instructs AOL to retrieve another screen full.
?	This is the Help button. Clicking on it requests information about the screen you are currently using.

Reading Articles

When you choose either the List Unread or List All button, you are eventually presented with a window similar to the one shown in Figure 8.12. In the body of this window, the subject line of each *thread* containing unread articles is listed, along with the number of articles included in the thread.

All articles in a newsgroup containing the same subject line are grouped together into *threads*. This makes it much easier to follow a conversation that may have taken place over a period of days.

If the AOL newsreader did not sort the articles into threads, you would need to scan the entire newsgroup article by article to follow a conversation.

FIGURE 8.12.

The Read Unread window displays all the unread articles in the currently selected newsgroups.

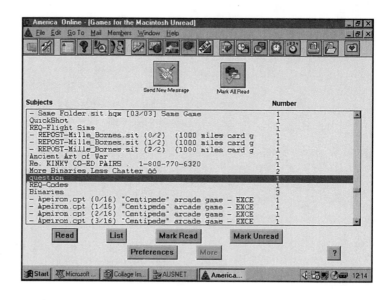

In addition to the list of threads, there are buttons across the top and at the bottom of this window that allow you to work with a selected thread. Table 8.5 contains a list of the actions performed by these various buttons.

Table 8.5. Actions performed by the buttons on the Read Unread window.

Button	Action
Send New Message	When you click on this button, a window opens that lets you compose a new message and post it to the currently selected newsgroup.
Mark All Read	Marks all the articles in the currently selected newsgroup as read.
Read	Before you click on this button, select a thread you are interested in reading. Then, when you click on the Read button a new window opens that displays the contents of the first article in the thread.
List	If you click on this button, a window listing information about each of the articles in the currently selected thread is displayed.
Mark Read	Marks all the articles in the currently selected thread as read.
Mark Unread	Marks all the articles in the currently selected thread as unread. This is the opposite of clicking on the Mark Read button.

Button	Action
Preferences	Clicking on this button opens a dialog box similar to the one shown in Figure 8.13, where you can adjust various settings. Currently, there are two options you can adjust.
	The More option lets you activate pauses during the loading of long messages. Leave this on by default.
	The Show messages option lets you determine the oldest message to be displayed. The default is 14 days.
More	If there are more threads in the current newsgroup than will fit on one screen, clicking on this button instructs AOL to retrieve another screen full.
?	This is the Help button. Clicking on it requests information about the screen you are currently using.

FIGURE 8.13.

The Preferences dialog box lets you adjust newsgroup reader-related settings.

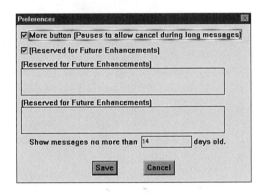

In most cases, when you open the Read Unread window you want to read the contents of the articles. To do this, highlight the thread you are interested in and select the Read Unread button, or just double-click on the thread itself. When you do this, the newsreader retrieves a copy of the first article in the selected thread and displays it in a message window like the one shown in Figure 8.14.

Once you open the message window, there are a number of additional functions to choose from, including reading the next or previous article in the current newsgroup and posting replies either to the newsgroup or the article's author. To take advantage of these functions, use the buttons displayed along the bottom and down the side of the message window. To help you better understand all these features, Table 8.6 has a listing of the buttons and the actions they perform.

FIGURE 8.14.

When you select a thread, the newsreader always displays the first article.

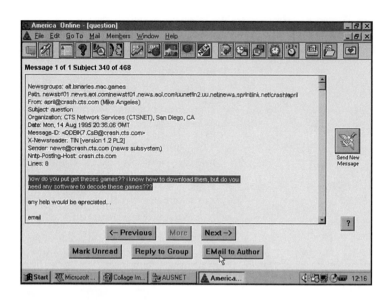

Table 8.6. Actions performed by the buttons on the Newsgroups Message window.

Button	Action
<-Previous	Clicking on this button instructs AOL to display the previous article in the current newsgroup.
More	If an article is very long, this button is activated. Clicking on it instructs AOL to retrieve another screen load of information.
Next->	Clicking on this button instructs AOL to display the next article in the current newsgroup.
Mark Unread	Usually, once you have read an article the newsreader marks it as read and won't display it the next time you enter this newsgroup. If you click on this button, however, the article is displayed again next time.
Reply to Group	Click on this button to send a reply back to the newsgroup.
Email to Author	Click on this button to send an e-mail message to the author of the current article.
Send New Message	When you click on this button a window opens that lets you compose a new message and post it to the currently selected newsgroup.
?	This is the Help button. Clicking on it requests information about the screen you are currently using.

Replying to an Article

After reading the articles posted to a newsgroup for a while, you will no doubt reach a point at which you feel the need to make your own comments or reply to statements made by other people.

To compose a reply based on an article written by another person all you need to do is follow these steps:

1. Before you start to compose the new article, highlight the text of the original article that you want to quote in your reply. In Figure 8.14, two lines of text were highlighted.

2. Using the copy-to-clipboard shortcut Ctrl+C or ⌘+C depending on your computer, make a copy of this selected text. You can also achieve the same results by opening the **E**dit menu and choosing the **C**opy option.

3. You now need to decide if you want to send your reply to the entire newsgroup or just to the article's author. Click on either the Reply to Group or EMail to Author buttons. The Reply to Author window shown in Figure 8.15, was accessed by selecting the EMail to Author button.

FIGURE 8.15.

The Reply to Author window also lets you send a copy of your message back to the newsgroup itself.

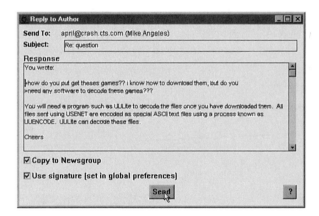

4. AOL has added Re: to the subject line of the original article. In most cases, the subject line field should be left unaltered so that the person who sent the original article will have some idea of what your reply relates to.

5. The next step is to enter your message. To begin with, the message area will be empty.

6. If you are including a quote from the previous message, type something along the lines of "In your message, you wrote" or as in Figure 8.15, simply "You wrote:".

7. On the next line you now need to paste the text you copied earlier. Position the cursor where you want the text to be placed and use the Paste shortcut key combination—Ctrl+V or ⌘+V. You can also achieve the same results by opening the **E**dit menu and choosing the **P**aste option.

8. Insert a '>' at the beginning of each line of the inserted text so that people know you are quoting from a previous message.

9. Once you have done this, enter your own comments as shown in Figure 8.15.

10. If you want to send a copy of the message to the newsgroup, select the Copy to Newsgroup checkbox. Note: If you are using the Reply to Group option this action is the default.

11. You can define a global signature for use with newsgroups in the Global Preferences window. If you have defined such a signature, and you check the Use Signature checkbox, a copy of your signature is appended to the message when you send it.

12. Once you are satisfied that your reply is complete, click on the Send button to post it to the Usenet. AOL responds with a message like the one shown in Figure 8.16, to indicate that your request was successful.

FIGURE 8.16.

AOL informs you that your message has been posted.

Posting a New Message

There are a number of windows in the AOL newsreader that give you the option of creating a new message via the Send New Message button. When you select this button, instead of creating an article in reply to a previous message, you are technically creating a new message thread.

To post a new message using the Send New Message button, you should follow these steps:

1. Using the Games for Macintosh Unread window discussed previously, click on the Send New Message button. When you do this, a window like the one shown in Figure 8.17 is displayed.

FIGURE 8.17.

Use the Post New Message window to post an article to a newsgroup.

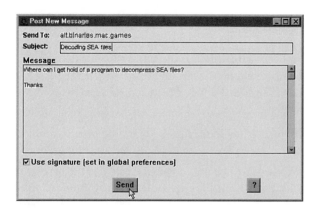

2. The newsreader automatically selects the correct newsgroup for you and displays its name at the top of the window.

3. Whenever you create a new article, there must always be something in the Subject field. You should come up with a subject line that accurately describes the point of your posting.

4. Once you have the "paperwork" out of the way, enter your message in the Message area located in the middle of the Post New Message window.

> By following the steps for sending an encoded file as discussed in Chapter 6, "The Internet E-Mail Gateway," you can send an encoded file as a part of a newsgroup article.

5. Click on the **S**end button to transmit your article to the nominated newsgroup.

Read Offline

In the most recent release of AOL's navigation software, a new type of FlashSession has been added that lets you read newsgroup articles while offline—in other words, while not connected to AOL.

To configure your system to take advantage of this type of FlashSession, click the Read Offline button on the Newsgroups main window. When you do this a dialog box like the one shown in Figure 8.18 is displayed.

FIGURE 8.18.

Select the newsgroups whose articles you want to read offline.

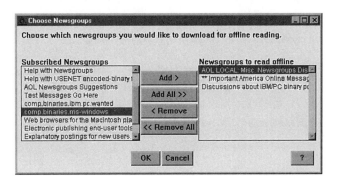

Using this dialog box, you select the newsgroups that you want to read offline. All the articles in each of the newsgroups listed in the right-hand column are retrieved automatically when you run your next FlashSession. You can then read these articles offline and post replies to them as well. Any replies that you create are uploaded to AOL the next time you run a FlashSession. (See Chapter 5 for more information on using FlashSessions.)

Note

> Because many newsgroups contain hundreds and sometimes thousands of articles that you may or may not even want to read, you should use the FlashSession option with some caution. If you have a few small newsgroups whose articles you are very interested in, then FlashSessions is a good option. On the other hand, if you only read a small number of articles in a large newsgroup, then downloading hundreds of articles that you won't read can be very time consuming.

Advanced Techniques

Now that you understand the basics of Usenet and the mechanisms required to send and receive articles stored in newsgroups, it's time to take a look at some of the more advanced options provided by AOL's Usenet newsreader.

Newsreader Preferences

To begin, let's look at some of the ways you can tailor the newsreader by choosing the Set Preferences button on the Newsgroups main menu. When you do this, the AOL displays the Perferences dialog box, shown in Figure 8.19. To explain the settings available in this dialog box, Table 8.7 contains a brief description of each and some comments on its use.

FIGURE 8.19.

The Preferences dialog box lets you tailor the way your AOL newsreader operates.

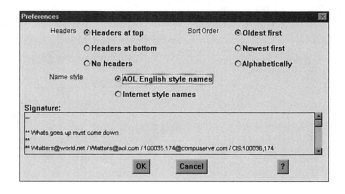

Table 8.7. Settings available using the Preferences dialog box.

Option	Description
Headers	In addition to the actual contents of each article, there is a considerable amount of other information that relates to the article stored in what is called the *article header*. This includes information about where and when the article was posted and the path it took to arrive at your computer.
	By default, the header details for each article are displayed before the message. You can choose the Headers at bottom or No Headers options to relocate or remove the headers entirely.
Sort Order	By default, articles in each newsgroup are stored in Oldest to Newest order. You can adjust this setting to Newest First or Alphabetically using the Sort Order option.
Name Style	In the examples discussed in this chapter, all the newsgroup listings have been displayed using what are called AOL English style names. If you would prefer all the newsgroup listings to use Internet style names, you can do so by altering the Name Style option.
Signature	If you want the newsreader to automatically append a signature to every article you send, enter the message you want to append in the space provided. When you do this, each time you post an article or send an e-mail message, the newsreader will append the contents of this field to the end of the message.

Parental Controls

With all the concerns currently being expressed about the somewhat explicit nature of parts of the Internet, AOL has decided to include a Parental Controls feature for the Usenet. These controls allow parents to disable certain newsgroups and prevent children from gaining access to them.

To set up Parent Controls on your system choose the Parental Controls button on the Newsgroups main window. When you do this, a list of all the screen names associated with your account are displayed on the screen. (See Figure 8.20.) Choose the screen name that you want to add controls to and click on the Edit button.

When you click on the Edit button you are then presented with a dialog box like the one shown in Figure 8.21. To explain the settings available in this window, the following section contains a short description of each option and some comments on its use.

FIGURE 8.20.

Select the screen name that you want to assign Parental Controls to and click on the Edit button.

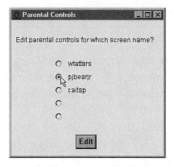

FIGURE 8.21.

The Parental Controls dialog box lets you disable access to certain parts of the Usenet.

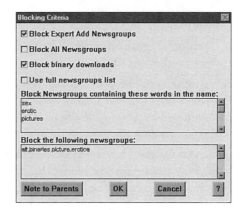

Block Expert Add Newsgroups

By default, only a selected list of newsgroups are displayed when you choose the Add Newsgroups or Search All Newsgroups options from the Newsgroups main window. Those newsgroups that are unsavory or distasteful are not displayed on these standard lists.

However, if you know the Internet name of a newsgroup already—and most kids will have already located the 'rude' ones before you know how to log on—you can still subscribe to it using the Expert Add button. To prevent this from happening, select the Block Expert Add Newsgroups option. This disables access to the Expert Add option.

Block All Newsgroups

This option is the most drastic of all. If you select it, all access to newsgroups is disabled for the selected screen name.

Block Binary Downloads

One of the areas that offers the most potential for abuse on the Usenet is the transmission of binary files using encoding methods similar to those discussed in Chapter 6.

If you select the Block Binary Downloads option, the person using the screen name you are working on will still be able to read articles but will not be able to download files using FileGrabber—a feature discussed later in this chapter.

Use Full Newsgroups List

Although AOL only displays an edited list of newsgroups by default, you can turn on the entire list by selecting the Use Full Newsgroups List option. When you do this all the newsgroups AOL has access to are searched and displayed on your screen when using the Add Newsgroups or Search All Newsgroups buttons.

Block Newsgroups Containing These Words in the Name:

If you don't want to disable access to binary files or Expert Add, but still want control over what groups a person can access, then this option is the one for you.

All you need to do is enter a list of names that you want barred. Any newsgroups that contain any of the words in this list will be disabled.

Block the Following Newsgroups:

Like the previous option, this one gives you control over which newsgroups are disabled. In this case, however, you need to enter the Internet name of each newsgroup using both the correct spelling and punctuation.

For most people this option is overkill, because the same results can be obtained more easily with the Block Newsgroups containing these words in the name: option.

UUENCODED Files and Usenet

In many different newsgroups, people use the UUENCODING techniques discussed in Chapter 6 to transmit binary files as a part of Usenet articles. Some of these articles contain graphics, others computer programs, and some even contain short movies or sound files. Basically, just about anything you would find on a computer system.

You can usually recognize such articles by both their description and the use of (1-1) type designations which indicate whether a file is split or contained in one message. Figure 8.22 shows the Models newsgroup that contains pictures of famous supermodels.

As discussed previously, before you can send a binary file across the Internet using e-mail, or in this case the Usenet, it first needs to be converted into a special ASCII text format. Then, when it is received at the other end, it needs to be reconverted to its original format.

Because this reconversion process is somewhat messy and at times difficult to accomplish, AOL has developed a tool called FileGrabber to help you out. When AOL encounters a UUENCODED file in a Usenet article, it pops open a window (see Figure 8.23) that gives you the option of letting AOL automatically download the file and decode it for you. To select this option, click on the Download File button.

FIGURE 8.22.

Newsgroups with the word binary in their name often contain articles which have UUENCODED files stored in them.

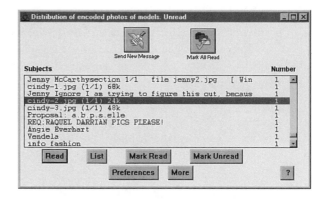

FIGURE 8.23.

FileGrabber automatically detects encoded files and gives you the option of decoding them immediately.

If you select the Download File option, AOL displays the Download Manager file requester shown in Figure 8.24. This dialog box gives you the option of nominating both the name and location where the file will be stored on your local hard drive.

FIGURE 8.24.

Using the Download Manager select the directory where you want the file to be stored.

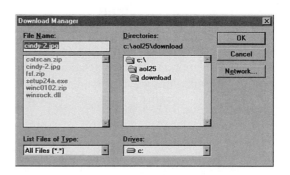

When you click on the OK button, AOL starts to transfer the decoded file to your computer. As an added bonus, if the file you are downloading is recognized by AOL, it attempts to display the file for you. For example, if the file contained a picture, AOL displays the image for you when it completes the file transfer. The cindy-2.jpg file highlighted in Figure 8.22 is, in fact, a picture of Cindy Crawford. If you chose to decode and download this article using FileGrabber, you would see an image like the one shown in Figure 8.25.

FIGURE 8.25.

AOL automatically displays Images, Sound Files and gives you the option of decompressing Zip'd files.

If you decide not to use FileGrabber, you can tell AOL to save a copy of the article as a text file so that you can decode it later using a program such as Wincode or UULite. To save a copy of the article, click on the Download Article button.

In a perfect world, FileGrabber would be the ultimate tool. However, because many people use different ways of encoding and decoding files, and because sections of a file are not always sent in order, FileGrabber is not always able to detect or decode every type of file. For articles where FileGrabber fails, you are going to have to rely on saving a copy of each article as a text file and decoding it later.

> You can also send your own files to Usenet newsgroups by first encoding them using a program like Wincode. Then, when you open the Send New message window, you need to copy the file into the article using the same steps discussed in Chapter 6 for sending a UUENCODED file.

Other AOL Newsgroup Resources

In addition to the Newsgroups window and the AOL newsreader, there are a number of other areas on AOL that may provide you with additional information about newsgroups.

Internet Questions

By clicking on the FAQ (Frequently Asked Questions) question mark icon, located on the Internet Connection window, you can gain access to the Internet Questions service shown in Figure 8.26.

This service contains answers to many of most commonly asked questions people often direct to AOL's support staff. Among these questions, you will find a section dedicated specifically to newsgroups.

FIGURE 8.26.

The Internet Questions area contains information about all the Internet services offered by America Online.

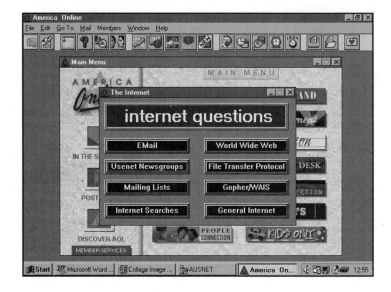

DejaNews Research Service

One of the latest additions to the Internet Connection resources list is a service called DejaNews. If you select this option, a World Wide Web page similar to the one shown in Figure 8.27 is displayed.

FIGURE 8.27.

DejaNews is an index and search tool that allows you to search through thousands of newsgroups.

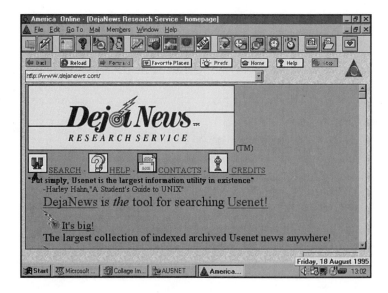

DejaNews is an index and search tool that allows you to search through thousands of newsgroups in a matter of seconds. To use the service all you need to do is enter the keywords you want to search for and click on the search button.

In no time at all, a list of articles is displayed (see Figure 8.28). To read any of these articles, simply click on the blue underlined text for the article you are interested in.

FIGURE 8.28.

DejaNews lists all the articles matching your search keywords.

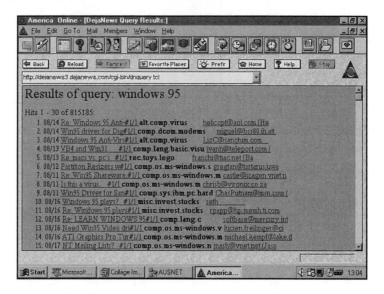

For more information about using the World Wide Web, refer to Chapter 12, "The World Wide Web."

Internet Exchange and Internet Chat

Both the Internet Exchange message boards and the Internet Chat online chat sessions contain discussions that relate to the use of Usenet and newsgroups in general.

There are message boards where you can exchange Usenet newsgroup names, debate the merits of Usenet versus message boards, or discuss the latest techniques to UUENCODING and UUDECODING. For those who prefer a more direct approach, many of the CJs (CyberJockeys or Forum Hosts) in the Internet Chat areas will be only too willing to assist you with answers to your queries.

For more information about the use of these two services see Chapter 15, "The Best of Both Worlds."

The Top 40 Newsgroups

With around 20,000 newsgroups now available, it isn't practical to even consider creating a long list of newsgroups you may or may not be interested in. Instead, to give you some idea of the diverse range of topics available, Table 8.8 lists the 40 most popular newsgroups, according to the information produced by the DEC Network Systems Laboratory in Palo Alto, California.

Table 8.8. The top 40 most popular newsgroups as of April, 1995.

Ranking	*News*	*Estimated Number of Readers*
1	alt.binaries.pictures.erotica	280,000
2	alt.binaries.multimedia	94,000
3	alt.binaries.pictures.erotica.female	140,000
4	alt.binaries.sounds.tv	37,000
5	alt.binaries.pictures.erotica.male	50,000
6	alt.binaries.pictures.erotica.orientals	87,000
7	alt.binaries.sounds.music	54,000
8	alt.binaries.pictures.misc	160,000
9	alt.binaries.pictures.supermodels	200,000
10	alt.binaries.pictures.celebrities	90,000
11	alt.binaries.pictures.erotica.amateur.female	28,000
12	rec.games.trading-cards.marketplace	22,000
13	alt.binaries.sounds.movies	41,000
14	alt.binaries.multimedia.erotica	28,000
15	alt.binaries.sounds.mods	37,000
16	alt.sex.pictures	110,000
17	alt.test	47,000
18	alt.binaries.pictures.tasteless	120,000
19	bionet.molbio.genbank.updates	11,000
20	alt.binaries.pictures.erotica.blondes	120,000
21	alt.sex.pictures.female	76,000
22	alt.binaries.warez.ibm-pc	6,800
23	alt.binaries.sounds.misc	91,000
24	alt.binaries.pictures.utilities	140,000
25	alt.binaries.pictures.erotica.bondage	22,000

Ranking	News	Estimated Number of Readers
26	alt.binaries.pictures.erotica.teen	4,300
27	alt.binaries.pictures.erotica.bestiality	19,000
28	alt.binaries.sounds.erotica	43,000
29	alt.binaries.pictures.erotica.fetish	22,000
30	alt.sex.stories	270,000
31	misc.jobs.offered	330,000
32	alt.binaries.pictures.anime	32,000
33	alt.binaries.pictures.erotica.anime	21,000
34	alt.binaries.pictures.erotica.breasts	15,000
35	alt.binaries.misc	25,000
36	alt.binaries.doom	41,000
37	alt.binaries.pictures.girlfriends	160,00
38	alt.binaries.pictures.erotica.cartoons	400,00
39	alt.binaries.sounds.cartoons	12,000
40	alt.religion.scientology	26,000

Summary

As you have seen in this chapter, Usenet offers America Online users access to an entirely new world. With thousands of newsgroups covering every topic imaginable, there is bound to be at least one area of discussion that interests you.

However, with all this discussion of e-mail, mailing lists, and now newsgroups, you are probably beginning to wonder if America Online offers any Internet services that don't involve discussions or the sending of messages. Well, you will be pleased to know that the answer is yes, it does offer other Internet services.

The next chapter takes a look at the first of these services, FTP, and looks at how you can use AOL to download files and computer programs from computers connected to the Internet.

FILE TRANSFER PROTOCOL (FTP)

What Is FTP?

AOL and FTP

Using AOL for FTP Connections

FTP Search Tools

The reason many people first purchase a modem is not to explore the World Wide Web or reap the benefits of electronic mail. Instead, it is to log on to local bulletin boards (BBS) and download copies of games and other computer files.

While they are connected to these BBS systems, most people inevitably discover e-mail and discussion forums, but for many the main attraction remains the downloading of files. This love affair with inexpensive access to copies of computer software and games has not been lost on the Internet world, either. Using the tools discussed in this chapter, it has been estimated that Internet users have access to more than 300 gigabytes, or the equivalent of over 400 CD-ROMs worth of computer files.

To obtain access to these files, the Internet uses a program known as the *file transfer program* and its corresponding communications protocol, the *file transfer protocol.* It is common practice to refer to both the program and the protocol by the common acronym *FTP.* Through FTP (the program and protocol), it is possible to log on to thousands of remote computer systems and transfer copies of the files they contain onto your own computer.

This chapter explores the use of FTP and some of the tools that assist you in locating files available via FTP by discussing these topics:

- ◆ What Is FTP?
- ◆ FTP Archives and America Online
- ◆ Using AOL with FTP
- ◆ Archie

What Is FTP?

The file transfer program is in many ways a special kind of remote logon or Telnet program. (See Chapter 10, "AOL and Winsock," for more information about Telnet.) As is the case for Telnet, you use FTP to log on to remote computer systems. But where Telnet lets you use the remote computer as though it were directly connected to your local computer, FTP lets you use the remote computer's files and download copies of them to your local computer.

The File Transfer Protocol

To achieve this, FTP uses a client/server environment that allows your computer and the remote computer to communicate using a *file transfer protocol.*

This is yet another example of a remote computer running special server software and your computer running a local client program. In this case, the remote computer needs to be running an FTP server while your computer runs an FTP client. Using this set of programs, you can open a connection with a remote host computer, access and retrieve copies of the files stored on its disk drives, and in some cases transfer files to the remote system as well.

In the early days of the Internet, the similarities between FTP and Telnet did not stop at just the logon process. Visually, running FTP was very much like running a Telnet terminal. To browse the directories on the remote computer, you entered commands such as `ls` or `dir` using a terminal-like command line interface, and to change directories you issued commands like `cd /pub`.

For people who were comfortable with the vagaries of DOS or UNIX, these commands were familiar. But as more and more people with little understanding of the workings of command line-based interfaces began to use FTP, more elegant interfaces were designed that allowed these commands to be hidden from the user. Modern FTP clients—like the one in AOL—now use point-and-click menus and action buttons to navigate though remote directories and send or receive files.

FTP Sites on the Internet

Obviously, if FTP allows you to log on to remote computers, there must be computers on the Internet that allow you to log on to them.

These computer sites fall into two basic categories: private FTP sites, which require you to have an Internet account at the site before you can FTP to it, and public sites, which allow anyone to log on. This chapter deals mainly with public sites. However, for those of you who have access to private FTP sites, the steps involved are identical.

Like the guest accounts provided by some computer systems, FTP also uses a special account to permit users to log on to public FTP sites. The account name used by FTP for this purpose is *anonymous*. To reflect the use of this account name, publicly accessible FTP sites are commonly known as *anonymous FTP servers*.

Domain Names

Like all computers connected to the Internet, FTP sites are referred to by domain names.

For the most part, these domain names are easily recognizable as belonging to an FTP server, due to the fact that they are usually prefixed with `ftp`. For example, the FTP site operated by my Internet service provider at `world.net` uses the domain name `ftp.world.net`. Although this is not a hard and fast rule, it is a handy way to work out the most probable domain name for an FTP site.

If you were trying to find the domain name for AOL's FTP server, it would be reasonable to assume it to be `ftp.aol.com`. The first part, `ftp`, describes it as an FTP server, followed by `.aol` to represent the name of the organization and `.com` to indicate that it is a commercial operation.

> When using AOL, you can substitute a site's IP address wherever a domain name is requested.

Internet Archives

Many of these sites have also become known by another name due to the nature of the files they contain. In recent years, the terms *FTP archive* and *Internet archive* have become popular when referring to a special group of FTP sites containing entire collections of files covering many types of computer systems. (See *AOL's Favorite Sites* later in this chapter for a discussion of some of these archives.)

These archive sites contain copies of literally thousands of public domain and shareware computer programs. In addition, there are copies of transcripts from popular newsgroups and mailing lists, graphics, photographs, sound files, and a wide variety of text files and documents covering just about every topic known to man. Basically, if a file has ever been publicly distributed by computer, chances are that a copy of it is available from one of the Internet FTP archives.

Hosts and Mirrors

As a result of the sheer number of files located in these FTP archives, the number of people who want to access them at any one time can become quite large. Like any computer system, there comes a point when the system cannot handle any more connection requests. When this occurs, any additional users attempting to open an FTP connection are effectively locked out.

To cope with this overload problem, some of the major FTP archives are now duplicated on other computer systems in different parts of the world. These sites are said to *mirror* the main FTP archive because they contain exact copies of all the files stored on the main site. As a result, if you are locked out of an FTP archive because it is overloaded, it is possible that the file you are looking for may be available from one of the archive's mirror sites.

For AOL users, America Online operates a site that contains mirrors of many of the major Internet archives. To access any of these mirrors, all you need to do is select the appropriate site from the AOL Favorite Sites list discussed later in this chapter.

> Although not all FTP sites have mirrors, in many cases copies of files can be found at completely unrelated sites as well. To assist you with the task of finding these files, a program called *Archie* was developed to create a global index of all FTP sites. (See the "Archie" section later in this chapter for more information.)

AOL's Software Libraries

When America Online announced the availability of FTP access using AOL, few AOL users realized the powerful resource they had been given. For the most part, this is due to the extensive library of files already available to America Online users in its various software libraries. Yet in reality, FTP is the ideal complement to America Online's file libraries.

There are files available at FTP sites that will never be available in any of America Online's own libraries, and likewise some of the files stored at America Online are not available on the Internet. In this sense, by combining the two resources, AOL brings the best of both worlds to its users.

AOL and FTP

As was the case for AOL's Usenet interface, America Online lets you use FTP in much the same manner as you'd use any of AOL's standard services. In this way, you don't need to learn a new program for each service. Instead, all you need to do is learn how to use one or two new windows displayed by AOL itself.

The Internet Connection

FTP is one of the services offered as a part of the Internet Connection channel. To access the Internet Connection window, click on the Internet Connection button displayed as a part of the AOL main menu shown in Figure 9.1. Alternatively, you can use Keyword: **Internet** to achieve the same result, or click on the Internet Connection icon (indicated by the mouse pointer in Figure 9.1) on the toolbar.

FIGURE 9.1.

Click on the Internet Connection button on the AOL main menu or use the icon in the toolbar.

Opening the Internet Connection window (see Figure 9.2) gives you access to all the tools and resources provided under the Internet Connection banner. From here you can move easily to any Internet service by clicking on the appropriate menu item or icon.

To access FTP via this window click on the FTP icon in the bottom left-hand corner. Or, you can jump straight to the File Transfer Protocol - FTP window using Keyword: **FTP**.

FIGURE 9.2.
The Internet Services window gives you access to all Internet tools and Forums.

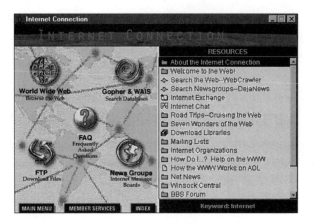

The File Transfer Protocol - FTP Window

The File Transfer Protocol - FTP window (Figure 9.3) provides you with the means of accessing all of the FTP-related services currently provided by America Online. From this window you can access information about FTP, explore AOL's FTP services or search for a specific FTP site.

FIGURE 9.3.
The File Transfer Protocol - FTP window.

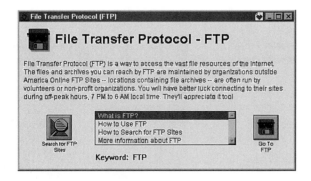

The following pages examine all the options available via this window and look at the steps involved in retrieving a file using FTP.

Keeping Up-To-Date

Before you proceed any further, now would be a good time to take a look at the information offered in the first four items listed in the File Transfer Protocol window. These items contain information about late-breaking FTP news and offer valuable assistance if you encounter any difficulties while using FTP.

AOL also provides you with answers to a number of Frequently Asked Questions about FTP and the Internet in general. To look at these answers, click on the FAQ icon located on the Internet Connection window.

> The Frequently Asked Questions area is designated as a Free Area. As a result, you will not be charged for connection time while in this area.

AOL's Search Software Libraries Tool

As was mentioned at the beginning of this chapter, access to FTP should be considered as a complementary service to the Software Libraries already offered by America Online. In many cases, copies of files you plan to retrieve using FTP are probably also stored in one of AOL's own forum libraries.

For this reason, it is a good idea to first search AOL's software libraries for any files you are trying to obtain before attempting to locate a copy using FTP. In the long run this can save you both time and money, especially if the FTP site you want to connect to is busy and no mirror sites are available.

To search AOL's software libraries, open the **G**o To menu and select the Search Software Libraries option, as shown in Figure 9.4. When you do this, AOL displays a Software Search window similar to the one shown in Figure 9.5.

> When you select the Search Software Libraries option, AOL opens the Search Software window that relates to the computer platform you are using. If you want to search for files on a different computer platform use Keyword: `Mac Software` or Keyword: `PC Software` to access the appropriate libraries.

FIGURE 9.4

Select Search Software Libraries from the Go To menu.

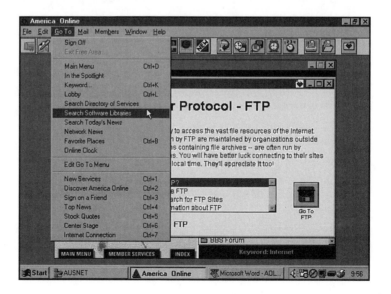

FIGURE 9.5.

Enter the keywords and select the categories you want to search for and then click on the List Matching Files button.

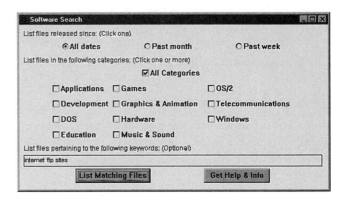

From this window, you can easily search the software libraries located on America Online by following these steps:

1. This example lets you look for any files stored on AOL that contain lists of FTP sites.

2. First you need to decide if you want to search all the files on AOL or just those that have been added in the past month or past week. For this example, select All Dates.

3. Next, you need to select the categories of files that you want to search. If you are unsure of exactly which category a file might be stored under choose the All Categories option.

4. Finally, to look for files containing lists of FTP sites, you need to enter some keywords in the field at the bottom of the search window. Where possible, try to give as many keywords as possible. This helps AOL limit the number of files returned as a result of the search. In Figure 9.5, I entered **internet ftp sites** as the keywords.

> A similar result would also be obtained by just entering **ftp** and **sites** as keywords. However, you should try to narrow down the search as much as possible. Even though it is highly unlikely that the **ftp** and **sites** keywords would be used in conjunction with files not related to the Internet, adding **internet** as a keyword ensures that all related files are found.

5. When you click on the List Matching Files button, AOL performs a search based on the settings and keywords you entered. When it completes the search, it reports the number of files found in a File Search Results window as shown in Figure 9.6.

FIGURE 9.6.

The File Search Results window lists all the files that meet the search parameters.

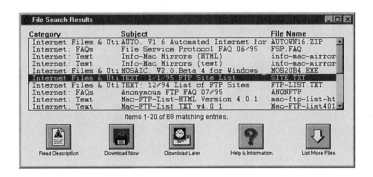

6. Judging from the list shown in Figure 9.6, it would appear that AOL does indeed have a file that meets our needs precisely. To make certain, double-click on the file's description line to request a more detailed description of the file's contents. (See Figure 9.7.)

FIGURE 9.7.

Click on the Download Now button to retrieve a copy of this file.

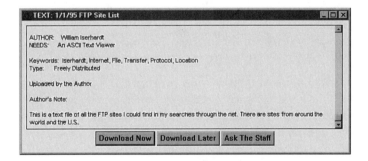

7. From this dialog box, you can download a copy of the file by clicking on the Download Now button or mark the file for retrieval later by clicking on the Download Later button.

Using AOL for FTP Connections

Now that you are familiar with the various support and information resources that America Online provides for FTP, it is time to look at how to use AOL to connect to an FTP site.

To get started, click on the Go To FTP button located on the right side of the File Transfer Protocol - FTP window shown in Figure 9.3. When you do this, AOL opens the Anonymous FTP window shown in Figure 9.8.

FIGURE 9.8.

*The Anonymous FTP
window lists AOL's
collection of Favorite Sites.*

Connecting to a Favorite Site

Using this window, you can either select one of the listed sites or click on the Other Site but-ton, to enter a site of your own. Listed in this window are nine of the most popular FTP sites currently available on the Internet. Between them, these sites provide access to files covering nearly every type of resource you could ever possibly need.

America Online has chosen these sites because they represent a good cross section of the sites available on the Internet, and also because they tend to provide access to files that may not be available as a part of America Online software libraries. Two of these sites are of special impor-tance as well, because they represent the primary locations for access to support files dealing with Borland and Microsoft computer software. Mac users will also find the FTP site for Apple Computers listed on their screen.

> To ensure that you get the fastest possible access to many of these sites, America Online has set up its own mirror site for many of the FTP sites on the Favorite Sites list. As a result, when you select these sites you are not connecting to the master site but instead to a faster AOL mirror site.

Logging On

To open an FTP connection with one of the sites on the Favorite Sites list, all you need to do is the following:

1. Highlight the site you are interested in and click on the Connect button. For this example, let's say you're interested in obtaining a new Internet add-on for Microsoft Windows, so highlight the `ftp.microsoft.com` entry.

2. Once the connection between AOL and the remote FTP site is complete, a welcome message appears, similar to the one displayed in Figure 9.9. This message provides you with information about the site you are connected to.

FIGURE 9.9.

The Microsoft FTP site Welcome message.

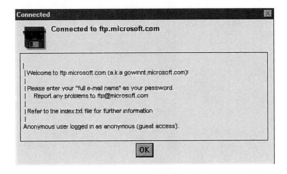

If AOL is unable to complete the FTP connection for some reason, it displays a message advising you of the problems it is encountering. The most common message you will encounter is one informing you that there are too many people connected to the site. In this case all you can do is try again later.

3. After reading the message, click on the OK Button to open the AOL FTP client window.

You should now be logged on to the Microsoft FTP site and looking at a window showing the contents of the site's root directory. The next section looks at how to use this screen to explore an FTP site.

Working with AOL's FTP Client

When the connection process is completed, your screen should look like Figure 9.10. The FTP client window is broken into three main areas:

◆ Directory location information
◆ The directory list box
◆ Navigation controls

FIGURE 9.10.

The AOL FTP client lets you navigate easily around remote sites.

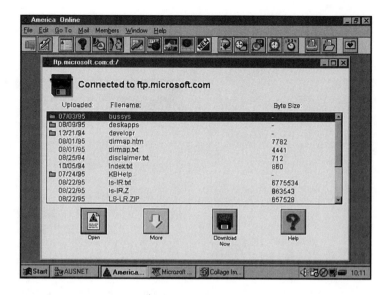

Directory Location Information

The first area is the directory location message line. The Connected to ftp.microsoft.com message in Figure 9.10 shows the location of this area.

Files at FTP sites are organized using a hierarchical structure similar to that used by MS-DOS. All files are stored in directories and subdirectories starting at a root directory. The directory location message line is used to display the directory or subdirectory you are currently connected to.

When you first connect to a site, you are usually placed in the root directory of the site, as indicated by the Connected to message. As you move around the site, this message is updated to reflect the directory you are currently viewing.

The Directory List Box

The second area of the FTP client window, and by far the most important, is the directory list box that takes up most of the screen.

The contents of the remote FTP site's current directory is listed here. In this box, subdirectories are designated by a folder icon and *linked directories* by a link icon. Files, on the other hand, don't usually have any sort of icon associated with them but can easily be recognized by a valid number in the Byte Size: column. This number indicates the physical size of the file.

By double-clicking on any of the subdirectories, you can move down the directory tree. As you move into successive directory layers, the directory location message in the top-left section of the window will change to reflect the location of the current directory.

Navigation Controls

Finally, the last area is occupied by the four buttons across the bottom of the window. Table 9.1 lists each of these buttons and explains their use.

Table 9.1. Control buttons on the FTP client window.

Error Message	*Comments*
Open	Click on this button to view the currently selected file. If a directory or link is selected, a new window is launched to display its contents.
More	This button is only active if there are more entries in a directory than AOL can handle in a single download. Click on the More button do retrieve more entries for the current directory.
Download Now	Click on this button to download a copy of the currently selected file.
Help	Click this button to display help information.

Important Files at FTP Sites

In the root directory of each FTP site, you will usually find a number of special files containing information that can help you find your way around the site. The next section shows you how to view and retrieve copies of these files, but for the time being, all you really need to be aware of is what they contain.

index.txt

A good place to start when connecting to any FTP site is the index.txt file, sometimes also called index.msg, index, or INDEX. This file usually contains a description of every file in the root directory. Reading this file gives you a good idea about which files contain information about the site's contents.

The root directory is not the only place that you'll find index.txt files. At many sites you will find an index.txt file in each directory as well, containing a list of the files that it contains.

ls-1R.txt

The ls-1R.txt file always contains a full directory listing of all the files held at the site. As a result, this file can often be quite large. When this happens, you may also find a file with a name such as ls-1R.ZIP or ls-1R.Z. If this file exists, it contains a compressed version of the ls-1R file, which you will need to decompress once you retrieve a copy of it.

On some sites, you will find that the ls-1R.txt file is listed as just ls-1R. In fact, this is the original name given to these directory files, and actually represents the command used on UNIX computers to generate the list.

dirmap.txt

A number of sites also provide an abbreviated version of the `ls-lR` file that lists just the directories without their contents. This file is often referred to as a directory map, hence the name `dirmap.txt` or `dirmap`.

readme.txt

You should also pay close attention to any `readme`, `read.me`, or `readme.txt` files stored in the root directory. These files often contain important information about the way the site is operated and special details regarding the files it contains.

.message

Some directories, including the root directory, contain special information that is displayed every time you change directories. However, because not all FTP clients display this information automatically, the `.message` file is included as a part of the directory list so that you can view it manually.

If you find that some strange things are happening in a directory containing a `.message` file, reading this file may help to explain what is going on.

links.txt

Some sites use a special process to create connections between their different directories. These connections, called *linked directories,* allow you to move quickly from one directory to a different directory, possibly on a different hard drive or in a completely different path.

For example, at `ftp.cdrom.com`, a number of its archives are stored in directories with names such as `/.1` or other cryptic descriptions. To get around this problem, they have a directory called `/pub/` that consists entirely of links to these cryptic locations. In `/pub/` these cryptic directories are described using names such as `/pub/doom` and `/pub/games`, which you must agree are much easier to understand.

However, not all FTP clients are able to handle these special links. To get around this problem, most sites that use these links include a file called `links.txt` that shows you how these directories are linked together.

> The current version of AOL fully supports the use of linked directories.

Retrieving a File

The Internet add-on for Microsoft Word mentioned in the "Logging On" section is stored in one of the subdirectories at `ftp.microsoft.com`.

You can describe the location of this file by writing down the path you need to follow to reach it, starting at the FTP site's root directory. The path to the file you are looking for is `/deskapps/word/winword-public/ia`.

This path indicates that the file is stored in the ia directory, which is a subdirectory of winword-public. In turn, winword-public is a subdirectory of word, and word of deskapps. Because deskapps is the first directory listed, this indicates that it is a subdirectory of the root directory.

To retrieve a copy of this file once you are connected to the Microsoft FTP site, follow these steps:

1. To get to the ia directory using AOL, use the directory list box to move from the root directory through each successively lower directory level. In Figure 9.11, you can see that the first subdirectory, deskapps, is listed as one of those available from the Microsoft FTP root directory. Click on this directory to highlight it, and then hit the Open button to make it the new current directory.

FIGURE 9.11.

Highlight the deskapps subdirectory and press the Open button.

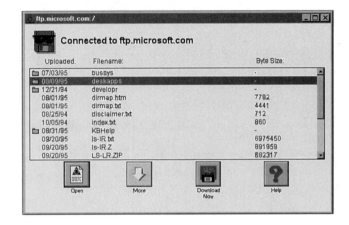

2. When you press the Open button, AOL sends a message to the remote FTP site to request a change of directory. When AOL receives a response from the FTP site, a new window is opened to display the contents of the new directory. (See Figure 9.12.)

   You should also note that the directory location message for this new window now contains the new path: /deskapps/.

3. Listed in this updated directory window you will find the word directory—the next directory listed in the file's path. Click on this subdirectory to highlight it and again press the Open button to move down another level. Alternatively, double-clicking in the subdirectory performs the same action.

If there are more subdirectories than can fit in the directory list box, you may need to use the scroll bar to the right of the window to display the rest of the list.

Tip

FIGURE 9.12.

Microsoft's deskapps *directory.*

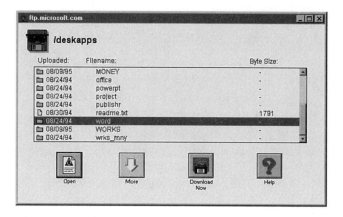

4. Now repeat step three two more times, once to move down into `winword-public` and then again to open the `ia` directory.

5. Once you reach the correct directory, it is time to turn your attention to the files stored in this directory. (See Figure 9.13.)

FIGURE 9.13.

The /deskapps/word /winword/winword- public/ia *directory.*

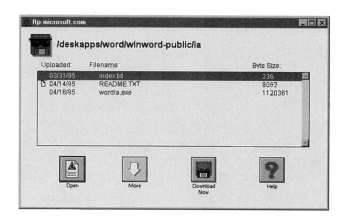

There are three files stored in this directory, each of which serves a different purpose:

`index.txt`   At most FTP sites, there is a special file stored in each directory that describes its contents. In this case the file is called `index.txt`, but at other sites it may simply be called `index`. To look at the contents of this file, click on it and then press the Open button. This tells AOL to request a copy of the `index.txt` file.

When you do this, AOL opens a window like the one shown in Figure 9.14. This window displays some basic information about the contents of the file including its expected type and estimated download time. It also gives you the option of viewing the contents of the file or downloading it.

FIGURE 9.14.

Click on the View File Now button.

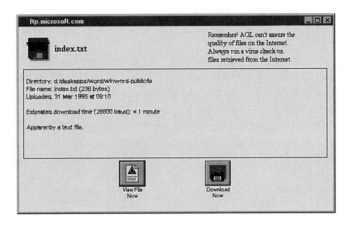

Click on the View File Now button to display the contents of the file, as shown in Figure 9.15.

FIGURE 9.15.

AOL displays the contents of index.txt *in a separate window.*

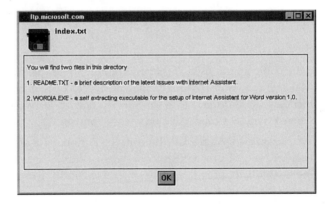

readme.txt   Depending on the FTP site, large files are often accompanied by a small description file. This file is designed to tell you about the contents of the larger file before you download it. The name of this file usually takes one of two forms: readme.txt, if there is only one main file in the directory, or *filename*.readme if there is more than one main file. For example, *filename* would be replaced by wordia.exe without its extension, resulting in wordia.readme. Like the index.txt file, the contents of these files can be viewed by pressing the Open Now button.

wordia.exe   After reading through the index.txt and readme.txt files, it would appear that this is the file you are looking for.

6. To retrieve a copy of this file, highlight wordia.exe and click on the Download Now button.

7. After a few seconds, AOL's Download Manager dialog box is displayed. (See Figure 9.16.)

Mac Users: Although the layout of your Download Manager dialog box may appear slightly different from the one shown in Figure 9.16, you need to follow the same basic steps.

FIGURE 9.16.

Click OK to store
wordia.exe in the
c:\aol25\download
directory.

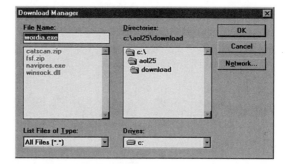

By default, all retrieved files are stored in your default download directory, using the same name as that used at the remote FTP site. However, using the Download Manager requester you can change the directory and even the filename before commencing the transfer. Once you are happy with the name of the file and the location where it will be stored, click on the OK button.

8. When you click on the OK button, the remote FTP site is then asked to begin the transfer process. Once the transfer begins, AOL displays a progress dialog box indicating how much of the file has been received and the estimated time remaining. (See Figure 9.17.)

FIGURE 9.17.

Click on the Finish Later
button to halt the transfer
and resume it a later time.

Depending on the number of requests an FTP site is handling, the transfer speed may sometimes fall below an acceptable standard. In these situations, it is often better to halt the transfer by clicking on the Download Later button. You can then resume the transfer at a later time using Download Manager.

9. When the transfer is complete, the progress dialog closes and you are returned to the FTP client window. From here you can retrieve additional files or close the FTP connection.

Uploading a File

The FTP client software built into AOL does not currently support the uploading of files to Internet sites. This situation may change in the future, but for the time being, if you really need to upload files to an FTP site, you will need to obtain a copy of a dedicated FTP client program and use the Winsock library discussed in the next chapter, "AOL and Winsock."

> The Windows version of AOL does allow you to upload software to your own private FTP site at America Online. See Chapter 14, "WWW Publishing with AOL," for more information about this feature.

Having said that, for those of you that would like to upload files to FTP sites, there are a few things you need to know about the different types of FTP sites in existence.

Archive Sites

Most archive sites that hold large collections of files allow people to submit new files through a special directory, usually called /incoming. At these sites, this is the only directory that allows you to upload files.

There are also usually strict guidelines and rules that need to be followed when you're submitting a file to one of these sites. In most cases, the file must be compressed using a program like WinZip (see Appendix D) and also must be accompanied by a readme file describing the file's contents.

Private Accounts

Some Internet service providers offer their users access to a private directory on their host system where they can store files using FTP.

For these people, this is a bit like having a filing cabinet stored in someone else's building. As a rule, only the owner of the directory has access to it, so these sites can often be used to store copies of private information with little concern about possible theft or copying.

> In September 1995, America Online launched a new feature called My Place. This effectively gives every America Online user their very own 2MG FTP storage area. (See Chapter 14 for more information.)

Connecting to Unlisted Sites

The only real difference you encounter when connecting to an unlisted site as opposed to one of the sites listed be AOL, is that you need to find the domain name on your own.

Locating FTP Sites

There are a number of ways to find the addresses of the different FTP sites dotted around the globe. To start with, the file located earlier in this chapter in AOL's Software Library offers an extensive list. Alternatively, AOL also provides an indexed database of FTP sites that you can search. (See the "Search Tools" topic later in this chapter for more information.)

However, both these methods offer a somewhat hit or miss approach to locating sites and, more importantly, files. As a result, most people find that the best approach is to use an FTP indexing tool called Archie. Archie is a globally accessible index containing a list of the contents of thousands of FTP sites. (See the "Archie" topic at the end of this chapter for more information on using Archie.)

Logging On to an Unlisted Site

Regardless of how you locate the domain name of a site from which you want to retrieve files, you need to follow these steps to make the connection:

1. On the Anonymous FTP window (see Figure 9.18), click on the Other Site button.

FIGURE 9.18.

Click on the Other Site button to connect to an unlisted site.

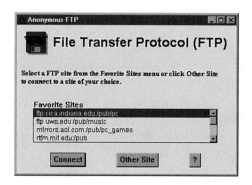

2. After a few seconds AOL displays the Other Site window shown in Figure 9.19. In the Site Address: field enter the domain name of the FTP site you want to connect to.

    For this example, enter **ftp.world.net**—the FTP site operated by my Internet service provider.

If you know the path name of the directory you want to access, you enter it as a part of the site name. To do this enter the domain name first, followed by a colon, and then enter the path. For example: `ftp.world.net:/pub/` would take you straight to the `/pub` directory at `ftp.world.net`.

FIGURE 9.19.

Enter the domain name of the site you want to connect to in the Site Address: field.

3. By default, AOL automatically attempts to log you onto the selected site using the anonymous username. If, however, you have an account at an FTP site or know the login name and password for a private FTP site, select the Ask for login name and password check box.

4. Click on the Connect button to instruct AOL to attempt a connection with the FTP site you have chosen.

5. If you select the Ask for login name and password check box, AOL displays the Remote Sign-On window shown in Figure 9.20. Enter the login name and password for the FTP site and click on the continue button.

6. Provided that AOL encounters no difficulties opening the FTP connection you will eventually be presented with an FTP client window similar to the one shown in Figure 9.21.

FIGURE 9.20.

Enter the login name and password for the FTP site and click on the continue button.

From here, you follow the steps discussed previously for downloading files.

FIGURE 9.21.

The root directory of
`ftp.world.net.`

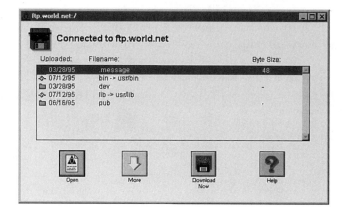

AOL's Favorite Sites List

The sites listed on the Anonymous FTP window represent a wide cross section of the files available via FTP. In the following sections, each of the sites currently listed are discussed briefly and their unique contents highlighted.

> Over time, this list of favorite sites may change based on the popularity of those sites included on the list currently and the demands of AOL users. If a site listed in the following pages no longer appears on the list, you can still reach the site using the Other Sites button. In addition, PC and Mac users may find that their respective lists differ slightly, with each list including sites more appropriate to the specific hardware.

ftp.cica.indiana.edu:/pub/pc

The CICA archive is one of the most popular sites currently available on the Internet. It is operated by the Center for Innovative Computing Application and Indiana University in Bloomington. To cater to the high usage level this site carries, AOL has created a mirror of this site. The mirror site is updated nightly so there is little need to ever visit the main site itself.

On this site you will find thousands of DOS and Windows 3.1 files along with software for UNIX systems and NeXT. To cater to the recent release of Windows 95, there is also an area dedicated to 32-bit software for both 95 and NT.

ftp.uwp.edu:/pub/music

If you're interested in music, this is the site for you. There are directories covering everything from hard rock to folk and classical, with just about every musical style in between catered to as well.

Depending on your needs, there are artist reviews, pictures, sound files, MIDI files, music scores, and thousands of sound tracks to download.

mirrors.aol.com:/pub/pc_games

This site is actually a mirror of five major sites in one. When you log on to this site you are presented with a root directory listing each of the five sites. The list below explains the content of each directory on the mirror site and also lists the home site for each archive.

Mirror Directory:	games
Site Name:	PCGA—PC Games Archive
Site Directory:	ftp.uwp.edu:/pub/msdos/games
Mirror Directory:	games_uml
Site Name:	PCGA—PC Games Archive
Site Directory:	ftp.uml.edu:/msdos/games
Mirror Directory:	programming
Site Name:	PC Games Developers' Archive
Site Directory:	x2ftp.oulu.fi:/pub/msdos/programming
Mirror Directory:	romulus
Site Name:	MS/DOS Cheats, Cracks, Hints etc
Site Directory:	ftp.uwp.edu:/pub/msdos/romulus
Mirror Directory:	doom
Site Name:	DOOM mirror
Site Directory:	ftp.cdrom.com:/pub/idgames

rtfm.mit.edu:/pub

This site contains a partial mirror of the rtfm.mit.edu site run by the Massachusetts Institute of Technology. What makes this site unique is the fact that it contains text transcripts of many of the newsgroups on the Usenet. Currently, this site contains archives of the following information:

◆ usenet-by-group

◆ usenet-by-hierarchy

◆ faq-maintainers

◆ post-faq

ftp.nevada.edu:/pub/guitar

This is another site for musicians, or more specifically, guitar players. As the home of OLGA— The On-Line GUITAR ARCHIVE, this site contains an extensive list of music-related files.

For both Mac and Windows users, make sure you read the readme files and other notices posted at this site. All the files here are archived using a UNIX storage format. To decode these files you need to download the appropriate utilities from the /resource directory on this site.

ftp.aol.com

This is America Online's own FTP site. Apart from copies of the latest versions of AOL, for all supported platforms, this site has little to offer.

For those of you that are interested, the new AOL Mac and Windows clients, including the Web browsers, are available from /aol_win and /aol_mac directories.

oak.oakland.edu

This site is provided as a service by Oakland University, Rochester Michigan. Among the many archives mirrored at this site is the SimTel archive. SimTel contains arguably one of the most extensive collections of MS DOS and Windows files in existence. In addition, there are also files for Mac users and UNIX systems as well.

World Wide Web (WWW) users can access files on oak.oakland.edu via http://www.acs.oakland.edu/oak/ and people using Gopher can access this site through gopher://gopher.oakland.edu:70/

Tip

Information about the SimTel archive is available on the World Wide Web at http://www.coast.net/SimTel/.

ftp.borland.com

If you use any of the software products developed by Borland, then this site may be of interest to you. Because this is Borland's support site, you will find product updates and support information on all of their software products located here.

ftp.microsoft.com

This extensive site, operated by Microsoft, contains thousands of files dealing with business systems, desktop applications, developer tools and information, Microsoft education and certification, Microsoft shareholder information, instructions and index for the software library, personal operating systems and hardware, and information on TechNet.

To help you find your way around this large FTP site, download the dirmap.txt file from the root directory when you first connect.

ftp.info.apple.com

For Apple users, this site operated by Apple Computers provides software updates and product related information. All new system updates are usually made available at this site within hours of their initial release. As a result, if you don't want to spend weeks or months waiting for your local supplier to get that update for you, then maybe you should try downloading it yourself.

`sumex-aim.stanford.edu:/info-mac`

If there is a mother lode for computer software, then for Mac users this site could be it. There are thousands of shareware and freeware software titles stored at this site, all specifically for Macintosh users. Stanford University in California maintains this site.

`mac.archive.emich.edu`

If you are looking for Macintosh games, system extensions, and other utilities, then this site is another good place to start. Operated by the University of Michigan in Ann Arbor, this site is dedicated entirely to Macintosh files and archives.

FTP Search Tools

As was mentioned earlier in this chapter, there are a number of search tools on the Internet that can assist you in your search for files stored at anonymous FTP sites. In this final section, two of these services, AOL's built-in FTP database and Archie, the Internet FTP database, are examined in some detail.

AOL's FTP Database

Clicking on the Search for FTP Sites button on the left-hand side of the File Transfer Protocol (FTP) window (see Figure 9.22) opens the FTP Search window shown in Figure 9.23.

To use this window, enter a list of words you want AOL to search its FTP database for and then click on the Search button. When you do this, AOL lists all the FTP sites that possibly contain files matching the words you entered in the search field at the top of the Ftp Search window.

FIGURE 9.22.

Click on the Search for FTP Sites button to open the FTP Search window.

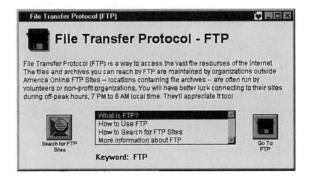

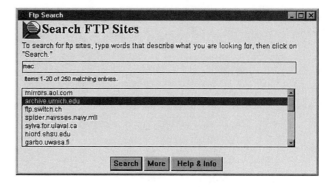

To find out more detailed information about any of the FTP sites returned by your search request, double click on the site you are interested in. After a few seconds AOL displays an information window like the one in Figure 9.24. Details covering the types of files available at this site, special access requirements, and the times of day when the site is available are displayed in this window.

While this database is a useful tool, when you are looking for interesting FTP sites to explore, it is of less use when you are looking for a specific file. When you consider the fact that some FTP sites can contain tens of thousands of files in hundreds or possibly thousands of different directories, locating a specific file in this maze can be a little like finding a needle in a hay stack.

To conduct a more thorough search of the Internet, you need to turn your attention to a program such as Archie.

Archie

With millions of files stored on FTP sites all around the world, locating the one you want by wandering onto sites by chance is a fairly remote possibility. To help you locate the file you want, a program called Archie was developed.

Archie is actually three separate computer programs, each of which performs a separate task. The first program's job is to search the Internet and collect copies of the indexes stored at each FTP site. It does this on a regular basis to ensure that it has a copy of the latest file information possible. The second component of Archie is responsible for taking these files and compiling them into a global database. This database, in theory, contains an index that holds the location of every file stored at FTP sites.

Now, having such a database is wonderful, but at the same time it's fairly useless if no one can use it. This is where the third component of Archie comes to the fore. To search this database, you use an Archie client program. There are four main ways to gain access to an Archie client with America Online.

The first, which I will look at in this chapter, is by sending an e-mail request to main Archie sites and the second by telneting to an Archie site and conducting an interactive session (see Chapter 10, "AOL and Winsock," for more information on using Telnet). You can also use a tool called ArchiPlex on the World Wide Web. (See Chapter 13, "World Wide Web Productivity.") Finally, you can use a dedicated Archie client program such as WSARCHIE (See Chapter 10).

Archie and E-mail

By far, the quickest way to start using Archie is by sending a search request via e-mail to any of the Archie servers listed in Table 9.2.

Table 9.2. Archie servers by location.

Location	Domain Name
North America	archie.rutgers.edu
North America	archie.internic.net
North America	archie.unl.edu
North America	archie.ans.net
North America	archie.sura.net
Canada	archie.mcgill.ca
Australia	archie.au
Europe	archie.funet.fi
United Kingdom	archie.doc.ac.uk
Middle East	cs.huji.ac.il

Usually, when I talk to people about which site they should use, I advise them to use the site located nearest to them. However, because of the America Online Internet gateway, this is not a practical consideration. As a result, any of the North American sites are probably a good place to start, although archie.rutgers.edu is recommended by America Online since it is the closest site to their head office.

You may find, however, that it takes some time for responses to arrive back from Rutgers, because it is often fairly heavily loaded down. As a result, you may like to experiment with the various U.S.-based sites to find the one that gives you the best response times.

Sending Your First Archie Request

To communicate with Archie via e-mail, follow these steps:

1. Open the Compose Mail window by clicking on the Compose Mail icon located in the toolbar—it is the second icon from the left. Alternatively, holding down the Control key and the 'M' key (⌘-M on a Macintosh) when using the Windows version of AOL achieves the same result.

2. In the To: field enter the e-mail address of the Archie site you have decided to use. The e-mail address is created by adding the username archie to the Archie servers domain name. As a result, the e-mail address for Rutgers is archie@archie.rutgers.edu.

3. Because you will probably use this address again, now would be a good time to add it to your Address book. Do this by clicking on the Address Book button on the left hand side of the Compose Message window.

4. When the Address Book window opens, click on the Create button. AOL opens an Address Group dialog box like the one shown in Figure 9.25 where you can enter a description and the e-mail address itself.

FIGURE 9.25.

Type the Archie e-mail address in the Screen Names field and a description in the Group Name field.

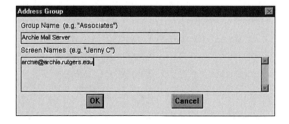

5. With your new address safely stored in your Address book, return to the Compose Mail window (see Figure 9.26) and enter a comment of some description in the subject field.

Archie, like most e-mail-based Internet tools, ignores the contents of the subject field. However, AOL does not allow you to send a message unless you enter something in this field.

Note

FIGURE 9.26.

AOL requires you to type something in the subject field even though it will be ignored by Archie.

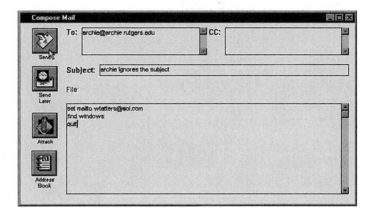

6. In the body of the message to the Archie server, you enter the commands you want it to perform for you.

You can enter as many commands as you like in each message you send to Archie, provided that each one starts on a new line.

Tip

7. In the first line of your message, type the command **set mailto** followed by your e-mail address at America Online. This command tells Archie where to send the results of your request. In Figure 9.26, I entered **set mailto wtatters@aol.com** so that Archie would e-mail the results to my AOL mail box.

Some Archie servers, like the one at Rutgers, will determine your return address automatically if you include a `set mailto` command. However, because this is not always the case, it is a good idea to include `set mailto` as the first line of every request you send to Archie.

Note

8. On the following lines you enter your search requests and any other special commands. Table 9.3, at the end of this section, lists the main commands supported by Archie. Alternatively, if you send the `help` command to Archie as a part of an e-mail message, a reply listing all the available commands will be sent back to you.

The command you will use most often is the find command. This command is the one that instructs Archie to make a search of its database. In this example, I asked Archie to search for files and directories that contain the word windows by entering **find windows.**

> *Note*
>
> Unlike the AOL database, which is cross-referenced by keywords, the Archie database only lists the names of the physical files and directories stored on each FTP site. As a result, when it conducts a search it will only locate files and directories that match your request exactly. For example, a win95 directory would not normally be located by the find window command. Instead, you would need to send find win or find win95. There is one exception to this rule. If there was a file named windows in the win95 directory, then both it and the win95 directory would be report by Archie.

9. The last line of each message must contain a quit command. This tells Archie that there are no more commands to follow.

10. Finally, click on the Send or Send Later buttons to post your message to the Archie server.

Understanding the Results of an Archie Search

Depending on the number of requests currently being handled by the Archie server you selected, you will eventually receive an e-mail response to your Archie request (see Figure 9.27).

FIGURE 9.27.

The result of your Archie request are posted to your AOL mail box.

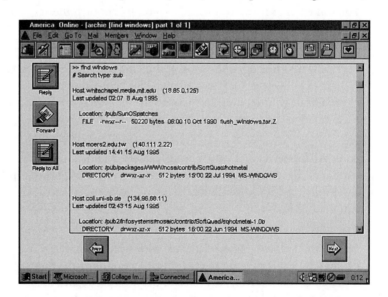

The results of each command you sent to Archie will be listed in the e-mail reply, in the same order that you sent them. Each command will be shown first—the >> find windows in Figure 9.27— followed by a list of files and directories, if any are found.

For each FTP site both the domain name and IP address is listed first, followed by a date indicating the last time that Archie updated its copy of the site's directory index. Below this, each directory and file—listed in alphabetical order—matching your search request are itemized, including file sizes and the date that the file or directory was uploaded to the FTP site.

> You can alter the order in which files are displayed by using the set sortby command discussed in Table 9.3.

Common Archie Commands

The table below describes the most important commands supported by Archie. To obtain a complete list, e-mail the command help to the Archie server.

Table 9.3. Common Archie commands.

Command	Description
help	Requests a copy of the Archie help file.
manpage ascii	Mails a copy of the Archie manual page to you.
find <query>	Locates files matching the contents of the <query> field. Exactly how Archie determines a match is dependent on the setting of the set search command.
set search exact	There are four possible types of search that can be performed by Archie. If a search is set to exact, the contents of <query> must match the name of a file or directory exactly.
set search sub	If search is set to sub (substring search), the contents of <query> only need to be a part of a file or directory. For example, find dos would located an msdos directory if search was set to sub, but would not return msdos as a part of the result if search was set to exact.
set search subcase	If search is set to subcase, a substring search is performed, but the search is case sensitive. In other words, find mac would not return a file or directory with the name Mac, but would still happily report one named macintosh or macmillian.
set search regex	You can use UNIX regular expressions as a part of a find <query> if search is set to regex.
set maxhits <num>	Set the number of results that Archie sends you for any one search. The default is 100.
set sortby <order>	You can set the order that Archie lists the results or your search to, filename order, hostname order, size order or time last modified.

Summary

For many people, the attraction of free computer software is reason enough to own an Internet connection. With FTP, you can obtain copies of just about any computer file ever made available to the public, either in the public domain or as shareware.

In this light, by bringing FTP to AOL, America Online now gives its members the best of both worlds. Not only do they have access to the extensive collection of files stored in America Online's software libraries, but they now have access to the millions of files located at FTP sites all over the Internet.

AOL's connections to the Internet don't stop at e-mail, newsgroups and FTP. As of August, 1995, America Online announced support for TCP/IP, and more specifically, access to Winsock-based programs while using AOL for Windows.

The next chapter examines the steps involved in configuring your computer to take advantage of Winsock support and also discusses the use of Telnet, IRC, and Archie clients.

10

AOL AND WINSOCK

Winsock for Windows

Popular Winsock Clients

Although the Internet tools provided by America Online give you access to the Internet, they do so using a very hands off approach. Every option you select when using Internet services needs to pass through AOL's internal gateways and filters before it reaches your computer screen.

Now while this sort of approach works admirably for services such as e-mail, FTP, and newsgroups, when you start to talk about services such as Telnet and IRC, using a gateway is not the best possible approach.

When the ARPANET was first proposed back in 1969, one of the main goals set down for the project was to develop the capability for remote computing using the ARPANET network, as opposed to dedicated telephone lines. The motivation behind this goal was the desire to share the capabilities and resources of the most powerful computers available at the time with as many scientists and researchers as possible. In addition, by using ARPANET to make the physical connections, the cost of maintaining separate dedicated lines for each user who wanted a connection was removed completely.

In the early developmental stages, all the work required to maintain these remote links was handled by the host computer system. This put a very heavy load on this computer, and was often the cause of system failures and other downtime events. As the need for remote computing began to increase, an alternate system was sought that could reduce these loads by sharing the workload between the host computer system and the remote computer.

The answer to this problem was Telnet. Using Telnet, the remote system oversees the physical screen display and keyboard processing, leaving the host computer free to get on with the job it was designed for. Telnet is yet another example of a client/server application that uses distributed processing techniques to share its work load.

Until recently, however, it was not possible to open a Telnet connection from America Online. But this all changed in August 1995, when America Online released an add-on utility called a *TCP/IP Winsock stack* for users of the Windows version of AOL. This software provides users with access to Telnet and also provides the link to many other Internet services such as IRC and Archie.

> Mac Users: At this stage, Winsock support is only available to people using the Windows version of AOL.

This chapter looks at the new capabilities offered by AOL when you install the Winsock program and also discusses some of the more popular Winsock client programs currently available. It does this by exploring the following topics:

◆ Winsock for Windows

◆ Telnet

◆ IRC –Internet Relay Chat

◆ Archie

◆ Other Winsock Clients

Winsock for Windows

As you discovered in Chapter 1, the Internet consists of many computers all connected together via a network that uses a communications and networking protocol known as TCP/IP. Therefore, to get the most benefit out of a connection to the Internet, ideally there needs to be a way to connect your computer directly to the network using TCP/IP.

So far, however, all the Internet services provided by America Online that this book has examined, have been connected to the Internet via special gateways that act as intermediaries. These gateways maintain the links to the Internet instead of direct connections via TCP/IP.

Gateways and the like are not suitable, however, for providing access to services like Telnet. As a result, to provide its users with efficient and effective access to services like Telnet and IRC, America Online decided to create a TCP/IP Winsock stack designed specially for AOL. This software gives America Online users direct access to TCP/IP and hence the Internet.

What is Winsock?

When you connect a computer to the Internet using TCP/IP, that computer physically becomes a part of the Internet. Making such a connection from a UNIX computer is a relatively straight forward process, because as a rule, such computers and their operating systems already understand the concept of networking and have well-defined standards and protocols for such actions.

In the PC world, on the other hand, there was no clearly defined standard. To compound this problem even further, MS-DOS, the operating system for the IBM-based PC, does not support or even understand the concept of computer networking. As a result, before PC's could be connected to the Internet using TCP/IP, a standard method for using TCP/IP software was needed.

Over a number of years a few approaches were experimented with, some under DOS itself and others which took advantage of Microsoft Windows. The result of all this experimentation was the release of a document, and accompanying computer software, that defined a standard method for connecting a PC running Windows to the Internet. The name given to this method was called *Windows Sockets* or *Winsock* for short.

To find out more information about Winsock you should take a look at the Winsock FAQ at: `http://mars.superlink.net/user/mook/winfaq.html`. Microsoft also provides a detailed description of the physical Winsock programming library, which you can download from `ftp://ftp.microsoft.com/Softlib/MSLFILES/WINSOCKW.EXE` and maintains a WWW page with Winsock- and Internet-related information at `http://www.microsoft.com/windows/pr/inetapps.htm`.

Note

Today, just about all Internet-related programs written for Windows include the ability to communicate with the Internet via Winsock. What this means is that regardless of the type of underlying Internet connection or TCP/IP software installed, the Winsock application or client, be it a Telnet program or a World Wide Web browser, will operate correctly.

FIGURE 10.1.

Winsock is the glue that links Internet client programs to TCP/IP and hence the Internet itself.

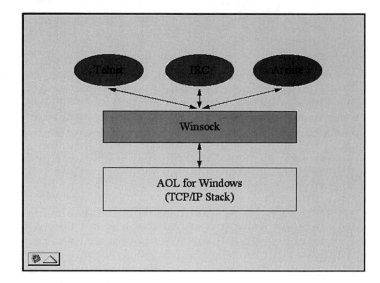

The diagram shown in Figure 10.1 displays the basic concept behind Winsock. Basically, Winsock acts as the glue that binds Internet-related computer programs such as a Telnet, IRC or Archie client to what is called a TCP/IP stack, which in turn provides the link to the Internet itself.

For America Online users, the AOL software effectively acts as the TCP/IP stack and provides the link, via your modem and America Online's host computers, to the Internet. What was needed then to allow support for Winsock client programs was a version of Winsock that could communicate with AOL and naturally with its Winsock clients.

Winsock Central

So what does this mean for you, the America Online user? To put it in the simplest of terms, by installing a single file called `winsock.dll` in your `c:\windows\system` directory you can instantly gain access to full TCP/IP Internet connectivity.

To obtain a copy of this file, select the Winsock Central option from the RESOURCES list on the Internet Connection window as shown in Figure 10.2.

FIGURE 10.2.

Winsock Central is listed as an option on the Internet Connection RESOURCES list.

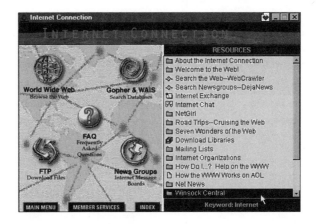

When you do this the Winsock Central window (see Figure 10.3) is displayed. This window contains links to a selection of Winsock client software, a FAQ covering all those difficult questions, a Message Board devoted especially to the use of Winsock and its related clients, and most important of all, the winsock.dll itself.

FIGURE 10.3.

To obtain a copy of winsock.dll, click on the button under the "Download it today!" message.

Installing Winsock for AOL

When you click on the button located below the Download it today! message, AOL opens a window similar to the one shown in Figure 10.4. At this stage select the **P**rint option from the **F**ile menu to obtain a hard copy print out of the installation instruction for winsock.dll. Then, click on the Download Now button to open the Download Manager dialog box.

FIGURE 10.4.
Click on the Download
Now button to open the
Download Manager.

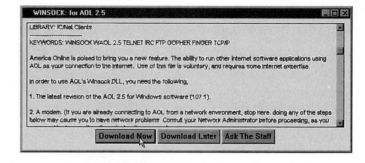

FIGURE 10.5.
Select OK to retrieve a copy
of winsock.dll.

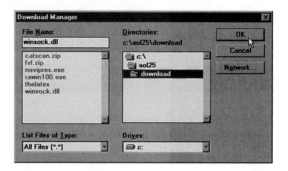

If you are sure that there are no existing copies of winsock.dll installed on your computer you can download the file straight into your c:\windows\system directory. Otherwise, download the file into a separate directory first, as shown in Figure 10.5. Finally, after making a copy of any existing version, copy the AOL version into the c:\windows\system directory.

> On occasion you may encounter a different version of winsock.dll. For example, Windows 95 comes with its own winsock.dll file. However, you can't use the Windows 95 version with AOL, instead you must use the one that was specially written for AOL.

> If you upgrade to Windows 95 after installing the AOL version of winsock.dll, the Windows 95 upgrade replaces the AOL version with its own. As a result, before you can use AOL, you need to copy the AOL version back into the c:\windows\system directory.

Winsock.dll is now installed on your computer—easy, huh? However, before you can begin using it you need to sign off from America Online and shut down your computer.

Popular Winsock Clients

Once the winsock.dll file has been successfully installed, all you need to do is obtain copies of a few Winsock client programs and you're on your way.

To get you started, America Online provides you with a list of software that gets their Cyberjockey's seal of approval, and in addition, there are a number of other files stored under the Download Libraries entry, listed on the Internet Connection window.

Alternatively, there are a number of excellent FTP sites and World Wide Web sites that maintain an up-to-date list of all the latest Winsock applications. To get started, you should take a look at the files available from the CICA archive, which is located at `ftp://ftp.cica.indiana.edu` in the `/pub/pc/winsock` directory.

If you prefer using the World Wide Web, E-Znet's Winsock Archive home page contains links to the most popular Winsock-based applications available on the Internet. The http address for this home page is `http://home.eznet.net/~rwilloug/stroud/cwsapps.html`.

This site is the home of the official FTP server for Forrest Stroud's Consummate Winsock Apps List. This list contains information about the latest release versions of each product, their status as freeware, shareware, or otherwise, and links to the host sites for each. As this site is often very busy, you should also consider using its mirror site at `http://www.tribble.com/cwsa.html`

After obtaining and installing your software, all you need to do is sign on to America Online in the usual way and then run the Winsock application you have chosen. Windows and AOL look after getting winsock.dll running and all the other connection issues.

The remainder of this book is devoted to an examination of some of the most popular Winsock applications requested by America Online users.

Telnet

Like many of the services previously discussed, Telnet is a tool that enables you to use the Internet for some form of communication.

In Telnet's case, you use the Internet to log on to computer systems located anywhere on the network and use them as though they were sitting in the room next to you. From a user's standpoint, running Telnet is a lot like using a communications program to connect to a local *bulletin board system* (BBS).

However, whereas communications programs create a physical connection between your computer and the host system, Telnet uses a client/server approach that physically separates the actions of the host and remote systems.

How Does Telnet Work?

This client/server mechanism, or more correctly, the *Telnet protocol*, allows two computer systems to share the workload required to perform a remote logon.

For this to happen, two separate computer programs are required. On the host computer—the one you want to connect to—there is a program called a Telnet server. It is this program's job to wait for Telnet *remote logon* requests to arrive from computers connected to it using the Internet.

When such a request arrives, the Telnet server opens a communications channel with the computer making the request. To make a remote logon request, the person on the remote computer needs to run a Telnet client program. (See Figure 10.6.) This program looks and feels very much like a standard VT100 terminal. Internally, however, it is actually conducting a conversation with the Telnet server instead of connecting directly to the remote computer system.

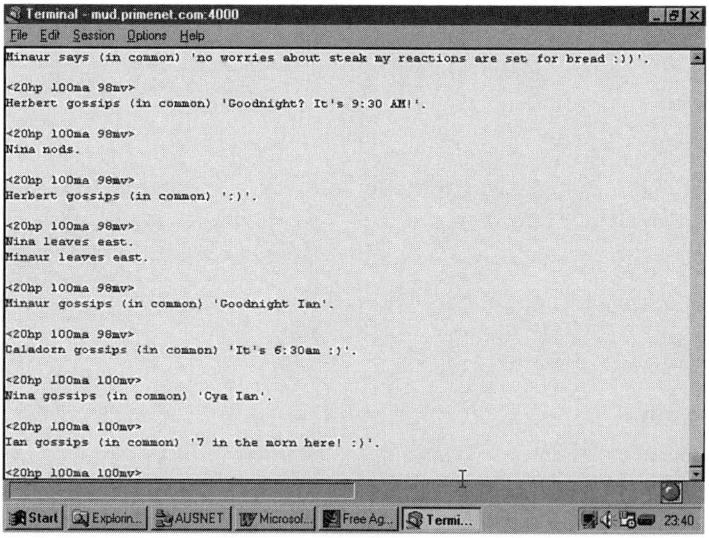

FIGURE 10.6.

EWAN— one of the most popular Telnet clients running in VT100 terminal emulation mode.

The VT100 terminal developed by DEC is the de facto standard terminal used by computer systems worldwide. Nearly every computer system available supports the use of VT100 terminals for both remote login and local connections. For this reason, it was also adopted as the default when using Telnet.

Getting Connected

To connect to a remote computer you usually need to know three pieces of information. First you need to know the remote computer's domain name. Second, you usually need to have a login name, and third, on some occasions, a password.

Once you have these pieces of information all you need is a Telnet client program, and you're on your way. When you start the Telnet client, it asks you to enter the domain name for the computer you are connecting to. For example: `archie.internic.net` is the domain name for a Telnet host at the InterNIC that lets you perform interactive queries of the Archie database.

When you enter the domain name, your Telnet client takes over and attempts to make a connection to the site you have requested. Once connected, you are then asked to enter a login name. For the InterNIC Archie site type in **archie**.

Port Numbers

During your travels, you may occasionally come across the address of a Telnet site that mentions something called a *port number*.

Port numbers are actually an internal addressing system used by Internet computers. Just as an IP address uniquely represents a computer connected to the Internet, a port number uniquely represents the different types of connections that can be made to a computer. For example, when you open a Telnet connection, you actually need to contact port 23 on the host system. A WWW client, on the other hand, needs to contact port 80, and a Gopher client port 70.

There is usually no need to worry about these port numbers, because each client program automatically appends the correct default port number to any address it uses. Where you encounter problems, though, is when for some reason you need to connect to a port number other than the default for a particular service. You may encounter this situation when using Telnet to connect to MUDs or MOOs or some other multiuser games. Although these games are accessed using a Telnet client, they are usually not assigned to the default Telnet port.

For example, the MUD server located at `mud.primenet.com` is described as using port 4000 instead of port 23. To inform Telnet that this is the case, you need to append the port number to the Telnet address by separating them with a colon (:). Therefore, to connect to the Primenet Mud site, you would enter the Telnet address as **mud.primenet.com:4000**.

Security Issues

A number of security issues arise when you begin to discuss remote login capabilities. Unfortunately, we don't live in a perfect world, and as a result sometimes people choose to abuse the services they are offered.

To protect yourself from such people and the effect they can have on computer systems, you need to consider the following issues when using services such as Telnet.

Passwords

The most important of these relates to the use of user IDs and passwords. Like your America Online screen name, it is most important that you keep your passwords a secret to prevent other people from illegally using and abusing your connection privileges.

Like America Online, you will rarely be assigned a password on Internet systems. Instead, you will usually be asked to make up your own password. You should take great care when making up passwords to ensure you use a combination of letters that only you know. Also, never use any of the following:

◆ Your name

◆ Your birthday

◆ Your initials

◆ The word "password"

Although this may sound crazy, many people use one or a combination of these items in their password, and doing so only serves to tempt disaster.

To complicate matters further, due to the nature of the Internet, you should change your passwords on a regular basis to ensure that no prying eyes have managed to obtain a copy of your password information.

Credit Cards

From the time that online computer services began, the concept of electronic shopping has become a popular part of the Internet.

To enable these services to operate in a society that expects payment before delivery, credit cards have become a popular method of payment for electronic purchases. Although using such services is certainly convenient, you should make sure that you know exactly who you are dealing with before you ever consider giving someone your credit card details.

This also raises an important point about the security of information you send across the Internet. From the time a message leaves your computer to the time it arrives at its destination, it may have passed through any number of machines that may be able to both intercept and copy the message.

Although such practices are illegal, this does not mean that they don't sometimes occur. For this reason, as a rule you should avoid sending any confidential or private information across the Internet.

Public Key Encryption

Although these warnings may sound like a lot of doom and gloom, you do need to take them into consideration when using any of the Internet's communication services.

In fact, they have become so critical that some people have begun to experiment with ways to encode information distributed on the Internet to prevent it from being read by the wrong people. Based on these experiments, a popular system known as *public key encryption* is now available to help protect your private information.

Appendix D examines one of these public key encryption systems and explains how to use it on the Internet.

Finding Telnet Sites Using HYTELNET

Without a doubt, the most comprehensive listing of Telnet sites is maintained by a program known as HYTELNET. This service contains the addresses of hundreds of Telnet sites located on computers in all parts of the world. Until recently, the University of Saskatchewan offered a public Telnet site running HYTELNET, but its popularity grew to such an extent that the service had to be closed.

In its place, a WWW page was created that offers the same capabilities without the problems associated with the direct Telnet connection version. You can reach this page at `http://www.usask.ca/cgi-bin/hytelnet`.

Other Favorites

If you're still hungry for more Telnet sites, here is a list of some additional sites that you might like to explore, in no particular order. For each site, I have listed the domain name and, where necessary, the port number. When you Telnet to most of these sites you will be logged on automatically, but for those where you aren't, I have also listed the appropriate user ID you will need to use to log in.

Table 10.1. Popular Telnet sites.

Address	Login	Description
`news.janet.ac.uk`	news	JANET news desk
`locis.loc.gov`	N/A	The U.S. Library of Congress information database
`madlab.sprl.umich.edu:3000`	N/A	Weather, crop, and ski reports
`consultant.micro.umn.edu`	gopher	The Online Electronic Books initiative
`quake.think.com`	wais	Wide Area Information server at Thinking Machines
`enews.com`	enews	The Electronic Newsstand
`info.umd.edu`	N/A	The University of Maryland Information Service
`leo.nmc.edu`	visitor	Traverse City Free-Net
`cdnow.com`	N/A	CDnow!: The Internet Music Store
`martini.eecs.umich.edu:3000`	N/A	The Geographic Name server
`baymoo.sfsu.edu:8888`	guest	BayMOO—Palo Alto, California

Telnet Clients

In the following section, two of the most popular Telnet clients are discussed. They are

◆ EWAN

◆ Trumpet Telnet

EWAN

EWAN in one of the most popular Telnet applications currently available. This is due both to its status as a Freeware program, and because it is by far the most configurable Telnet program.

You can obtain a copy of EWAN from AOL's software library or by downloading the latest version from `ftp://ftp.best.com/pub/bryanw/pc/winsock/`. The name of the file you are looking for will be something like `ewan1052.zip`, depending on what the current version is.

> The name EWAN is an acronym for "Emulator Without A Name."

Getting Connected

Once you have obtained a copy of EWAN and have installed it, you can connect to a remote site by following these steps:

1. Assuming that you have already signed on to America Online, and that you have installed winsock.dll, start EWAN as you would any other Windows program. When you do this your screen looks like the one shown in Figure 10.7.

FIGURE 10.7.

EWAN lets you create a list of Telnet sites you like visiting.

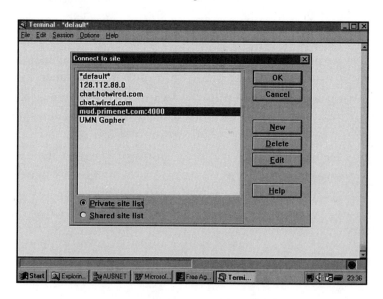

2. In the middle of the screen EWAN displays a list of Telnet sites that you can visit. When you first run EWAN this list is empty, so you need to know the domain name of a site that you want to connect to.

   To create a new site entry, click on the **New** button. When you do this the Add New dialog box shown in Figure 10.8 is displayed.

FIGURE 10.8.

Enter the connection details for the site you want to Telnet to.

3. For this example, let's connect to a site that operates a multiuser game called a MUD. (See Chapter 16, "Family Fun and Education," for more information about MUDs.)

   Enter a name for the site in the first textbox: `Primenet Mud`.

   Enter the domain name for the site: `mud.primenet.com`.

   Enter the port number for the site if it differs from the default for Telnet connections. This MUD uses port 4000 instead of 23.

   Click on the OK button to store this definition and begin your Telnet connection.

4. Back on the Connect to Site windows, select the site you have just defined and click on the OK button.

5. Unless EWAN encounters difficulties while attempting to open the connection, after a few seconds you will see a text-based logon screen describing the site you have connected to.

   Once you are connected, you need to follow the steps indicated on the screen, which vary from site to site. Some sites require you to enter a login name while others may automatically start a specific program.

Special Features

Unlike most other Telnet programs currently available, EWAN provides you with a wide variety of optional settings. To access these settings, open the **O**ptions Menu and select the **Con**figuration... menu item.

FIGURE 10.9.

EWAN gives you more control over both its appearance and operation than other Telnet programs.

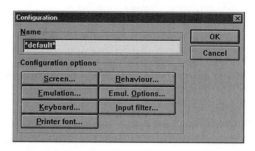

The configuration options (see Figure 10.9) are broken down into a number of sections. These include:

◆ Screen formatting and appearance

◆ Emulation & Options–VT100, ANSI VT52

◆ Keyboard Mapping

◆ Input Filters

◆ Printed Output

Trumpet Telnet

If you don't need a lot of control over the way your screen looks, or if all you want to do is occasionally connect to a Telnet site, then, Trumpet Telnet (see Figure 10.10) may be better suited to your needs.

FIGURE 10.10.

You can also use a host site's IP address instead of its domain name.

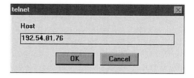

Trumpet Telnet is a simple, no frills Telnet client that gets in and does the job without any of the fancy options provided by the likes of EWAN. You can obtain a copy of the latest version from: `ftp://papa.indstate.edu/winsock-1/telnet/`. The file name to look for is `trmptel.zip`.

To use Trumpet Telnet follow these steps:

1. Sign onto America Online.

2. Start Trumpet Telnet.

3. In the Telnet dialog box, enter the domain name or IP address of the site you want to connect to. For example, to connect to the Carl Corporation Telnet site, you could use either: `database.carl.org` or `192.54.81.76`, as shown in Figure 10.10.

> If you need to nominate a port number using Trumpet Telnet, you do so by appending the number to the end of the domain name, as in `190.54.81.76:23`.

4. Once Trumpet connects to the Carl Corporation site, you are immediately presented with a menu. This menu asks you to nominate the type of terminal you are using. In this case select the vt100 option.

5. The main site menu, shown in Figure 10.11, is then displayed. From here you can explore any of the online databases and information services this site offers, including "Uncover"—the article and document delivery database.

FIGURE 10.11.

Select the number representing the service you want to use and then hit the Enter key.

> Uncover is a database containing over 5 million references to articles contained in 16,000 periodicals and magazines.
>
> By following the menus, you can search the database and obtain a list of articles matching search parameters you specify. Then, for a fee, you can instruct Uncover to fax you a copy of any articles you are interested in reading.

IRC: Internet Relay Chat

If you have ever spent more than a few seconds in one of America Online's online chat sessions, you are already familiar with the concept behind Internet Relay Chat—IRC.

IRC is basically a global version of online chat, where, instead of just communicating with other America Online members you can chat with people from all around the world.

Like America Online, IRC is composed of a number of separate rooms where people can meet. In these rooms you communicate with each other by typing messages on your computer, which are transmitted to every other person in the electronic room with you. Then, when any of these people enter a comment, a copy of their message is displayed automatically on your screen as well.

How IRC Works

While having an understanding of the ins and outs of IRC is not a prerequisite for enjoying the thrill of online communications, it may help you to understand some of the strange things that occasionally occur.

IRC Clients

To participate in any conversations on IRC you first need to obtain a copy of an IRC client. There are two very good ones discussed later in this section: mIRC and WSIRC.

These programs allow you to select which IRC channel you want to join, send and receive messages in real time, exchange private messages with individuals and even transfer files from one computer to another.

IRC Servers

Like most of the other Internet services covered in this book, IRC is yet another client/server-based system. As a result, once you have obtained a copy of an IRC client, you also need the domain name of an IRC server to communicate with. There are a number of good IRC servers currently available, however, you may like to consider

```
irc.eskimo.com
irc.texas.net
irc.colorado.edu
```

which are three of the best IRC servers currently available. Alternatively, there is also a very good list of IRC servers available for download from `ftp://cs-pub.bu.edu` in the `/irc/` support directory.

However, it does not really matter which IRC server you actually connect to, because most of the main IRC servers are connected to each other as well. As a result, the main factor that usually determines which IRC server you choose to use, is one of speed. This is why it is a good idea to experiment a bit with different IRC servers to determine which one seems to be the fastest.

Depending on the time of day that you are connected to IRC and also the distance from America Online's computer in Virginia to the IRC Server, you may find that the response times tend to vary greatly.

Putting It All Together

When you start your IRC client and tell it to connect to your IRC server, a number of things happen—basically without any intervention from you. Once your client has established a connection to the IRC server, it attempts to register your nickname—this is a name you choose as your screen name while on IRC. If no one else is using the name you have chosen, your server then proceeds to inform other IRC servers that you have arrived. These servers then pass the message on to more IRC servers until each one has been contacted. This passing of messages (or *relaying*) from one server to another is where IRC gets its name.

Now you need to select a room to visit. All the rooms on IRC start with the '#' symbol. To get a list of the rooms available you type the command /list or select the appropriate option from a list of buttons, depending on which IRC client you have. When you enter this command, your client sends the message to the server which in turn sends the list of rooms back to your computer for display. By default every room on IRC will be listed, but you can also limit this by using a version of the list command like /list -min 5. This version lists only those rooms with five or more people in them. Alternatively, /list #win would list all rooms with 'win' in their name.

Once you have chosen a room, the /join command is used to sign you into it. For example: /join #chatback would sign you into the #chatback room. When you join a room, the IRC server you are connected to informs each of the other IRC servers that you have joined the channel, and they in turn send a message to each of the people who are already in the channel, telling them that you have joined.

From then on, any messages that anyone connected to the #chatback channel types is displayed in a window specially for #chatback, and any messages you enter are sent to everyone else. Most IRC clients also display a constantly updated list of the nicknames for everyone who is in the room with you.

You can also send a private message to anyone on IRC by using their nickname. To do this you would type /msg nickname This is a message. The /msg command tells IRC that the message is not for public display, nickname is replaced by the nickname of the person you are talking to and This is a message is what actually gets sent to them.

Netsplits

There is one occurrence that you will no doubt encounter during your experiences on IRC. Because IRC operates by linking each IRC sever to only a small number of other IRC servers, which in turn relay messages to the rest of the network, if a part of the network breaks down, the servers on opposite sides of the break will no longer be able to communicate with each other.

This event is called a *netsplit*. When one occurs you will notice that many of the people in a room suddenly disappear. This is because they are connected to an IRC server on the other side of the network breakdown or netsplit. In most cases they will reappear once the connection has been fixed

DCC: Direct Client to Client

There is one other feature of IRC that has been rapidly gaining popularity over the last year. Most of the new IRC clients support a method of communication that bypasses the IRC server when conducting a discussion with another person. Hence the name Direct Client To Client or DCC.

DCC allows two people on IRC to start a private conversation that doesn't use the IRC server for its distribution. The advantage of doing this is one of speed, instead of relying on each server relaying your message until it reaches its destination. With DCC your messages are sent straight to the other person's IRC client.

DCC has also introduced some new capabilities to IRC, the most important of which is a means of exchanging files using IRC. To send someone a file using this method, you select the DCC Send option provided by your IRC client and enter the nickname of the person you want to send the file to, along with the name of the file.

When you do this the person on the receiving end receives a message asking them if they want to accept the file. If they answer yes, a copy of the file is then sent from your computer to theirs.

Note

> The developers of WSIRC have recently announced a new extension to IRC called DCC Video. In the future, you will be able to use this option, with the appropriate hardware, to conduct real time teleconferencing via IRC.

IRC Clients

There are a number of IRC clients offering a variety of capabilities currently available. However, there are two that stand out from the crowd as the current leaders.

In the section that follows, these two IRC clients are examined. They are:

◆ mIRC
◆ WSIRC

mIRC

mIRC (see Figure 10.12) is without a doubt the best freeware IRC client available today. To obtain a copy of the latest version of mIRC, check out the America Online software library or download a copy using FTP from `ftp://papa.indstate.edu/winsock-1/winirc/`. The file name for version 3.6, which is the most recent, is `mirc36.zip`.

Once you have installed it, use mIRC by following these steps:

1. Sign on to America Online using AOL.
2. Start mIRC as you would any windows program.
3. By far the most important part of using mIRC is getting it set up and running properly. To do this open the **F**ile menu and choose the **S**etup option. This opens a window similar to the one shown in Figure 10.13.

FIGURE 10.12.

mIRC—Chatting to the world.

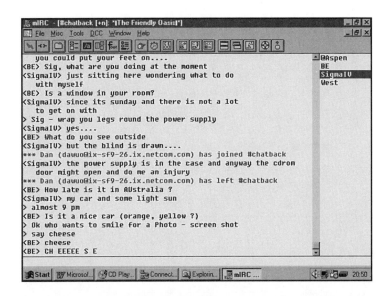

FIGURE 10.13.

Getting mIRC's settings right is the most difficult task you will ever face while using IRC.

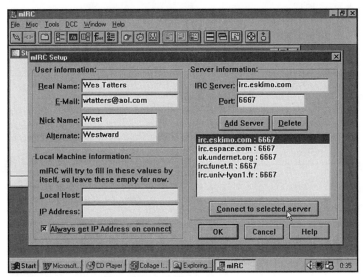

4. You should first configure the User Information.

   Enter your real name in the first field. I entered Wes Tatters.

   In the e-mail field enter your America Online Internet e-mail address.
   wtatters@aol.com is my e-mail address.

   Next you need to select a default nickname for yourself and an alternative one as well
   for those times when someone else has decided to use the same nickname.

> Nicknames can actually be changed at any time while you are online by entering the /nick <newname> command, where <newname> is replaced by your new nickname.

5. The local machine information area should be left blank, because mIRC needs to update this every time you log on.

   To make sure that this information is automatically updated, make sure that the **Al**ways get IP Address on connect check box is selected.

6. Finally, you need to select which IRC server you want to use. mIRC includes a list of popular IRC servers that you can select from, or alternatively you can add a new one by clicking on the **A**dd Server button.

> By default, most IRC servers use port 6667. If, however, mIRC appears to be having difficulties reaching an IRC server you may need to set the port number of 6668 or 6669.

7. Once you have selected a server, click on the Connect to selected server button to start an IRC session. If everything goes according to plan, after a few seconds mIRC displays a connection window like the one shown in Figure 10.14.

   This window displays a list of information about the IRC server you have connected to. You should always read this message to find out about any special events or limitations imposed by the server.

FIGURE 10.14.

Type /list -min 5 to obtain a list of all the active channels with at least five people in them.

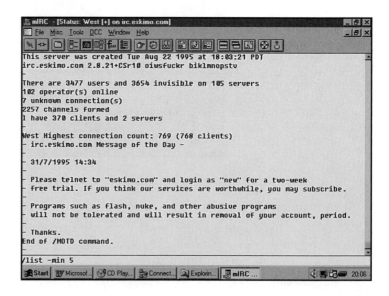

9. Now that you are online, the next step is to find out what channels are currently active. To do this type **/list -min 5** in the field at the bottom of the connection window. This tells mIRC that you want a list of all channels with five or more people in them.

Doing this creates a list similar to the one shown in Figure 10.15.

FIGURE 10.15.

Double-click on the channel you are interested in to join it.

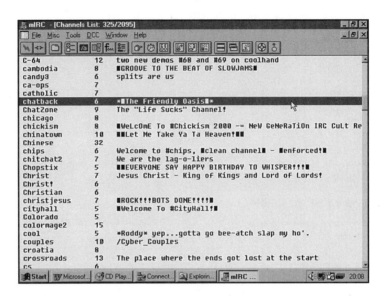

10. To join any of the groups shown on this list, all you need to do is double click on them. When you do this mIRC joins the channel and opens a chat window for you. (See Figure 10.16).

FIGURE 10.16.

A chat session in mIRC.

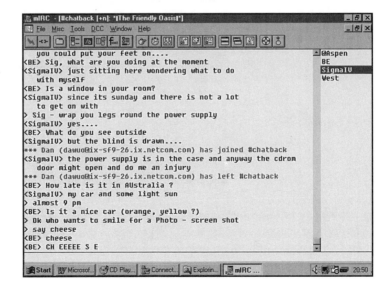

A list of all the people currently on the channel is displayed down the right-hand side of the screen and any messages in the box on the left.

To send messages yourself type them in the field at the bottom of the screen.

> IRC is far and away the most uncensored and unrestricted area of the Internet. As a result, there are going to be IRC channels that offend everyone. There is nothing you can do about these channels except ignore them. This is why use of IRC is one area that parents should monitor very carefully.

WSIRC

If mIRC is the best freeware IRC client, then WSIRC—according to the consummate Winsock list—is the best shareware IRC client.

You can obtain a copy of WSIRC via FTP at `ftp://papa.indstate.edu/winsock-1/winirc/`. The file you are looking for will be something like `wsirc20.exe`.

In the past, there were a number of noticeable differences between mIRC and WSIRC. Of these, WSIRC's capability of opening a number of chat sessions at the same time (see Figure 10.17) and superior DCC support were most noticeable. However, with the release of mIRC 3.6, most of these differences have been removed.

FIGURE 10.17.
WSIRC is the best shareware IRC client.

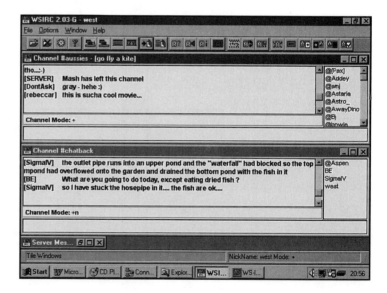

As a result, for most people it really comes down to usage. Your best bet is to download a copy of both programs and compare them for yourself. I have seen a number of passionate discussions on the merits of both programs and it seems that the vote is pretty much divided.

There is slightly better DCC support in WSIRC, but the freeware version is limited to only two chat sessions at once, so there are a few trade offs. On the plus side, WSIRC is supported software that is currently undergoing extensive development, and mIRC is listed as unsupported. This means WSIRC is more likely to contain all the most up-to-date IRC features.

Archie

Having discussed Archie in Chapter 9, "File Transfer Protocol (FTP)," you should already have a basic understanding of what an Archie client will do for you.

But for those of you that have been skimming, Archie is a database containing a listing of the directories for the many anonymous FTP sites available on the Internet. You use an Archie client to search this database and locate files stored at FTP sites.

There is only one Archie client available for windows. It is called WSArchie. You can download a copy of it from `ftp://ftp.coast.net/SimTel/win3/winsock/`. The file name for the latest version is `wsarch08.zip`.

Using Archie

To perform an Archie search using WSArchie follow these steps:

1. Sign on to America Online.
2. Start WSArchie.
3. In the Search for field enter the name of the file or directory you want to search for. (See Figure 10.18.) To locate a list of sites containing Winsock files enter **winsock**.
4. Select one of the Archie servers from the list provided. Depending on the time of day you may find that some sites respond to search requests faster than others.
5. The radio buttons under the Search button allow you to alter the type of search to be performed. See the Archie topic in Chapter 9 for more information about the different types of searches that Archie can perform.
6. Finally, click on the Search button.
7. Depending on the server you have selected, within a short while the Hosts and Directories fields will be filled with a list of sites that contain Winsock files or directories.
8. Select one of the sites and then double click on any of the directories it contains to retrieve a list of all the files stored in that directory. (See Figure 10.19)

FIGURE 10.18.

Enter the name of the file or directory you are looking for and click on the Search button.

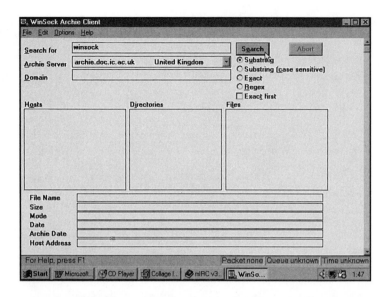

FIGURE 10.19.

Double-click on the file you want to retrieve.

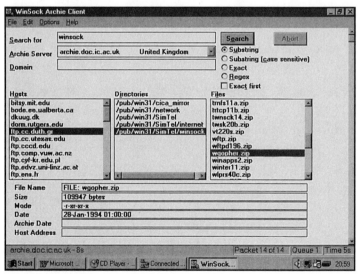

9. Once Archie displays a list of the files in a selected directory, you can use WSArchie's companion program WS_FTP to retrieve a copy the file for you. To do this all you need to do is double click on the file you are interested in.

Note

You need to have installed a copy of WS_FTP (see Figure 10.20) to take advantage of the automatic file retrieval facility in WSArchie. You can obtain a copy of WS_FTP from http://www.csra.net/junodj/. The file name you are looking for is ws_ftp.zip.

FIGURE 10.20.

WS_FTP is an FTP
Winsock client.

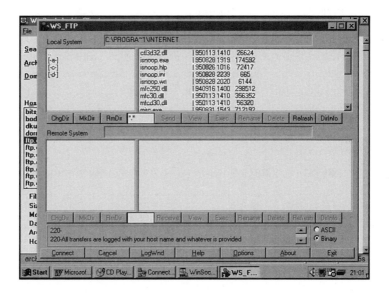

FIGURE 10.20.

WS_FTP is an FTP
Winsock client.

Locating Other Winsock Clients

Apart from the three types of Winsock clients discussed in this chapter, there are many other types of Winsock clients covering a rage of Internet services.

To help you locate many of these files, America Online has created a special download area (see Figure 10.21) as a part of the Internet Connection menu. This area is devoted entirely to Internet-related files, and more importantly, Winsock-based programs. To access this area use Keyword: **Net Software**, or select the Download Libraries option from the Internet Resources menu.

FIGURE 10.21.

All the Internet-related files
available for download
from America Online have
been grouped together in
the IC Download Libraries
area.

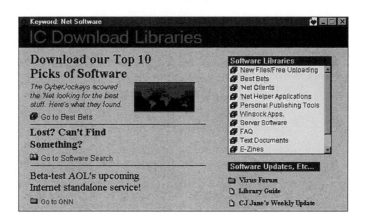

Summary

With the addition of Winsock capabilities to AOL, America Online now provides its members with total Internet connectivity. As a result, you can now use Telnet, IRC, and Archie-based clients while connected to the America Online.

But this list of Internet services doesn't stop here. America Online also gives you access to the two most powerful Internet navigation tools available today—Gopher and the World Wide Web.

The next section of this book looks at how you can access these two services via America Online.

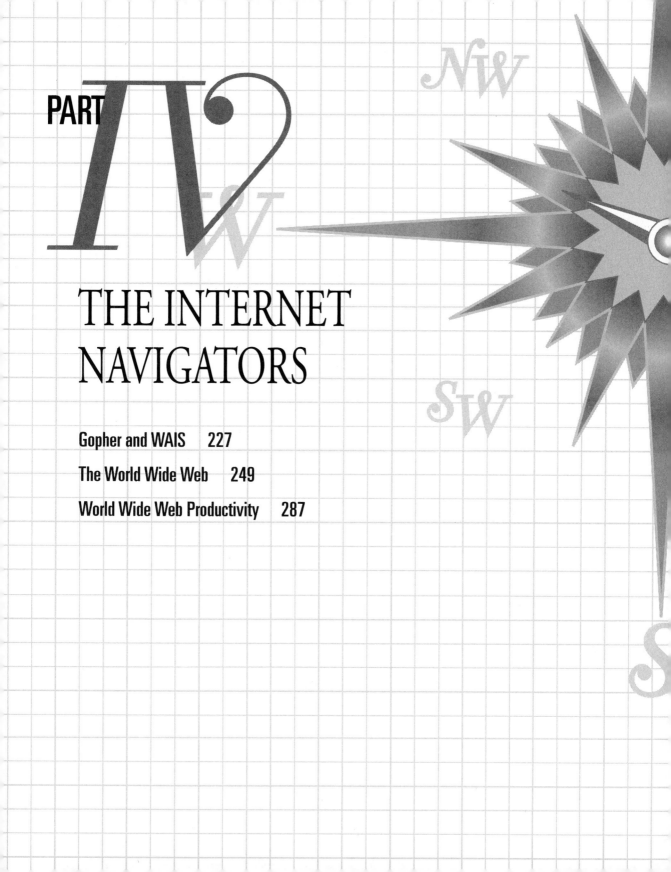

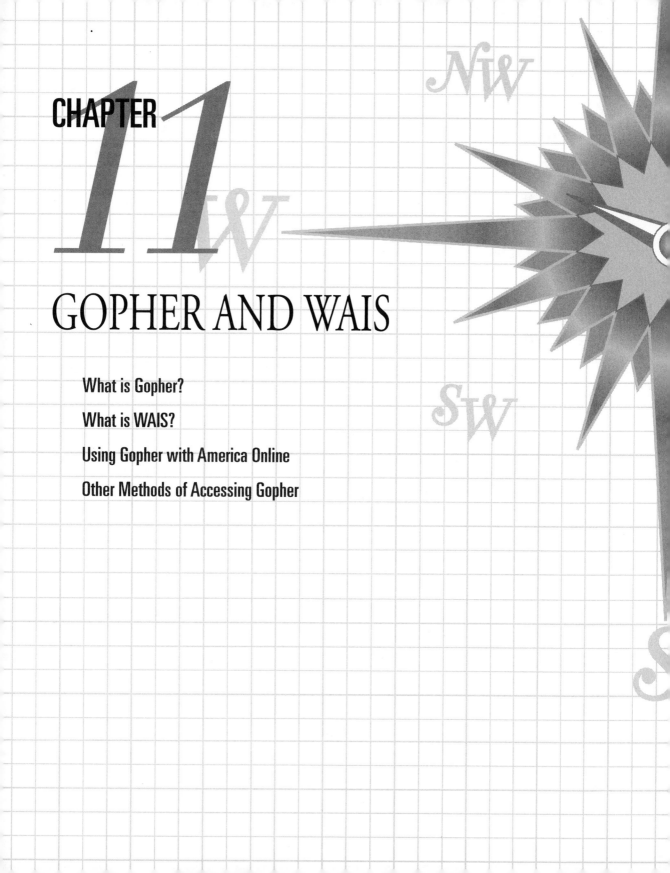

CHAPTER 11

GOPHER AND WAIS

Before the World Wide Web became popular, there was another Internet navigator that provided many of the features offered by a WWW browser. This navigator was aptly named the Internet Gopher, due to its ability to dig through the layers of information contained on the Internet and in the world it created, called *Gopherspace*.

Although Gopher has been replaced by the World Wide Web as the navigator of choice, there are still many Gopher servers in operation. This chapter looks at how you access Gopherspace by dealing with these topics:

◆ What is Gopher?

◆ What is WAIS

◆ Using Gopher with America Online

◆ Other methods of accessing Gopher

What Is Gopher?

Gopher was developed by the University of Minnesota to assist the members of its campus community who had access to the university's computer facilities. Gopher gets its name from the university's mascot, and from the play on words that gives the word "gopher" its alternate meaning. In many organizations a gopher is a person who fetches messages, runs errands, and picks up parcels—in other words, someone whose job it is to "go for" things. Both definitions accurately describe the activities provided by this service. Like the World Wide Web, Gopher is a navigator that allows you to move around the Internet, without many of the inherent difficulties. Whereas a spider's web is the analogy used to describe the World Wide Web, for Gopher the concept of a system that fetches things for you by burrowing though the Internet was adopted.

The History of Gopher

By 1991, the computer staff at the University of Minnesota was constantly being inundated with what were, as a rule, relatively easy queries to answer. But the sheer number of queries was consuming a considerable amount of staff time and resources. The plan for Gopher was to place all the answers to the more commonly asked questions into an electronic form. By doing this, the computer staff found that they could free up much of their time and also provide a service that, in most cases, would answer the questions of the past by acting as a tour guide for university computer systems.

What was unique about Gopher was its design. Instead of developing a simple menu-based help system, the developers decided to create a client/server-based system to cope with the massive number of people who were using the university's computer systems. By doing this, each campus community could use its own computing resources to access the Gopher-based information without putting an enormous load the main Gopher server.

Because of this design, people at other Internet sites soon began to realize that they could also take advantage of the Minnesota Gopher server and the extensive online help services it provided. All they needed to do was make a Gopher client available to their users and they too could access information via Gopher. During the period between 1991 and 1993, the popularity of Gopher grew at an astounding pace. By the middle of 1994, it was estimated that there were over 5,500 Gopher servers in operation worldwide, providing users with access to over 10 million items of information in documents and on FTP servers.

How Gopher Works

Gopher is yet another example of a client/server system, something that by now you should have grown accustomed to. On each Gopher server, directories of information are maintained in the form of text-based menus.

The items on these menus can contain a variety of information, including:

◆ A pointer to another Gopher menu located on either the local server or any of the other Gopher servers that populate Gopherspace.

◆ A file stored on the local server in a text-based format. When you select a menu item of this type, Gopher displays the contents of the file on the screen of your Gopher client.

◆ A link to an FTP server or a direct link to a file contained on an FTP server.

◆ A Veronica server that allows you to search the contents of Gopherspace.

◆ A link to a Telnet site.

◆ A link to specialized services such as WAIS.

When you select any of the menu items listed on your local Gopher client, it either performs the action demanded by the menu item or queries a Gopher server for a new menu if the item selected requires this.

Gopher vs. WWW

Despite all these capabilities, the popularity of Gopher has begun to decrease with the introduction of the World Wide Web. There are a number of reasons for this.

First, the Gopher environment is too sterile for many people. In a world that now demands fancy computer graphics and images, the text-based format of a Gopher menu simply cannot compete. In addition, until the development of Gopher+, an extension to the Gopher environment, it was difficult to handle many of the now-popular multimedia file formats, which included image files and audio clips.

So which is better, Gopher or the World Wide Web? Basically, this is a question that you don't even need to answer. The reason for this is because the World Wide Web has been designed in such a way that it can access a Gopher server as though it were a Gopher client. In a more literal sense, the World Wide Web is capable of doing everything that a Gopher server can do, and considerably more as well.

In fact, if you have been exploring some of the sites mentioned in this book—the InterNIC server or the Internet Society server, for example—it is highly likely that you have already encountered a Gopher server without actually realizing it. If a URL on a WWW page points to a Gopher server, it will contain `Gopher://` in the protocol section. (See Chapter 12, "The World Wide Web" for a full discussion of URLs and the World Wide Web in general.)

What is WAIS?

When you begin to explore Gopherspace you will rapidly become aware that the menus you are looking at are a bit like a Table of Contents for the Internet. Each Gopher menu item you select will, in turn, take you to another menu which provides you an expanded set of topics. These topics may be stored on the same Gopher server or on one at the other side of the world, it does not really matter, Gopher automatically collects the information for you.

Now, while this step-by-step method of locating information may be well and good when you have the time to explore, if you are pressed for time, a more direct approach is required.

To help people locate information in Gopherspace, a number of different search tools have been developed. These tools, like Veronica, which is discussed later in this chapter, provide you with a means of rapidly searching through all the menu entries in Gopherspace. When you conduct a Veronica search, a special Gopher menu is created that lists all the menu items one ever Gopher server that meet your search criterion.

What Veronica can't do, however, is examine the contents of each document referenced by a Gopher entry. Therefore, although a document may contain the material you require, if its menu entry does not contain an accurate description then a Veronica search will miss it.

As a result, when America Online set out to develop a Gopher client for its users, they decided to improve this weakness by incorporating a special kind of search tool called WAIS or a *Wide Area Information Server.*

History of WAIS

Where tools like Archie and Veronica provide you with a means of searching though directories and menu entries, a WAIS search tool allows you to search the contents of the physical files and documents that these entries point to.

As discussed in Chapter 3, WAIS was originally developed by the Thinking Machines Corporation to test the capabilities of its Connection Machine computer system. The Connection Machine was a computer system that used a principle known as massively paralleled computing. This type of computer system uses a large number of CPUs (central processing units) all housed in one enormous computer. Each of these CPUs are designed so that they can share the processing of computer tasks. By doing this, the Connection Machine can complete a task in a fraction of the time that a computer with only a single CPU would take, because each CPU can complete a separate part of the task.

> The computer sitting on your desk contains one CPU that must perform all the complex operations required to keep your system running.

Searching through the contents of millions of text files and documents was an ideal application for this type of computer system. The result was WAIS, a document indexing system capable of searching through the contents of hundreds of thousand of documents in a matter seconds.

Since WAIS was first released, a number of other organizations have also set up their own WAIS servers using software based on the original WAIS system but taking advantage of the less expensive computer systems available today. Mind you, although the computers that run these newer servers are not as powerful as the original Thinking Machines system, they still do the job admirably.

Using Gopher with America Online

Gopher, like most of the other services discussed in this book, can be accessed from the Internet Connection window shown in Figure 11.1. To open the Internet Connection window use the Keyword: **Internet**.

FIGURE 11.1.

The opened Internet Connection window.

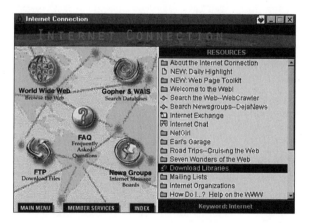

From here you can start AOL's Gopher gateway by clicking on the Gopher and WAIS icon or alternatively you can use either Keyword: **Gopher** or Keyword: **WAIS**. When you do this, the main Gopher and WAIS window shown in Figure 11.2 is displayed. From this window all the Gopher- and WAIS-based services provided by America Online can be accessed.

FIGURE 11.2.

The Gopher and WAIS window gives you access to Gopherspace.

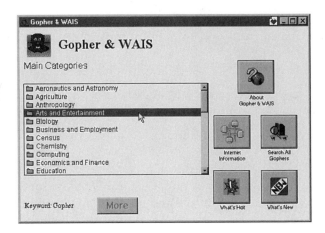

The Gopher and WAIS Main Window

The main Gopher and WAIS window can be broken into two main areas. Down the right-hand side is a group of buttons that take you to special Gopher areas. These buttons are discussed later in this chapter. On the left hand side, you see a list of all the main categories and topic areas that can be explored using Gopher. This list represents what America Online considers to be the top Gopher sites or Gopher 'holes' available on the Internet.

When you double click on any of the entries in this list, a new Gopher window is opened which reveals the contents of the selected menu item. For example, if you double click on the Arts and Entertainment entry highlighted in Figure 11.2, AOL opens a window similar to the one shown in Figure 11.3.

FIGURE 11.3.

The Arts and Entertainment Gopher menu at America Online.

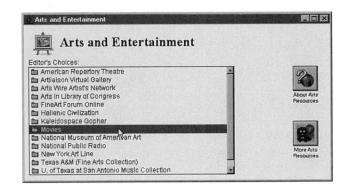

Gopher Categories

This menu contains a list of links to a number of different Gopher sites containing files and documents relating to the Arts or to entertainment. When you select any of the entries listed on this menu, America Online's Gopher client connects you to the site containing this information and retrieves a menu listing the current site's contents.

On each menu AOL uses a standard set of icons to indicate the type of information each entry contains. Items with a Folder icon in front of them represent links to other menus. Entries with a document icon (a sheet of paper) contain files that you can retrieve and read. While, entries using the Open Book icon represent WAIS or Veronica search databases.

For example, if you double click on the Movies entry, which is represented by a Folder icon, you will soon see a menu like the one shown in Figure 11.4. The site that you have actually connected to is the archive site for the USENET Movie Review newsgroup. Whenever anyone posts a movie review to the `rec.arts.movies.review` newsgroup, a copy of the review is stored at this archive site. By using Gopher, you can read any of the reviews that have been archived here or use the WAIS database search tool to quickly locate reviews that you are interested in.

FIGURE 11.4.

The USENET Movie Review archive.

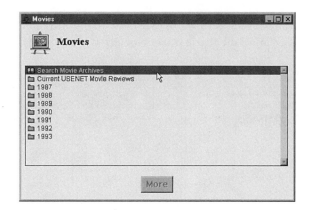

Gopher Searches

As you can see in Figure 11.4, this menu gives you access to a search database and a list of additional menus. If you click on the search entry represented by the Open Book icon, the standard Gopher search window is displayed. (See Figure 11.5). The name of the database that you are about to search is displayed at the top of the screen, in this case the Movie Archives, and just below the name there is a field where you enter the words you want to search for.

FIGURE 11.5.

Enter the movie name or other details that you want to locate and click on the Search button.

Figure 11.5 shows the results of a search for the words "indiana jones" which has brought up a number of entries mentioning these words. Some entries contain reviews of the movie itself, while others appear to contain reviews of other movies that mention the Indiana Jones movie in passing.

> Because most of the search databases displayed by the AOL Gopher are in fact WAIS databases, when you search one of these databases you will receive a far more complete list of information than you would receive by running a simple Veronica-based search. This is why the 'indiana jones' search turned up so many entries. It actually examined the contents of each article, instead of just its menu entry.

To read any of these reviews, double click on the entry in which you are interested. AOL then requests a copy of the article you have selected and displays it for you to read. (See Figure 11.6.)

FIGURE 11.6.

An "Indiana Jones and the Last Crusade" movie review by Jeff Meyer.

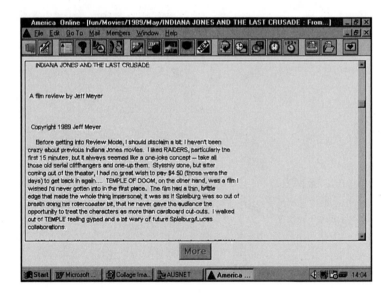

Gopher Folders

Instead of using the search tool, you can also explore the Movie Archive manually by selecting any of the folders listed below the search entry. If for example, you select the Current Reviews entry, a list like the one shown in Figure 11.7 is displayed. You can then choose any of these articles and read them in the same way that you did previously using the Search menu.

FIGURE 11.7.

The list of current movie reviews currently includes 66 articles about "Apollo 13."

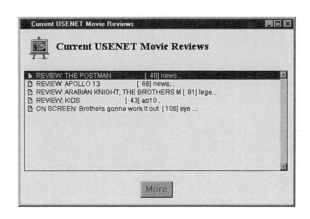

Other Gopher Services

Apart from the categories menu, on the main Gopher and WAIS window, there is a group of buttons down the right side that give you access to some special Gopher tools and menus.

About Gopher and WAIS

When you click on this button, AOL displays a message window that gives you some information about both Gopher and WAIS. In addition, it also discusses any new features included in the service. You should definitely read through the contents of this message file the first time you visit the Gopher and WAIS area, and it is not a bad idea to occasionally check back to see if there is any new information available.

Internet Information

This button acts as a gateway to a special set of Gopher menus (see Figure 11.8) developed by America Online that contain links to all the major Internet information Gopher sites. Sites such as the InterNIC and Internet Society Gophers can be reached from here along with information about all the major Internet services such as e-mail and naturally Gopher itself.

To help you determine what each of the sites on this list does, America Online has provided a brief description of each in a message file that can be accessed by clicking on the About Internet & Network button on the right side of the screen.

In addition, when you have exhausted all the sites on this list, you can access a list of addition sites by clicking on the More Internet & Network button located below the About Internet & Network button.

FIGURE 11.8.

The Internet and Network Information Gopher menu.

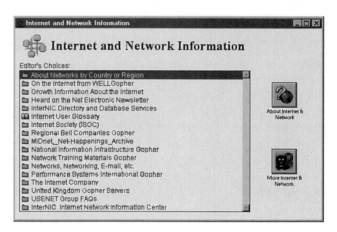

There is also a WAIS database search tool on this menu that contains an up-to-date glossary of Internet terms. If you ever encounter a word on the Internet that you don't understand, then a quick search of this glossary should be able to set you right.

Search All Gophers - Veronica

The databases that you have seen so far in this chapter have all been WAIS-based databases that were specific to certain areas of Gopherspace, be it an Internet Glossary or a Movie Archie. But what about searching Gopherspace itself?

To perform this sort of search, you need to use a search tool like Veronica—the Very Easy Rodent-Oriented Internet-wide Computer Archive.

Veronica lets you wade through the millions of menu items stored on Gopher servers all around the world, providing you with a quick and efficient means of searching through menu items in Gopherspace. It does this by creating a Gopher menu with a list of just the items you are interested in.

To access Veronica, click on the Search All Gophers button. When you do this, a window like the one shown in Figure 11.9 is displayed. In the field near the top of the window, enter a word or list of words that you want to search for and then click on the Search button. In a few seconds, all the Gopher menu entries on every Gopher server in Gopherspace containing the word or words that you entered are listed for you.

Note

Unlike a WAIS-based search, which examines the contents of each entry when using Veronica, only the item description on Gopher menus are searched.

FIGURE 11.9.

Enter a word or list of words for Veronica to locate.

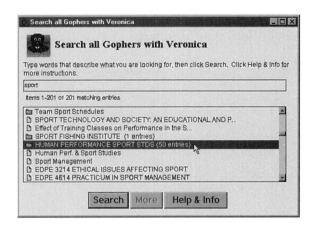

To explore any of these sites all you need to do is double click on the menu item listed and AOL takes care of the rest. It locates the Gopher server containing this entry, requests a list of all the menu items this entry contains, and then displays this menu on-screen for you in a window like the one shown in Figure 11.10.

FIGURE 11.10.

The results of a Veronica search can be used like any other Gopher menu to transport you automatically to the Gopher site and entry of your choosing.

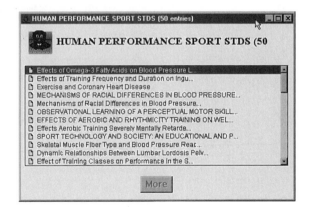

What's Hot Button

Clicking on the What's Hot button opens a Gopher menu containing America Online's pick of the hottest Gopher sites. To read a brief description of these sites, click on the About Hot button, which is located on the right side of the Hot sites window. (See Figure 11.11.)

FIGURE 11.11.

Hot sites in Gopherspace.

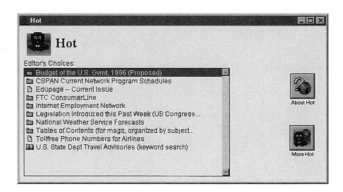

What's New Button

Because Gopherspace, like the rest of the Internet, is a constantly evolving place, America Online has added another new Gopher menu called the What's New list. (See Figure 11.12.) To access this menu click on the What's New button located at the bottom right side of the main Gopher and WAIS window.

FIGURE 11.12.

What's New in Gopherspace.

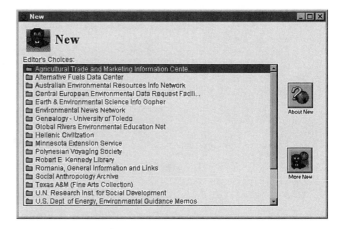

Like the What's Hot list, clicking on the About New button on the What's Hot window displays a brief description of each site to give you a better idea of what each one does. Because there are so many new sites constantly appearing, clicking on the More New button located below the About New button gives you a list of more sites to visit.

Other Methods of Accessing Gopher

Apart from using AOL's integrated Gopher system, there are a number of other ways that you can access Gopher via America Online. You can Telnet to Gopher, use a dedicated Gopher client, or connect to a Gopher site via the World Wide Web.

Telneting to a Gopher Site

By using a program like the EWAN Telnet client (see Figure 11.13) discussed in the previous chapter, you can log onto any one of a number of public Gopher Telnet sites operating Gopher clients that you can use remotely.

FIGURE 11.13.

Using the EWAN Telnet client, you can log on to any public Gopher client.

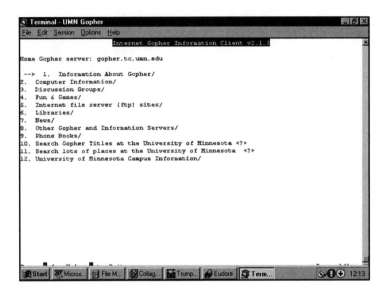

All you really need to know, to connect to one of these public Gophers sites is its domain name. According to the Gopher FAQ, the sites listed in Table 13.1 represent the major public-access points for Telnet connections to Gopher. For each site there is a domain name, IP address, and user ID you must enter to start the Gopher client. Each site's physical location is listed as well.

Table 11.1. Public Gopher clients available via Telnet.

Domain Name	*IP Address*	*Login*	*Area*
consultant.micro.umn.edu	134.84.132.4	Gopher	North America
ux1.cso.uiuc.edu	128.174.5.59	Gopher	North America
sailor.lib.md.us	192.188.199.5	Gopher	North America
panda.uiowa.edu	128.255.40.201	Panda	North America
gopher.msu.edu	35.8.2.61	Gopher	North America
gopher.ebone.net	192.36.125.2	Gopher	Europe
gopher.sunet.se	192.36.125.10	Gopher	Sweden
info.anu.edu.au	150.203.84.20	Info	Australia
tolten.puc.cl	146.155.1.16	Gopher	South America

continues

Table 11.1. continued

Domain Name	IP Address	Login	Area
ecnet.ec	157.100.45.2	Gopher	Ecuador
gan.ncc.go.jp	160.190.10.1	Gopher	Japan
gopher.th-darmstadt.de	130.83.55.75	Gopher	Germany
hugin.ub2.lu.se	130.235.162.12	Gopher	Sweden
gopher.uv.es	147.156.1.12	Gopher	Spain
hugin.ub2.lu.se	130.235.162.12	Gopher	Sweden
info.brad.ac.uk	143.53.2.5	Gopher	United Kingdom

Winsock Clients

There are a number of locations on the Internet containing copies of Gopher clients, including the sites listed in Appendix C, but by far the most comprehensive list is maintained by the University of Minnesota on its Boombox FTP server. To access this FTP site using the World Wide Web, use the following URL: ftp://boombox.micro.umn.edu/pub/gopher/Windows.

You will find copies of all the major Gopher clients for Windows and other platforms at the site, along with instructions for locating some of the less well known ones as well.

Note

> There are also a few Winsock-based Gopher clients in the America Online software library.

WSGopher

Archive Filename: WSG-12.EXE

WSGopher is a feature-packed Gopher client that uses the Windows environment to good advantage. All of the major functions are easily accessible through the toolbar across the top of the main window.

In addition, the latest version, 1.2, fully supports all the current Gopher+ extensions, which include simple forms entry and extended file views. You can open any number of Gopher menus at the same time, and even perform file transfers using the built-in FTP features while you explore Gopherspace in another window.

Once installed on your system, WSGopher automatically connects to its home Gopher server whenever you start it. From there you can select any of the items displayed on the Gopher menu or alternatively open the comprehensive bookmark listing shown in Figure 11.4. Many of the major Gopher sites and services have been included in this list to give you easy access to many parts of Gopherspace. Bookmarks are very similar to the Favorite Places database in the Windows version of AOL.

FIGURE 11.14.

WSGopher comes complete with a comprehensive list of bookmarks to help get you started.

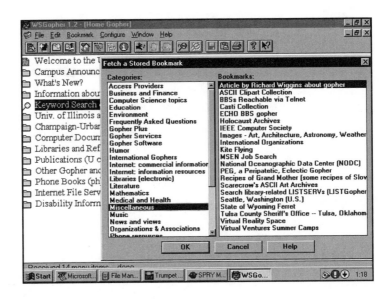

The authors have released WSGopher as freeware and place no limitations on its use. To obtain a copy of the latest version, visit the Boombox FTP directory.

HGopher

Archive Filename: `HGOPH24.ZIP`

Each Gopher client offers a slightly different approach to accessing the same basic information. Unlike WSGopher, HGopher does not provide you with a toolbar, but instead gives you a set of command buttons on the status bar at the bottom of the screen.

These buttons perform many of the same functions as those on the WSGopher toolbar, and also give you a means of controlling up to three simultaneous connections. (See Figure 11.5.) For example, this allows you to start a file transfer and then continue to explore Gopherspace while the file is retrieved in the background. The other major difference is how HGopher uses bookmarks. Whereas most other Gopher clients open a menu on a home Gopher when they are started, HGopher opens your bookmarks list as though it were a Gopher menu.

HGopher also provides a very comprehensive online help system that not only discusses the use of HGopher, but also contains some useful general information about both Gopher and Gopher+.

This program was released by the University of Illinois as freeware and is also available via FTP. But instead of using the Boombox site, you should first try the Consummate Winsock Applications list. This server always maintains a copy of the latest version of HGopher. The http address for this page is: `http://homepage.eznet.net/~rwilloug/stroud/cwsapps.html`.

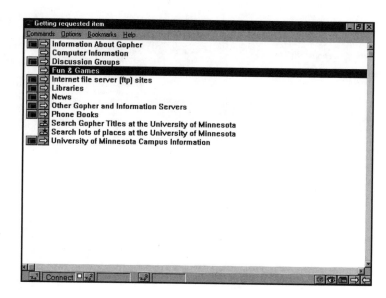

BCGopher

Archive Filename: BCG08B.EXE

BCGopher offers yet another way of displaying Gopher menus. This time, the approach involves big icons, a lot like the ones you find used throughout AOL, that represent the various types of information each menu item contains. (See Figure 11.16.)

These icons include folders for new gopher menus, Rolodex card files for Veronica search engines, and binoculars representing Gopher+ multimedia capable entries. You will also encounter other icons as well, representing graphics, audio files, and downloadable files.

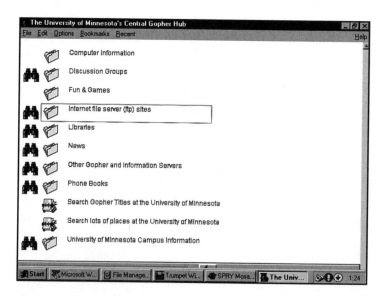

As already indicated, BCGopher does support Gopher+, although this client is beginning to show its age, because some of the newer features are not fully supported. It appears that this program is no longer supported, and because it was also released by Boston College as freeware, this makes getting any assistance unlikely.

Gopher for Windows

Archive Filename: WGPH32.ZIP

Gopher for Windows (Figure 11.17) is a fairly recent addition to the Gopher arena. It was released by the Chinese University of Hong Kong (CUHK) to provide students and faculty members with access to their Gopher server.

FIGURE 11.17.

Gopher for Windows displays each new menu in a separate window.

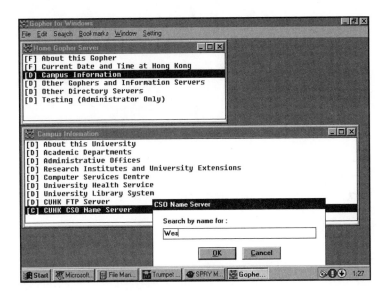

Many of its features are similar to those provided by WSGopher, but at this stage it still does not support all of the Gopher+ extensions. To obtain a copy of this Gopher client, you should use the CUHK FTP server located at ftp://ftp.cuhk.hk/pub/gopher/PC/.

Gopher and the World Wide Web

You can also use a WWW browser as a Gopher client. To do this, you need to use a special type of URL that takes the following form: gopher://<host>:<port>/11/<path>.

In place of the <host> field, insert the domain name of the Gopher site you want to connect to. The <port> field usually contains a 70, which indicates the standard port for a Gopher server. The /11/ area occasionally contains /00/. These numbers are used to indicate the type of link the URL points to. The /11/ indicates that the link is a Gopher menu. Following the /11/, you then enter the path and name of the Gopher menu or action you want to use.

For example, to access the Information About Gopher menu on the University of Minnesota Gopher server (Figure 11.18), you would use this URL: gopher://gopher.tc.umn.edu:70/11/ Information%20About%20Gopher. If you look closely at this URL, you notice that the spaces between Information, About, and Gopher have been replaced with a strange combination of symbols—%20. You need to do this because any URL you enter cannot contain spaces. The %20 symbol represents a space, which the WWW server translates into the correct form at its end.

FIGURE 11.18.

Use %20 to replace any spaces in the Gopher menu path or name.

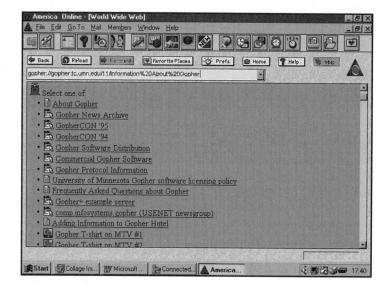

There is also a special form of the Gopher URL reserved for the top menu of each server. To open this menu, there is no need to include the /11/ or a menu name. As a result, to access the top menu of the Minnesota Gopher, use this URL: gopher://gopher.tc.umn.edu/1. (See Figure 13.19.) In these cases, the /1 alone gives your WWW enough information to locate the top menu.

Once you open a Gopher server using your WWW browser, you can then navigate your way around it using the World Wide Web's familiar hot links. You can access all the menus and features offered by Gopher from the World Wide Web and even request files via FTP. (See Chapter 12, "The World Wide Web" for more information.)

Note

> Although you can use the Gopher capabilities of AOL's WWW browsers to perform file transfers, you will sometimes find that the file names used by Gopher can cause strange things to happen when you try to start a download. In such cases you will need to use a dedicated FTP client, such as the one built into AOL.

FIGURE 11.19.

There is no need to use /11/ when accessing the top menu of a Gopher server.

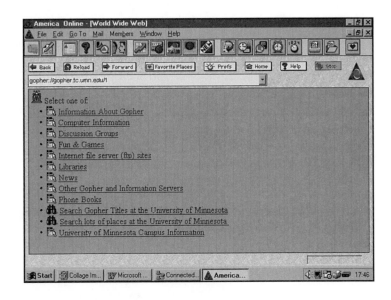

Searching Veronica via the World Wide Web

There is also a way to search the contents of Veronica via the World Wide Web itself. On most CUSI World Wide Web search pages, (see Chapter 13, "World Wide Web Productivity"), you will find a Veronica Search option. (See Figure 11.20.) There are a number of CUSI pages on the World Wide Web. To obtain a list of them all, use the following http address: `http://web.nexor.co.uk/public/cusi/cusi.html`.

FIGURE 11.20.

Select Veronica as your search tool and enter the words you want to search for.

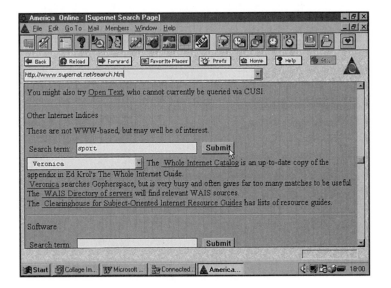

After selecting Veronica as your search option, all you need to do is enter the word or words you want to search Gopherspace for. Then, when you click on the search button, a Gopher menu is created for your World Wide Web browser, so that it can display the results of the search. (See Figure 11.21.) From here you can choose any of the Gopher menu items listed.

FIGURE 11.21.

A list of sports-related Gopher menus generated by Veronica and the World Wide Web.

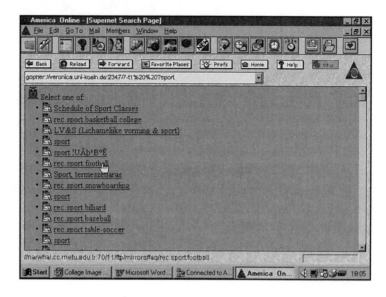

Popular Gopher Sites Accessible via WWW

Table 11.2 contains a list of URLs providing a wide cross-section of Gopher servers or facilities, along with a brief description of what each one does.

Table 11.2. Popular Gopher sites.

URL	Description
gopher://gopher.enews.com:70/11/newsletter	Business publications and resources (electronic newsstand)
gopher://free-net.mpls-stpaul.mn.us:8001/1	Twin Cities Free-Net
gopher://nceet.snre.umich.edu:70/1	EE-Link, the Environmental Education Gopher
gopher://jei.umd.edu:70/1	Joint Education Initiative Gopher site
gopher://avril.amba-ottawa.fr:70/1	French Embassy /Ambassade de France (Ottawa, Canada)
gopher://jupiter.sun.csd.unb.ca:70/11/FAQ	Internet FAQs

URL	Description
`gopher://gopher.nara.gov:70/1`	U.S. National Archives
`gopher://gopher.microsoft.com:70/1`	Microsoft
`gopher://gopher.voa.gov:70/1`	Voice of America and Worldnet Television
`gopher://winftp.cica.indiana.edu:70/11/pc/win3`	CICA Windows software archive (Indiana University)
`gopher://info.csc.cuhk.hk:70/1`	Chinese University of Hong Kong
`gopher://cexpress.com:2600/1`	Computer Express (online software & hardware)
`gopher://mudhoney.micro.umn.edu:70/10/Gopher.FAQ`	The Gopher FAQ
`gopher://ice.ucdavis.edu:70/1`	Information Center for the Environment
`gopher://mudhoney.micro.umn.edu:70/11/gplustest`	Gopher+ example server

Summary

As you have seen in this chapter, Gopher provides you with a simple yet effective means of exploring the Internet, that removes many of the complexities associated with remembering domain name, site addresses, and ports.

However, many people find that the Gopher menu system is a little too sterile for their liking. While it is effective when dealing with text-based information, when you start to look at latest multi-media developments, it has some difficulty competing.

To meet the push toward online multimedia head on, a new form of Internet browser was developed. The browser (and environment) I am referring to is the World Wide Web. In the next chapter, you discover how America Online is bringing the World Wide Web to its members.

CHAPTER 12

THE WORLD WIDE WEB

For many years the Internet was the domain of scientists and researchers who, for the most part, were willing to put up with its idiosyncrasies in return for the benefits it offered them. However, as more and more people began to understand the Internet's potential, these idiosyncrasies were deemed unacceptable and it was decided that a more efficient and user-friendly method of working with the Internet was needed.

The organization at the center of this debate was CERN—the European Particle Physics Laboratory. Since 1986, CERN has been one of the leading developers of Internet connectivity in Europe, allowing its researchers access to information and resources located on remote sites. However, its researchers were often forced to take extremely convoluted paths when trying to locate information using a combination of Telnet, FTP, and WAIS-based clients. Apart from being time-consuming, when new researchers were presented with such a task they were often left floundering and at a loss as to which way to proceed.

What was needed was a tool that could combine these different services into one easy-to-use program, a program that would give them easy access to the information they required and could also display any figures or graphics associated with this information. In answer to this list of requests, the *World Wide Web (WWW)* was born.

In this chapter you will learn about the World Wide Web's early history and explore the tools provided by America Online that allow you to access it. The following topics will be discussed:

◆ Early History

◆ Basics of the World Wide Web

◆ AOL's WWW Browser

◆ Advanced options

Early History

Unlike most other Internet tools whose history can be traced back to the formative days of the Internet and ARPANET, the World Wide Web is the relative youngster of the group.

It was not until late in 1990 that the first World Wide Web browser, designed by Tim Berners-Lee, appeared at CERN. Over the course of the twelve months following this initial release, this WWW browser (and a less-capable text-based version) was brought online at CERN and gradually enhanced to include all the capabilities requested by the project staff. These features included the capability to read newsgroups, access anonymous FTP sites, and make use of both WAIS and Gopher servers needing to access any other client program.

Note

> Kevin Hughes of Honolulu College, suggests that the actual birth date for the World Wide Web should be set to March 1989. This represents the period when Tim Berners-Lee first proposed the concept of the World Wide Web.

At the same time, they also adopted a new file format called HTML that has since become possibly the best-known file format in use on the Internet. HTML is basically an enhanced text file that contains embedded commands that let World Wide Web users easily create *hypertext* pages that can be displayed by a World Wide Web browser.

Although these browsers were still only available in-house at CERN, it wasn't long before people began to hear rumors about this exciting new tool and began to look for ways to make it available to the mainstream Internet world. To answer these rumors, in 1992 CERN began actively promoting the existence of the World Wide Web tool it had developed.

Following this announcement, a number of World Wide Web browsers began to appear on most computer platforms, including Windows, Apple Macintosh, UNIX, and even smaller platforms such as the Commodore Amiga. Since this time, the World Wide Web has erupted onto the Internet and single-handedly replaced many of the previously popular client applications, while giving people of different user levels simple and efficient access to all aspects of the emerging information superhighway.

NCSA Mosaic

Without a doubt, the best known of all World Wide Web browsers is the Mosaic browser developed by the National Center for Supercomputing Applications at the University of Illinois at Urbana/Champaign. Since the first NCSA Mosaic browser appeared in early 1993, it has become the de facto standard for World Wide Web browsers. (See Figure 12.1.)

FIGURE 12.1.

NCSA Mosaic.

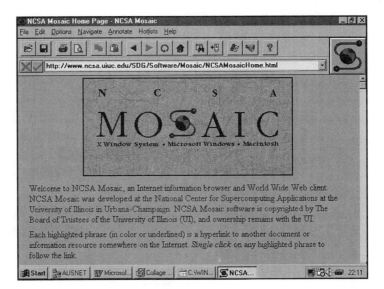

When the NCSA developed Mosaic, its aim was to create a World Wide Web browser that was freely available to all members of the Internet community. At the same time, the ongoing development of Mosaic, which will soon see the official release of version 2.0, will ensure that the World Wide Web continues to gain users and that it evolves to meet the new demands of an increasingly computer-literate community.

There are now versions of Mosaic available for Windows, Apple Macintosh, and a variety of X11/Motif-based UNIX machines. In addition, the full source code is also available to anyone interested in exploring the internal works or in developing their own specialized version.

To this end, many of the other World Wide Web browsers now available demonstrate their obvious heritage, which, for so many, lies in the NCSA source code.

> NCSA Mosaic is available free of charge from `http://www.ncsa.uiuc.edu/SDG/Software/Mosaic/NCSAMosaicHome.html` provided that it is for non-profit or private use. If you wish to use it for commercial reasons, on the other hand, the Mosaic license requires you to pay a licensing fee.

Netscape

If you are not using a copy of Mosaic or one of the browsers based on its code, chances are you are using Netscape. (See Figure 12.2.) For many people, Netscape is the *only* World Wide Web browser, but in most cases this is based purely on personal preferences and not on any performance or feature-for-feature comparisons between the two.

FIGURE 12.2.

The Netscape WWW browser.

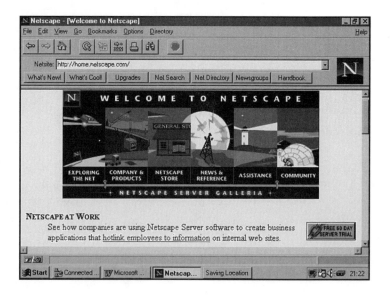

On the surface, these two programs' appearance is more than a little similar, possibly because many of the original NCSA staff who developed Mosaic now work for Netscape Communications, the company responsible for the Netscape browser. There are a number of features offered by Netscape that Mosaic does not support, not the least of which is that you can run Netscape on any Windows-based machine without the need for special 32-bit Microsoft libraries and support files.

Netscape is also fully compliant with the new Windows 95 environment, with version 1.2 adding support for Shortcuts and Personal Profiles. In addition, there are also versions of Netscape available for the Apple Macintosh, and for UNIX-based computers.

Like Mosaic, Netscape is also available for private use free of charge, although users are encouraged to purchase a copy of the identical commercial version that includes a comprehensive users' guide and technical support.

For more information about obtaining a copy of Mosaic or Netscape, take a look at Appendix C, "Internet Software." Both of these programs can be used in conjunction with the winsock.dll program discussed in Chapter 10, "AOL and Winsock."

W3 Consortium

Although CERN still maintains a presence on the Internet as the original developer of the World Wide Web, it is no longer directly responsible for the long-term coordination of the World Wide Web or the various standards such a global system now demands. To take over this responsibility, a group known as the W3 Consortium was formed by the Massachusetts Institute of Technology (MIT) and the French National Institute for Research in Computing and Automation (INRIA).

The purposes of the consortium are

◆ To support the advancement of information technology in the field of networking, graphics, and user interfaces, by developing the World Wide Web into a comprehensive information infrastructure.

◆ To encourage the industry to adopt a common set of World Wide Web protocols.

To achieve this, the consortium plans to design a common World Wide Web protocol suite, develop publicly available reference code, promote the common protocol suite throughout the world, and encourage industry to create products that comply with the common protocol suite.

If you are interested in finding out more about the consortium's activities and its members, a World Wide Web server has been set up to provide detailed information about many of the projects currently under development along with a wide variety of resource documents dealing with all aspects of the World Wide Web. The home page for this server, shown in Figure 12.3, can be found at http://www.w3.org/.

FIGURE 12.3.

*The W3 Consortium
home page.*

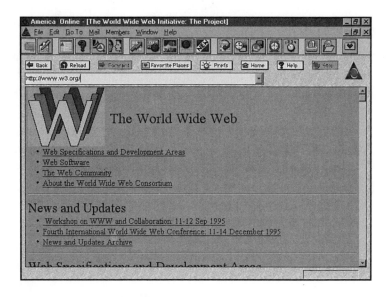

Basics of the World Wide Web

As mentioned previously, the tool used to access the World Wide Web—or more correctly, the Internet—is called a browser. This name stems from the way you can easily browse through many of the documents, files, and services provided by many different types of servers all over the Internet.

In this sense, a Web browser can best be thought of as an Internet client program for all occasions. Built into most browsers is the capability to communicate with FTP servers, Usenet newsgroup servers, and even WAIS or Gopher servers, and, more importantly, you can access all these servers using the same familiar interface. If this was all that the World Wide Web was capable of, it would already be a valuable tool to many people. However, with the addition of its own special type of server as well, the World Wide Web truly is *the* Internet navigator.

Hypertext

To assist you as you explore the World Wide Web, its developers adopted the now popular hypertext concept as the basis for the World Wide Web navigation environment.

Hypertext is a process that allows special connections called *hotlinks* or *hyperlinks* to be embedded in the text displayed on the browser's screen. Clicking on one of these links tells the browser to automatically load the document the link points to. With these links, you can very easily move from document to document without ever needing to know the actual name of the document or even its location. You simply click on a word that says "America Online," "bobsled," or "The Meaning of Life," and your WWW browser knows where to go to locate this new information.

What's more, these links can also take you to files on FTP sites, newsgroups, and other services offered anywhere on the Internet.

URLs

To make such a system a reality, a new type of addressing system needed to be developed that could describe not only the location of a file or server, but its type as well. The World Wide Web uses an addressing system known as a Uniform Resource Locator (URL) to achieve this.

A URL consists of up to four separate parts that, when combined, completely define the location of any file or service located anywhere on the Internet. These parts are the protocol, domain name, pathname, and filename. A completed URL usually looks something like this:

`http://home.mcom.com/home/internet-search.html`.

> Most URLs include all of the parts mentioned above. The exceptions are the `mailto:`, `telnet:`, and `news:` URLs.

The Protocol

The most important part of any URL is the protocol definition. This piece of information defines the type of server the selected link points to. Without this information, the WWW browser doesn't know which port and server it needs to talk to in order to obtain the information pointed to by the selected hyperlink. The main protocols are listed in Table 11.1.

Table 11.1. URL protocols.

Protocol	Service
`file:`	In addition to referencing information located on the Internet, most WWW browsers can also access files stored on your local hard drive. If `file:` is followed by a `///C¦`, this indicates that the URL points to a file on your local C: drive. Otherwise it performs the same function as the `ftp:` protocol listed below.
`ftp:`	If the selected link points to a file stored on an anonymous FTP server, the URL must begin with this definition.
`http:`	All HTML documents are usually stored on a WWW server. *HTTP (hypertext transfer protocol)* refers to the protocol used by these servers.
`gopher:`	All WWW browsers can also navigate their way around a Gopher server by using this protocol definition.

continues

Table 11.1. continued

Protocol	Service
`mailto:`	This is a special type of URL that lets you send an e-mail message. A `mailto:` URL does not contain a domain name, instead an e-mail address is required. For example: `mailto:wtatters@aol.net`. In addition, it does not require a `//` separator like standard URLs.
`news:`	Links that point to USENET newsgroups must be declared using this protocol. Instead of a domain name, `news:` URLs require a valid newsgroup. For example: `news:rec.arts.movies.reviews`. Also note that the `//` separator is not required here either.
`telnet:`	To indicate that a link needs to open a Telnet session, the URL begins with `telnet:`. Most WWW browsers can't open a Telnet session themselves. Instead, they usually launch a separate Telnet client when such links are selected.
`wais:`	In theory, all WWW browsers can access WAIS servers, but most users prefer to use WAIS gateways such as WAISgate, instead. (See Chapter 13, "World Wide Web Productivity.")

Domain Name

Following the protocol definition, the next item of information to be defined by a URL is the location of the server housing the file or information pointed to by the hyperlink. Like all other Internet services, this can be done by using either the domain name of the server or its corresponding IP address. However, the use of IP addresses is frowned upon by most of the WWW community because they do not describe in an easily understandable form the name of the site the URL refers to.

When the protocol definition and the domain name are combined using the `//` symbol, the result is a URL definition that accurately indicates the location and type of server. In addition, due to the nature of the World Wide Web, in most cases you can access a server's home page or root directory by using just these two pieces of information.

For example, this URL takes you straight to the home page of the America Online WWW server without the need for either a pathname or filename: `http://www.blue.aol.com/`.

Note

> WWW browsers use the protocol definition to determine the port number they should use to access a specific server. On certain occasions, however, this port number may need to be altered from the default port of 80. Simply append the port number to the domain name, separated by a colon, such as in `http://www.blue.aol.com:80/`.

Path and Filename

The last two components of a URL might or might not exist depending on the location and type of information any given hyperlink points to. In most cases, however, you will find that both a path and a filename are listed as a part of the URL.

When describing the path to a file, a URL uses the standard UNIX method for path definitions, separating each directory by a forward slash (/). Windows users should be careful not to fall into the trap of using the DOS backslash (\) because most WWW browsers will fail to understand what you have entered.

Relative Addressing

There is also a special type of URL that doesn't contain a domain name, but might still contain a path and filename.

This type of URL is referred to as a *relative* address. Instead of supplying a full domain name and path itself, this type of URL adopts the domain name and path of the last URL that the server accessed and looks for the specified file based on this information.

Many WWW servers use this type of addressing to move between pages because it makes for considerably easier site maintenance, especially if a group of pages needs to be relocated to a different server or directory.

> URLs containing a domain name are referred to as having an *absolute* address.

WWW Servers

To manage all these hypertext documents, a new type of server and a corresponding communications protocol were developed.

The protocol, known as the *Hypertext Transfer Protocol* (HTTP), lets WWW browsers communicate with special WWW servers containing collections of hypertext documents called *HTML pages*. These pages contain the information and links displayed by the WWW browser. There are now thousands of WWW servers in operation all over the world, joined together by the many hyperlinks in the over four million HTML pages that provide information as diverse as the Internet itself.

Although HTTP is the basic communications protocol of the World Wide Web, recent developments have seen the addition of new protocols and server capabilities which have enhanced greatly the functionality offered by both WWW browsers and WWW servers. These new protocols and server capabilities include secure transaction layers, firewalls, and proxy servers. Luckily, there is little need for you to learn about any of the capabilities in order to take advantage of the World Wide Web. For those of you who would like to know more, the best place to start is the HTTP information pages compiled by the W3 consortium at `http://www.w3.org/hypertext/WWW/Protocols/Overview.html`.

HTML

To easily define the contents of a WWW page, a simple method was needed that could encompass the large amounts of text many pages include and incorporate all the graphical elements and combinations of hypertext links that may be included on any given page. A system was also needed that could allow the same information to be displayed on a wide variety of both text and graphical WWW browsers.

As a result, it was decided that instead of defining WWW pages in a rigid typographical sense, a language would be developed to describe the information and the way its creator expected it to appear. The WWW browser could then take this information and display it in the best way possible, given its particular operating environment.

To do this, the *Hypertext Markup Language (HTML)* was developed. HTML uses text files that include a limited set of instructions to define special items such as hyperlinks, images, and a limited number of typographical elements. (See Figure 12.4.) This allows WWW pages to be created by anyone with a simple text editor or word processor. (See Chapter 14, "WWW Publishing with AOL," for a more in-depth discussion of HTML.)

> HTML is based on the language known as *SGML* or *Standard Generalized Markup Language*. SGML is a document description language used by producers of printed publications.

FIGURE 12.4.

The Hypertext Markup Language lets anyone with a text editor create pages that can be displayed by a World Wide Web browser.

Once a page of HTML has been created and stored on a WWW server, anyone can add a link to the new document from their own HTML pages. By doing this, the new page effectively becomes part of the World Wide Web and can then be called up by anyone with a WWW browser and Internet access. For example, the page of HTML shown in Figure 12.4 is actually a part of the home page for the America Online WWW Server shown in Figure 12.5. If you look closely, you can see how the various references made in the HTML document become pictures and hyperlinks in a WWW browser.

FIGURE 12.5.

HTML shows graphics and hypertext when dis-played by a World Wide Web browser.

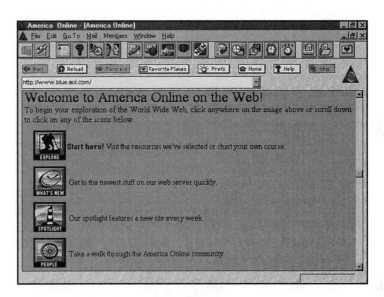

In your travels around the World Wide Web, you will occasionally encounter references to HTML 2.0 and HTML 3.0. HTML 2.0 is the current official version of HTML, while HTML 3.0 is a new standard that is being developed at the moment.

Not all WWW browsers—including the AOL WWW browser—fully support HTML 3.0. However, this does not mean that you won't be able to view pages constructed using the newer standard. You will, but some of the newer features such as tables, background images, and text colors, will simply not be displayed.

Home Pages

Because the World Wide Web effectively has no top or bottom, the concept of home pages was developed to give people some sort of reference points in what was otherwise a never-ending chain of links and interconnections.

There are many definitions of what actually constitutes a home page. Regardless of what the technical definitions are, most people consider a home page to be any location that acts like a front door to a collection of related WWW pages. For example, the WWW page shown in Figure 12.5 represents America Online's WWW server home page because it serves as an entrance point to all the other pages America Online provides.

The AOL WWW Browser

To give AOL users easy access to the World Wide Web, America Online has spent a considerable amount of time and effort developing a World Wide Web browser that closely integrates with the existing services provided by AOL.

As a result, starting AOL's World Wide Web browser is a simple matter of clicking on the World Wide Web icon located at the top left side of the Internet Connection window shown in Figure 12.6. In addition, you can also open the browsers by using the Keyword: **www**.

FIGURE 12.6.

Click on the World Wide Web icon to start AOL's WWW browser.

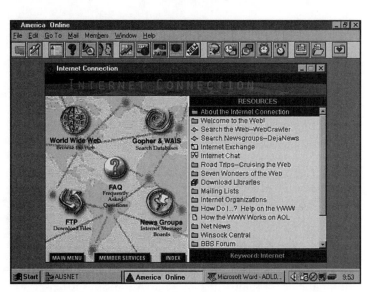

For users of the Windows version of AOL, America Online has completely integrated the World Wide Web browser into AOL. As a result, accessing the World Wide Web becomes simply a matter of opening a different window in AOL. In the next section, you learn more about how to use AOL for Windows and the World Wide Web.

When America Online set out to develop the Macintosh version however, they encountered some difficulties integrating the WWW browser completely with AOL. As a result, when you need to access the World Wide Web via the Macintosh version, a separate WWW application is started. There are a few advantages and disadvantages of doing this. First, because the two applications are not as closely integrated as the Windows version, some of the features that tie the two systems are not available. On the plus side though, the Macintosh version does give you a way to unload files to an FTP site—something you can't do under Windows. The section titled, "AOL for Macintosh WWW Browser" later in this chapter looks at using the Macintosh version.

> Before you can use either the Macintosh or Windows WWW browser you need to properly install it. See Chapter 4 for installation information and system requirements.

AOL for Windows WWW Browser

To take your first tentative steps onto the World Wide Web, all you need to do is use the Keyword: **www** or click on the World Wide Web icon. When you do this AOL automatically starts its WWW browser and retrieves a copy of the America Online WWW home page. This page is then displayed. (See Figure 12.7.)

> Depending on your modem speed, a page like the America Online home page can take a number of minutes to download. There are, however, a few ways that you can improve the speed. Obviously obtaining a faster modem is always an option, but you can also improve download speeds by telling AOL not to download graphics and images displayed as a part of a WWW page.

FIGURE 12.7.

AOL is initially configured to automatically open the America Online home page.

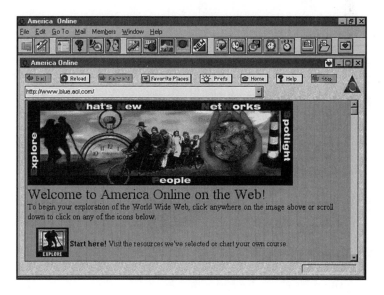

As you begin to explore the World Wide Web, the America Online home page will become very familiar to you, although the layout may appear slightly different from some of the figures you will encounter throughout this book. When AOL first starts the WWW browser, it places it in a window; however, depending on the type of display you have, you will probably find it best to expand the window to fill the screen as shown in Figure 12.8. Doing this helps AOL to display more of the current page on the screen.

FIGURE 12.8.

Expand the WWW browser window to fill the whole screen so that you can view more of a WWW page at once.

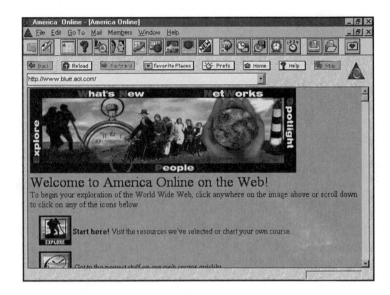

You are now on the World Wide Web. At this stage you can begin to explore it to your heart's content, but before you get too carried away, let's take a look at some of the features AOL provides.

The AOL World Wide Web window is broken into three main sections:

◆ The document area

◆ The control console

◆ The status bar

The Document Area

The most important part of any WWW browser is the *document area* where WWW pages are displayed. With AOL, as with most WWW browsers, the middle section of the screen is devoted to displaying WWW pages as they are retrieved from the Internet.

In addition, you'll often find that the information contained on a WWW page is larger than the space provided by the WWW browser. To read this information, use the scroll bars at the top and sides of the document area.

Hyperlinks

The first thing you need to know when working with any WWW browser is how to recognize a *hyperlink*. In AOL, all hyperlinks are defined in blue text and, optionally, are further enhanced by an underline. In addition, any graphics that have hyperlinks associated with them are highlighted by a blue border.

When you click on any of these hyperlinks, AOL opens a copy of the document the link points to and displays it in place of the current page. On the America Online home page you will find that all the hyperlinks are represented by pictures, but, as you explore further you will soon encounter text-based hyperlinks as well. For example, the America Online—Frequently Asked Questions about the Web page show in Figure 12.9 is composed entirely of text-based links.

FIGURE 12.9.

Click on any of the underlined text areas shown in blue to jump to a new WWW page.

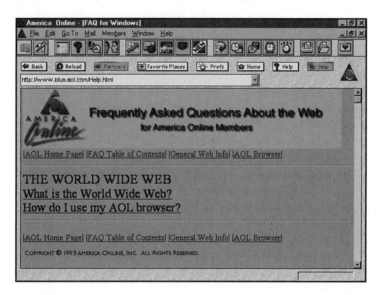

When you select a hyperlink to explore a new page, AOL remembers the original page for the duration of your current session. If you return to the original page, any of the hyperlinks that you have visited during the current session are now be displayed as purple text instead of blue text, or in the case of graphical hyperlinks, are surrounded by a purple box.

The Control Console

The area at the top of the AOL World Wide Web window, above the document area, is referred to as the *control console*. You can easily navigate your way around the World Wide Web by using the various tools provided in this area.

The Menu Bar

Because the AOL WWW Browser is a part of AOL itself, all the dropdown menus associated with AOL are still available. To access the options provided by this menu bar, click the various menu pad options listed. When you do this, a drop down menu appears displaying the options available.

All of the menu options listed will perform their functions in exactly the same way that was discussed in Chapter 5, "Working with AOL." However, there are a couple of options on the File menu that have been enhanced to support the World Wide Web browser. These functions are

Open   Using the **File O**pen menu option, you can load HTML files stored on your local hard drive and display them in the WWW Window.

Save   The **File S**ave option lets you save a copy of the HTML source code that defines the current page displayed by the WWW browser on your local hard drive. This is a good way to learn about HTML. If you encounter a page that you find impressive, save a copy of the HTML file and then open it with a program like Notepad.

Save **A**s   The **File Save As** option lets you save a copy of the HTML source code with a new name.

Print   You can print out a copy of any WWW page by selecting the **File P**rint option.

The Toolbar and Navigation Buttons

In addition to the toolbar discussed in Chapter 5, the WWW browser adds its own set of navigation buttons to the top of the browser window, as shown in Figure 12.10. These buttons let you to control various aspects of the WWW browser's operation and also help you to navigate around the World Wide Web.

FIGURE 12.10.

The AOL World Wide Web control console.

Here are the toolbar items.

Back   As you begin to move around the World Wide Web, AOL keeps track of where you have been. If you click on this icon the previous page is recalled.

Reload   Clicking on this icon forces AOL to reload the current page. For example, if you stopped the retrieval of a large page you can use this icon to retrieve the missing information.

Forward   If you've used the Back icon, you can then use the Forward icon to move up the list to the most current page.

Favorite Places   Clicking on this button causes AOL to open the Favorite Places window shown in Figure 12.11. When you select one of the items displayed and click on the Connect button, AOL jumps to the location it represents. This might be another WWW page or even an America Online forum or department.

You can manually add Favorite Places to this list using the buttons provided on the Favorite Places window. In addition, you can add the currently selected AOL service or WWW page, either by clicking on the heart-shaped icon shown in Figure 12.11 at the top right side of the WWW browser window or by choosing the Add to Favorite Places option from the **W**indow menu.

FIGURE 12.11.

The AOL Favorite Places window.

Prefs   Clicking on the Prefs buttons opens a window that allows you to alter a number of settings that relate to AOL's WWW browser. The "Configuring WWW for Windows" section later in this chapter discusses in detail all the available options.

Home   This icon always returns you to your own home page. When the AOL WWW browser is first installed, clicking on this icon opens the America Online home page, but you can adjust this to point to any page you choose by selecting the Prefs button.

Help   Clicking on this button causes AOL to open the America Online—Frequently Asked Questions about the Web page shown in Figure 12.9.

Stop   If you need to halt the loading of a document, click on this icon.

Document URL

Immediately below the navigation buttons, you will find a field that displays the URL of the current WWW page. This field also allows you to type in the URL of a WWW page directly instead of selecting it from the Favorite Places menu or via a hyperlink.

Doing this allows you to easily open any of the WWW pages listed in this book. For example, enter the following HTTP address into the document URL field: `http://www.webcom.com/taketwo/samsaol.html`.

Did you receive the special message left for you?

Note

By clicking on the drop-down arrow to the right of this field, you can call up a history list of all the WWW pages you have visited during the current session. (See Figure 12.12.) If you select any of the pages shown in this list AOL reopens that page for you.

Logo Animation

Apart from giving you something to look at, the spinning logo to the right of the document title is there to let you know when AOL is retrieving a WWW page. If the animation is spinning, AOL is busy. If it is static, no pages are currently being retrieved.

FIGURE 12.12.

AOL keeps a record of all the WWW pages you have visited during the current session.

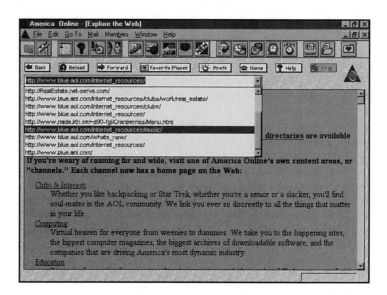

Status Bar

The last area of the AOL WWW window is the status bar. It is located below the main document display window. This area displays a variety of information depending on what the browser is doing. When you place your mouse pointer over a hyperlink, the URL of the page or server that it points to is displayed in the status area on the left side of the status bar. Alternately, when a new page is being loaded, a counter is displayed in this area to indicate the page size and the number of characters already retrieved. At the same time, on the right side of the screen a graphical bar is displayed to represent how much of the page has been loaded.

Configuring WWW for Windows

When you click on the Prefs button discussed in the previous section AOL opens a dialog box similar to the one shown in Figure 12.13. The items listed on this dialog box allow you to tailor the appearance and operation of AOL's WWW browser. This section examines each of these options and discusses their use.

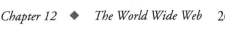

FIGURE 12.13.

AOL's WWW Preferences dialog box.

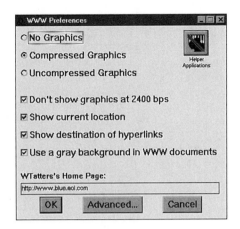

Graphics Options

When a WWW page is displayed, you will probably notice that the text of the document is displayed first and then any images associated with the page are loaded. By selecting from the first four options listed in the Preferences dialog box, you can alter the way that AOL treats images accompanying a WWW page.

Pictures displayed on a WWW page are referred to as *inline images.*

Don't Display Inline Graphics

If you select the No Graphics option, AOL loads only the text of the document and inserts placeholders where all the inline images are meant to go. (See Figure 12.14.)

The main advantage of doing this, is that loading the same document with all the images included, as shown previously in Figure 12.5, can take three to four minutes using a 14,400 bps modem, while loading it with placeholders takes only a matter of seconds. When you consider that some pages may take up to ten minutes to load with slower modems, selecting the No Graphics option makes a lot of sense.

Display Inline Graphics

While loading a page with the graphics turned off is the fastest option, there are times when you will want all the images to be displayed. To turn on inline images, select either the Compressed Graphics or Uncompressed Graphics option.

FIGURE 12.14.

The America Online home page takes less than 15 seconds to load with the No Graphics option selected.

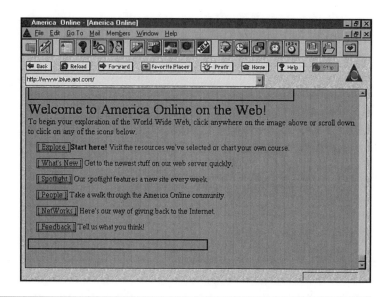

 Note

AOL can use a special method of transmitting images that compresses them before they are sent to your computer. Selecting this option will, in most cases, improve the speed of downloading and displaying inline images. However, if you are using a slower computer you may find that the added overhead of decompressing the image once it gets to your computer, may actually be slowing things down. This is why AOL gives you the option of using uncompressed graphics, in addition to compressed graphics.

One of the main reasons for turning on the display of inline images—apart from the aesthetic value—is that many pages now use a special type of inline image called an *image map*.

By default, clicking on an image that represents a hyperlink connects you to a single new page, however, if the inline image is an image map, when you click on different parts of the image you are taken to different pages. The image displayed on the Netscape home page, shown earlier in Figure 12.1, represents such an image map. Clicking on the different areas of this image takes you to different pages.

 Note

Most WWW sites give you the option of using either an image map or a more conventional set of links, as is the case for the America Online home page. However, you will occasionally come across pages that provide only an image map. To explore such pages you must display all graphics.

Don't Show Graphics at 2400 bps

If you occasionally use a 2400 bps modem to connect to AOL, or your AOL connection is limited to 2400 bps, selecting the Don't show graphics at 2400 bps automatically disables the display of inline graphics when AOL detects that you have connected at 2400 bps.

Appearance Options

The remaining check boxes on the WWW Preferences dialog allow you to control the appearance and layout of the WWW page itself.

Show Current Location

This option controls whether AOL displays the document URL line above the main WWW page area. In most cases you will want to leave this option active, however, if you do disable it, more room will be made available for displaying the actual contents of WWW pages.

Show Destination of Hyperlinks

By default, when you place your cursor over a hyperlink, AOL displays the URL for the page this link points to in the status area below the main document window.

Use a Gray Background in WWW Documents

AOL gives you the option of displaying WWW pages with either a gray or white background. Which option you decide to use really comes down to personal preferences; however, the use of a gray background is considered to be the default for WWW pages.

Setting Your Home Page

By default, whenever you start the AOL WWW browser, it automatically connects itself to the America Online WWW server and retrieves a copy of its home page.

However, as you begin to explore the World Wide Web, you may come across a different WWW server or WWW page that you would like to use as your home page. To set this page as your default home page, all you need to do is replace the `http://www.blue.aol.com` URL listed at the bottom of the Preferences dialog with the URL of the page you want to load in its place.

From then on, whenever you start the WWW browser or click on the Home button, this new WWW page will be loaded for you.

> To stop AOL from loading any page by default, delete the `http://www.blue.aol.com` reference entirely.

Advanced Preferences

At the bottom of the Preferences dialog box, there are three buttons: OK to accept any changes you have made, Cancel to ignore your changes and the Advanced… button. Clicking on the Advanced… button open the dialog box shown in Figure 12.15.

FIGURE 12.15.

AOL retains a copy of pages that you have visited during the current session if you select the Cache option.

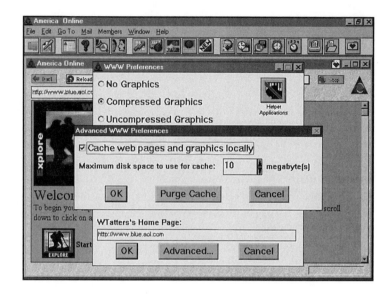

To speed up the reloading of pages you have visited during your current session, AOL can cache a copy of each page on your local hard drive. By doing this, when you return to a previously visited page, AOL attempts to load a copy of it off your local hard drive instead of downloading it from the WWW server.

The Cache web pages and graphics locally option controls whether AOL makes use of this feature and the Maximum disk space to use for cache: setting determines the number of pages that will be retained.

> If you want to free up the space currently being use to store cached pages, click on the Purge Cache button.

AOL for Macintosh WWW Browser

Although the WWW browser for Macintosh users is not integrated as a part of AOL itself, using it is no more difficult than using the Windows version. In fact, apart from the fact that the Macintosh version uses a separate program, there is very little difference in the operation of the two programs.

To start the Macintosh version, use the Keyword: **www** or click on the World Wide Web icon located on the Internet Connection window. When you do this, AOL starts the World Wide Web browser program running and attempts to display the America Online home page. (See Figure 12.16.)

FIGURE 12.16.

The America Online home page using on the Macintosh WWW browser.

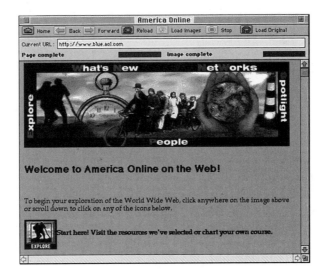

Like the Windows version, the WWW window is broken into three main areas:

◆ The document area

◆ The control console

◆ The status bar

In addition, because the Macintosh version is a separate program, there is also a set of drop-down menus that provide you with access to a number of different functions.

The Document Area

Regardless of which WWW browser you choose to use, whether it's the Macintosh or Windows version that comes bundled with AOL, or a dedicated one such as Mosaic or Netscape, the document area is basically the same.

In fact, this is one of the most important features of the World Wide Web. When the concept of the World Wide Web was first proposed, one of the guiding principals behind the project was the idea that any WWW page developed on any computer platform must be displayable on any other computer platfrom, including the most basic text-based computer terminal. Naturally, you could not expect a text-based terminal to display computer graphics such as inline images, but the text and hypertext links, at least, needed to be displayable.

As a result, the document area of the Macintosh and Windows version of the AOL WWW browser differs very little. Occasionally you will notice some asthetic differences in the area of layout and physical display, but a hyperlink is still a hyperlink and clicking on one will cause a new page to be loaded.

The Control Console

The area at the top of the World Wide Web window, above the document area, is referred to as the *control console.* (See Figure 12.17.) The information provided in this area and the navigation buttons allow you to navigate your way around the World Wide Web.

FIGURE 12.17.

The Macintosh World Wide Web control console.

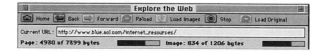

Navigation Buttons

The top section of the control console contains a row of buttons like the toolbar provided in the Windows version of AOL. These buttons let you to control various aspects of the WWW browser's operation.

The options provided by these buttons are

Home	When you first install the WWW browser, clicking on this icon opens the America Online home page.
Back	If you click on this icon, the last page you visited during this session is recalled.
Forward	Click on this button to move back to the most recently visited page.
Reload	Clicking on this icon forces AOL to reload the current page. If you stopped the retrieval of a large page, for example, you can use this icon to retrieve the missing information.
Load Images	If you have disabled the automatic loading on inline images, you can force the WWW browser to load the images for the current page.
Stop	If you need to halt the loading of a document, click on this icon.
Load Original	The WWW browser remembers the first page you visit at a WWW site. If you then go exploring the different pages con tained at a WWW site and then click on the button, the first page is reloaded.

Current URL

The URL of the WWW page currently displayed in the document area is always shown in the Current URL: field just below the navigation buttons.

You can also use this field to directly enter a URL for a WWW page. When you do this the WWW browser attempts to retreive the chosen page as though you had selected it via a hyperlink.

Status Area

Unlike the Windows WWW browser, the status area for the Macintosh versions is located just below the Current URL: field.

This area consists of two graphical display bars that represent the current display status of your WWW browser. On the left side, information about the WWW page itself is displayed, and on the right side, information about inline images is displayed.

Whenever the WWW browser is retreiving a WWW page or inline images, the size of the page and images is displayed along with the amount of information already retreived. Then, once the page has been fully received the messages `Page complete` and `Image complete` are displayed.

The Menus

Because the Macintosh WWW browser is a separate application, the dropdown menus accompanying it differ somewhat from standard AOL menu set. Of these menus, there are three that you will find yourself using on a regular basis.

- ◆ The Services Menu
- ◆ The Web Menu
- ◆ The AOL Menu

The Services Menu

The options listed on the Services Menu provide you with a means of accessing all major features provided by the Macintosh WWW browser. (See Figure 12.18.)

These features include the following:

FTP...   Selecting this option gives you access to an FTP client program similar to the one built into AOL itself. (See Chapter 9, "File Transfer Protocol (FTP).") For most purposes, you should use the version built into AOL because it is far easier to use and provides you with more information about the FTP site you are connected to.

However, there is one feature provided by this FTP client that is not available in the AOL version. You can upload files to an FTP site using this FTP client.

Gopher…	If you know the address of a Gopher site you can access it via this menu item.
Web…	To return to the WWW browser, if you have been using either the Gopher or FTP service, select this menu entry.
Open URL…	You can go to a new WWW page by selecting this menu item and entering its URL in the field provided. (See Figure 12.19.)
	This option is useful if you have turned off the display on the Current URL: field via the configuration options.
Add To Main Hot List	When you explore the World Wide Web, you will soon encounter a number of sites that you would like to revisit at a later date.
	Instead of writing the URL's of these sites down on a piece of paper, the Macintosh WWW browser provides you with a special feature called a Hot List. (See Figure 12.20.)
	From the Main Hot List window you can add new entries, edit exiting one or delete those that you are no longer interested in.
Hot Lists	You are not limited to having only one list either; by selecting the Hot Lists menu item you can create multiple hot lists.

FIGURE 12.18.

The WWW browser's Services Menu.

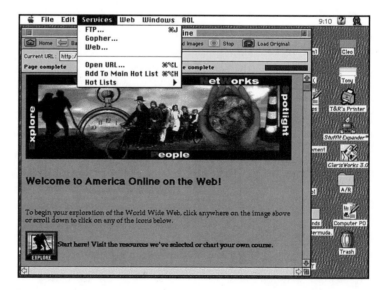

FIGURE 12.19.

Enter the URL of a site you want to visit in the field provided.

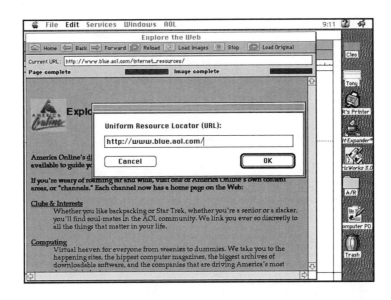

FIGURE 12.20.

Select any of the sites listed on your Hot List to retrieve and display it.

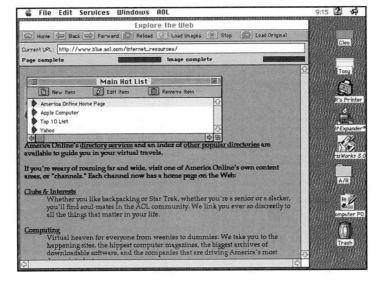

The Web Menu

Many of the options provided by the navigation button in the Control Console are duplicated on the Web menu shown in Figure 12.21. In addition, some of the more popular configuration options are also accessible from here.

FIGURE 12.21.

*The Web menu on the
Macintosh WWW browser.*

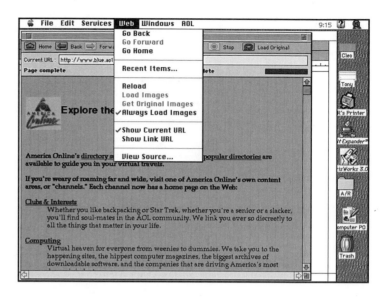

The functions provided by the Web menu include

Go Back	Return to the previous page.
Go Forward	Return to the most recent page.
Go Home	Open your home page.
Recent Items…	Select this item to pick a WWW page from a list of recently visited WWW pages.
Reload	Reload the current page.
Load Images	Load any inline images that have not yet been displayed.
Get Original Images	Reload the images for the current WWW page.
Always Load Images	This menu item is a selectable entry—each time you choose it its status changes. Use it to enable or disable the loading of inline images.
Show Current URL	Use the option to display or remove the Current URL: field from the Control Console area.
Show Link URL	This option enables or disables the display of URLs when you place your cursor over a hyperlink.
View Source…	If you select this option, the WWW browser opens a window that displays the HTML source code for the current WWW page.

The AOL Menu

Although this menu only contains two options, (see Figure 12.22) they are important enough to merit a discussion of their own.

FIGURE 12.22.

The AOL menu on the Macintosh WWW browser.

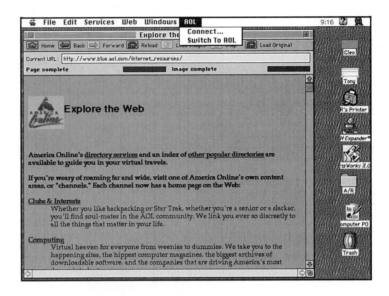

Connect...   To use the WWW browser, AOL needs to be running, and naturally it needs to be connected to America Online. If AOL is not currently running or is offline, selecting this option starts AOL and signs you on to America Online.

Switch to AOL   Because you are not actually using AOL to connect to the World Wide Web, you need some way of switching back to AOL. Selecting this option does just that.

Configuring WWW for the Macintosh

There is one option on the Edit menu that requires some special attention. When you select the Configure... option from the Edit menu, a window similar to the one shown in Figure 12.23 is displayed. The items listed on this window allow you to tailor the appearance and operation of your WWW browser. This section examines each of these options and discusses their use.

Down the left side of the AOL Internet Configuration window there are a number of icons that give you access to various options and settings. As a rule you should leave all these options as they are, except possibly those under the Web Icon. To examine the Web settings click on the appropriate icon.

Altering your Home Page

When you start the Macintosh WWW browser it attempts to load the page pointed to by the contents of this field. By default, the page that gets loaded is the America Online home page at `http://www.blue.aol.com`. In addition, when you click on the Home button, the same URL is used.

FIGURE 12.23.

You can adjust how the WWW browser looks by altering the settings on the AOL Internet Configuration window.

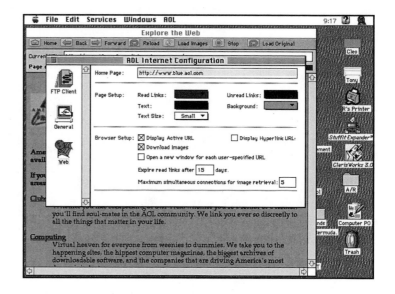

Setting the Folder for Web Files

When you save copies of WWW pages or download files via FTP, the WWW browser needs to know where you want them to be stored. By default they are saved in the same folder that the WWW browser is held in; however, by adjusting this option you can select any folder on your computer.

Adjusting Your Page Setup

The Page Setup options allow you to alter the color of several different elements on the WWW page. If, for example, you are tired of blue hyperlinks you can alter them to any color you want. You can also alter the color of links you have already read, the color of all the text on a WWW page, and the color of the background.

Depending on your screen resolution, you may find it handy to alter the size of the text displayed on WWW document pages. By doing this you can fit more information onto the screen at once.

Browser Setup Options

The options in the Browser Setup area let you control which parts of the WWW browser are active and which are not. These options include

Display Active URL	If this option is selected the Current URL: field is displayed in the Control Console.
Display Hyperlink URL	Select this option to display the URL of the hyperlink currently under the cursor.
Download Images	Inline images are downloaded if this option is set.
Open a new window…	If you enter a URL in the Current URL: field and this option is selected, the WWW browser opens a separate window to display the WWW page, instead of overwriting the current one.
Expire read links…	Enter the number of days the links will be shown as read.
Maximum connections…	When the WWW browser is downloading inline images it usually attempts to download them all at the same time. You can alter the number of images that are retrieved simultaneously by adjusting this setting.

Troubleshooting Tips for the Mac WWW Browser

For the most part, because the Macintosh WWW browser is not an integral part of AOL itself, a number of people have reported difficulties both installing and using it. In this section you will find a list of tips and suggestions compiled from a number of online discussions dealing with this issue.

> America Online is aware of the difficulties associated with using the Mac WWW browser and has indicated that they are currently investigating a solution to the problem.

Memory

By far, the biggest concern relates to the amount of memory required to run AOL and the WWW browser. Basically, you need a minimum of 8MB of physical memory before you can even consider using the WWW browser successfully. The term *physical memory* is important here too, because based on the comments some people have made, the use of RAM doubling software or virtual memory software appears to cause problems on some computers.

AOL itself technically requires at least 2000KB to run, but if you plan to display graphics or do any serious work, 3000KB is the practical minimum. The WWW browser needs at least 2560KB of physical memory to even start, but for practical purposes 3500KB should be considered the real minimum. This means that you need at least 4560KB, or in practical terms, 6500KB of memory. Depending on which version of the Macintosh Operating System you are using, it also requires around 2000KB of memory for its system services. So as you can see, 8MB is the barest minimum.

You will also need to have 8MB of memory to obtain support from Tech Support Live, Keyword: CSLIVE—AOL's online technical support service. If you have at least 8MB of memory, they will be able to assist you in getting your WWW browser operational.

Program Conflicts

The WWW browser also appears to have difficulties when it encounters any anti-virus, RAM doubling, or file backup programs such as Norton Filesaver, running in the background. As a result, you will need to disable any such programs before attempting to set up the Mac WWW browser.

Also, due to the memory requirements of AOL and the WWW browser, it is a good idea not to have any other programs or unnecessary system extensions running while attempting to use the WWW browser.

Version Conflicts

If your system meets the requirements discussed so far, but you are still encountering difficulties, the next logical step is to reinstall AOL 2.6 and the WWW browser. Although many people have indicated that they already have the latest version, in many cases, after doing a complete re-installation of both AOL and the WWW browser, everything starts to operate correctly.

You can download the latest version using the Keyword: Upgrade. The Upgrade window is a free area, so you can download the latest version without being charged for your online time.

Old System Preferences

When you install the upgraded version of AOL and the WWW browsers, there are a few files left lying around that can potentially cause difficulties. If you look in the Preferences folder located in the System folder on your hard drive, you will possibly find an America Online folder and an AOL Internet Settings folder. If either folder exists, delete them from your computer by dragging them into your trash can.

When you do this make sure that you "Empty the Trash" immediately afterward to ensure that the files are completely gone.

Old Cache Files

This step is more often associated with getting your WWW browser running if it stops working after you have been online for some time. However, you should cover all the bases when dealing with the Mac WWW browser.

Open the America Online v2.6 folder and locate the Online Browser folder. Open the Online Browser folder and then the Cache folder, which should be located inside the Browser Folder. If there are any files in the Cache folder move them to the trash can. (Note: Don't remove the Cache folder itself because the WWW browser needs it later.)

As before, "Empty the Trash" immediately afterward to ensure that all the files are completely removed from your computer.

Communication Errors

Assuming you have completed all the previous steps, the next error that you are likely to encounter is either `You must be signed on to AOL before using the Web` or `Error communicating with the Mac browser.`

At this stage, the Mac WWW browser occasionally has difficulties locating the AOL browser, which it needs when loading WWW pages. To resolve this issue, it has been suggested that the WWW browser should be started before you start AOL itself. To do this open your America Online v2.6 folder, then locate and open the Online Browser folder. In the Online Browser folder you will find an icon for the Web Browser. Double-click on this icon to start the WWW browser.

Once the WWW browser is running, start AOL itself by double-clicking on its icon, which is located in the America Online v2.6 folder. Finally, when AOL starts, sign on in the usual way.

You should now be able to use the WWW browser and switch between it and AOL by using the menus and options discussed previously.

Keyword: CSLIVE

If you are still encountering problems at this stage, then your best bet is in the America Online Technical support area. You can access this area using the Keyword: **CSLIVE** or Keyword: **TECHLIVE**.

In this area you will find America Online technical support personnel available online, who are only too happy to assist you with your problems. Remember, however, that you need at least 8MB of physical memory before they are able to be of any assistance.

Having said that, there are people on the WWW message boards who have indicated success with AOL and WWW while running RAMDoubler or Virtual memory with less than 8MB of physical memory. As a result, a visit to the WWW message boards that can be accessed from the Internet Connection window may also be time well spent.

Advanced Capabilities

Now that you have an understanding of how the World Wide Web works, let's take a look at some of the special features offered by World Wide Web browsers.

In this section, the AOL browser built into the Windows version is used for all examples. However, unless specified, similar functions are supported by most other WWW browsers.

mailto:

As you begin to explore the World Wide Web, you will occasionally come across a special type of hyperlink that looks something like this: `mailto:wtatters@world.net`. The hypertext link indicated by the cursor on Figure 12.24 indicates such a link, as shown by the URL information displayed in the status link at the bottom of the screen.

FIGURE 12.24.

Pointing to a link displays its URL in the status link at the bottom of the screen.

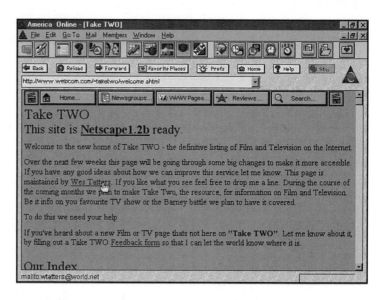

If you select a hyperlink like this, AOL opens the Compose Mail window and inserts the e-mail address indicated by the `mailto:` URL in the TO: field.

> This feature is currently only available in the Windows version of the WWW browser.

FTP

It is also possible to use your WWW browser as an FTP client. Simply enter the domain name of the FTP site you want to visit in the Document URL field. To tell the browser that you want to open an FTP session, first enter `ftp://` and then the domain name.

For example, if you want to visit America Online's FTP server discussed in Chapter 9, type the following in the Document URL field and hit the Enter key: `ftp://ftp.aol.com/`.

After a few seconds you should see a page like the one shown in Figure 12.25. All the files and subdirectories in the root directory of the Microsoft server are displayed down the left side of the main document, each represented as a hyperlink. All you need to do to enter any of these directories or retrieve any of the files is click on them.

FIGURE 12.25.

The root directory of America Online's FTP server.

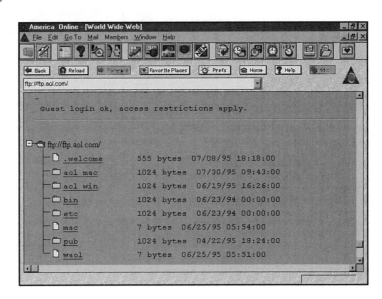

As an experiment, open the `aol win` directory. When you do this AOL retrieves a list of all the files in the selected directory and displays them for you. (See Figure 12.26.) You can then download any of the files in the directory by clicking on them. If the file is a text file or contains information that AOL can recognize, such as a picture or sound file, AOL opens the appropriate viewer and displays the file for you.

Alternatively, if AOL does not recognize the type of file you have selected, a Save As dialog box like the one shown in Figure 12.27 is displayed. Using this dialog box you can tell AOL where you want the file stored and alter its name if necessary.

Once you have told AOL where you want the file to be saved, click on the OK button to begin the transfer. AOL then transfers a copy of the file to your hard drive.

FIGURE 12.26.

Click on a file to retrieve a copy of it.

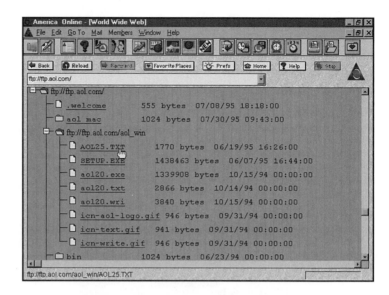

FIGURE 12.27.

When AOL does not recognize the contents of a file, it always asks you what you want to do with it.

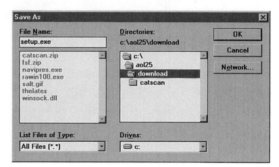

Newsgroups

The final major specification of the original WWW project was giving the user the ability to read articles stored in newsgroups by using a World Wide Web browser. Unfortunately, at this stage access to this level of functionality is not fully implemented in the AOL browser.

When the AOL browser encounter a news: URL it starts the AOL Newsgroup reader, but at this stage does not open the actual newsgroup for you to read. To get around this problem, if you right click on a hyperlink, a menu opens that lets you copy the URL onto the clipboard. Then click on the hyperlink to start the newsgroup reader and use the Expert Add option to subscribe to the newsgroup. In the Expert Add dialog, paste a copy of the URL into the required field—remembering to delete news: from the beginning. Once subscribed, you can then read the newsgroup using the standard functions.

There is no need to include a / / after the news: protocol.

Data Entry Forms

One feature of the World Wide Web that sets it apart from other Internet services is its ability to interact with users through *forms*.

On some WWW pages you will encounter fields like those in the form shown in Figure 12.28. These fields allow you to submit information to a WWW server by filling in the spaces provided. Depending on the WWW page, this information might relate to a membership application, a search form, delivery details for an online purchase, or even your responses to online messages on a service like WebChat.

FIGURE 12.28.

Data Entry forms allow you to interact with a WWW server.

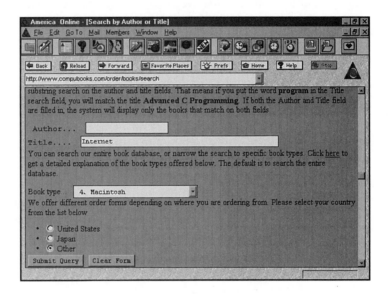

The form shown in Figure 12.28 is a part of a search form the Compubooks product list. By entering the name of a book or by selecting a book topic you can search their product list and locate books you may be interested in purchasing.

> In addition to providing you with a search tool to help locate computer books in print. Compubooks also gives you the ability to order a copy of any of the books on their product list. You can do this while online by following the simple steps outlined on the WWW pages. To visit Compubooks, point your WWW browser to `http://www.compubooks.com/books.html`

Note

In addition to data entry fields, many forms also contain *radio buttons* like the ones below the location message. These buttons allow you to choose a single option from the list provided. *Pick fields* like the Book Type field are also commonly used, because they allow you to choose from a list of options that don't take the entire screen to list. When you click on one of these fields, a popup menu appears listing all the possible options for the field. Other forms include *check boxes,* which allow you to select any or all of the corresponding options.

When you have completed the information requested by the form, you must then submit it to the WWW server. On most forms, you do this by clicking on a Submit button. In this example, however, you need to click on the Submit Query Register shown at the bottom on the screen.

> If you make a mistake in a form, you can often start fresh by clicking on the Clear Form button. Doing this removes all the information you have entered into the form. Not all forms include such a button, but those that do display it beside the Submit button in most cases.

Summary

Using the World Wide Web is both a simple process and one that offers you capabilities far beyond those provided by more conventional Internet clients. It allows you to explore the World Wide Web itself, retrieve files stored at FTP sites, and even do a bit of online shopping. So what else is it capable of doing?

The next chapter answers this question and takes a look at some of the more popular WWW sites and home pages and offers some suggestions about places that may be able to assist you further in your understanding of the World Wide Web.

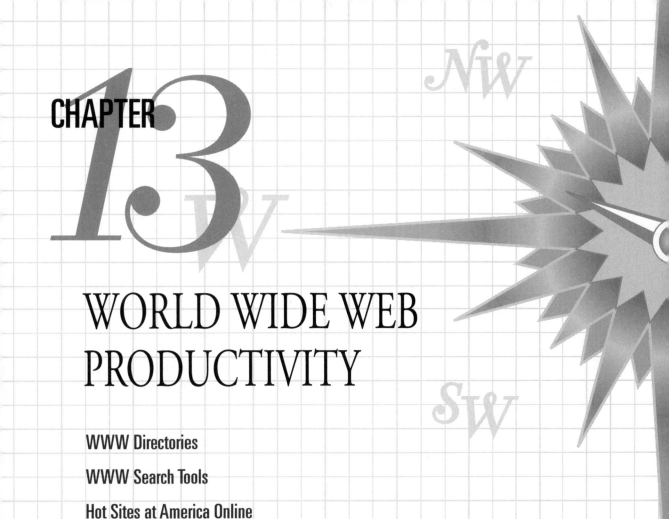

CHAPTER 13

WORLD WIDE WEB PRODUCTIVITY

WWW Directories

WWW Search Tools

Hot Sites at America Online

Cool and Unusual Places

Now that you have the world at your fingertips, so to speak, it's time to take a look at some of the ways you can locate home pages and WWW sites by using the World Wide Web. Instead of creating a shopping list of popular World Wide Web sites, this chapter demonstrates ways that you can use the World Wide Web to locate interesting sites yourself.

To do this, this chapter first examines some of the major WWW directories and then looks at ways in which you can search the World Wide Web and many other Internet services as well. America Online itself is also an ideal source of WWW sites with each of the major departments featuring a list of related sites. In the third section of this chapter, America Online's Hot Sites lists are examined. Then, for those of you who really want web addresses and URLs, the final section briefly discusses a few of the more unique WWW pages.

WWW Directories

With the mind-numbing growth of the World Wide Web over the last two years, it is not surprising that more than a few people have become overwhelmed by its enormity on their first few WWW outings. The fact that there is no front door or starting point is a concept that many people find difficult to grasp. This is to be expected, however, because our society is accustomed to the use of maps and step-by-step plans that have a logical beginning and end.

For this reason, a number of WWW sites have been set up for the sole purpose of providing you with at least a logical starting point. The endpoint is still up to you, but at the very least these pages give you some idea about where to start.

AOL's Internet Directory Services

For AOL users, by far the best place to start is the AOL Internet Directory Services pages at the AOL WWW site. While not necessarily the most comprehensive list of sites currently available, this site does contain links to many of the major directories.

To get to the AOL directory, open the Keyword dialog box (Ctrl+K or ⌘+K) and enter **WWW** or **Web**. Both of these keywords take you to the AOL home page at `http://www.blue.aol.com/`. (See Figure 13.1). Once the AOL home page has loaded, clicking the Explore icon or the word "Explore" in the image map at the top of the page, takes you to the AOL Internet Resources page. The URL for this page is `http://www.blue.aol.com/internet_resources/`.

The first two links listed on the Internet Resources page take you to the Internet Directory Services page and the Internet Directories page respectively. The former contains links to hundreds of different WWW sites categorized by type, while the latter contains a list of the most popular Internet Directory pages and search tools.

FIGURE 13.1.

Select the Explore icon on the AOL home page to load the AOL Internet Resources page.

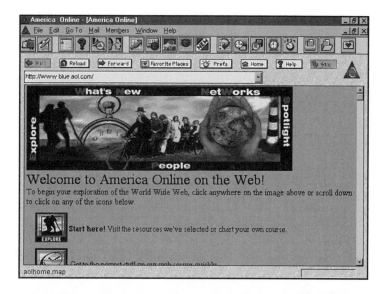

FIGURE 13.2.

The Internet Resources page provides you with links to many of the popular Internet Directories and related search tools.

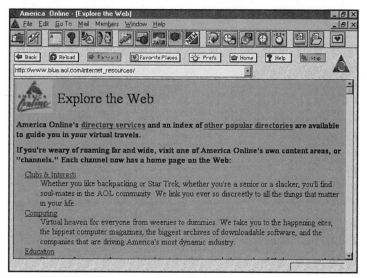

The URL for the AOL Internet Directory Services page shown in Figure 13.2 is: `http://www.blue.aol.com/internet_resources/directory/browse/`, and the URL for the AOL Internet Directories page in Figure 13.3 is `http://www.blue.aol.com/internet_resources/directories.html`.

FIGURE 13.3.

The AOL Internet Directory Services page.

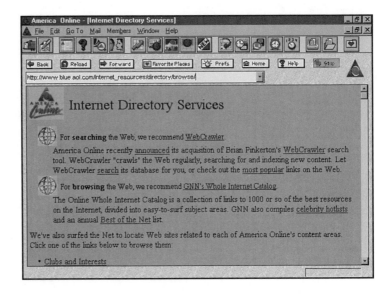

Scott Yanoff's Special Internet Connections

The Special Internet Connections list (see Figure 13.4) has been doing the rounds on the Internet in a variety of forms since 1991. When Scott Yanoff first published his personal list of Internet connections it contained just six Internet sites, but since then the list has grown to contain links to thousands of World Wide Web sites, FTP servers, Telnet ports, Gophers, and mailing lists.

FIGURE 13.4.

Scott Yanoff's Special Internet Connections list includes not only WWW sites but FTP, Telnet, and Gopher servers.

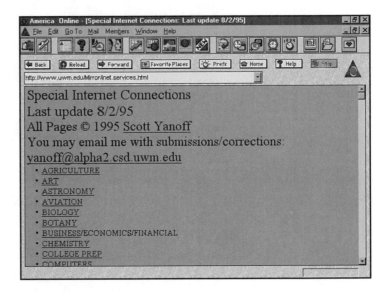

Since its inception, the list has been made available in a variety of formats, but with the growth of the World Wide Web, that version is now the most popular method of accessing the list. To explore the many links detailed in this list, use this http address: `http://www.uwm.edu/Mirror/inet.services.html`.

The list is sorted by category, but not by service type. As a result, when you use this list you will often be transported to Gopher servers and FTP sites when you select a hotlink. To check the type of service that any link uses, examine the protocol section of the URL shown in the status bar when you place your cursor over its hotlink.

Yahoo

Yahoo was created by David Filo and Jerry Yang who, according to *Newsweek*, are two of the 50 most influential people on the Internet. They prefer to describe themselves as "Yahoos," however, and will happily direct anyone who does not know what a Yahoo is to this URL: `http://c.gp.cs.cmu.edu:5103/prog/webster?yahoo`.

Yahoo contains a comprehensive listing of popular WWW pages categorized by type. (See Figure 13.5.) The site also contains a number of unique features, including:

◆ A What's New list, which is updated daily

◆ A What's Popular list, itemized by category

◆ David and Jerry's personal What's Cool listing

◆ An integrated search capability

◆ A random link page that takes you to a random WWW page

◆ The Yahoo rating system

FIGURE 13.5.

The Yahoo WWW sites listing.

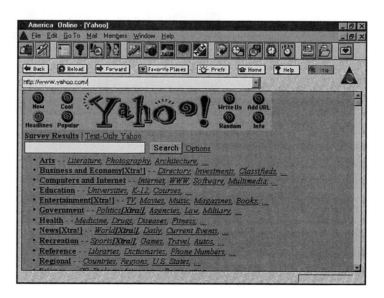

To explore Yahoo, point your WWW browser to this http address: `http://www.yahoo.com/` and select the topic you are interested in. Like most directories, Yahoo organizes its list of sites by category, but also provides a powerful search tool to help you rapidly locate sites you may want to examine more closely.

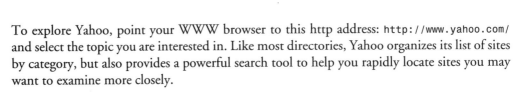

Note

`http://c.gp.cs.cmu.edu:5103/prog/webster?yahoo` is an automated version of Webster's dictionary, containing both definitions and full cross references. To look up the meaning of any word, replace `yahoo` with the word you are interested in.

The Whole Internet Catalog

This site is based loosely on The Whole Internet User's Guide & Catalog and contains links to all the sites this book mentions, along with many new updates and additional references. (See Figure 13.6.)

FIGURE 13.6.

The Whole Internet Catalog home page.

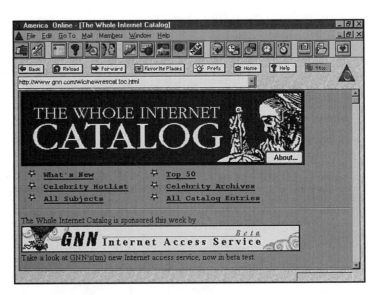

Like Yahoo, this site contains a hierarchical list categorized by resource type. It is not a comprehensive list, however, containing only what its publishers consider to be the best WWW pages for each category listed. The advantage of this sort of list is that it helps you wade through the many thousands of pages on the World Wide Web that each tend to cover a topic in many different, though not necessarily effective, ways. This catalog reduces the number of sites you need to explore in your effort to locate information.

In addition to the general resource list, there are also special pages that cover the following topics:

◆ The Celebrity Hotlist is a page where special Internet guest editors are invited to share their most popular WWW pages

◆ The What's New listing

◆ The Top 25 WWW sites

The Whole Internet Catalog is provided as a part of GNN—the Global Network Navigator. To explore the links this catalog provides, use the following http address: `http://www.gnn.com/wic/newrescat.toc.html`.

Global Network Navigator

GNN, which is provided through a partnership between O'Reilly and Associates and America Online, also contains links to many other popular sites and services. (See Figure 13.7.) To access this site use the following address: `http://www.gnn.com/`.

FIGURE 13.7.

GNN—The Global Network Navigator.

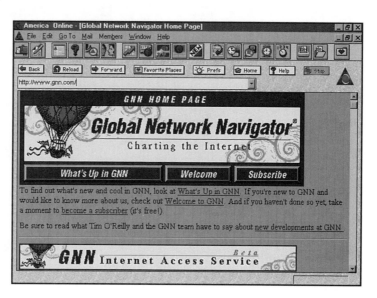

In addition to The Whole Internet Catalog, GNN maintains a number of specialized WWW lists that include the following subjects:

◆ Best of the Net

◆ Personal finance

◆ Education

◆ Net news

◆ Sports

◆ Travel

The table of contents for GNN also provides a very good list of major WWW sites and popular home pages at `http://gnn.com/gnn/wic/internet.toc.html`.

Note

> Before you can use many of the services offered by GNN, you need to become a subscriber. There is no cost involved in doing this. All you need to do is complete the Online Information form that is available from the GNN home page by selecting the Subscribe option.

The WWW Virtual Library

By far the most comprehensive list of WWW pages currently available can be found at the WWW Virtual Library, whose http address is `http://www.w3.org/hypertext/DataSources/bySubject/Overview.html`. (See Figure 13.8.)

FIGURE 13.8.

The WWW Virtual Library contains links to most WWW pages.

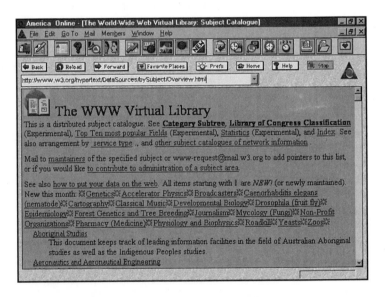

The WWW Virtual Library categorizes the pages it contains into over 150 major classifications, which themselves are often further broken down into more specific topic areas. As you may have already noticed by looking at the URL, this service is provided by the W3 Consortium as the primary resource for WWW-related indexes. There are also a number of special pages that provide you with additional information, including

◆ The Category Subtree
◆ The Library of Congress
◆ Top Ten most popular fields
◆ The Virtual Library Index

◆ The Virtual Library by service type

◆ A list of other Internet catalogs

The WWW Virtual Library also operates in a slightly different manner than most other major lists. If someone discovers a category that is not properly represented in the Virtual Library, instead of just letting the administrators know that they have been remiss, that person will often be asked to take over the maintenance of such a new area and keep the links it contains up to date. To make suggestions about new categories, select the "to contribute to administration of a subject area" hot link.

TradeWave Galaxy

TradeWave Galaxy (see Figure 13.9) is organized in a slightly different manner than the other major WWW directories. At its core, Galaxy is driven by a complex database system that uses a *manufacturing automation and design engineering* (MADE) program. This program allows the categories, or information structures, Galaxy maintains to be indexed and cross-referenced in a manner not permitted by conventional hierarchical lists.

FIGURE 13.9.

TradeWave Galaxy lets you search a variety of databases for WWW pages and other Internet resources.

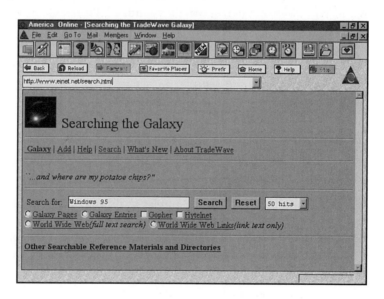

To access these indexes, Galaxy provides you with a navigation database that enables you to move easily around the Galaxy environment and quickly locate relevant information. Every information page on Galaxy contains a search field where you can enter words you want to locate. When you enter a word, a new information list is displayed that outlines all the related information structures.

To complement the navigation database, there are also service-specific databases that allow you to search for Gopher, Telnet, and WWW links separately.

If you are interested in exploring Galaxy, you can reach it via the TradeWave home page at `http://www.einet.net/`. Originally TradeWave was called EINET, hence the domain name. However, by the time this book goes to print, you will also be able to access TradeWave Galaxy using `http://galaxy.tradewave.com/`.

> This site also contains information about the services and tools offered by TradeWave, which include the WinWeb WWW browser and a variety of other browser and server products.

WWW Search Tools

If spending hours scanning endless lists of WWW pages is not your style, maybe a more direct approach would better suit your needs.

With more than an estimated six million pages of information now directly available via the World Wide Web, not to mention the countless FTP and Gopher sites, it didn't take long for a number of WWW search tools and utilities to appear. Many of these tools provide access to a variety of information sources, including WWW pages, FTP sites or files, and WAIS directories.

This section examines some of the more popular WWW search tools and provides you with details about the types of information indexed by each.

WebCrawler

For AOL users, the easiest WWW search tool to locate is WebCrawler. All you need to do is open the Keyword dialog box (Ctrl+K or ⌘+K) and enter **WebCrawler**.

When you do this, a WWW page similar to the one shown in Figure 13.10 is displayed by your AOL WWW browser. WebCrawler is operated by AOL as a part of its new Internet service in association with GNN. Alternatively, there is a link to WebCrawler listed at the top of AOL's Internet Directory Services page, or you can enter its URL directly—`http://webcrawler.com/`.

To use WebCrawler once the page is displayed on your screen, enter as many terms as possible into the search field. Doing this helps WebCrawler narrow down the number of WWW pages reported in its search results. You can also adjust the number of pages listed in the results by altering the Number of Results to Return: field. Then when you are satisfied with your query click on the Search button.

After a short break, a new page is displayed (see Figure 13.11) listing all the pages the WebCrawler located that contained words matching your query request. From this page you can jump to any of the listed pages by clicking on the hyperlink associated which each entry's description.

FIGURE 13.10.

Enter as many terms as possible to narrow down the search.

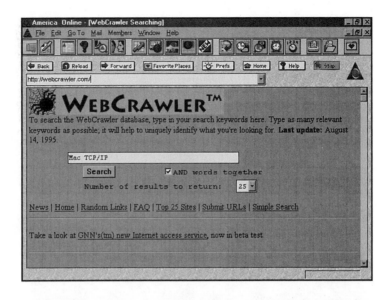

FIGURE 13.11.

To examine the contents of any of the pages listed, click on their highlighted descriptions.

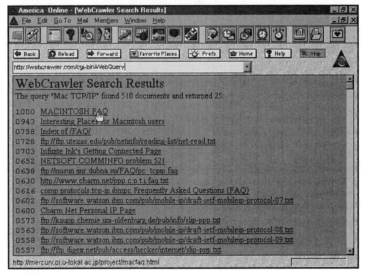

Lycos

By all accounts, the most comprehensive index of WWW sites is maintained by a search tool developed at Carnegie Mellon University. The name of this tool is Lycos. (See Figure 12.12.) As of the time of this writing, Lycos had indexed 5.6 million WWW pages and was adding thousands of new pages each day.

FIGURE 13.12.

Lycos is the most comprehensive WWW index currently available.

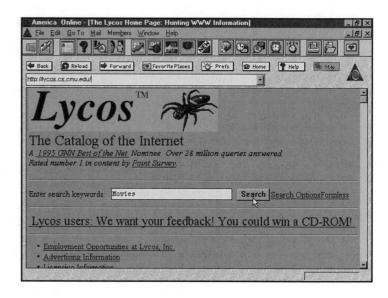

Like many of the WWW search tools currently available, Lycos has created its impressive index by automatically exploring the World Wide Web, page by page and link by link, following all the paths each page offers and recording each one as it visits it. In the last six months, Lycos has become one of the busiest places on the World Wide Web, with over 15 million requests for information being answered.

To access this index, Lycos provides you with a variety of search options that allow you to search either the full database or a smaller "recent pages" database. There is also a simple search page and a more complex form-based page that lets you configure details such as the number of matches reported and even the search benchmarks. On the home page shown in Figure 13.12, you can choose any of these search options and select from pages containing information about the use of Lycos. You can reach this page at `http://lycos.cs.cmu.edu/`.

When you type a word or combination of words into one of the search fields provided, Lycos searches its index and displays a list of results that match your query on a page similar to the one shown in Figure 13.13. From here you can select any of the links that Lycos has returned to take you directly to the WWW page described.

In addition, at the top of the search results page, Lycos also lists a set of links to search results for queries similar to the one you requested. If you select any of these links, Lycos runs the query again, this time using the word or words selected by this alternate link. (See the *The Web and Hubble* topic in Chapter 16, "Family Fun and Education," for more information on using Lycos.)

FIGURE 13.13.

You can select any of the links listed in the results of a Lycos search to move straight to the desired page.

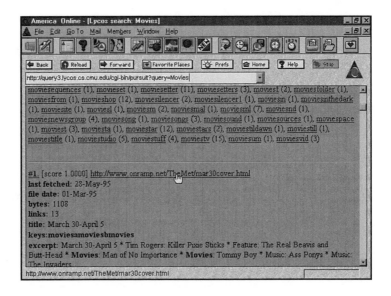

In spite of its popularity, Lycos is still only in beta release. It is common practice these days to release programs to the public before they are completed. Doing this lets the developer obtain feedback about their program and also locate bugs and faults they may not have been located by in-house testing. This process is known as Beta testing, or sometimes Alpha testing if the program is released while in the very early stages of development.

This testing process is helping Lycos' developers to refine the features and capabilities Lycos provides. In addition, as a result of the comments made by users, there are now plans to include extended Boolean features and possibly a search capability known as relevance feedback, which was made popular by WAIS.

ArchiePlex

The World Wide Web is not limited to providing WWW search tools. There are a number of other services currently available online that index many other popular Internet sources. Of these, one of the most popular is ArchiePlex. (See Figure 13.14.)

ArchiePlex is a World Wide Web extension to the Archie e-mail server discussed in Chapter 9, "File Transfer Protocol (FTP)." Instead of using e-mail or a dedicated Archie client, by taking advantage of ArchiePlex you can use the World Wide Web to locate files stored at anonymous FTP sites. In addition, once you have located a list of sites containing files you are interested in (see Figure 13.15), you can also take advantage of the FTP capabilities built into the AOL WWW browser to retrieve a copy of the files and store them on your local hard drive. (See Figure 13.16.)

FIGURE 13.14.

ArchiePlex, the WWW gateway to files on FTP servers.

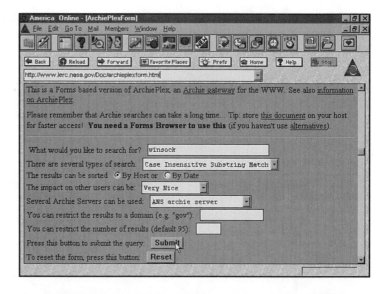

FIGURE 13.15.

ArchiePlex returns a list of links to FTP sites and directories that match the results of your search request.

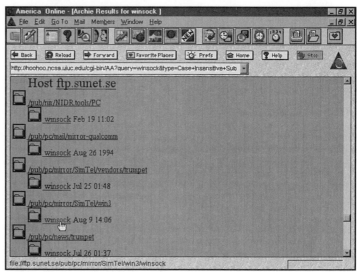

There are a number of ArchiePlex pages to choose from that are operated by WWW sites all over the Internet. To view a list of all the ArchiePlex pages currently available, point your WWW browser to `http://pubweb.nexor.co.uk/public/archie/servers.html`.

FIGURE 13.16.

Select any of the files listed to request AOL to download a copy of it to your computer.

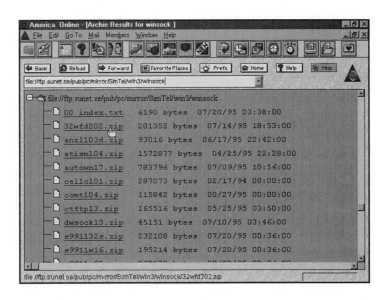

> Depending on the time of day, Archie servers respond to your queries with either promptness or downright tardiness. If you find that you have not received a response within a couple of minutes, you should cancel the request and try another server. You don't need to change ArchiePlex pages to do this. Simply adjust the Archie server field on the request form.

WAISgate

Although most WWW browsers are capable of directly communicating with WAIS servers, the results obtained when they do are often less than suitable. To get around this problem, America Online, in association with WAIS Inc—one of the leading WAIS publishers and developers—provides a WWW gateway called WAISgate. (See Figure 13.17.)

This gateway offers a form-based interface that greatly enhances the WWW/WAIS interface and provides a method of operation that seamlessly integrates the two services. (See the *WAIS and Hubble* topic in Chapter 16 for a demonstration of WAISgate.)

To access WAISgate, use the following http address: `http://www.wais.com/`.

FIGURE 13.17.

Enter a list of words to search for and click on the Search button to start WAISgate.

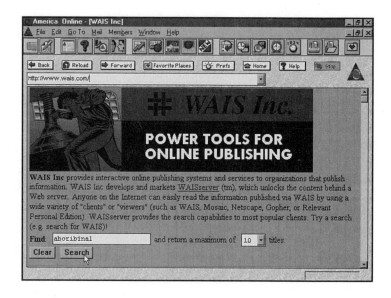

WAIS, Inc. is currently working on a new release of WAISgate dubbed WAISgate 2.0. To try a sample of what they plan to offer, select the WAISgate 2.0 demo option on the WAIS Inc. home page.

Popular WWW Search Pages and Locations

Apart from the four services already mentioned, there are about 20 other major WWW or Internet indexes and search pages, each of which offers a slightly different user interface and index. Most are not as comprehensive as those already discussed, but at the same time they often contain information that may not be available on other pages.

There are a number of ways to locate these different pages, the simplest of which is to follow the links on one of the WWW search tool pages. Figure 13.18 shows the list provided by Netscape on its WWW search page at http://home.mcom.com/escapes/internet_search.html.

This page also features a direct link to the new commercial InfoSeek WWW index, which aims to provide the most comprehensive Internet index ever created.

At the bottom of this page, there is also a link to a page known as the Configurable Unified Search Engine (CUSI). CUSI contains a list of all the known search engines that are accessible via the World Wide Web. These include

Lycos, WebCrawler, InfoSeek, and Jumpstation

ALIWEB, Yahoo, Global On-Line Directory, and the CUI W3 Catalog

Veronica, WAIS, and the Whole Internet Catalog

ArchiePlex, CICA & SIMTEL Archives, HENSA Micro Archive

FIGURE 13.18.

The Netscape list of search tools and utilities.

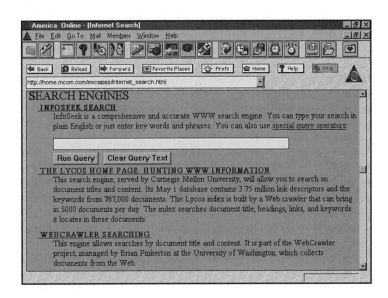

However, instead of just providing hotlinks to the appropriate pages, you can enter your search criterion in the space provided on the CUSI page (see Figure 13.19) and click the related search button. The search page takes care of connecting to the search engine you selected and the submission of your query request.

FIGURE 13.19.

Select the search engine you want to use and enter your query parameters. The CUSI page takes care of the rest of the job for you.

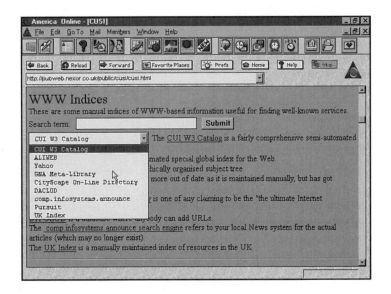

To use the CUSI interface, take a look at http://pubweb.nexor.co.uk/public/cusi/cusi.html, or for a slightly different service that provides many of the same features, try http://cuiwww.unige.ch/meta-index.html. (See Figure 13.20.)

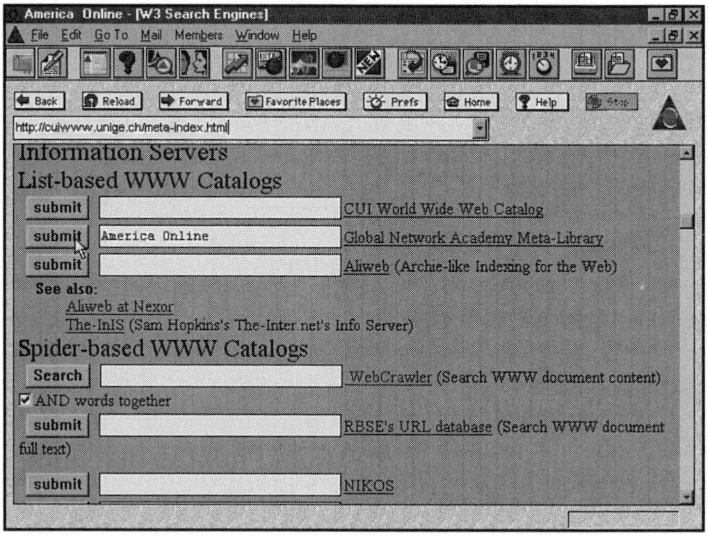

FIGURE 13.20.

Instead of drop-down boxes, this page lists each WWW search tool separately.

Hot Sites at America Online

Another good place to find WWW pages is in each of America Online's main channels. In each of these areas, you will find an option that takes you to a list of World Wide Web sites containing pages of information relating to that particular department or channel.

In this section each of America Online's Hot WWW Site windows are looked at briefly to give you a better idea of the amount of information and sites available. In addition, in Chapter 16, and Chapter 17, "Business on the Net," some of these windows will be examined in greater detail.

Top News Sites on the Web

The Today's News channel, accessible by using the Keyword: **News**, gives you access to Top News Sites on the Web window shown in Figure 13.21. To open this window click on the Top Internet Sites button on the right side of the Today's News window.

America Online has organized the WWW sites on this page into six separate categories:

◆ Top News Sites

◆ US News

◆ International News

◆ Weather Information

◆ Sports News

◆ Business News

FIGURE 13.21.

*Click on any of the buttons
displayed at the bottom of
this window to view lists of
additional WWW sites.*

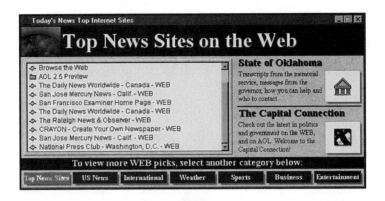

To view a list of WWW in each these categories, click on their corresponding button at the bottom of the Top News Sites on the Web window. If you find a WWW site that looks interesting, double-click on its entry using the mouse. When you do this AOL starts its WWW browser and attempts to retrieve the selected WWW page.

Publications on the Web

The Publications on the WEB window shown in Figure 13.22 can be reached via the America Online Newsstand at Keyword: **Newsstand**. All you need to do is select the Publications on the Web icon in the top left hand corner of the main Newsstand window.

FIGURE 13.22.

*There are a number of
publications now online as
a part of the World Wide
Web.*

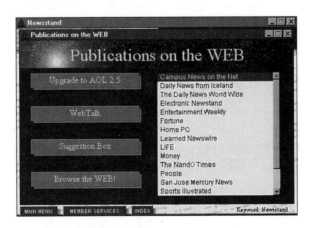

While not as comprehensive a list of publications as those available on America Online itself, a growing number of newspapers and magazines are beginning to experiment with providing services via the World Wide Web. In addition, there are now a number of WWW sites dedicated solely to publication via the Internet, of which, the NandO Times is one of the most impressive.

The Financial Web

Although the business and finance sector was a late comer to the Internet, since its arrival numerous financial advice and information pages have begun to appear all over the World Wide Web.

To help you explore the best of these services, America Online has created the Financial Web window shown in Figure 13.23. To access this window select the Internet Resources button from the Personal Finance channel's main window which can be accessed using Keyword: **Finance.**

FIGURE 13.23.

Want to find out what the World Wide Web offers in the way of finance tips?

WEBentertainment Sites

To catch up on all the latest entertainment gossip via the World Wide Web. Open the Entertainment channel, Keyword: **Entertainment** and select the To Internet Sites icon. When you do, AOL opens the WEBentertainment Sites window shown in Figure 13.24.

FIGURE 13.24.

Select any of the entertainment categories to display a full list of related WWW sites.

When you select any of the folders displayed on this window, AOL opens a new window displaying a list of WWW sites containing related information. Also, if you select the AOL Entertainment Channel – WEB option, the WWW browser is started and the Entertainment page of America Online's Resource directory is displayed.

Clubs & Interests Top Internet Sites

On the Clubs & Interests channel main window—Keyword: `clubs`—you will find a Top Internet Sites button. If you select this button a window similar to the one shown in Figure 13.25 is displayed.

There is a fairly diverse list of WWW sites displayed on this menu, covering topics such as aviation, food, real estate, women, and cultural diversity. If you are looking for something a little different then you may very well find it here.

FIGURE 13.25.

Religion, home builders, pets, and women's interests are all covered on the Clubs & Interests Top Internet Sites window.

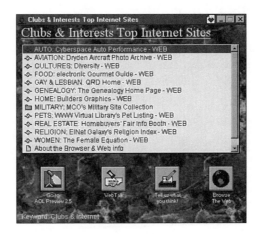

Hot Education Internet Sites

The Hot Education Internet Sites window shown in Figure 13.26 can be reached by clicking on the Top Internet Sites button located on the Education channel main window, Keyword: **Education**.

> To find out more information about education and the World Wide Web, take a look at Chapter 16, "Family Fun and Education."

FIGURE 13.26.

The Hot Education Internet Sites window contains links to many of the most popular education-related WWW pages.

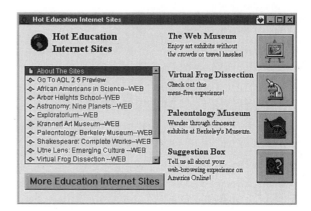

Computing Internet Sites

The Computing Internet Sites window shown in Figure 13.27 can be reached using the Keyword: **Comp Sites,** or alternatively by selecting the Top Internet Sites entry from the COMPUTING FORUMS menu of the Computing channel at Keyword: **Computing.**

The Internet Sites window lists four main categories or computing-related sites. When you select any of the entries a list of related WWW pages is displayed for you to choose from. The categories available include

- ◆ Top sites
- ◆ Graphics sites
- ◆ Computing magazines
- ◆ Hardware and software companies

FIGURE 13.27.

Believe it or not, there are sites on the Internet that relate to computing.

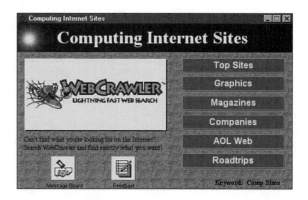

Reference Web

One of the most popular uses of the Internet is for research and study-related activities. To assist you in this area, America Online has compiled a list of the major online databases and reference resources currently available. (See Figure 13.28.)

To access this list, select the Top Internet Sites for Reference icon on the Reference channel main window, Keyword: **Reference**. The star attraction on this list of Internet sites includes the CIA World Fact book, the Internet Public Library, and the American Library of Congress.

FIGURE 13.28.

Visit the Internet Public Library or check out the CIA World Fact Book by clicking on the appropriate icons.

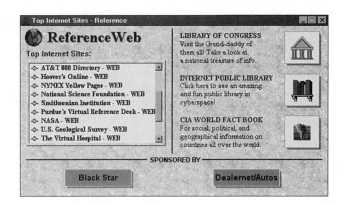

Travel on the Net

Another area of the Internet that is rapidly growing in popularity is travel-related WWW pages. If you select the Travellers! Cruise the world on the Internet icon located at the top of the America Online Travel window—Keyword: **Travel**—a window similar to the one shown in Figure 13.29 is displayed.

FIGURE 13.29.

Travel the world from the comfort of your desktop.

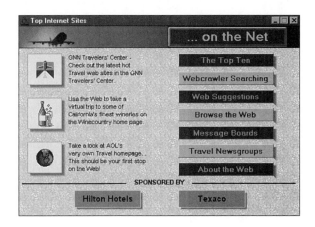

From here, you can visit a number of WWW pages dealing with the subject of travel, and as an added bonus, there is also a link to a list of travel-related newsgroups. Your first port of call on this page should be America Online's travel directory which is a part of the Internet Resource directory. To explore this directory select the world icon in the bottom left corner of Figure 13.29.

The Internet Connection RESOURCES Menu

At the risk of stating the obvious, the Internet Connection window (see Figure 13.30) also contains a number of links to WWW sites. Many of the forums listed in the RESOURCES menu maintain their own private list of pages, while others also house messages boards and software libraries.

FIGURE 13.30.

Many of the forums lists in the RESOURCES menu contain links to WWW sites.

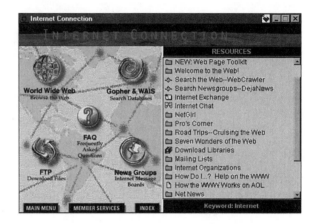

See Chapter 15, "The Best of Both Worlds," for a discussion of the major forums listed on the RESOURCES menu.

Marketplace Internet Sites

If you like to shop, then the World Wide Web should definitely be on your list of places to spend a few dollars. To help you get started, America Online's Marketplace, Keyword: **Marketplace** has compiled a list of some online shopping pages currently available via the World Wide Web. (See Figure 13.31.)

Chapter 17, "Business on the Net," contains additional information about a number of World-Wide-Web–based shopping malls and store fronts.

FIGURE 13.31.

The World Wide Web is rapidly becoming a global shopping mall. To find out more check out the Market-place Internet Sites.

AOL Sports

Click in the Top WEB Sites button at the bottom of the America Online SPORTS window, Keyword: **Sports**, to open the window shown in Figure 13.32.

Despite all the evidence to the contrary, it seems that many computer users are avid sports fans. So much so, in fact, that there are Sports pages popping up all over the World Wide Web covering sports as diverse as skydiving, rugby league football, basketball, the NFL, and athletics.

FIGURE 13.32.

If it's sports you want, then AOL sports has it covered.

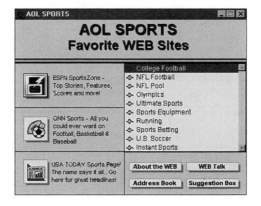

Kids Only Internet Pages

One of the feature services provided by America Online is its Kids Only area, Keyword: **Kids**. To complement this service, they have now added a list of special WWW pages, again for kids only. (See Figure 13.33.)

Chapter 16, "Family Fun and Education," contains a section devoted to America Online's Kids Only WWW pages.

Note

FIGURE 13.33.

America Online is the only major online service to provide special WWW services for kids.

Cool and Unusual Places

Because it seems that just about everyone else on the Internet now publishes their own list of favorite places, why should I be any different? As a result, all the WWW pages and links mentioned in this book are listed in chapter order at my private WWW site located at `http://www.webcom.com/taketwo/sams/nav-int-aol.html`. This is also the site of my Take Two film and television directory, among other things. (Cheap plug.)

As for the other things, in the pages that follow I have compiled a list of cool and unusual places for you to explore. This list is an ideal place to start your own exploration of the Internet and maybe even your own personal list—but more about that later. First the list: `http://www.webcom/com/taketwo/sams/cool.html`.

GNN's Best of the Net

GNN's Best of the Net (see Figure 13.34) was first proposed in 1994 as a way of recognizing expertise in all areas of World Wide Web development. The nominees for this year's awards are currently listed here, alongside the honorees for 1994. This list recognizes not just WWW pages, but also services such as Lycos and even programs like Netscape or NCSA Mosaic that have made an outstanding contribution to the development of the World Wide Web. It can be found at `http://gnn.com/gnn/wic/best.toc.html`.

Note

> If you find a service that you think should be listed here, there are instructions for making a nomination at the bottom of the Best of the Net page.

FIGURE 13.34.

It may not be the Academy Awards, but for netsurfers the Best of the Web is just as important.

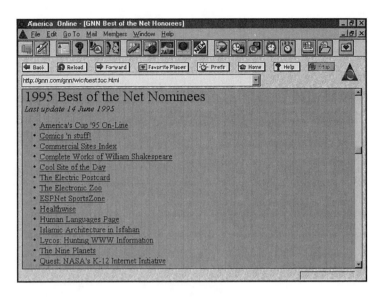

ESPNET SportsZone

If you're into sports or just like to watch, ESPNET SportsZone is the place to be. (See Figure 13.35.) Each day the latest news and information about many popular sports and sports personalities is brought to you live via the World Wide Web. The address is `http://web1.starwave.com/`.

FIGURE 13.35.

The home of Internet sportscasting.

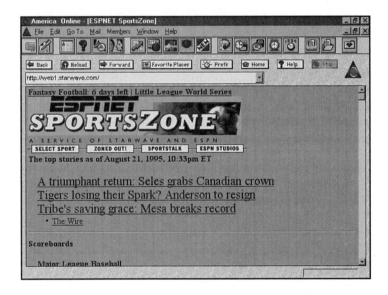

You can either select from the list of sports covered, find out who's zoned out, or catch up on all the latest sports talk. When you're done, drop by the ESPN studios for all the late-breaking excitement.

The Movie Database

Have you ever found yourself in one of those arguments that seem destined to occur over coffee? Frankly, who really cares what character Clint Eastwood played in the first movie he both directed and produced? Nevertheless, it's a debate that will often drag on into the small hours of the morning. To solve this dilemma, what you really need is your handy laptop computer, a cellular modem, and the Internet Movie Database (see Figure 13.36). It can be found at either `http://www.cm.cf.ac.uk/Movies/` or `http://www.msstate.edu/Movies/`.

FIGURE 13.36.

*A WWW interface to the
Internet Movie Database.*

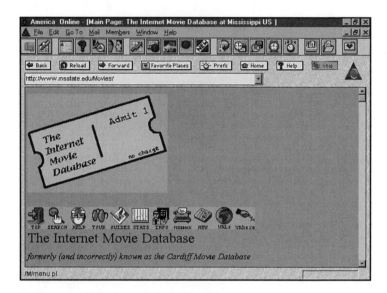

The Internet Movie Database is a classic example of what happens when a group of people with a good idea put their minds to making it happen. Since 1989, a small group of dedicated individuals have spent many thousands of hours creating what is one of the most comprehensive databases of movies, film, and television programs available today. To search this database, select the search option displayed on the home page shown in Figure 13.36. You will be presented with a list of search options that include

- ◆ Actors and actresses
- ◆ Producers, directors, and writers
- ◆ Editors, cinematographers, and costume designers
- ◆ Movie titles, release dates, and running times

Based on these parameters and many others, you can search the database and examine movie plots, cast biographies, and even lists of goofs or crazy credits.

For those of you who are interested in these things, the movie was *Firefox*, made in 1982. Clint Eastwood played Mitchell Gant while both directing and producing the finished product.

Note

The Electronic Zoo

For animal lovers, the Electronic Zoo (see Figure 13.37) offers links to every related WWW page, along with a number of non-WWW sites. The Zoo was created by Dr. Ken Boschert, a vet-erinarian who spends many a late night surfing the Internet. It can be found at `http://netvet.wustl.edu/e-zoo.htm`.

FIGURE 13.37.

Interested in Rabbits? Click on your animal of choice to see a list of related pages.

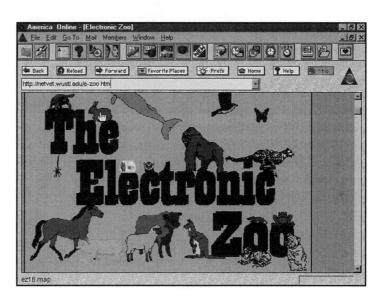

At the zoo, you will find sites categorized by both species and Internet service type. As a result, you can look for information by following a direct path to the animal of your choice or by a less direct, but often equally informative, path via a selection of Gopher, Telnet, mailing lists, electronic publications, and newsgroups.

To accompany this service, Dr. Ken also maintains the NetVet WWW and Gopher server, which contains information relevant to veterinary studies. The http address for NetVet is `http://netvet.wustl.edu/vet.htm`.

The White House

The White House site's biggest claim to fame is not the personal message recorded by the President or the Vice President. (See Figure 13.38.) It is not the guided tour of the White House by the First Family. Nor is it the list of publications and information about the executive branch of the United States government. Instead, it is the recording of Socks (the First Cat), which can be downloaded during the First Family tour. If you don't believe me, take a look for yourself. I won't tell you exactly where it is, but yes, it is in there.

The http address for the White House home page is `http://www.whitehouse.gov/`.

FIGURE 13.38.

Ever wanted to hear a personal message from the President of the United States? Click the President's Welcome Message button.

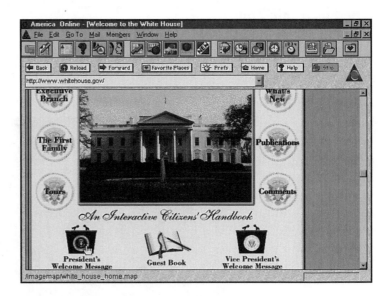

To hear any of the audio clips available on this site, your computer must be fitted with a suitable sound card. For those without a card, there is also a written transcript of each speech.

Useless Pages, or America's Funniest Home Hypermedia

It seems to be a fact of life that the moment you turn a video camera on even the most seemingly normal person, a strange metamorphosis takes place that often results in the most astounding actions. Now it seems this same affliction is starting to appear on the World Wide Web. Give a person the ability to publish their own WWW page, and you often get some strange results.

And like the popular *America's Funniest Home Videos* program, there is now America's Funniest Home Hypermedia page to catalog these pages. (See Figure 13.39.) If you really want to know all there is to know about homonyms, then this is the page for you. This is not to say that many of these otherwise useless pages are not worth paying a visit. Some, in fact, are extremely clever and in the past have resulted in their developers receiving considerable notoriety. This page is located at `http://www.primus.com/staff/paulp/useless.html`.

FIGURE 13.39.

More pages that exist because someone felt like creating them.

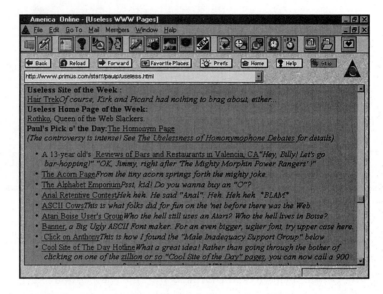

As a challenge, try to locate the HOTTUB page, which continually updates the temperature in Paul Haas's hot tub and refrigerator. (His WWW page efforts resulted in a high paying job, and not at "Hot Tubs R Us.")

Understanding the Internet

To accompany their television special "Understanding the Internet," produced in conjunction with the Discovery Channel, Cochran Interactive Inc. has created this special WWW site (see Figure 13.40) that provides over 200 links to information that new Internet users will find invaluable.

To explore this page point your WWW browser to `http://www.screen.com/start`.

FIGURE 13.40.

If you want to learn more about the Internet, check out this site.

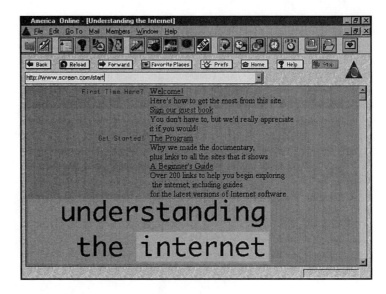

The Macmillan Web Site of the Week

The Macmillan Publishing WWW site at `http://www.mcp.com/` is the home of the Web Site of the Week competition (`http://www.mcp.com/hypermail/website/`). Web publishers are invited to nominate themselves as contestants in this competition. At the end of each week, a new WWW site is selected based on its design, content, and overall originality. (See Figure 13.41.)

> While you're visiting Macmillan, make sure you check out the Sams.net pages at `http://www.mcp.com/samsnet` to catch up with all the latest books in print.

If you have created your own WWW site and would like it to be considered, all you need to do is follow the steps outlined on the competition page. To take a look at the winner for the third week of August 1995, use this http address: `http://www.directnet.com/cybertown/`. (See Figure 13.42.)

FIGURE 13.41.

Nominate your entrant for the Web Site of the Week competition.

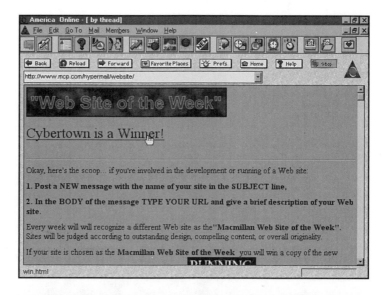

FIGURE 13.42.

Cybertown—site of the week as of August 21.

WebChat

In recent months, an innovation has appeared on the Internet that brings real-time communications like IRC to the World Wide Web. By taking advantage of the capabilities built into many new WWW browsers, it is now possible to use a site such as WebChat as an interactive alternative to IRC. (See Figure 13.43.)

Although they are still very experimental, many of these chat environments are rapidly gaining popularity as more and more people become aware of their existence. WebChat can be found at `http://www.irsociety.com/webchat/webchat.html`.

FIGURE 13.43.

IRC meets the World Wide Web.

To use WebChat, you need a modem capable of at least 9,600bps, with 14,400 or 28,800 offering better performance.

Summary

By now you should have come to the realization that with just a WWW browser you can take advantage of nearly everything the Internet has to offer. You can read newsgroups, download files, and even chat with other people in real time. By providing a single, easy-to use interface, the World Wide Web has done more to give people access to the Internet than any other tool.

So where do you go from here? If you've been look at all the WWW pages and are thinking, "I could do better than that," then the next chapter will interest you. America Online gives every member the ability to create their own private home page, that anyone on the Internet can visit.

In the next chapter, you will learn how to create your home page at AOL and also discover some of the secrets behind writing HTML.

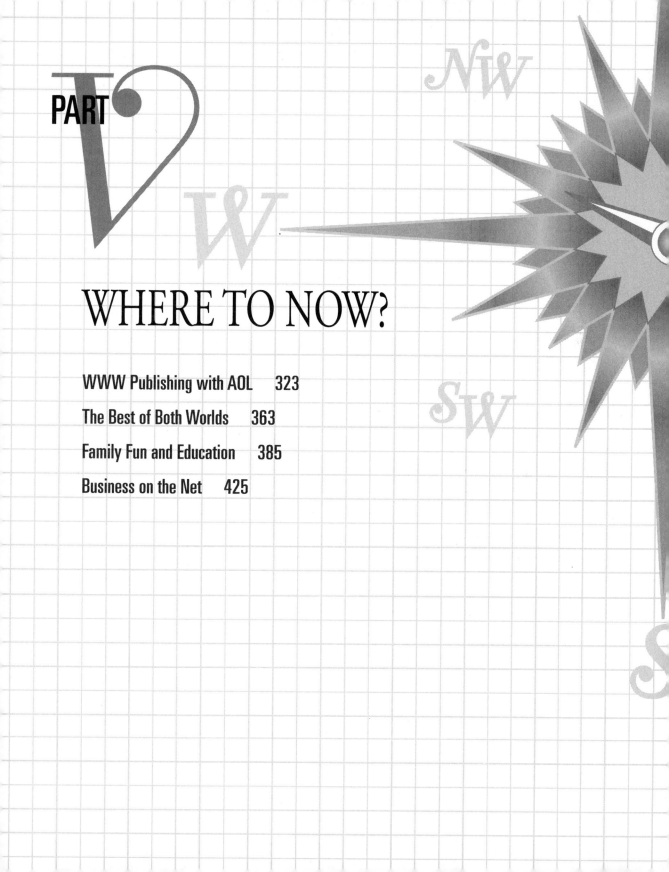

PART

V

WHERE TO NOW?

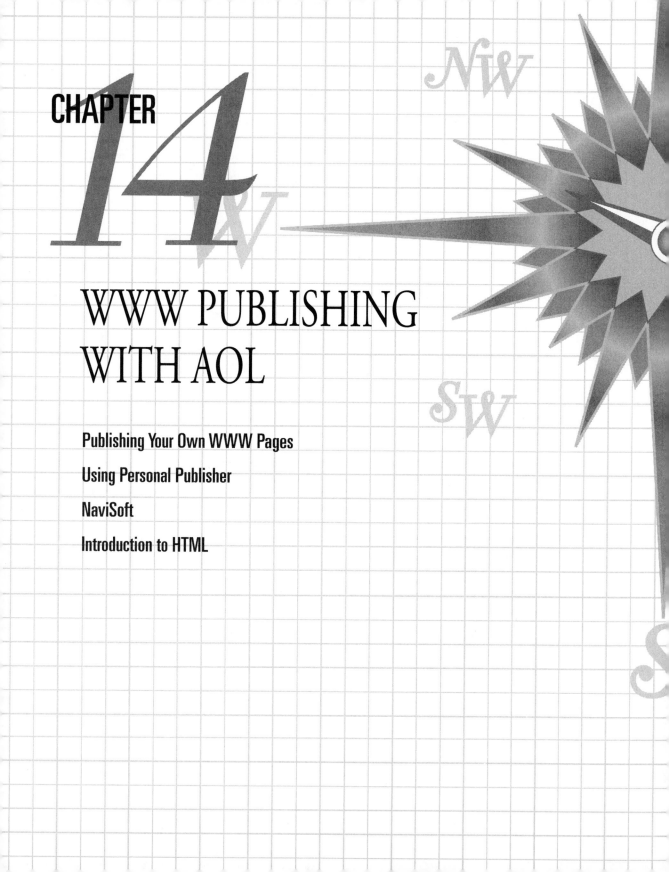

CHAPTER 14

WWW PUBLISHING WITH AOL

Publishing Your Own WWW Pages

Using Personal Publisher

NaviSoft

Introduction to HTML

By far the most impressive capability offered by the World Wide Web, and now America Online, is the ability to publish information in such a way that the entire world can see it.

Throughout history, events like the development of written language, the invention of the first printing press, the telegraph machine, and more recently, radio and television, have all brought with them an increased ability to disseminate information. In each case though, despite the fact that more information was being distributed, the number of people who had access to the transmission end of the system was always limited. There are many reasons for these limitations, but usually the cost of maintaining and operating the required equipment was the main reason.

However, with the rapid expansion of the Internet, and more significantly the World Wide Web, over the last three years, it is now possible for just about anyone to create their own WWW page and publish it for all the world to see. Because the World Wide Web is simply and extension of the Internet, information made available on the World Wide Web can be seen wherever an Internet connection is available.

In this chapter, you will learn about the new services provided by America Online that give each member their very own WWW page, and in addition you will also be given an introduction to HTML—the language used to create World Wide Web pages.

Publishing Your Own WWW Pages

America Online is one of the first major online service providers to make the move into the world of online publishing via the World Wide Web.

As of September 1995, every America Online member using the Windows version of AOL has been given the ability to create their very own home page or pages, and in addition, up to 10MB of hard drive space was set aside at America Online for each account. In this storage area, you can save WWW pages, graphics, multimedia files, or just about anything else you wanted to make available to people.

Each screen name you use can store 2MB of files at America Online. Therefore, because each account can have up to five screen names associated with it, this gives you 10MB of total storage space.

Mac users: Because Personal Publisher requires the use of AOL's built-in WWW browser, the Macintosh version of AOL is currently unable to access this feature. However, it is expected that a new release of AOL will soon be available that provides you with an improved WWW browser and all the features now available in the Windows version.

The Web Page Toolkit

To assist you with your move into the WWW publishing revolution, America Online has created a new service called the Web Page Toolkit. (See Figure 14.1.) To access this area you can either select the Web Page Toolkit option from the Internet Connection RESOURCE menu, or use the Keyword: **HTML**.

FIGURE 14.1.

The Web Page Toolkit.

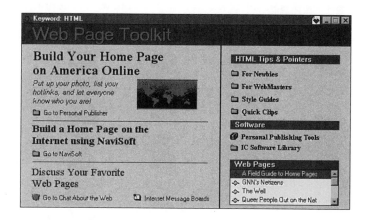

The Web Page Toolkit window is broken into three separate areas: Publishing Services, Online Discussions, and WWW Publishing Information.

Publishing Services

On the left side there are links to the two home page publishing services provided by America Online: Personal Publisher and NaviSoft. (These two links are discussed in greater detail later in this chapter.)

Personal Publisher is the home page publishing service provided free of charge to America Online members. It lets you create your very own WWW home page without ever needing to learn about HTML or WWW design. By following the simple steps outlined by Personal Publisher, in a matter of minutes your home page can be ready for viewing by anyone who has access to the World Wide Web.

Unlike Personal Publisher, NaviSoft is a separate commercial service more suited to business and corporate users who want to set up an online store front or information page. There is a low-priced service available to people who want to set up a more complex home page than would be permitted by Personal Publisher; however, doing so requires you to have some understanding of HTML and takes considerably more time to set up.

Online WWW Discussions

Below the link to NaviSoft and Personal Publisher there are two icons that give you access to an online chat area dealing specifically with the World Wide Web and the Internet Message Boards.

Chat About the Web

If you have never visited an online chat area before, now is definitely the time to do so. The Chat About the Web online area shown in Figure 14.2 is a great place to ask questions about the Internet and exchange tips with other users.

You will be amazed at what you can find during a visit to this area, because there will usually be at least one person online who can help you out with your problems. Also, because online chats are a two-way street, if you know the answer to other users' questions, why not jump in and help them out? Online chats are a good way to make valuable contacts as well, because a little bit of assistance often goes a long way.

FIGURE 14.2.

Chat with other America Online users about the World Wide Web and the Internet.

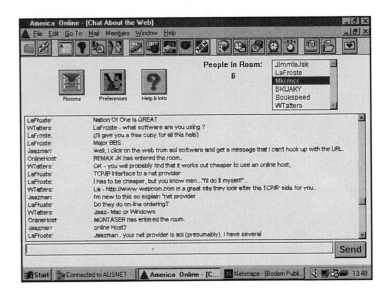

Internet Message Boards

Due to the popularity of the Internet and the number of people who have questions and queries about how it works, America Online has set up a special message board devoted solely to the Internet. (See Figure 14.3.)

FIGURE 14.3.

There are topics on the Internet message boards dealing with all the major issues surrounding the Internet.

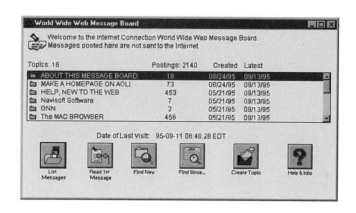

WWW Publishing Information

Down the right side of the Web Page Toolkit window, America Online has collected a number of information sources covering many aspects of WWW page design and the writing of HTML files.

If you want to learn more about home page development, this is the place to come.

HTML Tips and Pointers

The HTML Tips and Pointers section is broken into four main categories, each of which develops your HTML and publishing skills in different ways. These categories are:

◆ For Newbies

◆ For WebMasters

◆ Style Guides

◆ Quick Clips

For Newbies

Although using Personal Publisher doesn't require any knowledge of HTML, if you want to create your own WWW pages, in addition to the Personal Publisher home page, you need to use HTML.

In the For Newbies window shown in Figure 14.4, you find links to three of the best HTML guides currently available on the Internet. (There are also a number of good books on HTML currently available, including *Teach Yourself Web Publishing with HTML in 14 Days*, Premiere Edition by Sams Publishing.)

FIGURE 14.4.

Learn all about HTML on the For Newbies page.

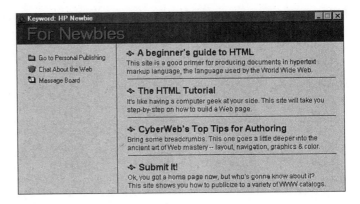

The other link included on the For Newbies window takes you to a special WWW service called Submit It.

Many of the Search Indexes and WWW Directories discussed in the previous chapter allow you to include a link to your own WWW pages as a part of their listings. After all, there is no point in creating a home page if no one is going to visit it. Until recently, however, the biggest problem was locating all of the appropriate application forms so that you could get your information displayed.

But now, Submit It has changed all that by providing the Internet with a single location for submitting applications to all the major WWW search engines and directories. When using Submit It you first complete some general information about your site and select the services that you want to submit your list to, as shown in Figure 14.5. This information includes the name of your site, your name, the site's URL, and personal information such a return e-mail address and postal contact address.

FIGURE 14.5.

Select all the services in which you want your site listed.

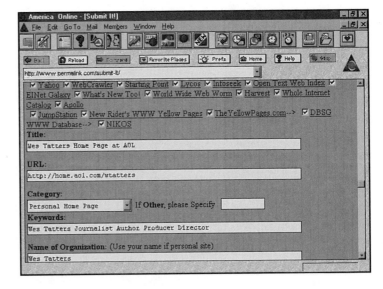

FIGURE 14.6.

Fill in any additional required information and click on the appropriate Submit button to register your home page with a directory or search engine.

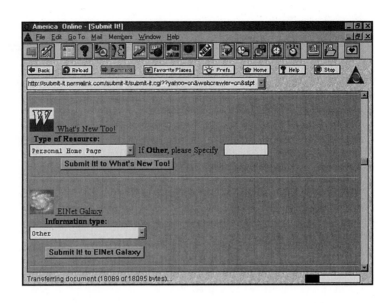

Once you have completed the main form, Submit It generates a new page like the one shown in Figure 14.6. This page lists all the sites you have selected, including any additional information specific sites require. To submit your application to each site, work your way down the page one site at a time, filling out any additional information and then clicking on the appropriate Submit button.

Each site reports back, informing you that your application has been received and describing when you can expect your listing to be included. Once you receive this notice, use the Back button to return to the page shown in Figure 14.6 and proceed to the next site.

For WebMasters

As your skills increase, you will want to take a look at the collection of Experts Only WWW pages and sites listed on the WebMasters windows shown in Figure 14.7. These pages are not for the faint of heart; however, if you are serious about creating a killer Web site, then the discussions and WWW pages listed here will certainly help you along the way.

The Interface Design case study should be of special interest to newer Web Masters because it gives a blow-by-blow description of the steps involved in creating the WWW site for SUN Microsystems, which you can visit at `http://www.sun.com/`. The case study not only discussed the technical aspect of HTML, but also looks at the more complex issues of layout and design that greatly affect the appearance, and often the useability, of a WWW site.

> Creating a good WWW site is not just about writing HTML, it's about developing a set of pages that look good, are easy to use, and provide people with information in a logical and organized manner. A messy WWW site is one that people will not return to.

Tip

FIGURE 14.7.

Find out what it takes to create a killer Web site.

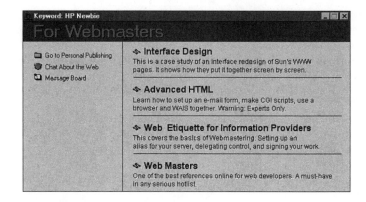

Style Guides

Luckily, there is no need to take a course in graphic design before you can create a good-looking WWW page, although no one said it wouldn't help. Instead, your best bet is to take a look at the excellent collection of WWW pages listed on the Style Guides window shown in Figure 14.8.

FIGURE 14.8.

Visit David Siegel's WWW site, arguably one of the best-looking WWW sites on the Internet.

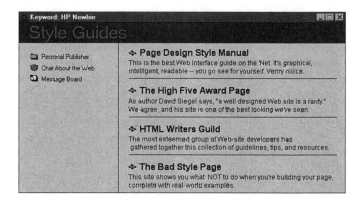

> Because David Siegel's WWW site makes extensive use of HTML 3.0 extensions, to view it in its best light you need to use Netscape 1.2N and the AOL winsock.dll file discussed in Chapter 10, "AOL and Winsock."

Each of the WWW sites listed on this page have been chosen because they examine or present important information about the design of a good WWW page. This includes the Bad Style Page, which provides a collection of real-world examples of the things you definitely should not do on a WWW page, and even lists the sites that have used them—kind of like a "Worst Dressed WWW Pages" listing.

Quick Clips

One of the ways to make your WWW pages look better is to add simple graphical images such as icons, bullets, and lines. To help you out in this area, America Online has created a collection of graphics that you can easily include in any of your WWW pages when using Personal Publisher, NaviSoft, or just about any HTML editor or WWW service provider.

To browse through the list of graphics currently available, click on the Quick Clips item and wait for the WWW browser to display the page shown in Figure 14.9. When this page opens, choose any of the options listed to obtain a list of all the images currently available.

FIGURE 14.9.

Select the type of Quick Clips you want to view.

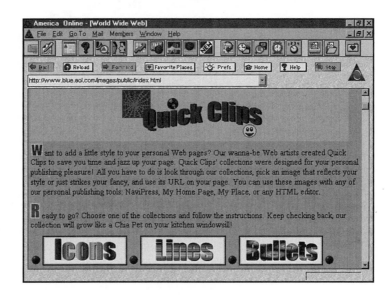

For example, if you click on the Icons item, AOL opens a new WWW page that graphically displays all the icon graphics you can choose from. (See Figure 14.10.) If you find an icon that you would like to use, click on it, and AOL displays a new page listing the URL for the icon you have selected. (See Figure 14.11.) Make a note of this URL, including all punctuation marks, for later use.

> If you plan to make frequent use of the icons, bullets or lines listed in the Quick Clips area, select the Print option from the File menu to create a printout of the page shown in Figure 14.11.
>
> *Tip*

FIGURE 14.10.

America Online provides you with a collection of icons that you can include on your WWW page.

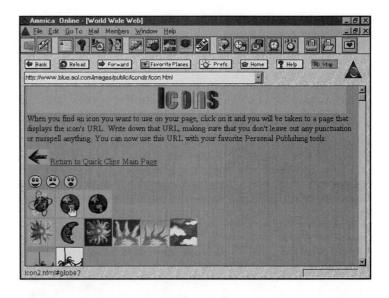

FIGURE 14.11.

The line of text listed below the icon you want to use represents the HTML code you need to use to include the icon on your WWW page.

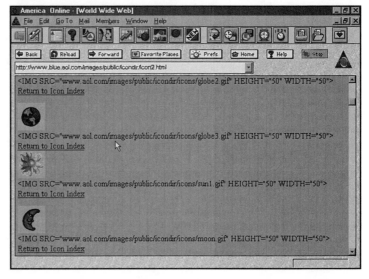

If you are using a modem or connection that operates at less than 14,400 bps, all the Quick Clips pages will take a very long time to load. This is because each page needs to download all the graphics one entry at a time.

Software

When you begin to create your own WWW pages, you will soon discover that, although you can develop very complex pages using just a text editor like Notepad, the task of remembering all the tags and other codes required by HTML can become quite daunting.

To help make life easier for WWW-page developers, a number of HTML editors have been created that greatly reduce the amount of time and effort required to develop WWW pages. America Online has collected a list of some of the more popular HTML editors into the new Personal Publishing Tools software library. (See Figure 14.12.) You can access this software library by clicking on the Personal Publishing Tools icon, located on the Web Page Toolkit window.

FIGURE 14.12.

Select any file you are interested in and click on the Download Now button.

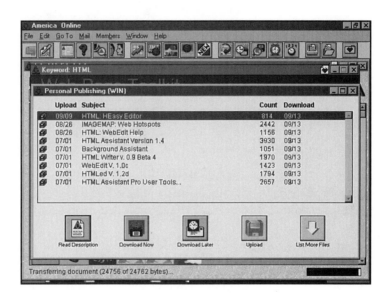

> You can also access the main Internet Connection software library by clicking on the IC Software Library icon.

Web Pages

The final section of the Web Page Tool kit, contains a list of WWW Pages and links to other sites that provide information about home pages on the World Wide Web. Sites such as GNN's Netizens and the WELL Community pages are included in this list. Also, to assist you further in promoting the existence of your WWW page, some of the home page collections listed also allow you to add your site to their list.

Using Personal Publisher

Personal Publisher (see Figure 14.13) is America Online's answer to the WWW page publishing question. Using a simple set of point-and-click WWW pages, you can create an effective WWW page without ever having to write a line of HTML code. To start Personal Publisher, either select the Personal Publisher icon from the Web Page Toolkit window or use the Keyword: **Personal Publisher**.

In this section you discover how to use Personal Publisher to create your own home page. You also learn about all the various features and functions America Online makes available to help you create additional pages and includes special elements such as sound and picture files.

Creating Your Home Page

To set up your home page, click on the Create/Edit My Home Page icon. When you do this, AOL starts a special version of its World Wide Web browser designed specially for Personal Publisher. Then in a few seconds, you will see a page similar to the one shown in Figure 14.14.

Tip

> There are Tutorial and Help buttons spread throughout the Personal Publisher pages. If you click on any of these buttons, AOL displays a new page that provides you with guidance and suggestions for using Personal Publisher.

If you scroll down through this page, you will find that AOL has included all the information entered in your Member Profile. (See Figure 14.15.) Don't be too concerned, however, if there is no information displayed at this stage, because you will be able to update the details in a few moments.

FIGURE 14.14.

Click on the Tutorial button to get online assistance for Personal Publisher.

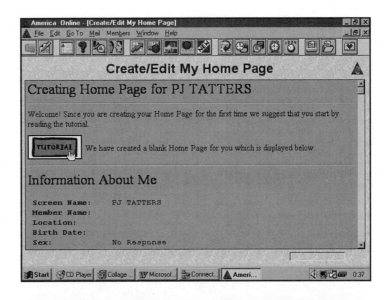

FIGURE 14.15.

Select the Create button to have AOL use this information to create your home page.

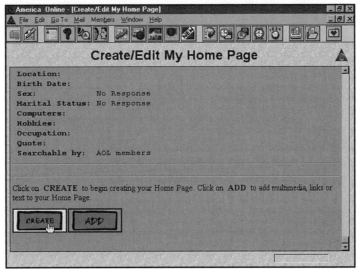

At the bottom of this page you see two buttons displayed: a CREATE button and an ADD button. For now, click on the CREATE button to have Personal Publisher prepare your home page for publication.

FIGURE 14.16.

Personal Publisher automatically updates the information in your Member Profile with the information you enter in these fields.

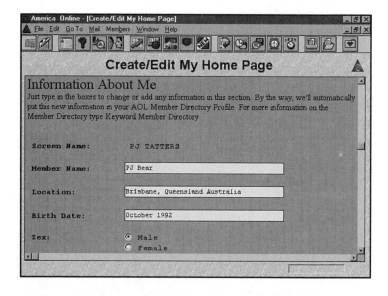

FIGURE 14.17.

Click on the See My Changes button to record your new information.

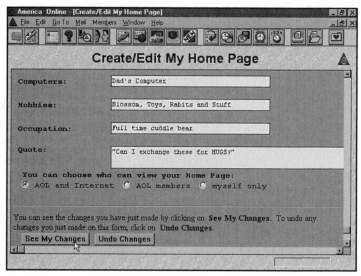

Before Personal Publisher saves your new page, you are given the opportunity to update the information about yourself. Work your way through the fields displayed in Figure 14.16 and Figure 14.17, and then click on the See My Changes button to view your new page as it will appear when anyone views it.

You are also given the opportunity to decide who can view your WWW page. Currently, there are three settings to choose from: AOL and Internet, AOL Members, and myself only. If you select AOL and Internet, your page is made available via the World Wide Web to everyone on the Internet. Alternatively, you can allow only other people using AOL access by selecting the AOL Members option, or hide your page from everyone but yourself.

> Whenever you alter your personal details, the corresponding information in your Member Profile is also updated to reflect the new entry.

When you click on the See My Changes button, Personal Publisher formats your home page as it will appear on the World Wide Web. (See Figure 14.18.) At this stage your home page is now ready for final publication.

FIGURE 14.18.

The Review page displays your home page as it will appear on the World Wide Web.

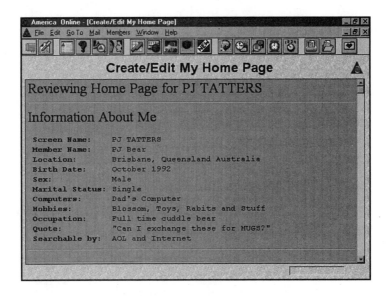

If you scroll down to the bottom of the Review page you find four buttons. These buttons control your next steps.

SAVE CHANGES   To commit your changes and install your new page on the World Wide Web click on the SAVE CHANGES button. When you do, a page is created at `http://home.aol.com/screenname`, where screenname is replaced by your screen name. For example: the PJ TATTERS home page would be addressed as `http://home.aol.com/PJ%20TATTERS`.

> Because you cannot include spaces in a URL, you need to use the special code `%20` to represent the spaces in your screen name.

EDIT	If you want to alter any of the information listed on your home page, click on the EDIT button.
ADD	To add extra information to your home page, such as images, text, and links, click on the ADD button.
CANCEL CHANGES	To revert back to your old home page information, click on the CANCEL CHANGES button. When you do this, any alterations you have made since you last selected the SAVE CHANGES option will be lost.

Adding Links and Images to Your Home Page

Once you have created your basic home page, you can add additional information by selecting the ADD button. When you select this button, Personal Publisher displays a page that provides you with a number of fill-in fields where you select the additional information you want displayed.

> As you add information using the Add page, each entry is added to the end of your home page. As a result you need to plan out how your page will look because there is currently no way to insert information into the middle of your page.

Add Text

The first area displayed on this page is the Add Text field shown in Figure 14.19. If you want to add a line or lines of text to your page, type the information in the field provided.

FIGURE 14.19.

Enter any text you want displayed on your page in the field provided.

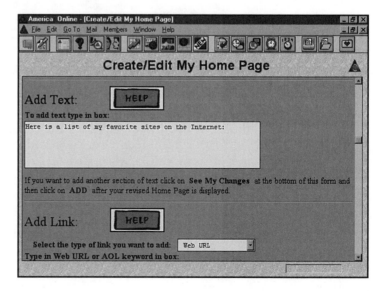

You then need to scroll down to the end of the page and locate the See My Changes button to add this information to your page. Personal Publisher then displays the Review page discussed previously, so you can check that your new entry looks correct.

If you are happy with it, click on the ADD button to add more information to your page or click on the EDIT button to alter the current information. If you do click on the EDIT button at this stage, you are presented with a page similar to the one discussed previously—the page where you edited your personal information. This time, however, in addition to your personal information, a new area will have been added to the bottom of the page where you can Update the text you have just added, or Delete it entirely.

Add Link

To add a hyperlink to your page, locate the Add Link area shown in Figure 14.20. Personal Publisher currently allows you to add a link to either a WWW page or an AOL keyword, although only people using AOL will be able to make use of links to keywords.

FIGURE 14.20.

Select the URL for the page you want to link to and enter a short description for it.

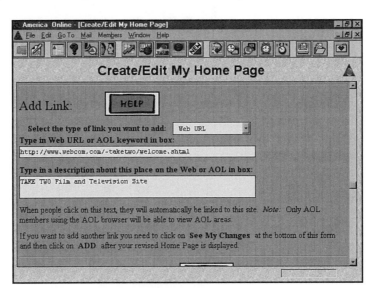

Enter the URL for the page you want to link to in the field provided, type a brief description below it, and then click on the See My Changes button to append the new link to your home page. The description you enter becomes the actual hyperlink when the link is displayed on your home page as shown on the Review page in Figure 14.21.

> After creating your home page, make sure you click on the SAVE CHANGES button before exiting AOL. If you don't, all your changes will be lost.

Tip

FIGURE 14.21.

Remember to click on the SAVE CHANGES button or your new home page will be lost.

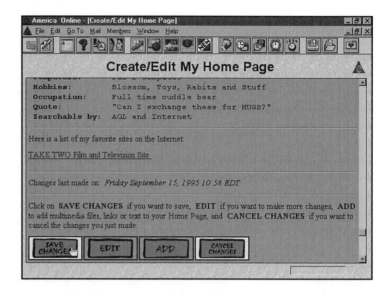

America Online plans to add a new link option to Personal Publisher in the near future that will allow you to define links using inline images.

Upload Multimedia File

Personal Publisher also gives you the ability to include images and sound files as a part of your home page. To do this, you first need to upload a copy of the file you want to use to a special software library called My Place. My Place is a 2MB storage area provided to you—free of charge—by America Online where you can store files, WWW pages, and images you want displayed on the World Wide Web.

You can access My Place either via the My Place icon located on the Personal Publisher window or you can upload a file using the Upload Multimedia File area on the Add page. (See Figure 14.22.)

To upload a file using the Upload Multimedia File option, enter the name that you want to give the file in the field provided, and then click on the Upload Multimedia File button. Personal Publisher then displays a page similar to the one shown in Figure 14.23, which includes a hyperlink using the name of the file you entered on the previous page. Click on this hyperlink to start the upload process.

FIGURE 14.22.

Enter the name you want to give the new file when AOL stores it in your My Place library.

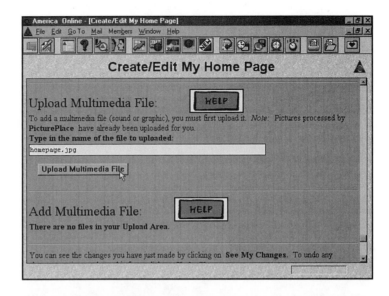

FIGURE 14.23.

Click on the hyperlink provided by Personal Publisher to start the upload process.

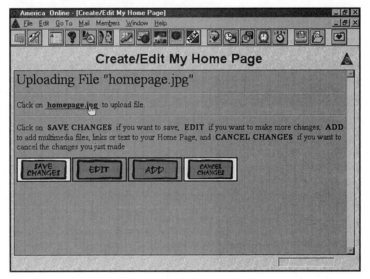

AOL then displays a window where you need to select the file to be uploaded that is stored on your local computer. You can do this either by entering the name and location of the file in the field at the bottom of the window or you can click on the Select File button to open the File dialog box. Then, once you have located the file, click on the Send button to upload it to America Online. (See Figure 14.24.)

FIGURE 14.24.

Select the Send button to upload the file to your My Place library at America Online.

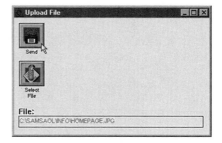

Add Multimedia File

Once you have uploaded the file or files you want to display as a part of your home page, you need to tell Personal Publisher where you want them to be displayed. You do this using the Add Multimedia File area on the Add page. (See Figure 14.25.)

FIGURE 14.25.

Select the Send button to upload the file to the My Place library at America Online.

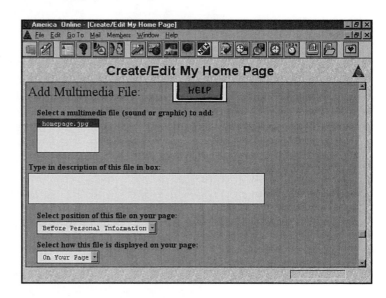

The first box in this area displays a list of all the files currently stored in your personal upload area at My Place. Currently, there is only one file, homepage.jpg, which is the file that was uploaded in the previous section. Below this box there is a description field. If you want a message displayed alongside the file, you can enter one in this box.

You can display either GIF format or JPEG format files on a World Wide Web page, however, JPEG (or JPG) files are rapidly becoming the format of choice because they take up less storage space and as a result can be downloaded in a much shorter amount of time.

The next field is used to tell Personal Publisher where you want the image displayed. It can either be added to the top of your page, above the Personal Information, or to the bottom of the page, like all the other elements discussed previously. In this example, the Before Personal Information option has been chosen.

The last option lets you control how the image is displayed. By default, the image will be displayed as a part of your home page, but alternatively, you can tell Personal Publisher to turn the description into a hyperlink that displays the image when a person clicks on it. For this example the default setting has been used.

Once all the correct information has been added, click on the See My Changes button to update your home page to include this new information. As before, Personal Publisher again displays the contents of your updated page as a part of the Review page. (See Figure 14.26.) From here you can either save the changes, edit them, add another entry, or cancel all the current changes.

FIGURE 14.26.

Personal Publisher lets you include graphics as a part of your WWW home page.

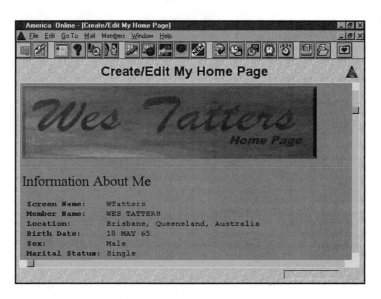

Figure 14.26 also demonstrates another important feature of Personal Publisher. In the examples earlier in this section, the screen name PJ TATTERS was used, but in Figure 14.26 my Wtatters screen name was used. Each of your five possible screen names can be assigned an individual home page. Whenever you sign on using a different screen name, Personal Publisher determines which screen name you are using and allows you to edit the home page with which it is associated.

Home Page Tutorial

To assist you in creating your home page, America Online provides you with a step-by-step guide that walks you through each of the options provided by Personal Publisher. You can visit the tutorial by clicking on the Home Page Tutorial icon located on the Personal Publisher main window.

The tutorial takes you through the steps that Roger and his dog, Byte, need to take to create their home page, shown in Figure 14.27. This page includes examples of text, images, links, and also provides you with a number of handy tips to help you get started.

FIGURE 14.27.

Learn how Roger and Byte created their home page.

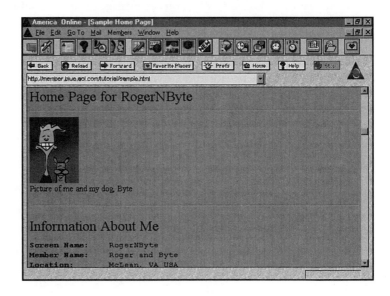

Search Home Pages

If you click on the Search Home Pages button located on the Personal Publisher main window, AOL starts its WWW browser and opens the search page at http://home.aol.com/. (See Figure 14.28.)

This page lets you search though all the pages created by America Online members using a list of keywords that attempt to match the entries in their personal profile.

Note

> Only those pages whose members have selected either the AOL and Internet or AOL Members option are located using this search tool.

FIGURE 14.28.

*You can search America
Online for a list of home
pages created by America
Online members.*

FIGURE 14.28.

*You can search America
Online for a list of home
pages created by America
Online members.*

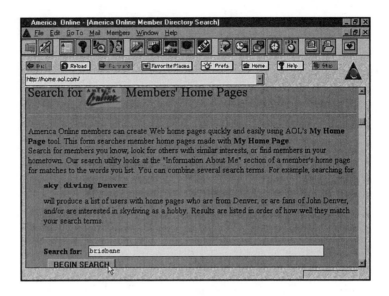

Home Page Graphics

The Home Page Graphics window, shown in Figure 14.29, which can be accessed by clicking
on the Home Page Graphics button on the Personal Publisher window, gives you access to two
very different services:

◆ Picture Place

◆ Downloadable Graphics

FIGURE 14.29.

*The Home Page Graphics
window.*

Picture Place

The Picture Place, shown in Figure 14.30, is operated by one of America Online's greenhouse
companies—an experimental partnership between America Online and selected businesses. This
project was designed to explore new ways of expanding the capabilities offered on America
Online by letting external business offer special services online.

FIGURE 14.30.

Send any two photographs to Picture Place and they will digitize them for you and save them in your My Place upload area.

The service offered by the Picture Place revolves around the digitizing of photographic images. What is more important for America Online members, however, is the special offer being made by the Picture Place. If you post them two photographs or slides, they will digitize the photos for you at no cost and convert them into JPEG files. Once digitized, copies of the two files will be uploaded to your My Place area. You can then include these images as a part of your home page.

> Digitizing is the process of converting an image such as a photograph or slide into a digital file that can be displayed on a computer.

Downloadable Graphics

To help you spice up your home page, America Online has collected a diverse group of graphics images that you can download by selecting the Graphics Available for use in your Home Page icon.

If you want to incorporate any of the files in this area as a part of your home page, you first need to download them to your computer and then upload them to My Place using either the Upload Multimedia File option or My Place itself.

> If you want files to appear in the list of available images when using Personal Publisher, you need to upload your files to the \Private subdirectory of your My Place area.

My Place

When you click on the My Place menu item listed on the Personal Publisher page, AOL opens the window shown in Figure 14.31. This window contains two buttons. Clicking on the top button causes AOL to display a list of Frequently Ask Questions about My Place, and clicking on the bottom icon opens My Place itself.

Working with My Place is basically identical to using the FTP client program discussed in Chapter 9, "File Transfer Protocol (FTP)." The only major difference that you will notice is the addition of three new buttons. (See Figure 14.32.) To help you understand the meaning of these new buttons, Table 14.1. lists each of the buttons on the My Place screen and explains its use.

FIGURE 14.31.

Select the Go To My Place icon to manage the files in your online storage area.

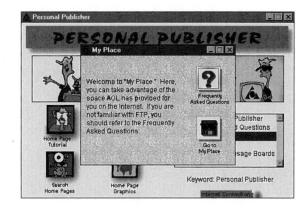

FIGURE 14.32.

The My Place window is basically the same as the FTP client discussed in Chapter 9.

Table 14.1. Control button on the My Place window.

Icon	Description
Open	Click on this button to view the currently selected file. If a directory or link is selected, a new window is launched to display its contents.
Download	Retrieves a copy of the selected file and stores it on your local hard drive.
Utilities	When you select this button, a small window opens that allows you to either delete or rename the currently selected file or directory.

continues

Table 14.1. continued

Icon	Description
Upload	To upload a file to My Place click on this icon. When you do, a window opens asking you to select a name for the file you want to upload. After you enter this name, the same upload window shown previously in Figure 14.24 is displayed to let you upload the file.
Create	If you select this button, a window is displayed so that you can create a new directory in your My Place storage area.
Help	Click on this button to display help information.
More	This button is only active if there are more entries in a directory than AOL can handle in a single download. Click on the More button to retrieve more entries for the current directory.

Advanced Issues

As well as storing images and audio files, My Place can also be used for the storage of WWW pages. Therefore, if you create a WWW page and save it in your My Place directory, you can then address this page like any other hypertext link.

For example: If you upload a page called `mypage.html` to your My Place area, you can then open the page using AOL's WWW browser by using the following URL: `http://users.aol.com/wtatters/mypage.html`.

> See the *Introduction to HTML* topic at the end of this chapter for a general discussion of HTML basics.

In addition, you can also add a link to your WWW page that allows people to download copies of files stored in your My Place directory. To do this use the URL: `ftp://users.aol.com/wtatters/filename.exe`, where filename.exe is replaced by the name of the file you want people to download. People can also access your My Page area using an FTP client by using the same address.

NaviSoft

Although Personal Publisher allows you to create reasonably complex WWW pages, it lacks a number of features that most people expect to find when visiting a WWW site. This includes features such as forms and searchable site indexes.

When you get to this level of Web page development, it is probably about time to consider using a full WWW publishing service. To meet this need in the market, America Online, has been developing a dedicated WWW publishing system called NaviService, which is now available via the World Wide Web.

Although this service is not a part of the standard America Online service, you can find out more information about access NaviService, by selecting the NaviSoft option in the Web Page Toolkit window. When you do this AOL displays the window shown in Figure 14.33.

FIGURE 14.33.

NaviSoft is an America Online company that provides commercial WWW publishing systems.

NaviService Online WWW Publishing

NaviService is a relatively late entrant into the online publishing game, being launched as recently as August 14, 1995. But the entirely new level of online support for World Wide Web publishing that it brings with it will rapidly make it a strong contender for anyone considering a WWW site or just a WWW home page. To find out more information about this service use the following URL: `http://www.navisoft.com/` or click on the NaviSoft Home Page icon shown in Figure 14.33.

What makes this service so unique is the way it integrates completely the online publishing process from page design to site maintenance as well as access to your WWW host site. All these activities are managed by a single program called NaviPress (See Figure 14.34).

> You can download a demonstration copy of NaviPress by selecting the Download NaviPress icon shown in Figure 14.33.

FIGURE 14.34.

NaviPress allows you to create WWW pages, maintain your WWW site, and communicate with its host server.

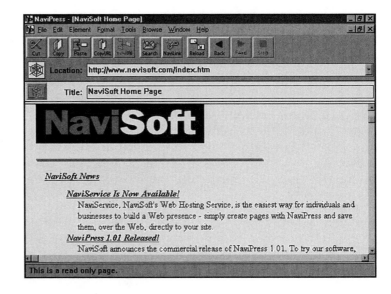

NaviPress Client Software

Instead of using a WWW browser or FTP client to communicate with the NaviService host computer, you use a dedicated client program called NaviPress. This program lets you design your WWW pages using a WYSIWYG-style interface and then, when you are satisfied with them, by simply selecting the Save option from its File menu you can download the pages to the NaviService host and install them as apart of your WWW site.

Like most of the WWW page designers now available, NaviPress takes the drudgery out of HTML page design by wrapping the hieroglyphics usually associated with a WWW page in an elegant graphical interface that displays each page as it will appear on the World Wide Web. All the HTML TAGs are replaced with a representation of their online visual appearance which takes much of the guess work out of page design.

Rates and Charges

The pricing structure for NaviService access is similar to that of most other online service providers, although initial connection fees are noticeably higher for personal users. But, on the plus side, you are given a far larger amount of hard drive space to play with and a copy of the NaviPress software. Table 14.2 lists the details of the NaviService pricing structure.

Table 14.2. NaviService pricing structure as of August 1995.

Fee Description	Home Page	Domain	Commercial
One-time setup fee	$99.00	$199.00	$199.00
Monthly fee	$14.95	$99.00	$199.00
Mo. disk sp. allowance	20MB	50MB	100MB

Fee Description	Home Page	Domain	Commercial
Max hits per day	1000	5000	10,000
Copy of NaviPress Incl.	Yes	Yes	Yes
Personal Domain Name	No	Yes	Yes

See Chapter 17, "Business on the Net," for information about other WWW service providers such as Web Communications.

Introduction to HTML

Whether you choose to use NaviPress, an alternative WWW Service provider, or just your My Place area at America Online, you will eventually need to learn a least a little bit about HTML, the language used to write WWW pages.

In addition to the list of HTML tutorials listed on the Web Page Toolkit window, there are a number of other sources of information about HTML including full tutorials and documents discussing all manner of design strategies. Many of these documents have been collated by the W3 Consortium and placed on the page shown in Figure 14.35, whose http address is `http://www.w3.org/hypertext/WWW/MarkUp/MarkUp.html`.

FIGURE 14.35.
The W3 HTML page.

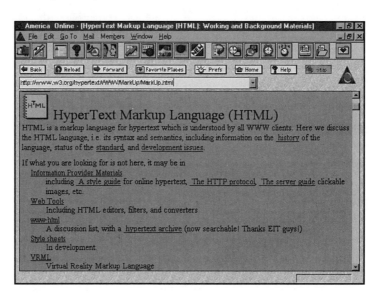

You should also take a look at the following pages as well, each of which provide additional information about using HTML to create functional and sophisticated WWW pages:

`http://www.ncsa.uiuc.edu/demoweb/html-primer.html`

`http://www.webcom.com/~webcom/html/`

`http://www.netscape.com/assist/net_sites/index.html`

`http://union.ncsa.uiuc.edu:80/HyperNews/get/www/html/guides.html`

`http://www.mindspring.com/guild/index.html`

Although creating WWW pages is not an overly complex task, it is a subject best left to the many online documents that do it the justice the subject deserves. One of the reasons for this is that the entire HTML specification is currently in a state of flux.

The HTML design standard has been through two major releases in its relatively short life, and is at the moment about to undergo another revision for the release of HTML 3.0. To keep track of all the latest changes and updates, you should keep a close watch on the pages maintained by the W3 Consortium, which is administering the current development and design strategies that will be implemented in version 3.

Hello World by HTML

Having said that, let's take a brief look at the contents of an HTML file and look at how you go about the development of a simple "Hello World" home page.

An HTML document is basically a simple ASCII text file with a number of special instructions included that tell the WWW client how it should display the page. I created a simple WWW page, shown in Figure 14.36, by entering the HTML information into a text file using the Windows Notepad. When this page is displayed using an HTML viewer or WWW Browser like GNNWorks, this information creates the page shown in Figure 14.37.

There are obviously many other commands available in HTML, but this example should at least take you some of the way toward the creation of your first page of HTML code.

Note

Not all the commands provided by HTML 3.0 are currently supported by all browsers. GNNWorks and AOL's WWW browser, for example, do not recognize heading alignment commands. As a result, where possible, you should test each page you develop on a number of different browsers to make sure that everything looks correct.

FIGURE 13.36.

You can create HTML pages using the Windows Notepad.

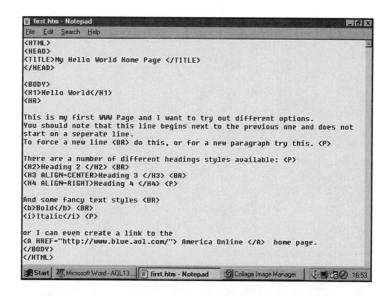

FIGURE 13.37.

Using GNNWorks you can display the page using the Open Local File option in its File menu.

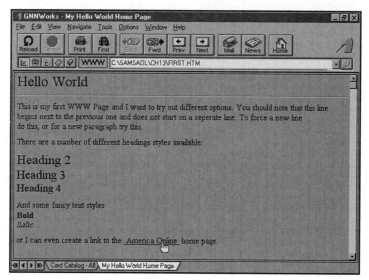

Building Blocks

To add an HTML command or *element* to an ASCII text file, enclose the element between a less than sign (<)and a greater than sign (>). When a WWW browser encounters a word contained within these symbols, it knows that it needs to interpret the command and perform some sort of action.

In Figure 13.36 you should be able to identify a number of such elements, including

`<HEAD>`

`<H2>`

`</BODY>`

Each of these elements tells the browser how it should format the text contained in the file or provide the information required to create hotlinks and display inline graphics. The best way to think of elements is like a switch. An element like `<H1>` tells the browser to turn on the Heading 1 print style for any text that occurs after it in the document. Until the text style is changed or Heading 1 is turned off by issuing a `</H1>` command, the text will be printed in large bold letters. The slash (/) after the < symbol acts as an off switch for the element command that follows it.

Let's go through this line by line:

`<HTML>`

The `<HTML>` element tells the browser where the start of the HTML information is. Although many browsers automatically assume that the start of the document is the start of the HTML information, you should always include a `<HTML>` element.

> If you want to add descriptive notes to a WWW page, place them before the `<HTML>` element so they won't be displayed by WWW browsers.

`<HEAD>`

At the top of every HTML document, you should always create a Heading section so that the browser knows some basic information about the page.

`<TITLE>My Hello World Home Page </TITLE>`

The Title element is not actually displayed on the page itself, but instead in the Document URL field mentioned in the previous chapter. If you have this field turned on, the words My Hello World Home Page will be shown.

`</HEAD>`

Use this element to close the Heading section of your WWW page.

> Although it is possible to insert displayable text into the Heading section, it is not technically correct to do so. You should only include information in the Heading section to describe the contents of the page.

```
<BODY>
```

All the text that is to be displayed on your WWW page should be included in the Body section. This element indicates the start of the body of your page.

```
<H1>Hello World</H1>
```

This is the first piece of actual text that is to be displayed on the WWW page. By placing it inside the `<H1>` `</H1>` element set, the WWW browser will display "Hello World" using the Heading 1 text format.

```
<HR>
```

The `<HR>` (horizontal rule) element is a graphical element that tells the WWW browser to place a line across the screen. (No `</HR>` is needed for this type of element.)

Any text that is typed into the document is displayed on the WWW page in normal text format unless any special formatting elements are active. You should also note that the WWW browser takes no notice of the text layout you have entered. It ignores any carriage returns, line feeds, or new lines you place in the text.

To force a new line to be inserted into the WWW page, place a `<BR>` element in the text. All the text appearing after this element is placed on a new line. Alternatively, you can use a `<P>` element to force a new paragraph, which is effectively a double new line element.

> In HTML 3.0, the paragraph option may support a `</P>` element. This allows you to define each paragraph as a separate block of text.

```
<H2>Heading 2 </H2>
```

There are six different heading type styles, which represent different size text formats. As the heading number increases, the size of the text decreases, with `<H5>` being approximately the same size as normal text and `<H6>` slightly smaller.

```
<H3 ALIGN=CENTER>Heading 3 </H3>
```

```
<H4 ALIGN=RIGHT>Heading 4 </H4>
```

By including the ALIGN command as a part of the Heading element, you can instruct the WWW browser to center or right justify the text contained within the element boundaries—that is, before the `</` element. For consistency's sake, there is also an ALIGN=LEFT command. However, this is rarely, if ever used, because it is the default option.

> The ALIGN command is a part of the HTML 3.0 specification, and as such, not all browsers currently support it for all elements.

```
<b>Bold</b>
```

```
<i>Italic</i>
```

There are also a number of style elements that allow you to alter the way text is displayed. At this stage, though, this feature is very much WWW browser-specific, especially if you use some of the less well-documented styles. Where possible, stick to bold and italic for the moment, at least until the HTML 3.0 specification is adopted by all WWW browsers.

> There is also an underline element (`<U>`), which has fallen into disuse due to the fact that so many people set their browsers to display all hotlinks with an underline. As a result, you should avoid using this element whenever possible.

```
<A HREF="http://www.blue.aol.com/"> America Online </A>
```

This is by far the most complex element on the whole page. It is used to define a hotlink to the America Online home page at `www.blue.aol.com`. The `<A ... >` element tells a WWW browser that the text between it and the `</A>` element should be marked as a hotlink. In this case, the words "America Online" becomes the hotlink.

The information contained inside the `<A ... >` element itself is used to indicate the action that will occur when this hotlink is selected. The `HREF="http://www.blue.aol.com/"` following the `<A` is the physical declaration of the location of America Online's home page. HREF can point to either an absolute address like this one or a relative address such as `HREF="index.html"`. It can also be used to point to a location within the current page using `HREF="#someplace"`, where `someplace` was defined by using

```
<A NAME="someplace"> </A>
```

> To find out more about creating links, check out the excellent documentation at `http://www.webcom.com`.

```
</BODY>
```

At the end of the Body section you need to remember to place a Close element. In most cases the browser assumes you have finished a page if you forget to include a `</BODY>` element at the very end of the document, but you should get used to including it, because in the future there may be other elements that require its existence.

```
</HTML>
```

Finally, close the HTML section by issuing an `</HTML>` command.

HTML Editors

As you become more familiar with the use of HTML, you will probably want to replace your text editor with a dedicated HTML editor. These programs provide you with a lot of special features that are designed specially for the creation of WWW pages.

There are currently about 15 different HTML editors available from various Internet sites, each of which offers slightly different capabilities. To give you some idea of the types of editors available, the following pages include short descriptions of the major contenders. For each site, you will find an FTP location where you can download a copy of the program and a home page address that contains additional information about it.

If you don't find an editor in this collection that suits your needs, there are a number of places on the World Wide Web that discuss the types of HTML editors available. By far, the most comprehensive list is maintained by Yahoo. To access this list, use the following http address: `http://www.yahoo.com/Computers/World_Wide_Web/HTML_Editors/MS_Windows/`.

Live Markup

FTP site: `ftp.mediatec.com/pub/mediatech/`

Home page: `http://www.digimark.net/mediatech/`

Live Markup (Figure 14.38) is one of the first of the new wave of HTML editors that bring true *what you see is what you get (WYSIWYG)* editing to the HTML world.

FIGURE 14.38.

Live Markup allows you to edit your page in HTML instead of text.

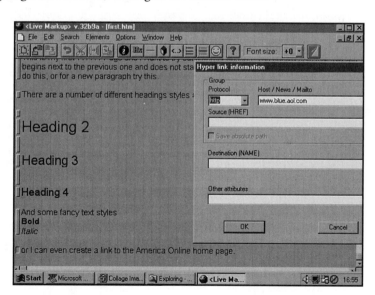

In Live Markup, you edit your HTML document in an environment that closely approximates the actual appearance of your finished document. By doing this, most of the HTML commands are hidden away, allowing you to get on with the job of designing WWW pages instead of worrying about whether you have used the correct element.

This approach also removes the need for switching back and forth between your editor and a WWW browser to check how your changes look. With Live Markup, you see the changes you make as they happen. On the downside, you will need at least a 486DX66 computer to cope with the amount of work the computer needs to do to maintain this environment, and 16MB of memory won't hurt either, although 8MB is the recommended minimum.

If you have the computer power and are serious about developing in HTML, this is one editor that you definitely need to check out. Included in the program is full support for inline graphics and all the new HTML 3.0 features, plus many of the special Netscape 1.2 enhancements, all of which are displayed on screen as you create them.

There are currently two versions of Live Markup available. The first is released as shareware, while the more powerful Pro version is available only as a commercial product. Depending on your needs, you can choose to use either version by visiting the Live Markup home page, which contains downloadable copies of the standard version and ordering information and comparison tables for the Pro edition.

Note

> In the words of one HTML editor developer, "HTML 3.0 is currently a moving target." As a result, this editor is still in a constant state of development. For this reason, the developers of Live Markup are offering special rates to new purchasers of the Pro version, which includes free upgrades for the remainder of 1995.

HoTMetaL

FTP site: `ftp://ftp.ncsa.uiuc.edu/Web/html/hotmetal/Windows`

Home page: `http://www.sq.com/products/hotmetal/hmp-org.htm`

HoTMetaL (Figure 13.39) is probably the most popular HTML editor currently available. It offers a powerful editing environment that represents each element as a tag. This allows for easy recognition of the element's purpose and correct placement. In addition, there is also a WYSIWYG viewing option, which approximates the appearance of your finished page, although it is not quite as accurate as Live Markup.

By far, the most popular feature of this program is its extensive error checking and document validation routines. Whenever you save a WWW page using HoTMetaL, it is first checked to ensure that the document complies with the HTML specification. If an element is out of place or has been incorrectly used, you will be given a message that tells you what needs to be fixed.

This program comes in a commercial version and a somewhat less-featured freeware version, but unfortunately the freeware version is incompatible with many of the new HTML 3.0 features. As a result, if you plan to do any serious work with HoTMetaL, you will need to purchase the commercial version. Ordering information and access to the downloadable version can all be found on the HoTMetaL home page.

FIGURE 13.39.

HoTMetaL represents elements as easily recognizable tags.

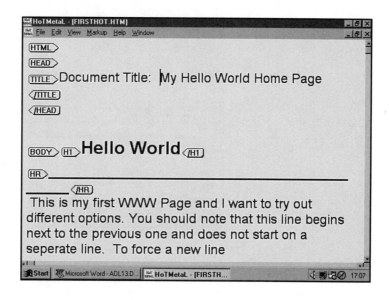

HTML Assistant

FTP site: `ftp://ftp.cs.dal.ca/htmlasst`

Home page: `ftp://ftp.cs.dal.ca/htmlasst/lernhtml.htm`

HTML Assistant can best be thought of as a text editor that helps you create WWW pages; hence the name. For this reason, you will need to have a fairly good knowledge of HTML design methods to take full advantage of this program.

There are no fancy WYSIWYG displays or error checking. Instead, you get a solid text editor that allows you to insert HTML commands with a click of a button on the toolbar. Just about every possible HTML command has a button assigned to it or a corresponding menu option. (See Figure 14.40.) This allows you to quickly add HTML elements to your WWW page without having to remember how each one is written.

Although the WYSIWYG style of WWW page design is gaining popularity, many people find that the straightforward, click-and-go approach of HTML Assistant can get their pages up and running just as fast, if not faster. What's more, the freeware version is full featured, with all the major commands already supported. There is also a commercial version with a number of additional features, including wizards that automate much of the creation process and special filters that can strip HTML commands out of documents.

FIGURE 14.40.

The toolbar gives you access to all the major HTML commands.

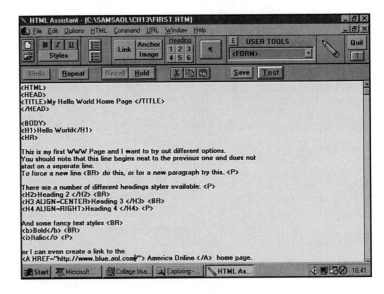

Note

The URL for the HTML Assistant home page is slightly different from those you have seen to date. Instead of starting with `http://`, it beings with `ftp://`. This home page is an example of an HTML document stored on an anonymous FTP server instead of a WWW server. Spry Mosaic displays the page correctly only if you use `ftp://`.

WebEdit

Home page: `http://wwwnt.thegroup.net/webedit/webedit.htm`

Like HTML Assistant, WebEdit (Figure 14.41) is a text-based HTML editor. Where it differs is how it helps you with the creation of your WWW page.

FIGURE 14.41.

The WebEdit URL builder guides you through the steps required to form a valid URL.

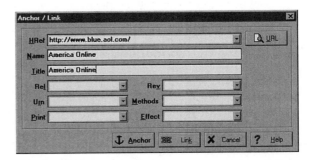

When you select any of the options on its toolbar, a dialog box opens to guide you though the steps needed to complete the information an element requires. This is especially valuable when you're designing complex forms and pages with many links. There is also a special feature that allows you to define your own commonly used tags so you can recall them for later use. For example, if you always place a `mailto:` link at the bottom of your pages so people can send you e-mail, you can easily add a copy to each page by placing this information in a tag.

Unlike all the editors mentioned previously, there is no freeware version of this program. Instead, the authors have released it as shareware. If you choose to continue using WebEdit after the 30-day trial period, you will need to pay a registration fee to the program's developers.

Internet Assistant for Word 6.0

Home page: `http://www.microsoft.com/pages/deskapps/word/ia/default.htm`

You may recall from Chapter 9 that the file downloaded in the FTP tutorial was an add-on module for Microsoft Word called Internet Assistant. (See Figure 14.42.)

Internet Assistant turns Word 6.0 into a WYSIWYG HTML editor. Once you install Internet Assistant on your computer, you can open an HTML document in much the same manner as a regular Word document, but instead of displaying the word processing editing tools, Word displays a special set of HTML editing tools. Using these tools, you can design WWW pages that include all the different heading and text styles and even URL links or inline graphics.

Then, when you have created your home page masterpiece, you can also use Internet Assistant as a fully featured WWW browser that even takes advantage of the Winsock utility discussed in Chapter 10, "AOL and Winsock."

FIGURE 14.42.

Edit WWW pages and browse the Internet as well.

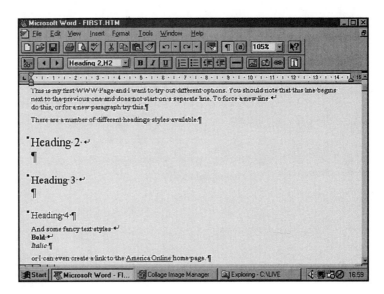

You must already have Microsoft Word version 6.0a running on your computer before you can install Internet Assistant. If, on the other hand, you have Word 7.0 for Windows 95, you need to download a separate version of Internet Assistant that is Windows 95 compatible. For more information about the Windows 95 version, point your WWW browser to http://www.microsoft.com/.

Summary

By giving every member their own home page, America Online has become the first online service provider to totally embrace the concept of integration with the Internet in the fullest sense of the word.

And now, with the completion of this chapter, you have seen all the Internet tools and services currently provided by America Online. At this stage you should now be able to work with all the tools currently available and begin your own exploration of the Internet.

To guide you through this new phase of your life on the Internet, the next section of this book, "Where to Now?" contains information that can act both as a starting point for your explorations and as a resource tool.

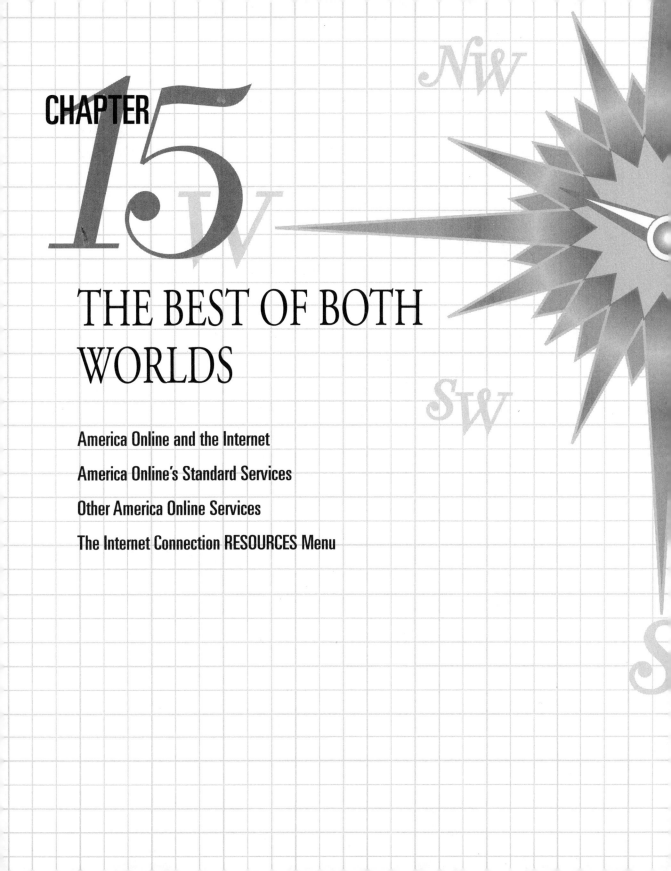

CHAPTER 15

THE BEST OF BOTH WORLDS

America Online and the Internet

America Online's Standard Services

Other America Online Services

The Internet Connection RESOURCES Menu

With the integration of so many Internet services into America Online, its users now have the best of both worlds: the flexibility and simplicity of AOL and the expanded resources offered by the Internet. But how do these new services compare with those already available on America Online, and more importantly, why would anyone want to use them instead of America Online's existing services?

Because answering this question in any definitive way is an impossible task, this chapter looks at how the services offered by the Internet compare and contrast with the better-known America Online services. Once you have an understanding of the differences and similarities inherent in these services, you will be in a better position to answer this question for yourself.

This chapter looks at the Internet services that complement America Online's message boards, and also at some of the more dedicated tools, by discussing the following topics:

- ◆ Message boards and newsgroups
- ◆ FTP and software libraries
- ◆ Conferences and IRC
- ◆ The World Wide Web and AOL
- ◆ The Electronic Mall and Internet shopping
- ◆ The Internet Connection RESOURCES Menu

America Online and the Internet

Before I dive in and look at specific America Online services, let's take a look at why people would choose to use AOL for their connection to the Internet as opposed to using a dedicated *Internet Service Provider* (ISP).

Despite a number of recent advances in Internet software from companies like Microsoft, the prospect of getting connected to the Internet is a daunting one for many users. Even with the preconfigured software and install disks that are now available, many people are still reluctant to make the move to the Internet.

At the same time, there are many people who would like access to the Internet, but who are simply not willing to fight their way through a host of different programs and manuals just to get their system up and running.

One Stop Connectivity

For all these people and many others, the simplicity of installing AOL and having instant access to the Internet is a dream come true. No more fighting with IP addresses and domain name servers and no more "Which program do I need to run to read e-mail?" questions. Instead, you get an easy-to-use program that gives you access to e-mail, the World Wide Web, Gopher, and more.

In addition, by downloading one extra file to your computer—winsock.dll—you also gain access to all those Internet programs people are talking about today. These include programs such as Netscape, IRC, Telnet, and even experimental tools like IPhone—the Internet's answer to long distance phone charges.

As a result, AOL is the ideal 'soft' option for new Internet users. It gives people the freedom to explore the Internet, while at the same time protecting them from many of the pitfalls and hitches that so often plague a new user's first encounter with TCP/IP and the Internet.

Of these difficulties, by far the most common problems relate to installation problems. There are IP addresses, domain names, and MTU settings that need to be configured, and in a number of cases, connection scripts that need to be written, before a new user ever makes it onto the Internet using an ISP. On the other hand, with AOL all you need to do is sign on in the usual way and you're there.

Affordability

Although America Online may not offer the cheapest Internet connection around, it certainly does offer users an Internet service that gives them value for their money. This is especially the case when you consider the level of support and value-added resources it offers.

Unfortunately, the level of support currently available to people using the Internet via an ISP is for the most part, less than they would expect or, in many cases, hope for. This tends to be especially so for those services offering cheap access to the Internet. If you are comfortable with getting your hands dirty crawling around inside your computer, then one of these cheaper connection options may be just right for you. However, if like many new users you want to click on a big friendly button that says "GO", then a service like America Online is what you need.

That said, like any online service, how you get the best benefit out of a service really depends on your particular circumstances. However, if you find yourself spending more and more time on the Internet and less using America Online's own services, then you may need to consider a dedicated TCP/IP connection such as AOL's new GNN MegaWeb TCP/IP service.

Online Support

One of the biggest difficulties many people face when dealing with the Internet—and the issue of getting connected via an ISP—is the problem of finding anyone who is willing to help you out. While some of the larger Internet Service Providers are starting to introduce improved customer support services, many of the smaller operators tend to take the attitude of "Here is your user ID, now you're on your own."

America Online cuts through all these problems by offering its members a toll free customer service number, and an online chat area where people are only to happy to answer even your most difficult questions. To visit the online chat area use the Keyword: **CSLIVE**.

Enhanced Services

For many home users, there is another very attractive reason for using the combined service America Online offers. Although the Internet is growing at a rapid pace, and new features and capabilities are being introduced on a regular basis, there are services offered by America Online that don't have an Internet equal as yet.

Of these—by far the most important for many families—are the parental control options, which, while still giving America Online's younger users access to the Internet, can at the same time protect them from many of the more sensitive subject areas.

Each of the other main areas of America Online also provides a collection of unique features that sets them apart from their Internet counterparts. In the next section of this chapter you will learn more about how these services compare.

America Online's Standard Services

Unlike the Internet, which is made up of many varied services, America Online on the whole revolves around 14 main menus, or *channels*. In some ways this makes it difficult to compare Internet and America Online services directly. What you need to do is look at the various components that make up an America Online channel and contrast them with their correlating Internet services.

At the same time, it is the very nature of America Online that highlights one of the many differences between it and the Internet. Although there are many different topic areas on America Online, the subjects and categories they deal with are limited to those chosen by the staff of America Online. The Internet, on the other hand, gives almost anyone with a computer the ability to provide services such as access to files via FTP or entire multimedia extravaganzas using the World Wide Web.

As a result, due to the anarchic nature of the Internet, it is far easier for people to create their own "places" on the Internet than to open a service area on America Online. At the same time, though, on the Internet there is still currently no direct equivalent for the combination of services provided by America Online, although the World Wide Web promises to equal this potential in the future. For the moment, the Internet is still a place of differing services that make up a whole, whereas America Online is still basically a single all-in-one service.

Message Boards and Newsgroups

Where better to start the comparison than with the Internet's main conversation facility, Usenet newsgroups, and America Online's message boards? (See Figure 15.1.) Both services are basically discussion areas that allow people to publicly exchange messages and opinions on a wide variety of topics. At the same time, they both maintain the distribution of these messages without any user intervention. Where they do tend to differ, however, is in their content and in the way they are moderated.

FIGURE 15.1.

Each America Online channel contains message boards where members can discuss topics of interest.

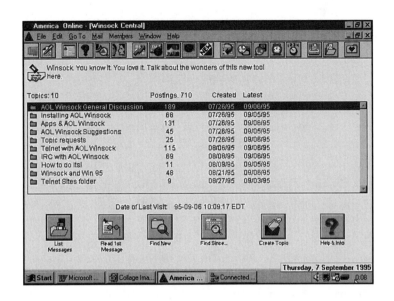

First, let's look at the moderation issue. On America Online, message boards are administered by forum operators or "CyberJockeys" who ensure that discussions are conducted in an orderly fashion and that, for the most part, decency and adherence to each message board's topic is maintained. Although message boards aren't moderated in the strict mailing list sense of the word—where each message is approved by an administrator before being posted to the message board—most CyberJockeys do keep a fairly close watch on the discussions that take place and will intervene when necessary.

> A surefire way to attract the wrath of America Online is to use foul or abusive language on a message board. This may also be the reason for the relatively small number of flame wars—bouts of electronic insults and name-calling—that occur on America Online message boards.

Newsgroups, on the other hand, tend to be less controlled, although many do still have a person who acts as moderator. One of the main reasons for this is due to the way that Usenet operates. A new newsgroup message can come from any of the thousands of Usenet servers around the world. When such a message is posted, it is gradually distributed to all other Usenet sites and may not even be seen by some people, including the administrator, until days later. As a result, even if a message is unwelcome, in most cases it has already wound its way across the Internet before anyone can stop it. That said, as discussed in Chapter 8, "Usenet Newsgroups," most newsgroup members tend to conduct their own form of moderation and policing when unacceptable messages are received. This often takes the form of a *flame* or a *mail dump*, where sometimes thousands of messages are sent to a person's e-mail address telling them to behave.

A flame is the Internet equivalent of hate mail. If you make comments on a newsgroup that people take offense to, you can wind up with a mailbox full of messages all telling you that you're wrong, and not necessarily in the kindest of terms. When you consider that America Online only allows around 500 unread messages to be stored in your mailbox before it starts rejecting new ones, you will soon start to miss important messages because your mailbox is full of junk mail.

This brings us to the second point: content. The diversity of Usenet newsgroups and the relative freedom of expression they allow—including the ability to easily create new newsgroups—means that there are discussions taking place on Usenet that deal with just about every topic known to man. At last count there were over 20,000 newsgroups on the Usenet, compared to a considerably smaller number of message boards on America Online.

Not all Usenet sites provide access to all these newsgroups. Depending on your service provider, some of the less savory newsgroups in the alt section may be edited out. On AOL, however, if you do know a hidden newsgroup's name, you can still read it by entering the name directly using the Subscribe by Name option.

Based on the number of newsgroups and the variety of discussion topics, the Usenet would seem to be a better place to hang out. However, this is not always the case. Depending on what you are looking for, there are many reasons why you should consider using both services. For America Online's part, there are many discussions that take place in forums that have no corresponding newsgroups on Usenet. This is in part due to the attitude services like Usenet take towards commercial activities on the Internet.

FTP and America Online's Software Libraries

Both America Online and the Internet offer an extensive collection of public domain and shareware computer programs that can be downloaded to a person's local computer. As to how these two services compare, the answer lies not so much in how they operate but in the files they contain and how you locate them.

For general PC or Macintosh shareware and public domain software, there is relatively little difference between FTP and America Online. In most cases, if a program has been uploaded to America Online, it has also been uploaded to an FTP site. Where the two services tend to differ, however, is in the maintenance of more specialized files. Due to the UNIX-based nature of the Internet, you are more likely to find the UNIX file you are looking for on one of the many FTP sites than in the UNIX Forum archive. On the other hand, if you are looking for Mac and PC software support files or upgrades, including all the latest Winsock files (see Figure 15.2), America Online would be a good place to start your search.

FIGURE 15.2.

Look no further than America Online for an up-to-date collection of PC software.

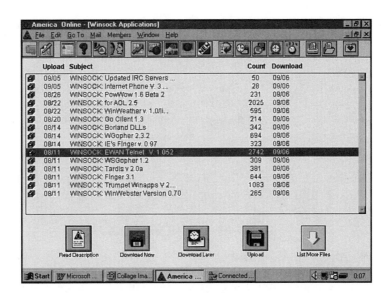

Upload	Subject	Count	Download
09/05	WINSOCK: Updated IRC Servers ...	50	09/06
09/05	WINSOCK: Internet Phone V. 3 ...	28	09/06
08/26	WINSOCK: PowWow 1.6 Beta 2	231	09/06
08/22	WINSOCK: for AOL 2.5	2025	09/06
08/22	WINSOCK: WinWeather v. 1.0/li..	595	09/06
08/20	WINSOCK: Go Client 1.3	214	09/06
08/14	WINSOCK: Borland DLLs	342	09/06
08/14	WINSOCK: WGopher 2.3.2	694	09/06
08/14	WINSOCK: IE's Finger v. 0.97	323	09/06
08/11	WINSOCK: EWAN Telnet V. 1.052	2742	09/06
08/11	WINSOCK: WSGopher 1.2	309	09/06
08/11	WINSOCK: Tardis v 2.0a	381	09/06
08/11	WINSOCK: Finger 3.1	644	09/06
08/11	WINSOCK: Trumpet Winapps V.2....	1083	09/06
08/11	WINSOCK: WinWebster Version 0.70	265	09/06

Note

> Unlike files found on America Online, there is no guarantee that files you download using FTP have been checked for viruses. To be sure there are none, always scan any new files with a virus checker before using them on your system. Unfortunately, the open nature of the Internet provides the ideal environment for the distribution of computer viruses.

Apart from the different files each service contains, the other major difference springs from how the two services organize their files. At America Online, all the files are held on the one system and stored in the America Online software library. The Internet, on the other hand, consists of many unrelated FTP sites, each with its own organizational structure and unique naming conventions. For this reason, how you locate and retrieve files using the two services tends to differ greatly.

Archie and AOL's Search Software Libraries

On America Online you locate files using the Search Software Libraries tool. (See *AOL's Search Software Libraries Tool* topic in Chapter 9.) This tool allows you to search America Online's software libraries and identify files using keywords, dates, categories, and descriptions. As a result, you can very quickly narrow down your search and locate specific files.

Unfortunately, locating files stored at FTP sites can be a more difficult task. The most reliable way to search for files located on FTP sites involves the use of Archie. But, unlike AOL's internal search tool, you can only search for files by file name or directory name. This means that in most cases you need to know the name of the file before you begin your search. The other difficulty you face when using Archie is that not all FTP sites are currently indexed. This means that in some cases the file you are looking for may exist on an unindexed site even though Archie reports that it does not exist.

To reduce this problem to some extent, a number of FTP sites also allow access to their files using Gopher. For these sites, you can locate files using Veronica, the Gopher search tool. (See Chapter 11.) This approach allows you to perform basic keyword searches using Gopher's file descriptions, which can greatly assist you by narrowing down the number of files located by a search request.

Tip

> If time is important to you, AOL Search Software Libraries tool offers the best approach. You'll be able to find files quickly and can be assured that you are downloading virus-free software.

Conferences and IRC

The last major component of America Online is the online conferencing and chat system and its Internet counterpart, IRC or *Internet Relay Chat.* Like IRC, America Online's conferencing system allows users to conduct real-time discussions with other people.

Both of these two systems have many features in common, yet in some respects they are worlds apart. While both systems allow you to participate in real-time conversations with other people, the scope of the two services varies greatly. For starters, IRC is a global chat system where people from all over the world can get together; America Online's service, on the other hand, lets you communicate only with other America Online users.

The second major difference relates to the number of people that can participate in a conversation. On IRC there is technically no limit to the number of people that can gather in one room. America Online limits regular chat rooms to 23 people. This number does increase for online conferences where there is usually a guest or guests who make most of the responses.

While on the subject of online conferences, this is a major feature of America Online that has yet to be fully replicated on the Internet. This is due in part to America Online's ability to pull the big names. (See Figure 15.3.) Movie stars, sports heroes, celebrities, and a host of software and hardware developers have all been special guests at America Online conferences.

FIGURE 15.3.

Even the Dalai Lama found time to chat at America Online.

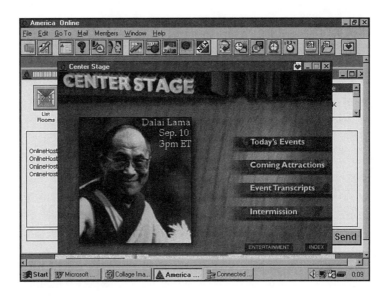

Other America Online Services

Apart from the standard America Online services, there are a number of feature services offered by America Online that also have complementary offerings on the Internet.

The following pages look at some of these services and discuss the different benefits each provides.

The World Wide Web and AOL

By far, the most difficult Internet service to compare with America Online and AOL is the World Wide Web. This is because in many ways a World Wide Web browser it is not unlike AOL itself when you consider how a browser allows you to navigate around the Internet.

Like AOL, the World Wide Web lets you explore the electronic world without being concerned with all the complex technical issues such activities entail. As a result, America Online has put a considerable amount of time into developing a World Wide Web tool that complements the services already offered by America Online. Moreover, the area in which the World Wide Web excels, Netsurfing, provides a major contrast between the two services that indicates why each service is so valuable in its own right.

Each of America Online's channels provide its members with access to a dedicated, but in some ways limited, list of services. However, with the inclusion of a list of related World Wide Web links in each of these channels, all of a sudden the doors of the electronic world are open to all America Online users, with AOL's channels acting as the gateways.

With America Online's incorporation of a World Wide Web browser, its members have truly been given the best of both worlds. But more importantly, they can now pick and choose between the different services, allowing them to tailor their exploration of the information superhighway to suit their own particular needs.

The Marketplace and Internet Shopping

It seems these days that if you run an online service and don't offer access to electronic shopping, then you are not a part of the 'In crowd.' This aspect of online communications is, in fact, becoming so popular that even local bulletin boards have started to get on the bandwagon.

For America Online, the Marketplace is their answer to the online shopping question: A one-stop service where many of the most popular and respected businesses currently online sell their wares. Through the Marketplace, America Online offers its members a diverse range of products from many different sectors of the business community. Yet now it seems that the Internet is positioning itself to expand these services with its own brand of electronic commerce. So how do these two types of services shape up? And more importantly, which should you choose for your shopping explorations?

Probably the most significant difference between the Marketplace and the online shopping services that are beginning to appear on the Internet is the location of these services. The Marketplace is located on America Online and can be entered using the Keyword: `Marketplace`. Doing this opens the Marketplace main window, as shown in Figure 15.4. From this menu, you can easily access all the stores operating storefronts here.

America Online has recently opened a new service on the World Wide Web called AOL Downtown that opens up the Marketplace to the Internet.

Finding stores on the Internet is a very different prospect. Following the near-global acceptance of the World Wide Web as the Internet navigator of choice, a number of inventive users realized that, due to its nature, it was an ideal platform for online commerce. In recent months, this has led to a deluge of new World Wide Web sites selling products and services online.

This has led to two problems. The first is, how do people find these stores on the World Wide Web? Because there is no starting point to the World Wide Web—no electronic front door—in order to locate WWW pages where businesses are located, you need to put in some legwork. This is one of the big plusses for America Online's Marketplace—everything is in one place. However, if you use any of the World Wide Web search tools, this is not an insurmountable problem.

FIGURE 15.4.

America Online's Marketplace.

> To help you get started, the Top Internet Sites button on the Marketplace window opens a short list of businesses on the World Wide Web.

Note

There is also another way that businesses are seeking to promote their wares on the Internet. A number of businesses have proposed the creation of shopping malls on the Internet similar to America Online's Marketplace. (See Chapter 17, "Business on the Net," for a list of the major sites.) By doing this, they increase their chances of being discovered and also benefit from the increased credibility such services provide.

The second problem is a lot more difficult to deal with. Because of the lack of security on the Internet, there have always been concerns about the safety of personal financial details, particularly information such as credit card numbers. Until recently, this was a serious concern for anyone considering a purchase using the Internet. In the past, this was, in fact, the main argument for using services like America Online's Marketplace. It offers protection for your account details and the additional security of knowing that the store was approved by America Online.

To counter these concerns, a number of developments are currently taking place on the Internet in the search for secure World Wide Web servers. Among these developments are those being pursued by Netscape and Terisa Systems. These two companies are currently working on secure WWW protocols in an attempt to make secure financial transactions a reality on the Internet.

At this stage, however, there is no official standard. Netscape Communications, the developers of the Netscape WWW browser, has released their own secure transaction system (SSL), which only works if you are using their browsers. While Terisa is working on a separate system based on S-HTTP, which some other WWW browsers already support, there is possibly a third standard in the pipeline as well. For this reason, the whole secure transaction concept is still somewhat up in the air.

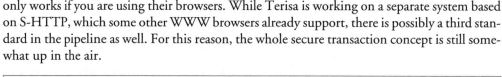

Warning

As with any shopping experience, consider the old saying "Let the buyer beware" whenever you venture out into the world of electronic commerce and online shopping.

First, always deal with respectable or well-known businesses when possible. Secondly, *do not* give out your credit card number or other financial details if you don't know who you are dealing with.

Electronic News Services

Following closely on the heels of electronic shopping in the popularity stakes is the ability to read the latest news of the day electronically.

For some time, America Online has offered access to direct newsfeeds from services such as the ABCNEWS On Demand (see Figure 15.5) and Reuters, giving its members the news of the day (or in most cases, of the minute) long before it could ever be delivered to their doorsteps.

FIGURE 15.5.
ABCNEWS On Demand.

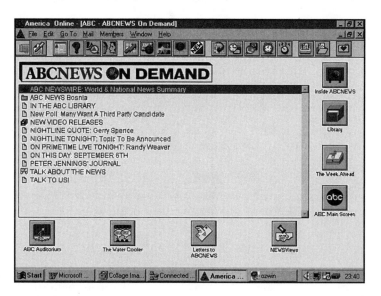

To complement this almost instant coverage, the addition of direct access to electronic magazines and newsletters heralds the next wave of electronic news services. To the forefront of this new growth area comes the World Wide Web, which is ideally suited to the delivery of such services. (See the section on HotWired in Chapter 16 for a look at one of the more popular online magazines.)

Where this particular area of Internet development will end is very hard to say at this time. Already, a number of major newspapers are considering the possibility of offering online editions. Others, like the Internet Daily News at `http://tvp.com/`, are exploring the merits of operating a newspaper purely in the electronic realm. What is certain is that within a few years you will just as likely read your newspaper online as buy a copy from the newsstand on the street corner.

> Where better to find online newspapers than an electronic newsstand? Using the World Wide Web, go to the ENEWS home page at `http://www.enews.com/` to browse through the publications it offers.

Tip

The Reference Desk and WAIS

There is one America Online service that at the moment has no direct equal on the Internet, although that's not to say that in the future this will remain the case. America Online's Reference Desk (see Figure 15.6) is an extensive collection of databases that America Online members can search when conducting research on a wide variety of topics. To find an equivalent resource on the Internet, you need to look at the combined services offered by WAIS and those provided by the growing number of World Wide Web search tools that are rapidly attempting to index the Internet.

FIGURE 15.6.

The online Reference Desk.

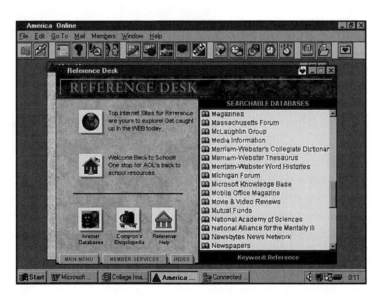

The Reference Desk highlights yet another example of the unique services that both America Online and the Internet offer. For the home user, student, or educator, the databases available via the Reference desk provide access to some of the largest commercial databases in the world.

On the other hand, when you use search tools such as WAIS via the Internet, you have access to thousands of research papers, newsgroup discussions, and educational documents.

Again, each service offers you something different: one offers a collection of databases all located in a single, easy-to-find location, while the other offers the entire breadth of the global online community. This is the reality of both the Internet and America Online. Depending on what you are looking for, you need to choose the service that is right for the task.

The Internet Connection RESOURCES Menu

On the right side of the Internet Connection window shown in Figure 15.7, you will find the RESOURCES menu. This menu contains a list of forums and other special areas that give America Online users an added edge when they begin to explore the Internet.

FIGURE 15.7.

Double-click on any of the items listed in the RESOURCES menu to open the corresponding forum.

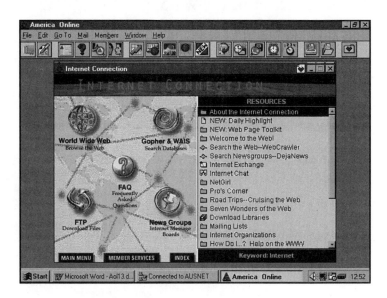

Because the Internet is such an expansive environment it has the tendency to be somewhat impersonal. America Online, on the other hand, is composed of a community of people, who for the most part are willing to help each other out. By integrating its Internet services so closely with existing channels and forums, America Online is bringing this community spirit to the Internet.

In this section, you learn about some of the forums and services that make this possible. At the same time, you will also learn more about the potential of the Internet and the World Wide Web.

Welcome to the Web

To assist you in your early exploration of the World Wide Web, America Online has developed a special area titled, "Welcome to the Web." (See Figure 15.8.)

FIGURE 15.8.

The Internet Connection's Guide to the Web.

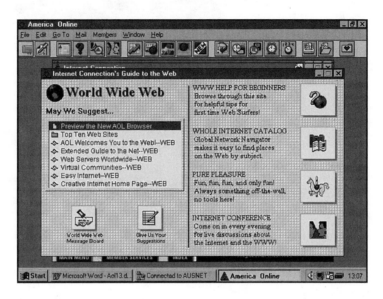

This area is basically a self-starter kit for the World Wide Web. Each of the WWW pages listed here have been chosen because they are designed to give you a better understanding of the World Wide Web and some of the many sites it contains. Of all the sites listed here you should definitely spend at least a small amount of time exploring the following:

◆ WWW Help for Beginners

◆ Extended Guide to the Net

◆ The Whole Internet Catalog

Internet Exchange

America Online provides message boards where you can discuss the Internet and the World Wide Web. To gain access to these message boards select the Internet Exchange item, Keyword: **Net Exchange**.

There are three main Internet-related message boards on the Internet Exchange window. (See Figure 15.9.) The first is the World Wide Web message board where you can talk about the Web and exchange URLs for favorite sites. The second board (Earl's Garage) is designed for technical discussions and Internet Experts. You can also visit this area via the Pro's Corner item on the RESOURCE menu. Finally, the third message board is for general Internet discussions.

FIGURE 15.9.

Discuss the Internet with other AOL users by using the message boards provided in the Internet Exchange forum.

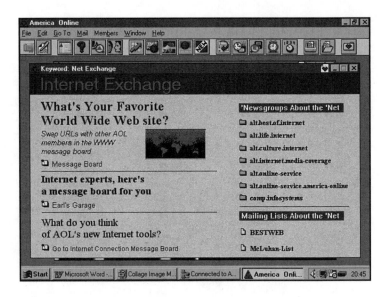

In addition to the message boards, this page also contains a list of newsgroups and mailing lists dealing with general discussions of the Internet. If you select any of these options, AOL displays a message window describing the mailing list or newsgroups, and how you can access it.

Internet Chat

If you prefer the immediacy of online chatting to the slower message-based approach of message boards, then the Internet Chat area, shown in Figure 15.10, may be better suited to your needs. You can also access this area by using the Keyword: **Net Chat**.

Nightly, between 8 pm and 11 pm ET, the Internet Connections CyberJockeys are in attendance at the Chat About the Web area. If you have any questions about the World Wide Web, or the Internet in general, this is the place to come.

There are also a number of Internet- and communications-related conferences happening each week on America Online. To find out about any of these conferences, select any of the conference links displayed on the Internet Chat window.

NetGirl

Tired of 'bozos' annoying you online? Do you want to find a group of people you can relate to? Then NetGirl (Keyword: **NetGirl**) may be a good place to start. (See Figure 15.11.)

FIGURE 15.10.

Chat online about the Internet.

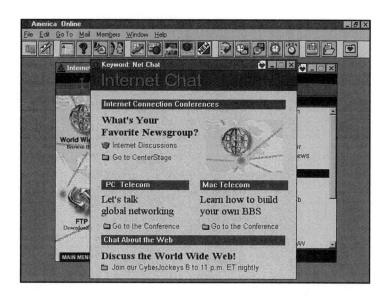

Unlike many online services that cater to a predominantly male audience, the ratio of males to females on America Online is surprisingly close. To cater to the growth in the number of females interested in the Internet, America Online has created NetGirl. Mind you, don't expect the stereotyped hair and makeup tips when visiting NetGirl. This forum deals with real issues, as a quick look through NETGIRL'S pick of favorite sites attests to. (See Figure 15.12.)

FIGURE 15.11.

Online relationships: The 90s social issue.

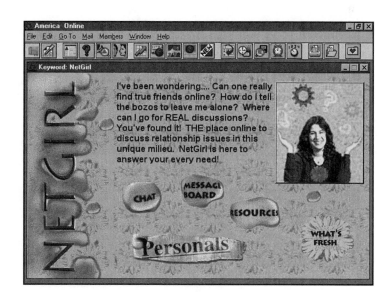

FIGURE 15.12.

NETGIRL'S Picks:
Favorite WWW sites
and services.

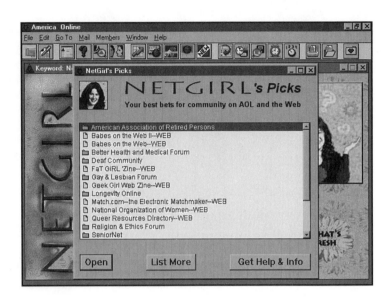

Road Trips—Cruising the Web

One of the most unique features provided by AOL is the concept of Road Trips around the Web. (See Figure 15.13.) Instead of exploring the World Wide Web alone, why not explore it with a group of other "AOLers." Using a special version of AOL's WWW browser, shown in Figure 15.14, you are guided around the World Wide Web by one of AOL's forum staff.

FIGURE 15.13.

Take a guided tour of the
World Wide Web.

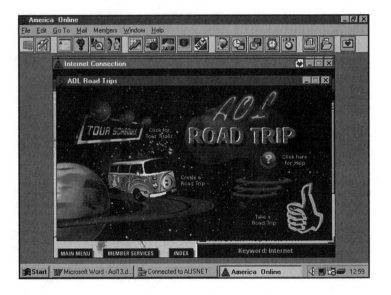

FIGURE 15.14.

See the sites and meet new people while exploring the Web.

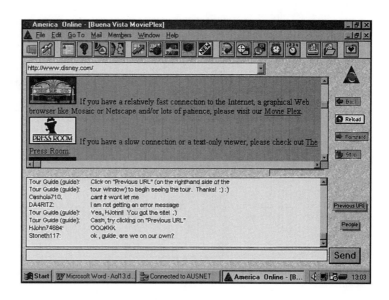

There are a number of different tours available, most of which start on the hour or the half hour. To find out what tours are coming up, click on the Tour Schedule sign shown in Figure 15.13 or join a Road Trip by clicking on the Take a Road Trip sign.

> If you have found some special places on the World Wide Web, you can also create your own Road Trips and act as a Tour Guide yourself.

Note

Seven Wonders of the Web

Seven Wonders of the Web is a weekly competition run by America Online that gives you the opportunity of winning 10 free hours of connect time. All you have to do is solve the weekly clues listed in the Question window shown in Figure 15.15.

To answer these questions you will need to get out and explore the World Wide Web, which means you'll not only be solving the puzzles, but exploring the Internet at the same time.

Internet Organizations

There are a number of organizations and societies that have been formed in recent years whose goals and interests are directly related to the Internet. America Online has created a special area for these forums under the Internet Organizations banner, Keyword: **Net Orgs**. (See Figure 15.16.)

Of these organizations, the two most well known are the Electronic Frontier Foundation, one of the principal advocates for electronic rights, and the Internet Society, which now administers the Internet Engineering Task Force and other global Internet discussion forums.

FIGURE 15.15.

Win 10 free hours of connect time by solving the weekly challenge.

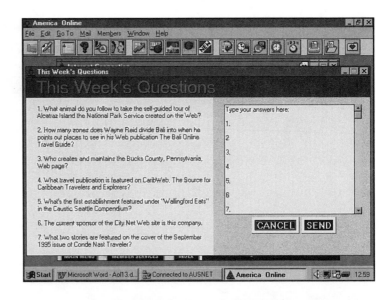

FIGURE 15.16.

Find out about Electronic Frontier Foundation and the Internet Society by visiting the Internet Organizations forum.

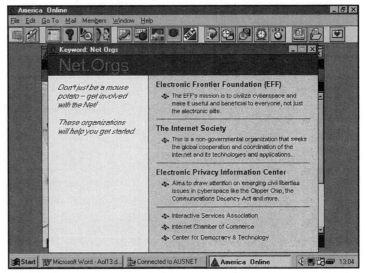

Net News

With all the near daily changes and developments occurring all over the Internet, it is almost an impossible task to keep yourself up to date. For America Online users, however, the task has been made considerably easier thanks to the Net News area shown in Figure 15.17, Keyword: `Net News`.

On this one page, America Online has brought together a list of the top Internet-related online news services. As a result, all you need to do to keep up-to-date is spend a bit of time visiting the sites provided. Of these, the GNN Net News service is a good first choice, with MecklerWeb's iWorld site coming a close second.

FIGURE 15.17.

Keep up-to-date with Net News, the best source for all the latest Internet happenings.

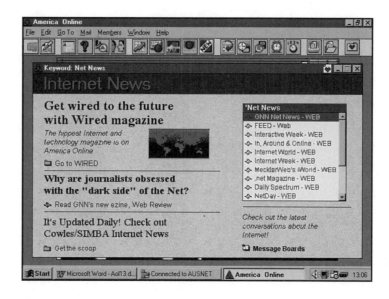

Zen and the Internet

First there was Motor Cycle Maintenance and now, "Zen and the Art of the Internet." (See Figure 15.18.) If you want to read more about how the Internet operates, then this online book has plenty of additional information for you to examine.

FIGURE 15.18.

Zen and the Art of the Internet, an online guide for everyone.

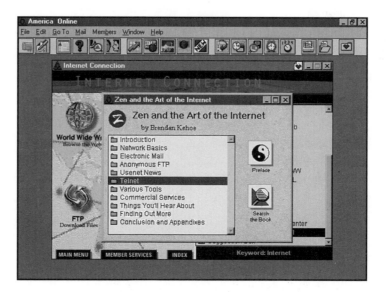

Summary

Despite the fact that many of the services offered on the Internet are similar to those offered by America Online, each service brings with it a certain uniqueness of character.

With this uniqueness comes diversity and the ability to explore more widely the electronic world developing on the computer networks that now link the real world. Yet at the same time, the Internet services that America Online now offers don't so much reduce the need for its existing services as enhance and complement them. In doing this, they truly do combine the best of both worlds for America Online members.

With all this theory and comparison of services and resources, by now you are probably feeling a bit overloaded with computer terminology. So it's time to put your feet up for a while and simply explore some of what the Internet has to offer.

The next chapter takes you on a tour of the lighter side of the Internet, exploring family, fun, kids, and, oh yes, we'd better look at education as well just to give the chapter some redeeming value.

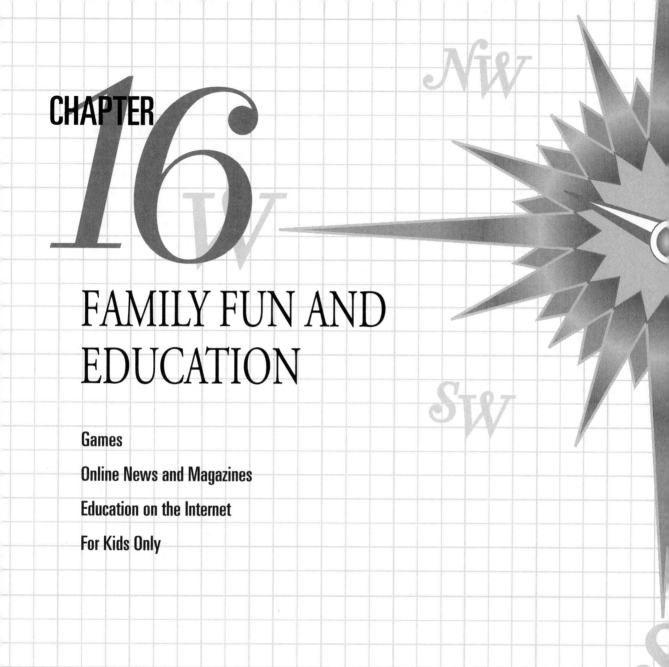

Although the ARPANET was originally designed as a tool for scientific research and distributed computing, it didn't take its users long to discover that it could also be used for many not-so-scientific endeavors.

For example, consider one of the early mailing lists devoted to science fiction. Despite the wide variety of technical and scientific discussions available, this list rapidly became one of the most popular mailing lists ever. What was more interesting, however, was the fact that although the early administrators frowned on this non-scientific use of their new network, they were effectively forced to tolerate this non-standard usage due to the number of people choosing to use these mailing lists. In addition, people rapidly discovered that because of the interconnected nature of the Internet, if an administrator attempted to block one avenue of access, another would soon appear to replace the blocked one.

As ARPANET grew and was eventually replaced by NSFNET, this level of tolerance became the accepted norm for the emerging Internet. Despite many guidelines dealing with acceptable usage, the Internet has grown to become a veritable electronic playground. Ironically, it is the same level of freedom that eventually permitted the development of a number of Internet-based education and community-based services.

It is these services and some of the more "fun" resources that will be covered in this chapter by discussing the following topics:

- ◆ Games and other stuff
- ◆ Online news and magazines
- ◆ Education on the Internet
- ◆ Study and research

Games

"When you're tired of the Internet, you're tired of life," to misquote a well-known saying. While making such a comment may at first sound a bit trite, when you look at what the Internet has to offer, it isn't far from the truth. In the future this same saying will probably become even more appropriate when the promised delivery of live television over the Net becomes a practical reality.

But enough of future dreams, what you want to know, I'm sure, is what's available now!

Without a doubt, one of the biggest software growth industries on the Internet—apart from writing WWW navigators—is the development and distribution of shareware or public domain computer games. You would be very hard-pressed to locate an FTP site anywhere on the Internet that doesn't have at least one directory devoted to computer gaming.

Major Game-Related FTP Sites

To cater to this growing need, a number of FTP sites maintain archives containing a wide assortment of both DOS- and Windows-based computer games. These sites include these DOS game archives:

```
ftp://ftp.cdrom.com/pub/games
ftp://ftp.uml.edu/msdos/games
```

They also include these Windows game archives:

```
ftp://ftp.minash.edu.au/pub/win3/games
ftp://ftp.cica.indiana.edu/pub/pc/win3/games
```

In these archives you can find copies of public domain and shareware games, plus demonstration versions of many popular commercial games. Although these sites contain a large number of games, there are many other sites on the Internet that also contain various files—some dedicated to specific games and others holding more general archives.

To help you locate these sites, the best place to start is the World Wide Web, and more specifically, a WWW site called the Games Domain. (See Figure 16.1.) This WWW site has been designed to provide easy access to every Internet resource related to computer games. The links it provides include access to all of the major FTP sites, WWW servers for many commercial games, newsgroups, gaming FAQs, and one-click downloading of many shareware and public domain games. The home page for the Games Domain is `http://wcl-rs.bham.ac.uk/gamesdomain/`.

FIGURE 16.1.

The Games Domain.

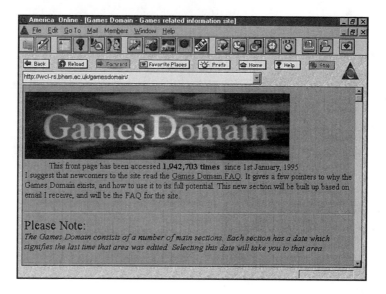

DOOM

The distribution of computer games using the Internet has become so popular that one company in particular, id Software, has nearly turned the concept into an art form. In case you've been "out to lunch" for the last two years, id Software, Inc. is the developer of DOOM, DOOM II, and Heretic. By offering fully playable versions of all their games on the Internet, this company created an instant market for itself when the final release (commercial product), with all the bells and whistles was released. In addition, they also encouraged the development of what can only be described as a new aftermarket industry, which now sees new shareware support tools and many additional playing fields or *wads* being placed on the Internet each month.

There are a number of id Software game archives stored at various FTP sites, including mirrors of the host FTP archive at `ftp://ftp.cdrom.com` in the `/pub/idgames` directory. Alternatively, you can find a wealth of information about DOOM, including pointers to many World Wide Web FTP sites at DOOMGate. Figure 16.2 shows the home page for DOOMGate, which is by far the most up-to-date DOOM WWW site. Its http address is `http://doomgate.cs.buffalo.edu/`.

FIGURE 16.2.

DOOMGate: The gateway to DOOM.

 id Software has recently decided to set up a WWW server of its own at `http://www.idsoftware.com/`.

Apogee

If id Software is the writer of the most popular game, Apogee is the most prolific publisher. With a software catalog that includes Wolfenstein 3D, Commander Keen, and Duke Nukem, it is only natural that the shareware versions of most of Apogee's software should also be available on the Internet.

For fans of Apogee software, the Games Domain has created a page providing direct access to all FTP sites containing Apogee shareware games. The http address for this page is `http://wcl-rs.bham.ac.uk/gamesdomain/apogee`.

Newsgroups

Accompanying the many shareware games available using FTP, there are hundreds of newsgroups that discuss many of the more popular computer games.

alt.binaries

The `alt.binaries` area of Usenet contains a few newsgroups that distribute the latest computer games as UUENCODED files stored in messages. Some of these are shown in Table 16.1. (See Chapter 8, "Usenet Newsgroups," for a discussion of UUENCODE and Usenet.)

Table 16.1. `alt.binaries` newsgroups.

Newsgroup	Description
alt.binaries.descent	The latest DOOM-like incarnation.
alt.binaries.doom	DOOM I and II wads and editors.
alt.binaries.games.vga-planets	Not another DOOM game—but a popular online computer game.
alt.binaries.heretic	Another DOOM-like game from id Software.
alt.binaries.mac.games	Games for the Apple Macintosh

alt.games

If fighting with UUENCODE isn't your style, some of the newsgroups in `alt.games` may be more to your liking. These newsgroups contain discussions ranging from hints and tips to game cheats. To get you started, Table 16.2 offers a list of some of the more popular newsgroups; however, just because a game isn't listed here doesn't mean that it isn't covered on the Internet.

Table 16.2. Popular `alt.games` newsgroups.

Newsgroup	Description
alt.games	Watch this newsgroup for announcements about new newsgroups and computer gaming in general.
alt.games.apogee	A lively discussion of the many games released by Apogee.

continues

Table 16.2. continued

Newsgroup	Description
alt.games.dark-forces	Having trouble winning at Dark Forces? Ask here for help.
alt.games.descent	Discussions and playing tips for Descent.
alt.games.doom	Enough said.
alt.games.doom.announce	This newsgroup is reserved for announcements about new wads, game editor, and any other late-breaking DOOM news.
alt.games.doom.ii	When you've tired of DOOM, you're ready for DOOM II.
alt.games.doom.newplayers	This is a good place to start if you're new to DOOM. There are always people around who are willing to lend a helping hand.
alt.games.dune-ii.virgin-games	Dune, the computer game, not the book (or the movie).
alt.games.heretic	DOOM with a crossbow.
alt.games.playmaker-football	It's not a shoot-em-up, but for football fans it's just as much fun.
alt.games.tiddlywinks	Yes, there is even a newsgroup for this one.
alt.games.ultima.dragons	Adventure gaming at its best.
alt.games.x-wing	Star Wars for your PC.

To locate other game-related newsgroups, use the Search All Newsgroups button in AOL's Newsgroups area, Keyword: **Newsgroups**. For example: type the words **game and pc** into the Search Phrase: field and hit the **S**earch button as shown in Figure 16.3. After a few seconds, AOL displays a Search Results dialog box similar to the one shown in Figure 16.4. This dialog box displays a list of all newsgroups matching your search request. From this dialog box, you can subscribe to any newsgroup that catches your eye by selecting it and clicking on the Add button.

FIGURE 16.3.

Click on the Search button to locate other computer game newsgroups.

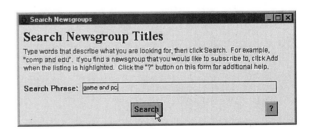

FIGURE 16.4.

AOL reports that there are 12 newsgroups containing the words game *and* pc *in their name.*

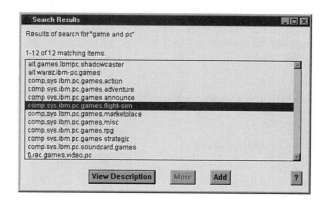

The rec.games **Newsgroups**

If you thought that the alt newsgroups covered the topic of computer games well, you're in for a big surprise. The rec.games area of Usenet is also crammed full of game-related newsgroups. To get you started, Table 16.3 lists some of the more active discussion areas.

Table 16.3. Popular rec.games newsgroups.

Newsgroup	Description
rec.games.backgammon	In this newsgroup you don't even need a computer. Backgammon anyone?
rec.games.computer.doom.editing	You guessed it, more DOOM stuff.
rec.games.corewar	One of the more popular online games.
rec.games.diplomacy	Diplomacy buffs need look no further than this newsgroup.
rec.games.rpg	Role-playing games of all descriptions also receive good coverage on Usenet.
rec.games.mud	There are also a number of newsgroups dealing with multiuser dungeons.
rec.games.pinball	If you've ever played pinball, check out this newsgroup.
rec.games.programmer	This is a good place to talk with people about writing computer games.
rec.games.xtank.play	If you haven't heard about Xtank, have a look here.

Hardware-Related Newsgroups

To close out this topic, there are a number of other newsgroups dealing with computer games written for specific computer platforms. Some of these newsgroups are listed in Table 16.4.

Table 16.4. Hardware-specific games newsgroups.

Newsgroup	Description
`alt.mac.games.binaries`	Computer game files for the Apple Macintosh.
`comp.os.os2.games`	OS/2- and Warp-related computer gaming issues.
`comp.sys.acorn.games`	Devoted to computer games written for the Acorn Microcomputer system.
`comp.sys.amiga.cd32`	Commodore may be dead, but its computer games live on in the `cd32` newsgroup.
`comp.sys.amiga.games`	For Amiga gaming discussion, this newsgroup is a good place to start.
`comp.sys.ibm.pc.games.flight-sim`	Flight simulators for those who love to fly.
`rec.games.video.3do`	The `3do` newsgroup.
`rec.games.video.atari`	Atari computer game machines also get a look in here.
`rec.games.video.cd-i`	CD-I, for those who have one.
`rec.games.video.nintendo`	Nintendo game machines are the topic of discussion here.
`rec.games.video.sega`	You can't mention Nintendo without someone saying Sega, so there is a newsgroup for it as well.

Online Games and the Internet

The Internet is not only a great source of computer game software, but it also offers a number of games and gaming environments that you can play with while online.

These games tend to follow one of three main threads. The first relates to role-playing games (RPGs) not unlike the adventure games made popular by software houses like Sierra—the makers of King's Quest, Leisure Suit Larry, and Space Quest, just to mention a few. The second group falls into the category of interactive games, such as chess or checkers, which allow you to play with other people across the Internet. Finally, the last group is literally play-by-Internet games, where you play against a remote computer.

MUDs

Without a doubt, the most well-known role-playing game environment on the Internet is the MUD (*multiuser dungeon* or *multiuser domain*, depending on who you talk to).

MUDs are in many ways similar to text-based adventure games. When you enter a MUD, you are placed into an electronically generated world that you can explore by typing commands such as "north," "south," "up," and "down." As you enter commands, the MUD responds with descriptions of your location, plus other important information. If you've ever played a text-based adventure game, you will probably recognize the basic idea by now.

However, MUDs contain one vital element that separates them from your run-of-the-mill adventure game—the human element. When you join a MUD, you enter a world that is populated by other people—people like yourself who have entered the MUD and, like yourself, want to win. But win what? Fame, fortune, power, strength, magical abilities, or maybe the hand of a fair maiden or a prince. It really depends on which MUD you are playing. There are a number of different types with varying rules and goals.

To participate in a MUD, as a rule, you need to have installed the Winsock program discussed in Chapter 10, "AOL and Winsock," and obtained a copy of a Telnet program such as EWAN. Apart from this, all you need is the domain name of a MUD and away you go. Figure 16.5 shows the Telnet client supplied with Windows 95, connected to the Login screen for a MUD called "The Final Challenge," whose domain name is `mud.primenet.com:4000`.

> Mac Users: Currently there is no direct support for Telnet connections using the Macintosh version of AOL. As a result, you will need to use a direct TCP/IP connection via an Internet Service Provider.

> The `:4000` following the domain name refers to the port address of the MUD. You must include this number to ensure that your Telnet client connects to the MUD and not to a Telnet server associated with the same domain name. This address may be different for each MUD, so make sure you check out exactly which port you need to connect to.

The first time you log on to a MUD, you are asked to choose a name and a password. In addition, depending on the MUD, you need to enter other configuration information. You may be asked to select your sex, your character type (human, elf, ghost, shaman, and so on), and select properties such as initial strength, wisdom, health, and level of magical ability.

> If you find that your Telnet connection displays symbols such as ^M when you hit the Enter key, you may need to use Ctrl+J instead of the Enter key.

FIGURE 16.5.

You can use any Windows-based Telnet client to access a MUD.

Once you enter the MUD itself (see Figure 16.6), basically you are on your own. After all, part of the fun of playing a MUD is finding out how it works and learning its layout. There are often thousands of rooms to explore, objects to find, and people to meet (or sometimes do battle with). All MUDs are operated by gods and other minor deities who can be called upon for assistance, although some will expect adoration and worship in return. If you are really good, maybe one day you too can become a god—the highest level of achievement in any MUD game.

FIGURE 16.6.

Finding out how a MUD works is all part of the challenge.

Playing a MUD does not need to be all guesswork. Most sites have a help facility offering many useful tips and guidelines. To request the main help page, simply type the word **help**.

Tip

With over 450 MUDs of various types to be found on the Internet, listing them all here would be impractical. So instead, let's turn again to the World Wide Web and the Games Domain for a list of some popular MUDs and links to other MUD information pages. The http address for this page (see Figure 16.7) is `http://wcl-rs.bham.ac.uk/GamesDomain/mud.html`.

FIGURE 16.7.

The Games Domain MUD home pages listing.

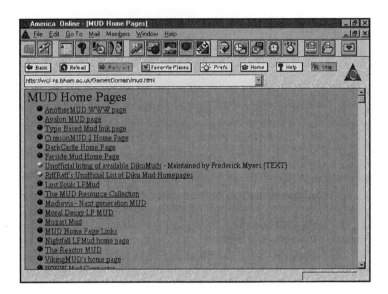

MOOs, Mushes, and MUSE

In addition to MUDs, there are a number of other multiuser environments on the Internet. Like MUDs, they allow people to interact with each other online. However, where MUDs lean toward combat with the forces of evil, these other environments tend to be places for social interaction.

These environments fall into three main categories—MOOs, Mushes, and MUSE. MOOs and Mushes are different types of social MUDs, some of which feature worlds that often simulate places made popular by novels and movies, while others feature historical or futuristic worlds. Of the two, Mushes tend to more closely adhere to the rules of dice-based role-playing games, with some closely replicating tabletop games of the same name. MUSE, on the other hand, are educational or tutorial worlds used by schools and colleges to teach human interaction and social sciences.

The best place to find information about MOOs, Mushes, and MUDs in general is a WWW site called the MUD Resource Collection. (See Figure 16.8.) This site contains links to many games, plus related information including player guidelines, historical archives, and programming tutorials. The address for this site is `http://www.cis.upenn.edu/~lwl/mudinfo.html`.

FIGURE 16.8.

The MUD Resource Collection.

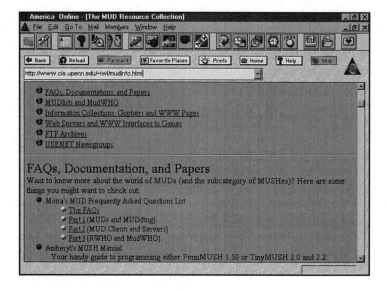

However, for those of you who want to get started right away, Table 16.5 contains a short list of popular Mushes and MOOs for you to explore.

Table 16.5. Popular MOOs and Mushes.

Site Address	Name	Description
`sarcazm.resnet.cornell.edu:9000`	AngrealMOO	This is a role-playing MOO based on Robert Jordan's novel, *The Wheel of Time.*
`omega.ru.ac.za:4201`	Elenium MUSH	This game is set one hundred years after the events told in David Eddings' *Elenium Trilogy.*
`colossus.acusd.edu:4444`	ChromeMUSH	This is a cyberpunk MUSH set in Sacramento, California, in the year 2030.
`omega.acusd.edu:9999`	Danse Macabre	A world based on the cult movie, "World of Darkness"—well, at least loosely. This time, the setting is Paris in 1356.

Site Address	Name	Description
`dana.ucc.nau.edu:1892`	Elendor MUSH	This MUSH is based on J.R.R. Tolkien's *The Lord of the Rings*.
`baymoo.sfsu.edu:8888`	BayMOO	This MOO is designed as a virtual reality world based around the San Francisco Bay Area.

Where to Find Other Games

As mentioned earlier, there are many other games on the Internet, some terminal-based and others built around the World Wide Web. To play any of these games, all you really need to know is the address of the site operating the game. Once you log on or open the appropriate WWW page, there are usually instructions provided to get you going.

There can be no doubt that the most concise list of online games ever compiled is Zarf's List of Interactive Games on the Web, a tiny section of which is shown in Figure 16.9. This site contains links to every known WWW-based game and a number of Telnet-based games as well. The http address for this site is `http://www.cs.cmu.edu/afs/andrew/org/kgb/www/zarf/games.html`.

FIGURE 16.9.

Zarf's List of Interactive Games on the Web.

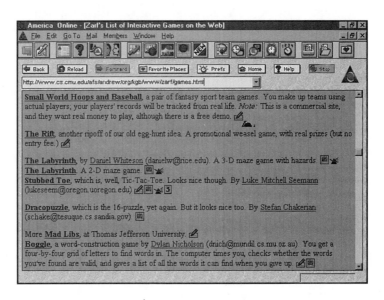

If your thirst for online games still isn't satisfied, you should also check out some of the game-related sites listed at the Games Domain. Many of these also contain links to online games.

Online News and Magazines

If playing games isn't your style, maybe browsing though online newspapers and electronic magazines is more your speed.

Ever since the first text editor was developed for computers, people have sought ways to publish their comments, criticisms, and views of the world. In the early days, many of these commentaries, or *e-zines* (electronic magazines), were disk-based. A number of articles would be collected on a disk with some pictures and maybe a game or two, or possibly the source code of some computer program. The disks would then be distributed by the postal service or spread from hand to hand around university campuses and offices.

With the advent of widespread access to bulletin boards and modems, the popularity of disk-based magazines began to dwindle. In their place came electronically distributed versions. On the whole, the content did not change much, but now the publishers of these e-zines could reach a wider audience without the hassles and limitations of disk-based publication. Then came public access to the Internet, and again e-zine publishers adapted to meet the new technology.

Today, there are thousands of electronic magazines and newsletters published all over the world on a variety of topics, ranging from general interest to highly specific publications. Many of these e-zines are now distributed on the Internet. Some e-zines are delivered by e-mail using mailing lists, while others can be downloaded from various FTP and Gopher sites.

E-zines are not the only type of electronic publication available on the Internet. Since the arrival of the World Wide Web, a popular new concept has been sweeping the Internet—Web publishing. Of all the services offered on the Internet, none is more suited to the widespread delivery of electronic news and magazines than the World Wide Web. As a result, over the last two years hundreds of publications of all descriptions have begun to spring up all over the Web.

This section looks at some of the different types of e-zines, WWW publications, and even electronic newspapers that are now available on the Internet. In addition, it also looks at some of the best places to find new publications.

E-Zines

To get the ball rolling, let's first take a look at one of the oldest forms of electronic publishing, and still one of the most popular—electronic magazines, or e-zines.

The Internet is by far the most effective, and possibly the cheapest, method of electronic publishing currently available. If you have access to a word processor and a modem, you can become an Internet publisher. While this may not be everyone's idea of a great way to spend the weekend, for many people it is just that—a hobby or, in many cases, a labor of love.

One of the more popular e-zine WWW pages currently lists over 350 well-known e-zines. These publications cover topics as diverse as cyberculture, independent film making, time-wasting, and philosophical discussions at Phil and Bernie's Philosophical Steakhouse. In addition, there are literally thousands of other private publications devoted to just about every topic imaginable.

A large majority of these magazines are delivered by e-mail, although some of the more popular ones also operate World Wide Web pages containing copies of not only the current edition, but also archives of back issues and, in many cases, subscription information as well. A small number are also available using FTP or Gopher, but most of these e-zines are being phased out in favor of the more popular World Wide Web distribution method.

To find one of the more popular e-zines, let's look first at the WWW site operated by a guy called John Labovitz. When John discovered that there was no concise listing of e-zines on the Internet, he set off on a personal journey to bring such a list to the world. The result was John Labovitz's E-Zine List (see Figure 16.10) which can be found at `http://www.meer.net/~johnl/e-zine-list/index.html`.

FIGURE 16.10.

John Labovitz's E-Zine List.

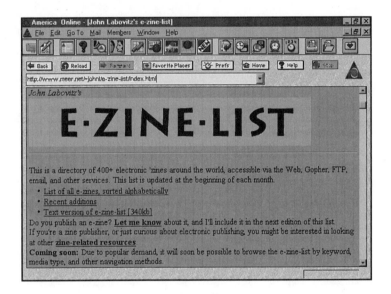

Many people regard this site as the most up-to-date and accurate listing of e-zines available today. At the moment, the list is available online in alphabetical order, or you can download a copy using FTP. However, by the time you read this book, a search tool should have been added to assist you with your e-zine exploration. There are currently over 400 e-zines listed on this site, which includes instructions on how to subscribe to each, as well as links to those e-zines whose publishers operate WWW, Gopher, or FTP sites.

One of the more impressive e-zines pointed to by this list is the Netsurfer Digest. This e-zine, published on a weekly basis, contains up-to-the-minute information about the latest and greatest WWW sites, along with other Internet-related information. It is available via e-mail or online via its World Wide Web site at `http://www.netsurf.com/nsd/index.html`. There is also a link on John Labovitz's e-zine listing that takes you straight to the Netsurfer WWW home page. (See Figure 16.11.) From here you can browse though the latest edition, look up articles from past editions, and subscribe to the e-mail version.

FIGURE 16.11.

The Netsurfer Digest home page.

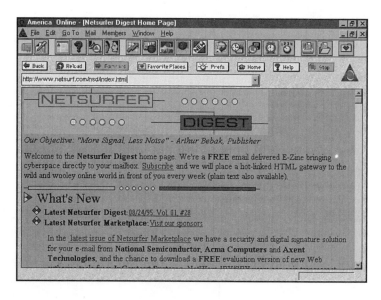

Subscribing to an e-mail version of any e-zine is by far the best way to read one because you can read it offline without being connected to the Internet. The Netsurfer Digest provides you with such an option. As a result, each week the latest edition can be delivered to your America Online mailbox as an HTML page ready for you to load into any World Wide Web browser. You can subscribe to the Netsurfer Digest by clicking on the word "Subscribe" in the first paragraph of the Netsurfer Digest home page. Doing this opens a WWW form where you can enter your e-mail address and request a subscription. (See Figure 16.12.)

FIGURE 16.12.

Enter your America Online e-mail address to subscribe to the Netsurfer Digest.

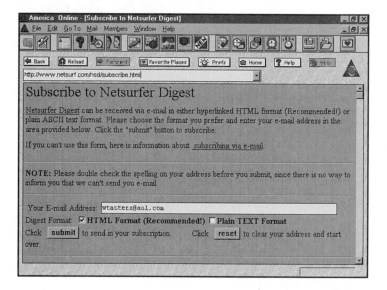

> When entering your America Online e-mail address, remember to remove any spaces from your screen name and use @aol.com as the domain name.

Once you have subscribed to Netsurfer, you will begin to receive a weekly e-mail message containing the latest edition. To read Netsurfer, save a copy of this message as a file with an .htm extension. You then need to use a World Wide Web navigator such as GNNWorks or Netscape. (See Chapter 18, "The GNN Internet Access Service," for more information.) Using GNNWorks, open the **F**ile menu and select the **O**pen Local File option. (See Figure 16.13.) This opens a dialog box similar to the one shown in Figure 16.14. From here, select the file in which you saved a copy of the Netsurfer Digest e-mail message and click on the OK button.

FIGURE 16.13.

Select the Open Local File option to load the Netsurfer Digest in GNNWorks.

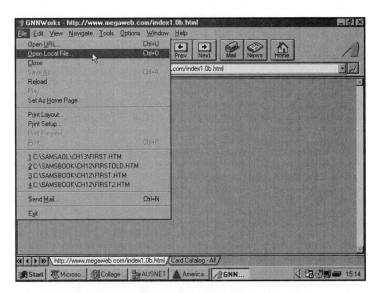

FIGURE 16.14.

The GNNWorks File Open dialog box.

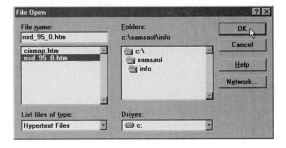

In this example, the e-mail message is saved as `nsd_95_0.htm` and stored in the `c:\samsaol\info` directory. To keep track of past publications, you may wish to create a special directory to save all your Netsurfer Digest e-zines and name each one with a date, but remember that to load them into a WWW browser you must save them with an `.htm` extension.

> Mac Users: Macintosh users can also utilize the separate WWW browser included with AOL for displaying local files.

After a few seconds, GNNWorks loads the Netsurfer Digest and displays the text in your GNNWorks browser. You can now read any of the articles in this edition. (See Figure 16.15.) In addition, many articles also contain links to other WWW sites you can explore by simply clicking on the appropriate hypertext hotlinks, assuming of course that you have configured Winsock as discussed in Chapter 10 or are using a direct TCP/IP connection via GNN. (See Chapter 18.) Alternatively, Windows users can also load the file into AOL itself—while online only—by selecting **O**pen from the **F**ile menu.

FIGURE 16.15.

Hot places on the Web this week.

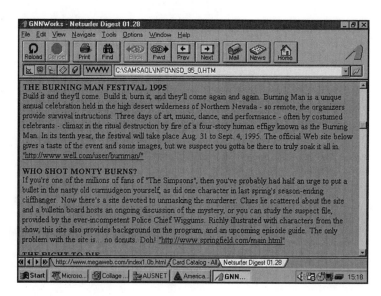

HotWired

Since the arrival of the World Wide Web, a new type of electronic magazine has begun to appear on the Internet—the interactive magazine. Unlike a traditional e-zine that you read and then put away, an interactive magazine invites you to become an active participant. After reading an article, you can add your own comments, criticisms, or even editorials.

At the leading edge of this type of publication technology, it isn't surprising to find one of the leading-edge magazines—*Wired*. In a bold move, *Wired* has created an alter ego on the Internet called HotWired. (See Figure 16.16.) To open HotWired, use `http://www.hotwired.com/`.

> Before you can participate in HotWired, you must first become a subscriber. Although there are no costs involved in using HotWired, you must be a subscriber and have a valid user ID and password. To do this, follow the steps outlined on the HotWired home page.

FIGURE 16.16.

HotWired = Wired
on the Web.

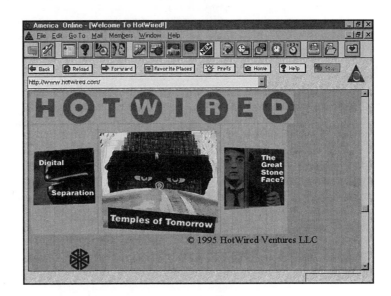

This Web site is styled after *Wired* and offers the same level of insight into the emerging online world that people have come to expect. Where HotWired is different, however, is that it lets you become a part of the magazine by allowing you to make your own editorial comments, much like a global online letter to the editor. These commentaries are categorized into threads and grouped by subject, as shown in Figure 16.17. This level of interaction means that HotWired is always changing and growing as new members add their thoughts and ideas to the mix of cultures and ideologies.

FIGURE 16.17.

HotWired's threads take you on a journey into the Wired world.

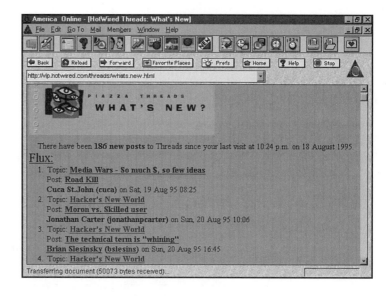

The Trib

Reading magazines may pass the time, but there are situations when what you really want is the latest news from around the world.

There's no better place to turn when you want the news than a newspaper or, in this case, the Internet newspaper shown in Figure 16.18. At `http://www.trib.com`, the news of the day is available online as it happens. Operated by the *Casper Star Tribune* in Wyoming, this WWW site provides you with up-to-date national and global news, as well as links to many newsfeeds and newspapers operated by news organizations all around the world.

FIGURE 16.18.

The Trib online.

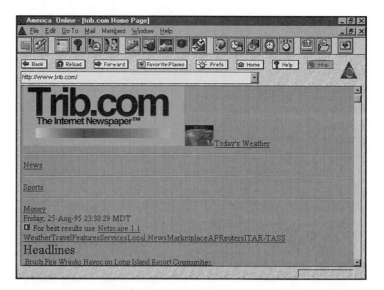

One of the main features of this service is its direct link to the Associated Press online news service—a first for the Internet—which enables you to read about the latest news as it happens. You can also search the Associated Press archives via this link and follow up on past news stories. The Trib also provides a link to CNN (Cable News Network), which offers the unique ability to download video clips of news stories.

In addition, by installing a special program called RealAudio, you can listen to the latest ABC radio news while online. To obtain a copy of RealAudio for either Macintosh or Windows, point your WWW browser to `http://www.realaudio.com/products/player.html`. (See Figure 16.19.)

FIGURE 16.19.

RealAudio on the World Wide Web.

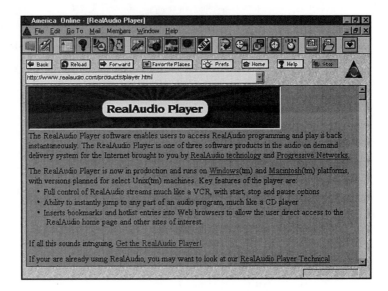

The Electronic Newsstand

Wherever there are magazines and newspapers, you can be sure that a newsstand isn't far behind, and the World Wide Web is no different.

So far you have looked at some of the magazines and journals published on the Internet, but what about the thousands of print magazines published each month? Many of these publications are also represented on the Internet at the Electronic Newsstand (see Figure 16.20), whose address is `http://www.enews.com/`.

Every month the magazines with a listing on The Electronic Newsstand upload copies of various articles and features published in their current print editions. Many also upload a copy of the table of contents to give you a better indication of what the magazine contains. Using The Electronic Newsstand, you can browse through any of the magazines and read the articles that have been uploaded.

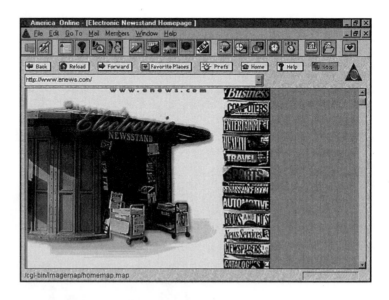

After reading the articles, if you like what you have read you can also use The Electronic Newsstand to subscribe to the printed edition. Due to a special arrangement with publishers, in most cases you can receive significant discounts or other benefits by subscribing online.

To give you some idea of the variety of magazines available online, here is a short list of randomly selected publications.

AV Video
Best Friends Animal Magazine
Guitar Player
NBA Inside Stuff Magazine
Technology Review!
World Politics

News Filtering

The Usenet is another good source of news and information, but for many people the sheer number of newsgroups available make it nothing short of impossible to keep track of all the various conversations. To help people keep track of what's happening on the Usenet, Stanford University has developed a news filtering service called Netnews as a part of its electronic library project.

Netnews lets you define search profiles for the Usenet. In these profiles you nominate keywords that you want Netnews to watch out for. Then, every day Netnews scans the thousands of articles posted to newsgroups all over the Usenet and captures any containing the keywords you have defined. All these captured messages are collated and sent to you on a regular basis via e-mail. By using Netnews, you can reduce the number of hours spent wandering around the Usenet looking for interesting conversations.

Access to Netnews is available either through an e-mail list server-style service or a more flexible World Wide Web page. People interested in investigating the e-mail service should send mail to `netnews@db.stanford.edu` with the word HELP in the body of the message. On the other hand, if you prefer the World Wide Web, the Netnews World Wide Web home page can be found at `http://woodstock.stanford.edu:2000/`.

On this page you will find links to information about Netnews and a link to the Service Request Form shown in Figure 16.21. You use this form to define search profiles, update profiles you have already set up, as well as cancel profiles in which you are no longer interested.

FIGURE 16.21.

The Stanford Netnews profile form.

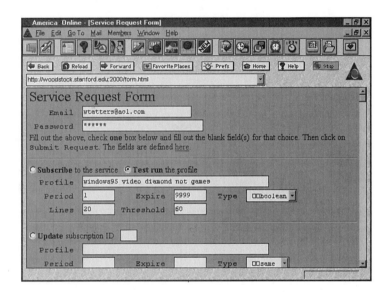

> Before defining any profiles, it's a good idea to test them using the Test Run option. This option scans the current day's newsgroup discussions and generates a list of messages that meet your profile's requirements.

Tip

Education on the Internet

Although many people are often amazed by the fact that I like to talk about education and fun in the same breath, access to the Internet has changed the face of education forever. For the first time, even students are equating education with fun—especially when the Internet is involved.

One of the major strengths of the Internet is its capability to enable people to communicate with each other and share resources and information. This is an enormous boon to the educator. By providing access to resources that in the past have been simply unattainable or too expensive, the possibilities for expanding the education experience are abundant.

In fact, the Internet has become so popular with educators that an entire service has been developed specifically for education purposes. Known collectively by the title "K12," these services offer a number of benefits to educators and students alike.

AskERIC

The Educational Resources Information Center (ERIC), shown in Figure 16.22, is a federally funded information service providing access to education-related resources using Gopher and the World Wide Web. To access this site, use the following http address: `http://ericir.syr.edu/`.

FIGURE 16.22.

The Educational Resources Information Center home page.

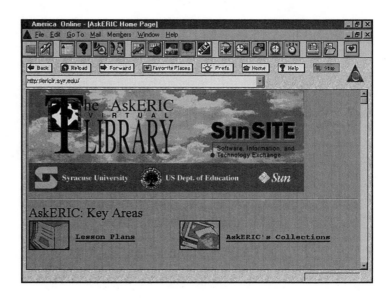

For educators at all levels, ERIC offers resources and teaching aids covering a wide range of subjects, including

- Lesson plans
- Digests and publications
- Reference tools
- Internet guides and directories
- Archives of education-related mailing lists
- Access to other education-related sites

To support these resources, the Educational Resource Information Center also operates AskERIC. This service is an e-mail feedback service that allows teachers, library media specialists, administrators, and other people involved in any field of education to send resource queries to the AskERIC staff. Because many educators are unfamiliar with the resources available on the Internet, AskERIC was created to help them locate the information they need. To quote from the information published about AskERIC:

The hallmark of AskERIC is the human intermediary, who interacts with the information seeker and personally selects and delivers information resources within 48 working hours. The benefit of the human-mediated service is that it allows AskERIC staff to determine the precise information needs of the client and to present an array of relevant resources, both from the ERIC system and from the vast resources of the Internet.

To send an inquiry to AskERIC using e-mail, address your message to `askeric@ericir.syr.edu`.

Web66

Unlike ERIC, which is still strongly based on Gopher, the Web66 project shown in Figure 16.23 is built around the World Wide Web. To explore this site, open its home page: `http://web66.coled.umn.edu/`

FIGURE 16.23.

Web66—The World Wide Web Education Project.

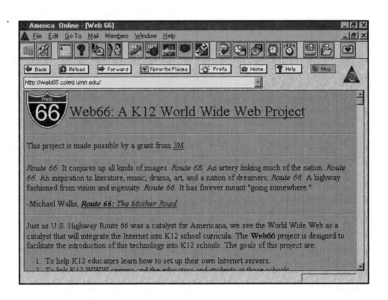

Begun by the University of Minnesota to facilitate the introduction of Internet and World Wide Web technology into K12 schools, this project aims to

◆ Help educators set up their own Internet servers.

◆ Assist educators in linking these servers to the World Wide Web and other K12 schools connected to the Internet.

◆ Help educators locate K12-related resources on the Internet.

One of the main features of this page is the Web66 What's New page, which is updated daily. If you want to keep up-to-date with all the latest happenings in the online education world, this is the place to look.

Note | Mac Users: For Apple Macintosh users, this site contains a very good discussion of exactly what's involved in using a Mac as a WWW, Gopher, or FTP server.

GNN's Education Center

Another good source of educational information is the Education Center (see Figure 16.24) operated by GNN (Global Network Navigator), located at http://www.gnn.com/gnn/meta/edu/index.html.

FIGURE 16.24.

The GNN Education Center.

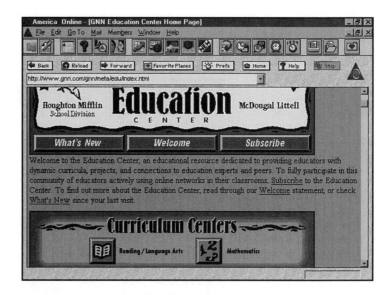

Although this site contains links to many of the same pages as Web66, it also maintains its own What's New catalog called K12 Weekly. The Education Center also operates a classifieds service where teachers can advertise for collaborators when planning school projects and Internet-based classroom activities such as Travel Buddies. The Travel Buddies concept is an inter-classroom activity in which students from schools in distant locations—often on opposite sides of the world—exchange a small stuffed animal and report on the activities these Travel Buddies participate in while on vacation.

This page also features links to the GNN Library of Links, which is the ideal place to look for those hard-to-find K12 resources. There is also a link to a selection of notable quotes and humorous tales for those times when you really need to relax.

Before you can take advantage of the services offered by GNN, you need to register as a user. You can do this from either the Education Center index page or the GNN home page at `http://www.gnn.com/`.

Tip

Keyword: Education

The AOL Education Channel, Keyword: **Education**, also provides you with access to a number of education-related WWW sites via its Top Internet Sites icon. (See Figure 16.25.) When you click on this button, the Hot Internet Sites window, shown in Figure 16.26, is displayed on your screen.

FIGURE 16.25.

The AOL Education Channel.

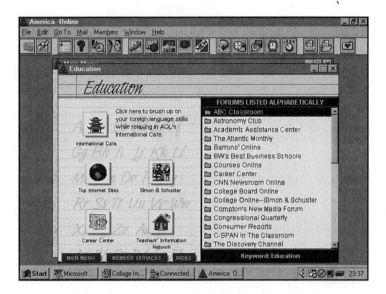

FIGURE 16.26.

Select from the list of education sites provided by America Online.

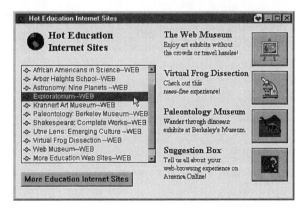

An important feature of all the sites listed in this window is the fact that when you select any of them, AOL launches a special version of its WWW browser that is designed specially for kids. (See Figure 16.27.) Options such as the URL document line, Preferences button, Favorite Places button, and Home button have been removed from this version of the WWW browser to prevent younger users from gaining access to areas of the World Wide Web that might not be suitable. At the same time, by reducing the number of options available they have made using the World Wide Web a lot less daunting task for a new user.

> **Note**
>
> This feature is currently only available for the Windows version of AOL.

FIGURE 16.27.

When using the Kids Only WWW browser to visit sites like ExploraNet, all the more complex or "unsafe" features of the standard WWW browser are removed from the screen.

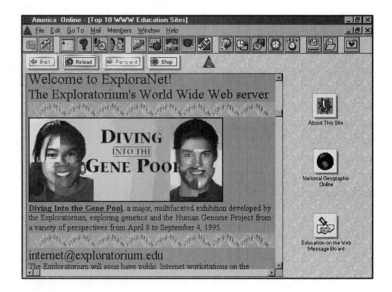

In addition to the links provided by the Hot Education Internet Sites page, AOL also maintains a directory of other education-related pages on its WWW server. To access this directory, click on the More Education Internet Sites button, or use its corresponding URL: `http://www.blue.aol.com/internet_resources/education/`.

FIGURE 16.28.

Try out the AOL education Map of the Month, you never know what you might find.

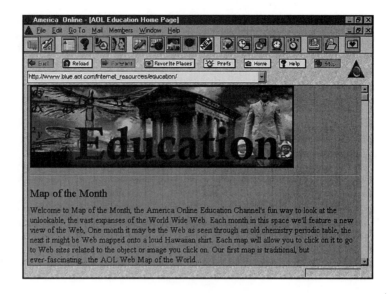

Study and Research

As a research tool, the Internet offers capabilities unheard of in even the recent past. Many people wish that Internet access had been freely available during their time at school and college. With services such as the World Wide Web and WAIS now bringing the world to your desktop, finding information on many subjects is often just a few keystrokes away.

For example, assume that you are doing an assignment on the Hubble space telescope and want to find some information about what it does, and maybe locate a picture or two as well to show what it looks like. There are a number of places you can begin a search, but by far the best approach is to again use of the World Wide Web. From the World Wide Web, you can access two of the main Internet research tools: WWW search pages and WAIS.

The Web and Hubble

The weapon of choice for this Web search is Lycos, which was discussed in Chapter 13, "World Wide Web Productivity." To search for information on the Hubble space telescope using Lycos, follow these steps:

1. Call up the Lycos home page, shown in Figure 16.29.

   The home page for Lycos is `http://lycos.cs.cmu.edu/`.

FIGURE 16.29.

Enter hubble picture *in the search field.*

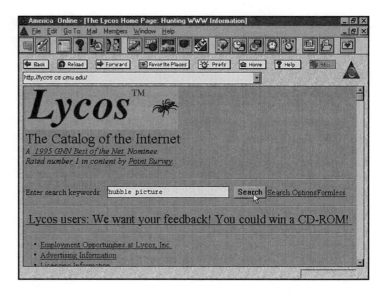

2. In the Enter Search Keywords: field, type a list of keywords you want to search for. For this example enter **hubble picture.** This should find pages that are relevant to the Hubble space telescope.

   Once you have entered the parameters, click on the Search button to begin the search.

3. After a short wait, Lycos begins to display the results of your search showing its name, http address, and a partial listing of its contents. (See Figure 16.30.)

   After looking through the results of the search, find a site that looks right for your needs. Figure 16.31 shows part of the results list, which includes a site that seems to contain a number of pictures dealing with the Hubble telescope and possibly some that may be useful for your assignment.

   To open this page, click on the highlighted http address shown at the beginning of the entry.

Tip

Using the search field on the Lycos home page, Lycos displays the first 10 entries it locates. To request additional entries, select the Search Options link located next to the Search button.

4. When AOL finishes loading the selected page (see Figure 16.31), it turns out that this is really the Hubble information mother lode. In fact, this site contains more information than you would ever need for your assignment, including a large collection of photos taken by the Hubble itself.

FIGURE 16.30.

Lycos lists the results on each search, including the http address of the site.

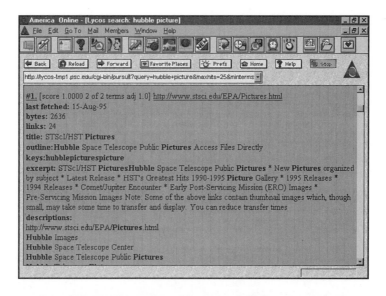

FIGURE 16.31.

The Hubble space telescope images page at the Space Telescope Science Institute WWW site.

All things considered, these steps would probably take no more than five minutes to complete, and in that time will have located all the information you need as well as some suitable photographs.

> Obviously, you will not always be so lucky, but when you consider that by the end of this year, some experts estimate that there will be over 8 million pages of information available on the World Wide Web, the odds of not finding what you are looking for are being reduced by the day.

WAIS and Hubble

Like Lycos, WAIS enables you to search for information stored on the Internet. But this time, instead of searching through WWW pages, you search the many databases linked by WAIS. To access WAIS, you can use either a dedicated WAIS client or a Web-based client like WAISgate. Both the dedicated client and the World Wide Web client achieve the same results, although each is somewhat different in its operation.

For this search you will use WAISgate, because you are already connected to the World Wide Web. (See Appendix C for information about obtaining dedicated WAIS clients.) To begin the search you need to follow these steps:

1. To open WAISgate, call up the WAIS, Inc. home page shown in Figure 16.32, which is located at `http://www.wais.com/`.

FIGURE 16.32.

The WAIS, Inc.
home page.

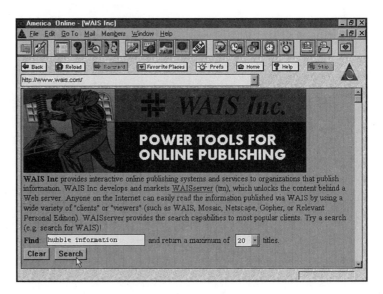

2. For this example, to find some up-to-date information on what the Hubble space telescope is doing, enter the words **hubble information** into the search field as shown in Figure 16.32. Click on the Search button to get started.

3. When WAISgate completes the search, it generates a list of databases matching the search parameters. (See Figure 16.33.)

   Because you are trying to find information about Hubble's status, the `sci.astro.hubble` database seems like a good place to start. To open this database, click on its hotlink.

FIGURE 16.33.

WAISgate lists every database that matches search parameters.

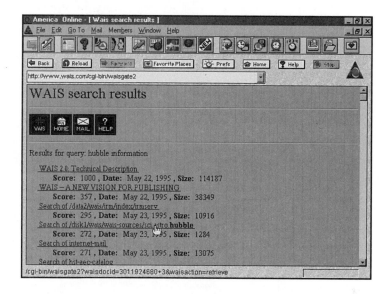

4. When you click on the `sci.astro.hubble` item, WAISgate displays another search form similar to the directory of servers form. This time, however, it shows the name of the selected database. (See Figure 16.34.)

   To narrow down the search a little bit, this time type **status** into the Search field and then click on the Submit Query button. You could also type any other word that would narrow down the files selected.

5. After WAISgate completes its search, it again creates a list showing all the files matching the search parameters. (See Figure 16.35.)

   From here you can request copies of each of the files listed, all of which contain information pertaining to the status of the Hubble Space Telescope.

Like World Wide Web search tools such as Lycos, or AOL's own WebCrawler, WAISgate offers you another powerful research tool with hundreds of databases containing an extensive collection of text resources. How each of these resources will suit your needs may differ greatly, but between the two of them, you have access to a large percentage of the information available on the Internet.

FIGURE 16.34.

To search the `sci.astro.hubble` *database, type* **status** *and click on the Submit Query button.*

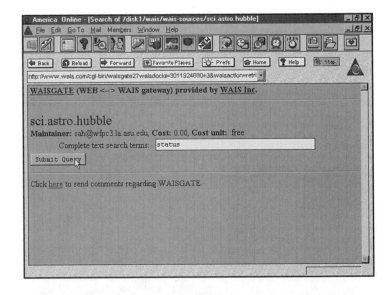

FIGURE 16.35.

The `sci.astro.hubble` *database contains a collection of text files.*

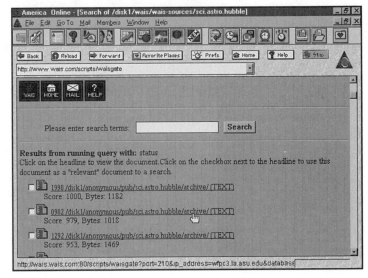

For Kids Only

Unlike a lot of other online services, America Online places a great deal of interest in the needs of its younger users. To cater to this rapidly growing population of online users, America Online operates a special Kids Only channel (see Figure 16.36), which is filled to the brim with information and activities for kids, both young and old.

FIGURE 16.36.

The Kids Only channel.

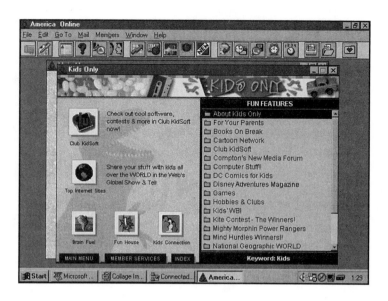

With the advent of World Wide Web access, AOL has decided to update the Kids Only channel to include a range of Internet-related links (see Figure 16.37) using the special WWW browser mentioned in the previous section. To access this list, click on the Top Internet Sites icon displayed in the Kids Only window.

FIGURE 16.37.

Kids Top Internet Sites at America Online.

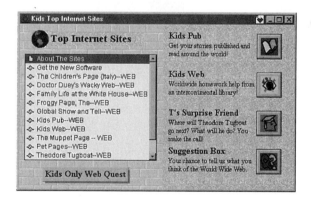

KidPub

By far, the most tempting element of the World Wide Web is the ability to publish information that all the world can read. With the introduction of KidPub, even the youngest members of the family can get into the act and have their literary creations and pictures displayed on the World Wide Web.

FIGURE 16.38.

Publish stories on the World Wide Web with KidPub.

To get a story published at KidPub, all you have to do is send it as an e-mail message to `KidPub@ engarde.com`. KidPub's administrators will do the rest. They will format the story into an html page suitable for viewing on the World Wide Web and include a link to the story on the list at the KidPub home page. In addition to the story itself, kids can also include a brief note telling everyone who they are. This note should include things like their favorite hobbies and sports, what type of pets they have, or maybe the types of shows they like to watch on TV.

For the more adventurous, you can also submit pictures by e-mail using a MIME format encoder. (See Chapter 6, "The Internet E-Mail Gateway," for more information.) Or if you have access to an FTP client that supports file uploads, you can upload the file to `ftp://en-garde.com/ incoming/`.

Kids Web: The Digital Library for School Kids

For those of you that remember spending hours in the school library searching though stacks of books for information that always seemed to be in either the last book you checked or the only book currently checked out of the library, Kids Web will probably make you green with envy.

As the name suggests, Kids Web is a library just for kids that contains information they will find invaluable when doing research for school assignments and class projects. Categorized into subjects such as the Arts, Sport, History, and Science, this site contains hundreds of pages of useful information, along with pictures, diagrams, and even the occasional audio clip. (See Figure 16.39.)

FIGURE 16.39.

The World Wide Web Digital Library for School Kids.

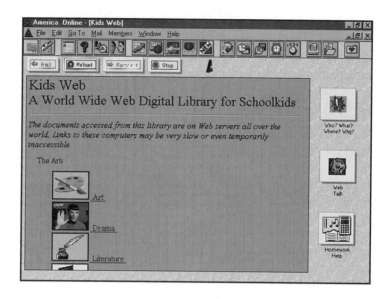

FIGURE 16.39.

The World Wide Web Digital Library for School Kids.

T's Surprise Friend

And now for something completely different. Theodore is a Tugboat who generally enjoys life and good friends. To find out about his latest escapade, click on the T's Surprise Friend button and follow the story. (See Figure 16.40.)

FIGURE 16.40.

Follow the adventures of Theodore and choose the outcome of the story.

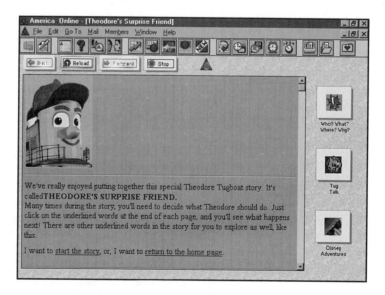

This series of stories is based on the interactive storytelling concept made popular by "choose your own outcome" books and magazines. This time, however, the story comes to you via the World Wide Web. Apart from that, the concept is the same. As you read the story, you are presented with different choices that determine the outcome of the story.

Kids Only WebQuest

Another good way to learn about the World Wide Web is by participating in WebQuest—a game run by America Online. WebQuest provides you with a list of links to different sites all over the World Wide Web, where you will find clues to the WebQuest riddle.

What makes this game such a good tool, however, is the fact that while they are exploring the Web looking for clues, they are also learning about a host of different concepts and useful information. Then, once they think they know what happens next, they can send a message to the Kids Department to find out whether they are correct.

Kids Resources on the World Wide Web

As an adjunct to the sites listed on the Kids Top Internet Sites window, AOL also maintains a more extensive list of sites as a part of its Internet Resource directory. You can explore this directory by double-clicking on the More Kids Web Sites entry, shown previously in Figure 16.37. Alternatively, you can select this page (see Figure 16.41) using its URL which is `http:/ /www.blue.aol.com/internet_resource/kids/`. This page is also the location of the Kids Only WebQuest and also contains a link that returns you to the Kids Top Internet Sites window.

Finally, you may also like to look at the links display as a part of the AOL Internet directory itself. This page can be viewed by pointing the WWW browser to: `http://www.blue.aol.com/ internet_resource/directory/browse/6Kdsl.htm`.

FIGURE 16.41.

The AOL Internet Resource directory also contains a list of kid's Web sites.

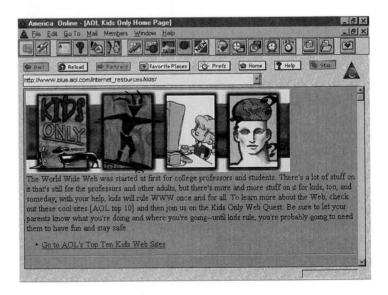

Summary

As you have seen in this chapter, the Internet contains resources suited to the different needs of all members of the community, whether it's games, magazines, newspapers, educational information, study tools, or even specialized WWW pages just for kids.

However, there is one aspect of the community that has not yet been discussed—the business community. To rectify this, "Business on the Internet" is the topic of discussion in the next chapter.

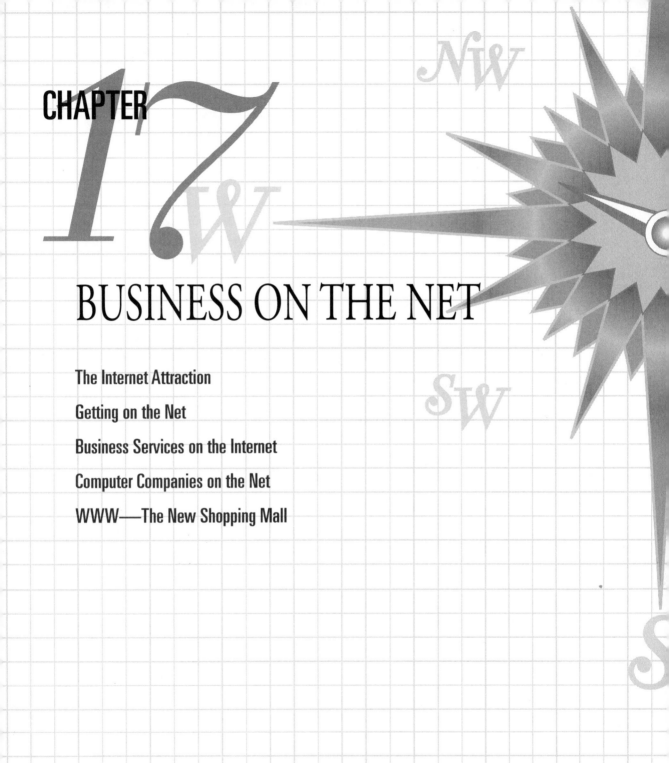

CHAPTER 17

BUSINESS ON THE NET

Until recently, many Internet users weren't open to the idea of companies doing business on the Net. For a long time there was strong resistance to any business activities on the Internet, with the operators of many network backbones actively participating in the lockout of business activities.

In fact, it was not until the formation of the *Commercial Internet Exchange* (CIX) that business activities began to be tolerated by much of the Internet. Gaining this acceptance came at a considerable cost, however, because CIX was effectively forced to set up its own communications backbone to bypass those areas of the Internet that insisted on locking it out. Thankfully, that period of conflict in the life of the Internet is pretty much behind us now, and businesses, educators, and the public alike are now permitted to roam the Internet at will.

Since the resolution of this conflict, the commercial sector has consistently maintained its position as the fastest growth area on the Internet. As a result, the Internet Society reported that by the end of 1994 there were over 1.2 million commercial hosts connected to the Internet.

This chapter looks at why so many businesses are connecting to the Internet and explores some of the ways that even the smallest business can get a foothold. It looks at the following topics:

◆ The Internet Attraction

◆ Companies and Services

◆ Business Services on the Internet

◆ Computer Companies on the Net

◆ WWW—The New Shopping Mall

The Internet Attraction

There are many reasons why companies of all sizes are now looking to the Internet. Some see the benefits of electronic mail, others see the potential of the World Wide Web, and some just want to use it because it's there. Regardless of the reason, it is a fair assumption that in the not-too-distant future, most businesses will be connected to the Internet in some way.

Commercial E-Mail

As the pace of daily life increases at near breakneck speed, people have come to expect, and in many cases demand, instant feedback and around-the-clock support.

Unfortunately, the postal and courier services have reached a point where they simply cannot meet the turnaround requirements of 1990s business in the fast lane. To cope with these demands, the first innovation was the telex machine, an expensive device that required constant maintenance and trained operators—but at least they got the job done. Then came the fax machine, heralded as the business development of the century. No longer was there a need for telex operators, and even CEOs could be taught to use them.

From a resource perspective, the fax machine is a wasteful tool, spewing out streams of paper when often all that was required is a simple one-line answer. It is also less useful within the office environment itself, although people have been known to send faxes from room to room just to make a point. Now, with the widespread acceptance of computer networking, electronic mail is rapidly replacing the fax in many business situations as the primary communications tool.

E-mail offers a new level of interaction to the business community. Using e-mail, messages can be sent and received almost instantly for considerably less cost than a corresponding letter or fax. This rapid transmission also leads to increased productivity because turnaround times for responses to messages can be reduced to a matter of hours or sometimes even minutes.

Global Presence

E-mail is a powerful tool, but the big attraction for many businesses is the potential for global exposure through services such as the World Wide Web.

To any business, the potential for greater public exposure, and hence the possibility of increased sales or greater market share, is a carrot that is hard to ignore. When this also means the possibility of international exposure, it becomes obvious why so many commercial sites are springing up all over the Internet.

Not since the invention of the telephone has a single communications service done more to bring about the advent of a global economic community. In real terms, it is now possible for even the smallest business to market its products and services to a global market for less than the cost of a good meal in a restaurant. Businesses are not the only ones to benefit from the global reach offered by the Internet. For the first time, many consumers now have direct access to products and services that only a few years ago would not have been available to them.

Riding on the heels of this new consumer gold mine are the many credit card services, which also stand to benefit greatly from the upturn in online shopping. For their part, many of these services are very active in the area of secure transaction processing development, with both Visa and MasterCard now promoting these much-needed Internet security enhancements.

Warning

> The AOL WWW browser does not currently support the use of secure transaction processing. If you want to order products online, you should consider downloading a copy of Netscape and using the AOL winsock.dll file discussed in Chapter 10, "AOL and Winsock."

The Internet Industry

In addition to offering new opportunities to existing businesses, the growth in popularity of the Internet has fostered the development of an entirely new industry. This industry is devoted solely to the support and maintenance of the Internet and the services it provides.

To accompany the astounding growth of the Internet, new businesses offering Internet connections, WWW development assistance, FTP and HTML page storage, electronic shopping malls, and Internet-related software are popping up all over. If you want to get your business on the Internet, these companies are the place to start. And where do you find these companies? On the Internet, of course.

Is it any wonder that so many people are talking about the Internet? While some regard it as a passing fad, others are calling it the overnight success story of the century. However, what it is now and what it has the potential to become suggest that the Internet is most definitely the place for businesses to be.

Getting on the Net

All this sounds great, right? But how do you go about actually getting your business on the Internet?

The are two basic ways that you can do this. The first is by purchasing a direct TCP/IP connection from an Internet service provider and setting up your own Internet WWW server, FTP site, e-mail gateway, and possibly a gopher server as well. Or alternatively, you can rent space from an existing site and install your WWW pages or FTP files there.

> Because a discussion of the concepts involved in setting up your own WWW site with the TCP/IP links, hardware, and server software complexities that includes, are beyond the scope of this book, you should refer to *The World Wide Web Unleashed*, also from Sams.net, for additional information.

Online Service Providers

If setting up an Internet server is not within your budget, there is another option that may be more suited to your financial constraints. A number of companies have begun to set up servers on the Internet where you can rent space. Using one of these servers, you can set up your own FTP site or WWW home page without having to worry about operating your own permanent Internet connection or World Wide Web server.

The following pages look at two very different types of online service providers. The first service offers almost total access to its WWW server and allows you a high level of customization but also requires a considerable amount of effort on your part. The second service offers you little or no access to its WWW server and requires very little work on your part. On the downside, this type of service usually does not provide a high level of flexibility and adaptability.

Chapter 14, "WWW Publishing with AOL," discusses two alternative WWW publishing services provided by America Online itself. These are Personal Publisher and NaviPress.

Web Communications

One of the most popular online Web servers is operated by a company called Web Communications—WebCom. (See Figure 17.1.) Using WebCom, you can create your own WWW pages and make them available to people on the Internet. The WebCom home page is located at `http://www.webcom.com/`.

FIGURE 17.1.

At Web Communications you can set up your own private WWW home page or FTP server.

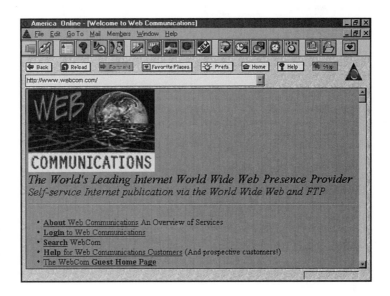

Registration

The main feature of Web Communications' server is that the entire service can be managed using the World Wide Web. This includes the registration process and all contractual negotiations.

To open an account with WebCom, all you need to do is fill out an application form using your WWW Navigator and select a preferred payment method. If you choose to take advantage of the credit card payment facility, your WebCom account will be up and running about four hours after you make your request.

When you fill out your application, you will need to nominate the type of account you want to apply for. At WebCom, this is based on how you intend to use the account and the size of your business. For private users, there is a personal account that can only be used for non-profit purposes. For companies with less than 15 employees, there is a special business rate. All other companies will need to select the corporate rate.

Regardless of which account you select, using a service like WebCom can save you thousands of dollars, not to mention the time and effort required to maintain an Internet server. To give you a better idea of the costs involved, Table 17.1 lists the current pricing structure for WebCom.

Table 17.1. WebCom pricing structure as of Sept, 1995.

Fee Description	Personal	Business	Corporate
One-time setup fee	$14.95	$44.95	$145.00
Monthly fee	$9.95	$29.95	$95.00
Mo. disk sp. allowance	5MB	5MB	10MB
Addtl. disk space/mo.	$1.95/MB	$2.95/MB	$4.95/MB
Net traffic allow./mo.	200MB	200MB	400MB
Optional addtl. traffic	$1.95/100MB	$3.95/100MB	$5.95/100MB

WebCom Services

Once you have created an account at WebCom, you can log on to your own private WWW server at any time. To maintain the WWW pages on this server, you use the online tools provided on the Web Communication - Customer Online Services page shown in Figure 17.2. From this page you can access your private directories on the WebCom server, configure the various accounting and traffic reports available online, and keep track of your monthly account fees.

Note

Due to the current AOL WWW browser for Windows being unable to support all the new HTML 3.0 features required by sites such as WebCom, you need either an FTP client that supports file uploads or a dedicated WWW browser such as GNNWorks or Netscape to set up your WWW pages.

FIGURE 17.2.

Web Communications lets you maintain your WWW pages online.

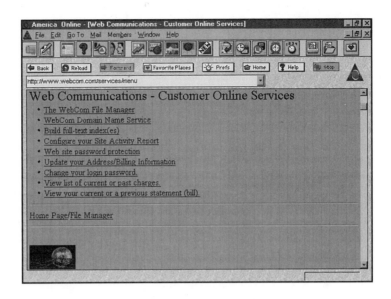

WWW Home Pages

For many people, the main reason for opening a WebCom account is the ability to create a personal WWW home page. The moment you open an account, a home page is automatically created for you using the account name you gave during the registration process.

The address for this home page is http://www.webcom.com/~ plus your account name. When I opened an account at WebCom for Take Two—my film and television site—I selected the account name taketwo. As a result, anyone who wants to access this home page uses the address http://www.webcom.com/~taketwo/welcome.shtml. (See Figure 17.3.)

FIGURE 17.3.

Take Two, the film and television home page.

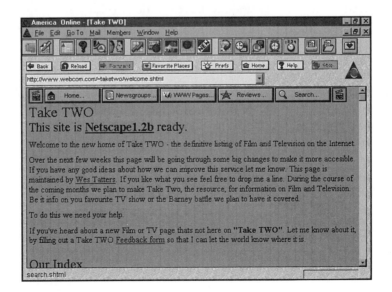

Depending on the type of WWW browser you are currently using, you may also be able to access my home page by using just `http://www.webcom.com/~taketwo/`. However, the AOL WWW browser currently requires you to add the welcome.shtml page name as well.

> `Welcome.shtml` is the name of the home page itself. On some sites you will find that this page may also be called `index.html`, `index.htm`, `welcome.html`, `welcome.htm`, or possibly even `home.html`. It really just depends on the service you choose to use.

> By the time you read this book, there will also be no need to include the tilde (~) as a part of your URL. As a result, `http://www.webcom.com/taketwo/` will also become a valid URL.

If you are interested in film and television, why not drop in sometime and say hi? I have links to every major film and TV page on the World Wide Web, and all the popular newsgroups as well. Oh, and if you like what you see, don't forget to nominate it for the Best of the Web. (So much for the shameless plug <G>.)

When it comes to online WWW maintenance, about the only thing that you can't easily do online is design your home page extravaganza. WebCom does allow you to edit the HTML text of your WWW pages online, but for any serious work you need to consider using one of the many HTML editors now available. (See Chapter 12 for information about designing HTML pages.)

FTP Sites

In addition to World Wide Web access, you can also use FTP to access your directory area at WebCom and selectively make directories available to the public as well.

Using the AOL FTP client, you can log on to WebCom using its FTP server. To access the WebCom FTP server, use this domain name: `ftp.webcom.com`.

Once connected, you will find that your files are stored in the subdirectory `/pub/` with the same name as your account. In Figure 17.4, I located my TakeTwo files in the `/pub/taketwo` directory. The subdirectories of `/pub/taketwo` store any HTML pages I have created and can also be configured to hold files that other people can download just like a normal anonymous FTP server.

> If you log on to `ftp://ftp.webcom.com` as an anonymous user, only those files and directories marked as public on the WebCom WWW Directory Management page can be downloaded. To access protected files using FTP, log on using your WebCom account name and password.

FIGURE 17.4.

Take Two via FTP.

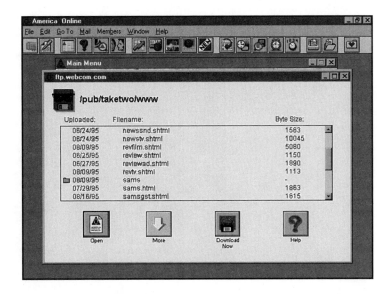

Mailing Lists

Probably the most unusual service offered by Web Communications is the ability to operate a simplified type of mailing list. (See Chapter 7 for a discussion of mailing lists.)

Using the instructions outlined online, you can create any number of mailing lists—called *exploder lists*. These mailing lists can contain any sort of information you wish to distribute.

This system works by assigning you an e-mail address for each mailing list. When anyone sends a message to this address, all the people whose e-mail addresses are included in a special text file set up for this purpose, are automatically sent a copy of the message.

While exploder lists don't offer all the capabilities of Majordomo or LISTSERV, they do provide you with a simple, but effective means of distributing information as a part of a mailing list. In addition, WebCom also provides you with a special WWW form that can be used to let people subscribe to these lists via the World Wide Web.

WebCom Support Services

To help you create your home pages, WebCom offers possibly the most comprehensive online guide to HTML ever produced. (See Figure 17.5.) There is information here for everyone who has ever considered using the World Wide Web, discussing topics as diverse as:

Tutorials on HTML
Forms management and WebCom
WWW marketing and advertising
A beginner's guide to the World Wide Web
Online help for all WebCom tools

FIGURE 17.5.

WebCom's Comprehensive Guide to the World Wide Web.

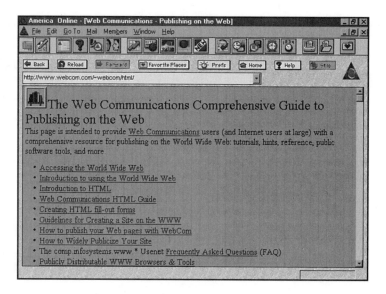

BizPro—Billboards on the Internet

For businesses that don't want to have to learn about HTML, there is another option. For a fee, some WWW operators will create the electronic equivalent of a billboard on their server where you can advertise your products and services.

One such server specializing in this type of service is BizPro. When you purchase a billboard from BizPro (see Figure 17.6), all you need to do is give them a copy of the text you want to display on your billboard and any images, such as corporate logos or product graphics. BizPro then takes this information, creates your Web HTML pages, and places links to your billboard in their customer directory.

FIGURE 17.6.

Advertise your products on BizPro's Electronic Billboard.

To find out more about the services offered by BizPro, take a look at their WWW server on `http://www.bizpro.com/bizpro/bilbord.html`.

Rates and Charges

Instead of charging a flat rate for space on their WWW server, BizPro charges you by the page, because they are actually doing all the maintenance work for you. To give you some idea of the costs involved in using this type of service, Table 17.2 lists the current charges for a listing on BizPro.

Table 17.2. BizPro billboard charges as of January, 1995.

	1/4 page	*1/2 page*	*Full page*
Page rental per year	$60.00	$120.00	$240.00
Each addtl. page per year	$30.00	$60.00	$120.00
Text updates	$10.00	$10.00	$10.00
Graphics updates	$20.00	$20.00	$20.00

Forms and Customization

If yours is a small business, or one that doesn't plan to make many changes to their listing, this type of service can provide a quick way to get your business on the Internet. However, if you plan to change your information on a regular basis or would like to use features like forms, services like BizPro should be considered only as a short-term option. At this stage, BizPro is strictly a billboard service and as such does not permit the use of data entry forms of any description.

If this is the case, you will probably be better off investing some time in learning about HTML and opting for a service like the one offered by WebCom or the NaviPress service discussed in Chapter 14.

Business Services on the Internet

With the rapid growth of interest in the Internet from the business community, it didn't take long for some astute minds to realize that the Internet itself could be used to offer much-needed support.

As a result, several Internet business centers are now beginning to appear on the World Wide Web. These centers offer assistance to businesses interested in moving onto the Internet as well as support for existing services. This section looks at some of the businesses now available on the Internet and some of the major directories that will assist you in locating others.

AOL and Business on the Net

To accompany the already extensive list of online business and finance tools provided by America Online, they have recently added a new Internet Resources area that links you to business- and finance-based pages located on the World Wide Web.

To access this area, click on the Internet Resources icon shown in Figure 17.7. When you do this AOL opens a window like the one shown in Figure 17.8.

FIGURE 17.7.

The AOL Finance Channel contains links to many business- and finance-related WWW sites.

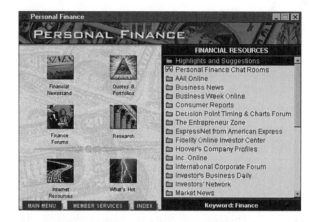

FIGURE 17.8.

Select any of the sites listed and AOL starts its WWW browser to retrieve the chosen page.

All the sites on this list have been chosen by AOL because they represent much of the best of what the World Wide Web has to offer. If, however, you want to view a more extensive list of business- and finance-related sites, you can do so by selecting the Other Web Sites entry shown in Figure 17.8. This opens AOL's Personal Finance Resources On the Web directory as shown in Figure 17.9. This page contains a list of the top 100 finance pages on the Internet and is a part of the AOL Resource Directory. You can also visit this page using the following URL:
`http://www.blue.aol.com/internet_resources/personal_finance/top_hundred/`.

FIGURE 17.9.

The top 100 finance sites on the World Wide Web are listed here.

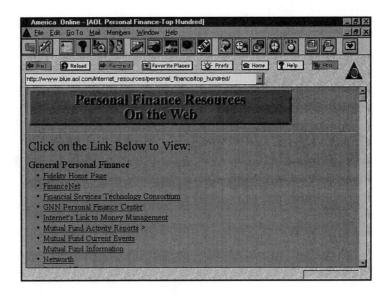

CommerceNet

CommerceNet is a non-profit corporation formed in 1993 to facilitate Internet use for electronic commerce. According to the CommerceNet charter, it aims to:

◆ Operate an Internet-based World Wide Web server with directories and information to facilitate an open electronic marketplace for business-to-business transactions;

◆ Accelerate the mainstream application of electronic commerce on the Internet through fielding pilot programs in areas such as transaction security and electronic catalogs;

◆ Enhance existing Internet services and applications and stimulate the development of new services;

◆ Encourage broad participation from small, medium, and large companies and offer outreach programs to educate organizations about the resources and benefits available with CommerceNet;

◆ Serve as a common information infrastructure for northern California and coordinate with national and international infrastructure projects.

By doing this, CommerceNet hopes to stimulate the growth of a communications infrastructure that will be easy to use, oriented for commercial use, and ready to expand rapidly.

The first and most visible outcome of this project was the creation of the CommerceNet WWW server, shown in Figure 17.10. If you are interested in finding out more about what CommerceNet is doing or how you can take advantage of the services it offers, this is the best place to start. The http address for this WWW site is http://www.commerce.net/.

FIGURE 17.10.

The CommerceNet home page at http://www.commerce.net/.

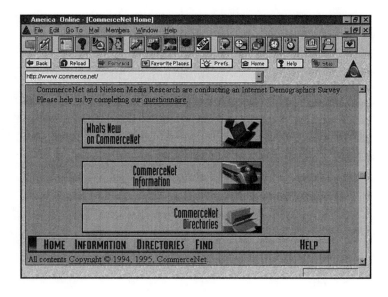

The Internet Business Center

While CommerceNet offers you a considerable wealth of information about commerce on the Internet, there is another site that offers more general business-orientated information. The service I am referring to is the Internet Business Center (see Figure 17.11), located at `http://www.tig.com/IBC/index.html`.

FIGURE 17.11.

The Internet Business Center offers a wide variety of business information.

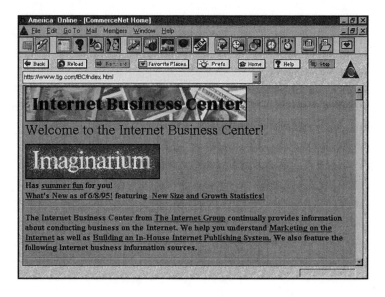

If you are planning to set up any sort of business venture on the Internet, spending a few hours browsing through the information stored at this site could save you many sleepless nights further down the line. Of all the information stored here, the section called "Building an In-House Internet Publishing System" should be considered required reading. In addition, there are some valuable insights into the art of marketing on the Internet and a good collection of facts and figures that can help make your case for an Internet server to even the most wary board of directors.

This site also provides links to many other business-related sites, including financial and legal services, and graduate business schools, through the Internet Business Center Hot Sites list (see Figure 17.12), which can be found at `http://www.tig.com/IBC/Servers.html`.

FIGURE 17.12.

The Internet Business Center Hot Sites list.

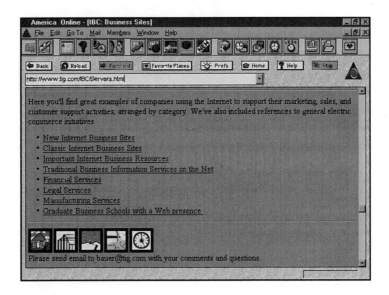

TradeWave Galaxy Business and Commerce Directory

The most comprehensive directory of business- and commerce-related Internet sites is maintained by TradeWave Galaxy in its Business and Commerce directory. (See Figure 17.13.) This directory is maintained as a part of the Galaxy directory service discussed in Chapter 13.

You can access the directory from the Galaxy home page or jump straight to it at `http://galaxy.einet.net/galaxy/Business-and-Commerce.html`.

> To coincide with the name change from EINET to TradeWave, the Galaxy Business and Commerce directory can now also be accessed using `http://galaxy.tradewave.com/galaxy/Business-and-Commerce.html`.

Note

FIGURE 17.13.

The TradeWave Galaxy Business and Commerce directory.

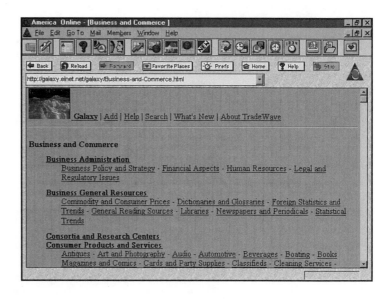

Other Popular Listings

There are many other business-oriented lists on the World Wide Web dealing with a wide variety of business-related topics. To get you started, Table 17.3 lists some of the more popular business listings.

Table 17.3. Other popular business pages and listings.

Site Name	HTTP Address
Yahoo	`http://www.yahoo.com/Business/`
GNN	`http://www.gnn.com/gnn/bus/index.html`
Career Mosaic	`http://www.careermosaic.com/cm/`
Legal Information Institute	`http://www.law.cornell.edu/`
GE Corporate Toolkit	`http://ce-toolkit.crd.ge.com/`
Networth Info Page	`http://networth.galt.com/www/home/networth.htm`
Dow Jones Industrial Averages	`http://www.secapl.com/secapl/quoteserver/djia.html`
BizInfo	`http://www.dnai.com/~sharrow/bizinfo.html`

Computer Companies on the Net

As you would probably expect, many of the major computer manufacturers and software companies now present a variety of services on the Internet. Some companies offer online support to their customers, others provide software updates and patches, and a few even allow you to purchase software products online.

Software Manufacturers

To help you locate some of these companies, and because most of these companies now operate a server on the World Wide Web, Table 17.4 provides you with a list of World Wide Web sites operated by software manufacturers.

Table 17.4. Computer software manufacturers on the World Wide Web.

WWW Home Page	*Company Name*
http://www.adobe.com	Adobe Systems, Inc.
http://www.microsoft.com	Microsoft Corporation
http://www.ncd.com	Network Computing Devices
http://www.novell.com	Novell, Inc.
http://www.sco.com	Santa Cruz Operations, Inc.
http://www.sgi.com	Silicon Graphics, Inc.
http://www.sun.com	Sun Microsystems, Inc.
http://www.synopsys.com	Synopsys

Hardware Manufacturers

Like software manufacturers, many hardware manufactures also operate WWW servers to support their various products and services. Table 17.5 lists the World Wide Web sites of the some of the better known computer hardware manufacturers.

Table 17.5. Computer hardware manufacturers on the World Wide Web.

WWW Home Page	*Company Name*
http://www.amdahl.com	Amdahl Corporation
http://www.apple.com	Apple Computers, Inc.
http://www.cisco.com	Cisco Systems, Inc.
http://www.cray.com	Cray Research, Inc.
http://www.dell.com	Dell Computers
http://www.digital.com	Digital Equipment Corporation
http://www.hp.com	Hewlett Packard
http://www.ibm.com	IBM Corporation

continues

Table 17.5. continued

WWW Home Page	Company Name
`http://www.intel.com`	Intel Corporation
`http://www.qms.com`	QMS, Inc.
`http://www.racal.com`	Racal-Datacom
`http://www.rockwell.com`	Rockwell International
`http://www.tandem.com`	Tandem Computers

WWW—The New Shopping Mall

As discussed in Chapter 15, "The Best of Both Worlds," the Internet is rapidly becoming the shopping mall of the 1990s, offering goods and services to a global market that is just beginning to realize the potential of online shopping.

Discussing the diverse range of products and services now being offered is a job that begs for a book of its own. Instead, this section takes a look at some of the more popular electronic malls offering access to these stores.

The AOL Marketplace

Before stepping onto the Internet boardwalk itself, let's take a short detour to the AOL Marketplace, Keyword: **Marketplace**. AOL has for some time offered its members the benefits of online shopping via its Marketplace channel. (See Figure 17.14.)

FIGURE 17.14.

You can reach the AOL Marketplace using its Keyword: **Marketplace**.

Whether it's flowers, gifts, car prices, or even grocery and pharmaceutical delivery, AOL has had it covered. But now with the advent of the World Wide Web, it seems that everyone is setting up an online shopfront. To keep up with these latest developments, AOL now offers both a directory of online services and their very own WWW shop front.

Top Internet Sites

To open the Marketplace Internet Sites window shown in figure 17.15, click on the Top Internet Sites icon displayed in Figure 17.14. This window contains a list of some of the most popular WWW stores and shopping malls currently available.

To select any of the sites in the menu list double-click on them. This will tell AOL to start its WWW browser and retrieve a copy of the home page for the selected site.

FIGURE 17.15.

Select any of the sites listed and AOL opens its WWW browser to display them.

Downtown AOL

In addition to providing a list of links to other World Wide Web sites, AOL now operates its own WWW Marketplace called Downtown AOL. (See Figure 17.16). You can visit this site by either clicking on the Downtown icon shown in Figure 17.14 or by using its URL, which is `http://downtown.www.aol.com/`.

The Internet Mall

The Internet Mall is operated by Meckler Media—the publishing company that produces *Internet World* magazine—on its MecklerWeb site at `http://www.mecklerweb.com/`. (See Figure 17.17.)

Designed around the concept of a true shopping mall, the Internet Mall is divided into virtual floors (see Figure 17.18) with different products and services available on each level. This site is by far the most comprehensive listing of commercial WWW sites currently available.

FIGURE 17.16.
Downtown AOL.

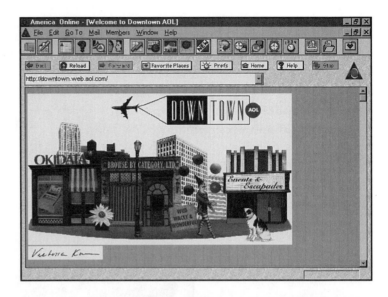

FIGURE 17.17.
*Meckler Media's World
Wide Web site is the home
of the Internet Mall.*

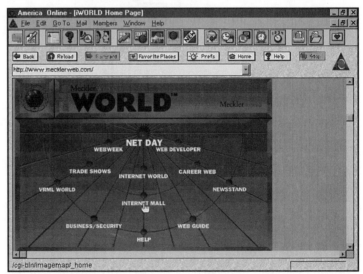

MecklerWeb also provides you with access to WWW pages dedicated to the various publications produced by Meckler Media: *Internet World, VR World, WebWeek,* and *Net.Day.* There are also links to information on Internet-related trade shows, the Career Web, and business activities on the World Wide Web.

FIGURE 17.18.

The Internet Mall uses virtual floors to categorize the products and services available online.

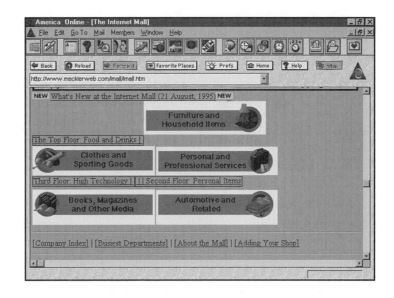

Netscape Galleria

Netscape, the developers of one of the most popular WWW navigators ever written, maintains its own listing of commercial WWW sites at the Netscape Galleria, `http://www.netscape.com/escapes/galleria.html`. (See Figure 17.19.) To find out more about Netscape itself and the list of products and services—including WWW navigators and servers—it provides, use `http://www.netscape.com/`.

FIGURE 17.19.

Click on a letter to display a list of all the sites whose names start with that letter.

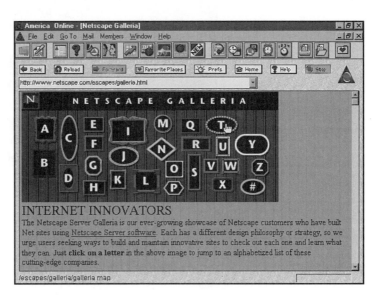

What is special about all of these sites is that they all use a Netscape WWW server. In addition, many of them also support the use of secure transactions, which encode your purchase and credit information—protecting it from prying eyes.

> There are currently a number of different secure transaction specifications making the rounds of the Internet. As a result, it will take some time before an official standard is agreed to and all WWW clients support each of the different protocols. Check with your WWW client provider to find out which protocols it supports.

The Open Market

Open Market (see Figure 17.20), like Netscape, is a developer of World Wide Web server software. Where Open Market servers differ, however, is in the way they operate. Unlike other WWW servers, which provide services to other businesses by allowing them to create their own home pages, Open Market servers oversee all the billing and accounting details for all the stores they contain. To find out more information about the products and services that Open Market provides, use the following http address: `http://www.openmarket.com/`.

FIGURE 17.20.

One-stop billing on the Open Market.

This means simpler online shopping for customers because all your billing details only need to be entered once. The first time you enter an Open Market server, you are asked to create a demonstration account by selecting a user name and password. Doing this allows you to explore some of what the Open Market offers. If you decide to make a purchase, you register your billing details and your account is activated. After this, every time you purchase products and services from businesses in the Open Market, your accounting details are automatically updated and your credit card is billed based on your previous instructions.

> The Open Market supports secure transactions using the S-HTTP protocol. At this stage, however, only people using the latest version of NCSA Mosaic or Netscape 1.2 can take advantage of this capability. Check with your WWW client provider to find out if their latest version supports S-HTTP.

In addition to information about its own products, Open Market also operates one of the most extensive directories of commercial WWW sites currently available. (See Figure 17.21.) To explore the 5,000 commercial WWW sites listed in this directory, use the following http address: `http://www.directory.com/`.

FIGURE 17.21.

The Open Market commerce directory.

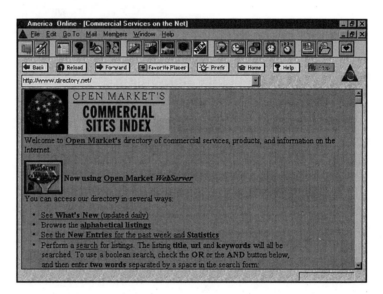

The Internet Shopping Network

If you enjoy the Home Shopping Network, you're bound to find something of interest on its new Internet service, the Internet Shopping Network, whose home page is located at `http://www2.internet.net/`. (See Figure 17.22.)

Like the Home Shopping Network, the Internet Shopping Network strives to offer you the best products at the cheapest prices, with overnight delivery of most products.

Before you can purchase any products on the Internet Shopping Network, you must become a member. To do this, select the Member option from the home page or any of the main product pages. When you fill out the membership application, you will be given your own private account number to use whenever you want to make a purchase.

FIGURE 17.22.

The Internet Shopping Network home page at `http:// www2.internet.net/`.

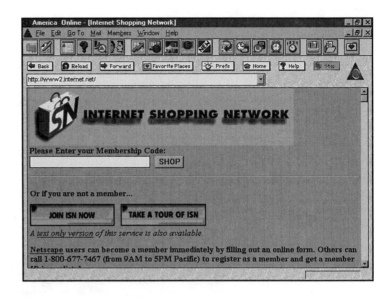

More Malls and Internet Shopping Centers

In addition to these sites, there are a number of other WWW pages that provide lists of commerce-related Internet sites. Table 17.6 contains a list of other popular sites that you may like to explore.

Table 17.6. Shopping malls on the World Wide Web.

Mall Name	HTTP Address
BizWeb	`http://www.bizweb.com/`
Canadian Business Pages	`http://cban.worldgate.edmonton.ab.ca`
Companies on the Net	`http://www.primenet.com/links/companies.html`
iMall	`http://www.imall.com/`
The Commerce Center	`http://www.save.com/`
Shopping 2000	`http://shopping2000.com/`
GNN Direct	`http://www.gnn.com/gnn/gnndirect/index.html`

Summary

Over the past two years, businesses all around the world have begun to realize the potential of the Internet, and the World Wide Web in particular.

As you have seen in this chapter, businesses of all descriptions are now using the Internet for communications, commerce, product support, and customer service. Where this growth will end is hard to say, but it would appear that if you want to remain in business in the very near future, you will need to be connected to the Internet. Eventually, consumers will come to expect this type of access in much the same way that people now simply assume that a business has a fax machine.

As this book goes to press, AOL will be launching a new service offering full TCP/IP connectivity to its users. Currently, the service code named MegaWeb is in public beta testing. As a special bonus, the next chapter examines the potential of this new service and takes a look at its flagship WWW browser—GNNWorks.

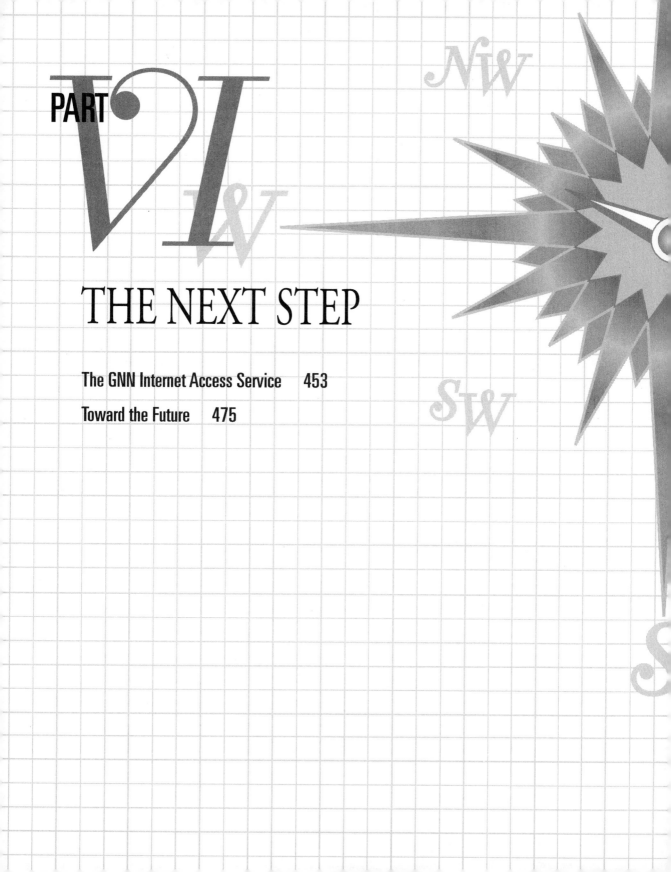

PART

VI

THE NEXT STEP

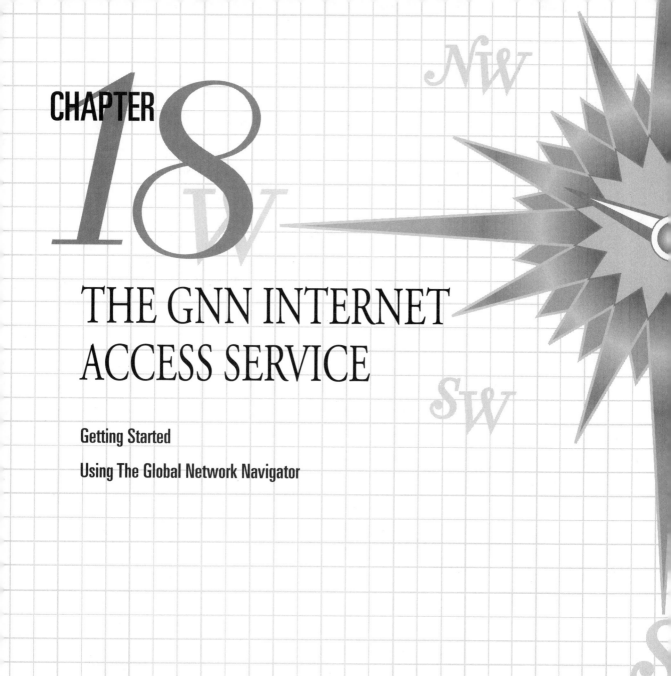

CHAPTER 18

THE GNN INTERNET ACCESS SERVICE

Getting Started

Using The Global Network Navigator

Although America Online now provides you with access to all the major services and tools available on the Internet, it does so through the use of gateways and other interfaces sitting between your computer and the Internet itself.

While this additional interface layer is—for most people—of little concern, there may come a time when a direct TCP/IP connection to the Internet becomes a necessity. One of the main reasons for this usually comes from the area of performance or the desire to use programs not currently supported by America Online itself.

In areas such as e-mail management, newsgroup support, and even to a certain extent the World Wide Web, America Online currently limits you to using its built-in tools. For example, there is a very good newsgroup reader called Free Agent that lets you read articles offline in a much smarter way than by using AOL's FlashSession approach. However, although you can run Free Agent under windows—assuming you have installed the `Winsock.dll` file discussed in Chapter 10, "AOL and Winsock"—there is currently no way to access the America Online news server and retrieve the articles it contains.

For this reason, America Online has decided to set up a dedicated TCP/IP service that is independent from the America Online service discussed previously in this book. As this book goes to press, this new service—the GNN Internet Access service—is in the final stages of beta testing.

You will occasionally find this new service referred to by its beta codename—MegaWeb. This was the name used to describe the GNN Internet service during the public beta testing cycle.

So to give you a sneak preview as a special bonus, this chapter takes a look at what GNN will offer by exploring the following topics:

◆ Getting Started
◆ The GNN Center at America Online
◆ Signing On
◆ Working with GNN

Because America Online has not yet finalized all the details of this new service, you may find that some of the features discussed in this chapter will be subject to change before GNN is finally released to the public.

Getting Started

Following the acquisition of GNN—the Global Network Navigator—in June 1995, and shortly thereafter, the WebCrawler search and indexing tool, America Online announced its intentions to create an easy-to-use, one-stop, TCP/IP service that removed all the hassles so often associated with getting connected to the Internet.

By taking advantage of its existing AOLnet data network, and through the release of a feature-packed Internet navigation tool, America Online aims to provide a service that is second to none, and that can also be accessed by either a local phone call or AOLnet's 1-800 toll-free number from anywhere in North America.

In this section you will find out how easy it is to get connected to the Internet using GNN and also learn about the online registration process.

GNN Center at America Online

To help America Online users get connected to the GNN Internet access service, a new area called the GNN Center (see Figure 18.1) has been opened as a part of the existing America Online service. To visit this area while online, use the Keyword: **GNN**.

FIGURE 18.1.

The GNN Center provides you with everything you need to know about GNN.

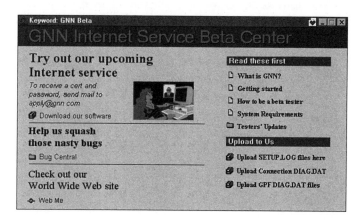

By the time you read this book the look of this page will have changed somewhat to reflect the move from a beta program to full commercial operation, but apart from that, most of the options listed will still be displayed. Of these, by far the most important option available is the Download our software option.

Before you can connect to GNN, you need to obtain a copy of the latest version of the GNN software either by downloading it from the GNN Central software library, or alternatively using FTP from the GNN site at `ftp://ftp.gnn.com/`.

Signing On

Once you have obtained a copy of the navigator software, you are ready to install it and sign on to GNN. To do this, follow the steps listed below:

1. If you downloaded a copy of the GNN software from America Online or from `ftp://ftp.gnn.com/` you first need to obtain a registration certificate number.

   To do this, send an e-mail message to `apply@gnn.com`. When you do this, you usually receive an e-mail response in a matter of minutes listing your registration certificate number and a corresponding password.

   If you are installing the version from the CD-ROM that accompanies this disk, you will need to use the GNN registration certificate number printed on the page opposite the CD-ROM.

2. Using File Manger or Explorer if you have Windows 95, locate and run the file that you downloaded previously. The file will be named something like SETUP.EXE or SETUP28.EXE depending on what filename was assigned when you downloaded it.

The SETUP.EXE file is a special type of compressed archive containing an installation utility and all the programs you need to get GNN installed onto your computer.

3. Once you start the SETUP program, a window like the one shown in Figure 18.2 is displayed on your screen. Click on the Install button to start the installation process or click on the Cancel button to exit without installing GNN.

   If you click on the Review button you can alter the directory in which the GNN software will be installed, but for now, let the setup program install it in the C:\GNN default directory.

4. After you click on the Install button the setup program unpacks all the required files into the selected directory and then displays the message window shown in Figure 18.3.

   When you click on the OK button, setup starts the GNN online registration system and allows you to sign on as a new GNN user.

FIGURE 18.2.

Click on the Install button to unpack the GNN software onto your computer.

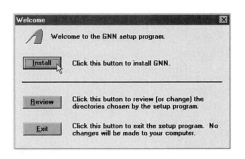

FIGURE 18.3.

When you click on the OK button, the GNN online registration process begins.

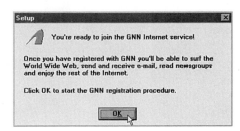

5. By now this process should be beginning to remind you of the online registration process for America Online itself, because all the steps involved are nearly identical.

   When the registration program starts, you first need to enter the Registration number and password obtained in Step 1. You cannot complete the installation without this information. (See Figure 18.4.)

FIGURE 18.4.

Enter the Registration number and password you obtained previously.

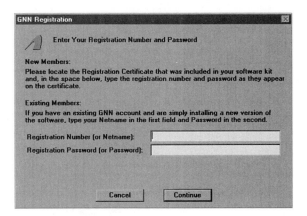

6. After a few screens of Welcome information, on which you can safely click Continue or OK, the installation program asks you to enter the area code for your phone number. (See Figure 18.5.)

Once you have entered this number, the installation program signs you on to GNN and displays a list of numbers in your local area. Pick the number that best suits your needs with regard to location and modem speed. You are then asked to select a second number as a secondary number for those times when your primary number is busy.

FIGURE 18.5.

When you enter your area code, the registration program signs on to GNN and obtains a list of numbers in your local area.

7. Even if you are already an America Online user, you are now asked to complete a Registration information form like the one shown in Figure 18.6, and then select your billing preferences and enter credit card and bank account details.

Although AOL and GNN are both owned by America Online, you will be billed separately for each service.

FIGURE 18.6.

You cannot proceed until you complete all the details on the Registration form.

8. The last step of the registration process requires that you select a Netname (see Figure 18.7) and an access password. When choosing a Netname, the same rules apply as those for a screen name:

   ◆ It must be at least 3 characters and no more than 10 characters in length.

   ◆ It must begin with a letter from 'A' through 'Z'.

   ◆ It may contain letters, spaces, and numbers, but no punctuation marks, however, you should avoid the use of spaces where possible.

   ◆ It can not already be used by another member.

FIGURE 18.7.

Selecting a Netname is a lot like choosing a screen name, in fact, if you want, they can be the same.

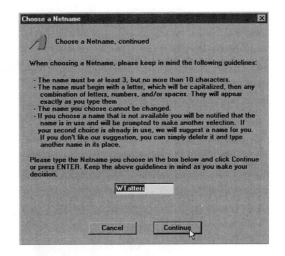

9. With the online registration complete, you are now ready to sign on to GNN for the first time; however, at this stage you still do not have access to all the Internet utilities comprising the GNN software package. There appear to be a number of reasons for taking this approach, but the main one seems to be for security reasons. When you downloaded the SETUP.EXE file previously, the only components you actually received were the programs allowing you to sign on to GNN and register yourself as a new member.

   As a result, before you can make use of all the services provided by GNN, an additional set of files needs to be installed. The installation program is aware of this requirement and automatically starts the download after you enter your Netname and password.

> If this step does not occur the first time you sign on, don't be upset. All this means is that you already have a full copy of the latest version of GNNworks on your computer. The dialer program automatically checks which version you have and updates your system accordingly.

10. After the download is complete, the installation program tells you that it needs to shutdown Windows and re-start your computer before proceeding any further. You must accept this option or the additional GNN utilities will not be properly installed onto your computer.

Using the Global Network Navigator

During the installation process, a new folder is created in your Program Manager window or on the Start menu if you are using Windows 95. In this folder (see Figure 18.8), the installation program places an icon representing each of the utilities provided as a part of the GNN software package.

FIGURE 18.8.

The installation program creates a new folder to hold all your GNN software.

The Internet services these programs allow you to access include the World Wide Web, newsgroups, Gopher, e-mail, and as an added bonus, an IRC client. To give you some idea of how you make use of this software, and to also put in perspective the extensive list of capabilities offered, the remainder of this chapter is devoted to a brief discussion of each of these programs.

GNNconnect

At the heart of GNN lies a program called GNNconnect. (See Figure 18.9.) This is the program responsible for negotiating your connection to the Internet.

As a rule, you will never need to run GNNconnect on its own unless you need to alter your connection or modem settings. This is because when you run programs like the GNNworks browser, GNNconnect is started automatically for you. In fact, the only interaction you will usually have with GNNconnect is when you enter your password during the sign on process and when you click on the **Hangup** icon to finish an online session.

> During the initial registration process, if you interrupt the online registration you can restart it again by opening GNNconnect and selecting the **Register** option from the Connection menu. You can also log onto GNN manually by selecting a location from the list provided and then clicking on the **Login** button.

FIGURE 18.9.

Unless you need to alter your settings you will rarely need to use GNNconnect.

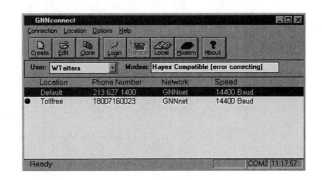

GNNworks

For most people, the main reason they want to connect to the Internet—apart from receiving e-mail—is to explore the World Wide Web. Naturally, from a service called the GNN—the Global Network Navigator—you would expect a top class WWW browser to get you surfing the Internet.

This is where GNNworks comes into play. To start GNNworks and explore the World Wide Web, click on the GNNworks icon, or select it from the Start menu in Windows 95. In a few seconds you will see a window like the one shown in Figure 18.10. Once GNNworks starts, GNNconnect is started in order to sign you on to the Internet. Your Netname has already been entered into the top field, but you will need to enter your access password.

Once you enter your password and click on the connect button, GNNconnect takes over, dials GNNnet, logs you on, and then advises GNNworks that it can start retrieving WWW pages. If everything goes to plan, in a few minutes your screen will look something like the one shown in Figure 18.11.

During the beta-testing period, the default home page for GNNworks was configured to `http://www.megaweb.com/index.1.0c.html`, however, by the time you read this book it will most likely point to `http://www.gnn.com/`. There is basically little difference in the appearance of these two sites, although only GNNworks users can access the `http://www.megaweb.com` site where `http://www.gnn.com` is open to the general public.

FIGURE 18.10.

When you start GNNworks, GNNconnect is automatically started to sign you on to the Internet.

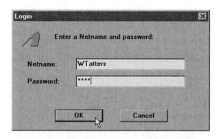

FIGURE 18.11.

Although the layout of GNNworks is slightly different from AOL's WWW browser, the basic concepts remain the same.

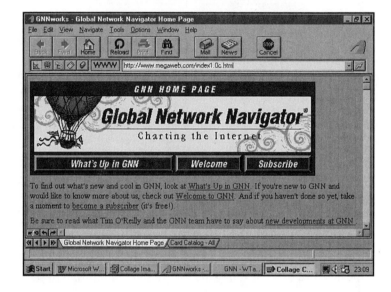

At this point take a few moments to experiment with GNNworks and get the feel for how it operates. You will soon notice, that apart from some additional control buttons and a tab bar below the main document area, GNNworks operates in basically the same way as the AOL WWW browser discussed earlier in this book. This is in fact one of the main features of the World Wide Web. Basically, once you have used one WWW browser you will be able to use a different version with very little difficulty at all.

Like the other WWW browsers discussed in this book, the GNNworks screen is separated into a number of main areas, but unlike the other browser that had three main areas, GNNworks has four. These are:

◆ The Document Area

◆ The Control Console

◆ The Tab Bar

◆ The Status Bar

The Document Area

In the center of the GNNworks screen lies the document area. This is where the contents of WWW pages retrieved from WWW servers or loaded from your own hard drive are displayed. You will find very little difference in the document area of most WWW browsers, because basically all this area is designed to do is display WWW pages. (See Chapter 12, "The World Wide Web," for more information about the contents of the Document Area.)

Having said that there is very little difference, there is one variation in the GNNworks browser that does deserve mention. In the bottom left hand corner of the document window, beside the scroll bar, you will find three small buttons. The two-curved arrow button duplicates the Back and Fwd buttons located on the toolbar, while the button that looks a bit like a broken key is used to display information about the current WWW page.

If you click on this button, a small window is opened that displays information about the currently displayed WWW page. While this information may be useful to WWW experts, it is a piece of information indicated by the actual appearance of the button which will be of interest to most people. This information relates to a feature called secure transaction processing.

Many commercial WWW sites, especially those giving you access to online shopping and ordering systems, now operate what are called secure transaction servers. What this basically means, is that when you send a page of information to one of these servers, it is encoded before it leaves your computer, so that no one else can read it. This is especially important when you are sending information such as credit card numbers and personal billing details.

If you are connected to a secure server, GNNworks lets you know that you are doing so by displaying a solid key instead of the broken key. When this solid key is displayed, you can send your personal details over the Internet, safe in the knowledge that only the people you intend to see your information can do so.

The Control Console

Like its counterparts, GNNworks provides you with a collection of navigation tools in a control console directly above the main document area. (See Figure 1812.) Many of the elements on this control console should be familiar to you by now, but there are a few items that you may not have encountered before.

To give you a brief overview of the new functions, the following sections examine the main navigation options provided by GNNworks.

FIGURE 18.12.

The GNNworks control console helps you navigate your way around the Internet.

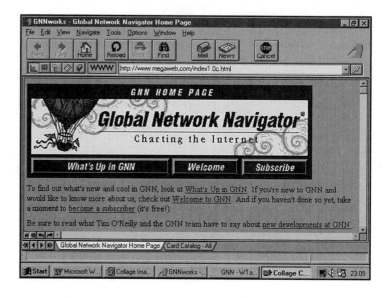

The Menu System

Because this chapter is designed to give you an introduction to GNNworks and not to fully explore its operation in every detail, a complete discussion of the options provided by the drop-down menus is better left for another time. However, to give you an idea of the options provided by each menu tab, Table 18.1 listed below contains an abridged list of features.

Table 18.1. Menu tabs on GNNworks.

Menu Tab	Description
File	The File menu lets you open local WWW pages, save WWW pages, set your default home page, and print out hardcopies of WWW pages.
Edit	You can copy text from a WWW page, paste text into WWW fields, and even copy URLs embedded as hyperlinks using the Edit menu. There is also a Find option on this menu that allows you to search for text in the currently displayed WWW page.
View	This menu lets you control whether the Toolbar, tabs, and status bar are displayed. Also, you can view the document information or the HTML source code for the current page.
Navigate	For the most part, the items in this menu duplicate those on the Toolbar, but there are also some additional options relating to management of Hotlinks—GNNworks Favorite Places look-alike.
Tools	Currently you can open the Mail and Newsgroups tools via this menu, however it is likely that this may be eventually expanded to include GNNchat as well.

Menu Tab	Description
Options	This menu gives you access to the GNNworks Preferences window. When you first install GNNworks, all the preferences are set up for you, so for the time being it is a good idea to leave them at their defaults.
Window	You can control the layout of all the currently open windows using this menu.
Help	GNNworks contains an extensive online help system. To access this system select the Contents option.

The Toolbar and Navigation Buttons

The functions provided by most of the buttons on the GNNworks toolbar are probably familiar by now; however, for those of you who may have skipped straight to this chapter, here are the actions performed by all the toolbar buttons:

Back	When you click on this button the last place you visited before the page currently displayed on the screen is recalled.
Fwd	After using the Back button, you can use this button to move up the list to the most recently visited page.
Home	Selecting this button returns you to your home page. To adjust the home page, select the Set As Home Page option from the File menu.
Reload	Clicking on this icon forces GNNworks to reload the current page. For example, if you stopped the retrieval of a large page, you can use this icon to retrieve the missing information.
Print	When you click on this button, GNNworks prints a hardcopy of the currently selected WWW page.
Find	This button opens a dialog box that lets you search the contents of the currentl WWW page.
Mail	To start GNNmessenger, click on this button.
News	If you want to read newsgroup articles, click on this button.
Cancel	If you need to halt the loading of a document, click on this button.

URL Buttons

Just below the Toolbar on the left side of the screen you will find a group of five small buttons. When you click on any of these buttons GNNworks places an empty URL in the Document URL field. For example, if you click on the first button, which looks a bit like a spider's web, the http:// URL is placed in the Document URL field.

Working from left to right, these buttons insert the following URLs:

World Wide Web page	`http://`
Gopher site	`gopher://`
FTP server	`ftp://`
USENET Newsgroup	`news:`
E-mail address	`mailto:`

Note

> In the version of GNNworks available at the time of publication, there was no built-in FTP support. As a result, you will need to install a copy of WS_FTP to gain access to FTP. See Appendix C for more information on WS_FTP.

Document URLs

The document URL field, to the right of the URL buttons, functions in basically the same ways as it does on other WWW browsers. The only minor difference you will encounter, is the fact that if you select any of the previous pages you have visited using the drop-down history list, you need to click on the small button to the right of the document URL field to get GNNworks to retrieve a copy of the chosen WWW page.

Logo Animation

Apart from giving you something to look at, the animated logo to the right of the Toolbar is there to let you know when GNNworks is retrieving a WWW page. If the animation is moving, GNNworks is busy. If it is static, no pages are currently being retrieved.

The Tab Bar

Located immediately below the main document area, you will find a collection of small tab-like buttons. Whenever you open a new WWW page, GNNworks adds a new tab to this bar, and places on the tab either the name or URL of the new page.

Once added to the tab bar, a tab will stay there for the remainder of your current session. You can then return to this page at any time, by simply clicking on its corresponding tab. Basically, the tab bar can be thought of as a visual history of all the sites you have visited during a session.

There is only a limited amount of space on the tab bar itself, however, so once it fills up, GNNworks simply keeps adding tabs to the area outside the right-hand side of the screen. You can then access any of these tabs by using the four navigation buttons at the left-hand end of the tab bar.

Status Bar

As was the case for AOL's WWW browser, the GNNworks status bar is located below the document window. Although this time there is obviously a Tab bar below the document window as well.

The status bar is used by GNNworks to provide you with information about the current WWW page. When you place your mouse pointer over a hyperlink, the URL of the page or server that it points to is displayed in the status area on the left side of the status bar. Also, when a new page is being downloaded, on the right-hand side of the screen a graphical bar is displayed to represent how much of the page has been retrieved.

GNNmessenger

The third major component of the new GNN Internet service is the GNNmessenger program. This program is actually responsible for two separate activities: e-mail and newsgroups.

To access either of these services, you can start GNNmessenger manually by selecting its icon from the Global Network Navigator folder, shown previously in Figure 18.1, or alternatively you can click on the appropriate button in the GNNworks toolbar.

E-Mail Manager

The GNN messenger screen, shown in Figure 18.13, consists of three areas: a toolbar and drop-down menu, a message list window, and finally the message contents window. To help you better understand the purpose of each of these areas the follows sections will examine each separately.

FIGURE 18.13.

GNNmessenger automatically checks for new mail and downloads a copy to your In Box whenever you start it.

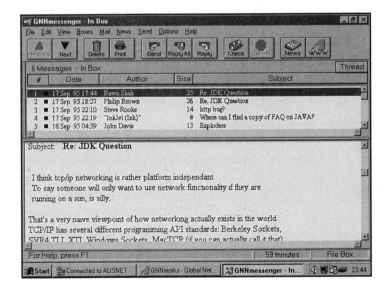

The Menu System

In Table 18.2 you will find a brief discussion of the main features provided by the GNNmessenger menu system.

Table 18.2. Menu tabs on GNNmessenger.

Menu Tab	Description
File	The File menu lets you create new message boxes, open existing ones, and update their contents. In addition to the standard In and Out boxes, you can configure any number of personal message boxes where you can store copies of messages you have sent or received. They are a bit like the personal folders available in the AOL filing cabinet.
Edit	This menu gives you the ability to copy messages and move them from message box to message box. You can also control the selection of messages highlighted in the message list window.
View	The options in this menu let you alter the appearance of the GNNmessenger screen.
Boxes	Using this menu, you can select which message box you want to see. By default, whenever you start GNNmessenger the In Box is displayed. At the same time, GNNmessenger also logs on to your private GNN mailbox and retrieves a copy of any new messages.
Mail	The Mail menu lets you control the delivery of new mail and also allows you to configure Signature lines for all your mail.
News	This menu option is only active when you select the Newsgroups option.
Send	The options listed on this menu let you choose the type of messages you want to post. You can create a new message, reply to a message you have received previously and forward or redirect any message you have received.
Options	The Options menu gives you access to a list of preferences and settings that control how GNNmessenger looks and operates.
Help	This menu lets you access the online help system.

The Toolbar

All the controls and options available while using GNNmessenger can be accessed by using either the Toolbar or the drop-down menu system. You will find that all of the major functions are accessible via the Toolbar, while the least-used options are only available via a drop-down menu item.

The functions available via the Toolbar are:

Previous	In the message box you currently have selected, this reads the message prior to the one you are currently reading.
Next	Reads the next message in the message box you currently have selected.
Delete	Marks the selected message for deletion at the end of the current session.
Print	Prints a hard copy of the current message.
Send	Click this button to open a new window where you can compose a new message.
Reply All	Composes a message in reply to one you have previously received and sends a copy to all of the recipients of the original message.
Reply	Composes a message in reply to one you have previously received, and only sends it to the person who sent you the original message.
Check	Checks your GNN mailbox for any new messages.
Cancel	Cancels the current message transmission or retrieval.
News	Reads newsgroup articles.
WWW	Click on this button to return to the GNNworks WWW browser.

The Message List Window

The area directly below the toolbar contains a list of all the messages stored in the currently selected message box. By default the messages are listed in the order that they were retrieved from your mail box, however, you can change the order by clicking on the buttons that act as headers for each of the columns of information.

The Message Contents Window

When you select any of the messages listed in the Message List window, the corresponding message is displayed in the Message Contents window at the bottom of the GNNmessenger screen.

Newsgroup Reader

If you take a close look at the newsgroup reader shown in Figure 18.14 you will probably notice that apart from an additional window, there is very little difference in appearance from the GNNmessenger screen discussed previously. The reason for this similarity is that GNNmessenger is actually used for both newsgroup and e-mail management. However, having said that, the way GNNmessenger manages your newsgroups is worthy of a separate discussion.

FIGURE 18.14.

When reading newsgroup articles, an additional window is added to the GNNmessenger screen listing all the newsgroups to which you currently subscribe.

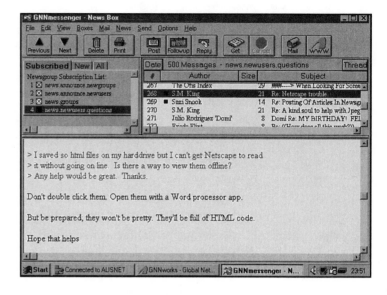

Reading Newsgroups with GNNmessenger

Unlike most of the newsreaders currently available, GNNmessenger supports a special method of newsgroups management that greatly reduces the amount of time you spend online reading newsgroup articles. If you have experimented with using FlashSessions for reading articles offline, then you will be very impressed by the improvements in offline message reading incorporated into GNNmessenger.

Basically, GNNmessenger can be configured to automatically log on to the GNN news server and retrieve a list of unread articles for each of the newsgroups you subscribe to. Once the GNNmessenger finishes this process, you then sign off from GNN and work your way through the list of article headings retrieved by GNNmessenger, selecting only those articles that you are interested in reading.

> By reading articles and looking through headers offline you can save a considerable amount of money, by not racking up hours of wasted online time.

Once you have selected all the articles you want to read, sign on to GNN again and tell GNNmessenger to download a copy of all the articles you have selected. As before, GNNmessenger takes care of connecting to the GNN news server and the retrieval of your chosen articles. Then, when GNNmessenger has collected all the articles, you can sign off from GNN and read your articles while offline.

The Groups Window

When you select the News button, GNNmessenger adds a new window to the screen and places it next to the Message List window. In this new window, by default, GNNmessenger lists in alphabetical order all the newsgroups you currently subscribe to.

Alternatively, by selecting the New tab displayed at the top of the Groups window you can also examine a list of all the latest newsgroups added to the GNN news server. In addition, by selecting the All tab, a list of every newsgroup currently available from GNN is displayed. Using these three lists, you can subscribe to newsgroups or delete newsgroups you are no longer interested in.

The Message List Window

Where the Message List window listed the contents of your current message box when working with e-mail messages, when you work with newsgroups this window is used to display a list of all the articles and headers in the currently selected newsgroup. When you select a newsgroup in the Groups window, a list of all the articles associated with that group are displayed in the Message List window.

You can then select any of the listed articles and GNNmessenger displays its contents in the Message window. If, however, you have not retrieved a copy of an article's message body, only the header information for the article will be displayed. In this case you need to mark the article for retrieval and tell GNNmessenger to download it for you.

> To find out more about reading newsgroups with GNNmessenger, check out the online help system that provides detailed descriptions of all the major features and options.

GNNchat

The last major Internet utility bundled with GNN is a program called GNNchat. GNNchat is an IRC client that allows you to conduct realtime conversations with people all over the world in much the same way as AOL's online chat sessions. (For more information about IRC, take a look at Chapter 10.)

At this stage, GNNchat is not integrated with the rest of the tools mentioned previously, however, this may change before GNN is finally launched. As a result, currently, the only way to start GNNchat is by double-clicking on its icon in the Global Network Navigation folder shown previously in Figure 18.1.

Once you start GNNchat, it automatically connects you to the GNN IRC server and displays the information window shown in Figure 18.15. From here, you can obtain a list of all the available rooms and join any discussion that catches your attention.

To join a room, first request a list of rooms using the List option of the Channel menu. When you do this GNNchat retrieves a list of all the active rooms. If you find one you like, double-click on it and GNNchat opens a chat window like the one shown in Figure 18.16. Once you are in a room, all the messages typed by people are displayed in the main window. To send a comment of your own, use the field below the main window and hit return to transmit the message to everyone else.

FIGURE 18.15.

GNNchat gives you direct access to IRC—the Internet's global online chat system.

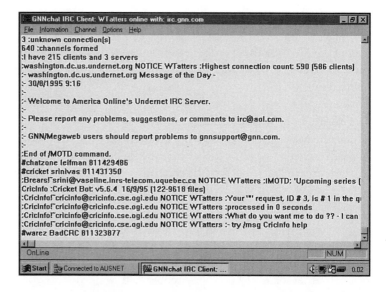

FIGURE 18.16.

Enter your own comments in the field below the main chat window.

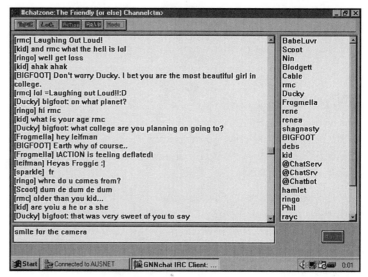

Summary

As you have seen in this chapter, the GNN Internet Access service offers a whole new level of Internet connectivity. However, because the service is still in development, don't be too surprised if there are even more features available in the final release.

With this chapter drawing to a close, you are nearing the end of your exploration of the Internet using America Online. So where do you go from here? The Internet offers many new avenues for research, education, business, fun, and entertainment. All you need to do is open the door and explore it.

The final chapter of this book takes a look at where you go from here and recaps some of the better departure points and places where you can find information about the Internet and its various uses and applications.

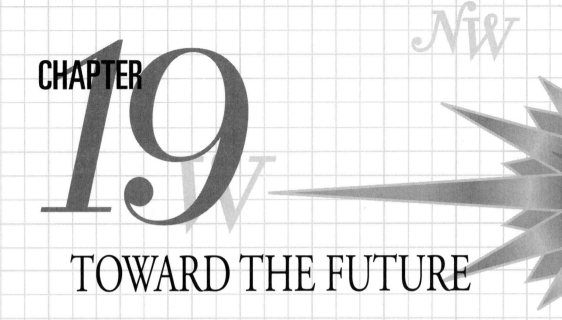

CHAPTER 19

TOWARD THE FUTURE

The Future of the Internet

Where to Now?

Sadly, our time together is almost at an end. You now hold in your hands the final chapter, apart from the good stuff at the back—the appendixes, the glossary, and the all-important index.

By now you are probably asking yourself, "What else is there to talk about?" You have already looked at

- Sending messages using e-mail
- Mailing lists
- Usenet and newsgroups
- Remote connections via Telnet
- File transfers with FTP
- Winsock connectivity
- Gopher and WAIS
- And of course, the World Wide Web

Well, the simple answer to "What else is there to talk about?" is "Nothing," and yet at the same time "Everything." If you have been following all the examples and exploring the many sites discussed in this book, by now you should have a good understanding of the Internet and the many tools that America Online provides to give you access to it.

With all this knowledge under your belt, you should now be able to confidently explore the Internet. Yet at the same time, the Internet is so large that it continually offers up new sources of information, new means of accessing this information, and in some cases, entirely new technologies as well.

The Future of the Internet

If I had told you five years ago that there would be a computer network spanning the globe by 1995, allowing people to communicate with each other for little more than the cost of a local phone call, you would probably have laughed in my face.

Today that story, which many would have considered a work of fiction, is a reality, and the Internet is its name. But what if we take our crystal ball and try to look forward another five years? What sort of place will the Internet be, or will it even exist? Trying to answer such a question is at best a difficult proposition, but there are a number of pointers that can give you some indication of what the Internet may become.

Performance

For most people, the biggest single difficulty in using services like the World Wide Web, and to a certain extent, FTP, is one of speed. Until modems capable of maintaining speeds in excess of 9,600bps became commercially available, even attempting to use the World Wide Web for any practical purpose was far from a viable proposition. When you consider the fact that many WWW pages are over 50KB in size, not including images and other graphics, that can easily push the size of a complex page to close to 200 to 300KB, downloading such a page and displaying it on your computer can take a considerable amount of time.

With the introduction of 28,800 bps modems, which can effectively achieve speeds of between 56,000bps and 110,000bps using on-the-fly data compression, the time it takes to load these pages can be considerably reduced. But at the same time, the complexity of WWW pages is also increasing to a point where even these high-speed serial modems are finding it difficult to keep up.

To keep pace with this increased need for improved performance, the next logical step seems to be ISDN. ISDN (Integrated Services Digital Network) is an emerging standard that provides both voice and data communications via a single cable. A number of major Internet service providers, including America Online, are currently either experimenting with the use of ISDN or are already offering ISDN as an alternative to slower dial-up modem options. Depending on the type of ISDN service you choose, it is possible to transfer data at rates of between 64KB and 128KB, providing much higher performance when you're using the World Wide Web.

> Unlike the audio tones system used by your modem when communicating with another computer, ISDN is an entirely digital system. When the telephone company installs an ISDN connection, they are actually creating a connection that connects directly to their high speed digital network without the need for modems and slow analog to digital data conversions.

Even ISDN may only be a temporary step, and one that may already be doomed to fall by the wayside as the world's communications giants prepare to meet the Internet head on.

Cable TV and the Internet

One of the major disadvantages of ISDN in the past has been the high costs associated with maintaining the service and the expensive equipment required to connect your computer to it.

Yet in many households around the world, there is already another cable that may be able to provide direct access to the Internet in the very near future. This cable is the cable TV connection that currently brings you all the latest movies, the *Home Shopping Network* and a continual stream of *I Love Lucy* reruns.

Since late 1993, a number of cable TV providers and commercial telephone companies have been experimenting with the delivery of services such as the Internet using existing cable TV connections and through even higher-speed services such as fiber-optic cable. Although these systems are still in the early stages of development for the most part, the information that has begun to surface describing their potential is enough to make the mouth water.

The ambitious goal of much of this research is the delivery of video on demand, offering as many as 500 TV channels via a single cable. In addition, the same cable will be able to handle your telephone calls, including multiple lines, as well as provide you with a direct connection to the Internet at speeds approaching a megabyte of data per second.

When—not if—such services become available, you are likely to see full-motion video on your World Wide Web page, with IRC replaced by online video conferencing, and newspapers, magazines, and even virtual reality games all available in the comfort of your own home. The other change that you are also likely to see is a change in the appearance of your computer, which may eventually look more like the VCR sitting on top of your television. But what about the keyboard? Well, maybe voice recognition will become a practical reality as well.

Basically, who really knows? However, judging by the rapid growth in the popularity of the Internet and the imminent release of some exciting new technology, chances are you won't have to wait another five years to find out for yourself.

The Future of America Online

With all these new developments taking place, what is the future of services like America Online? For America Online at least, the answer appears to be a bright future. However, that does not mean that you won't begin to see substantial changes in the way America Online looks and feels over the coming months and years.

What you will most likely see is further integration of America Online's services such as its Channels, Message Boards, and chat areas, into the structure of the Internet. Having said that, all the existing services will most likely remain, but in the future it is likely that they may be accessible using the World Wide Web or some future navigation tool based on WWW technology.

We are already seeing such integration occurring through the acquisition by America Online of services such as the Global Network Navigator (GNN), WebCrawler, and WAIS, Inc. When these acquisitions are considered in the light of the new developments surrounding GNNWorks, it is a reasonable assumption that in the future you will see even more moves by America Online into the Internet.

Where to Now?

But enough of this stargazing—what about now?

Where should you go next in your exploration of the Internet? The answer is really up to you. Depending on your interests, there are many directions that you can choose. However, there are a few possible steps that you should consider.

Winsock and Direct Internet Connections

One of your first ports of call should be Appendix C, "Internet Software." This appendix contains a brief introduction to the many Winsock-based Internet clients currently available and discusses many of the programs available on the CD-ROM accompanying this book. Although the capabilities offered by America Online via AOL and its various gateways are indeed very useful, to get the most out of the Internet, your computer really needs to be connected as a physical part of the network.

This is where programs such as GNNWorks and MegaWeb's dial-up PPP connection come into their own, and in reality it is where the future direction of services such as America Online lie. Already we are beginning to see the gradual paralleling of services such as the AOL Marketplace and Downtown AOL on the Internet, and in the future, maybe you will one day even be able to access AOL Channels and Message Boards using the World Wide Web.

There is one important aspect of dial-up PPP connections and Winsock-based applications that makes them a valuable addition to your Internet resources. When you connect your computer to the Internet using a program such as GNNWorks, the computer itself becomes a physical part of the Internet network. This has been mentioned before, but what you probably didn't realize is that once you're connected in this way, you can take advantage of all the capabilities offered by Windows when using Winsock-based applications that communicate with the Internet via the dialer program.

Of these capabilities, the most interesting is both the Macintosh and Windows' ability to run more than one program at the same time. This means that it is possible to have GNNWorks displaying a home page while an FTP client retrieves copies of files in the background, with a Usenet newsreader at the same time searching for the latest articles in your favorite newsgroups.

By taking advantage of these multitasking capabilities, you can greatly reduce the amount of time you spend online while at the same time getting more done.

Surfing the Net

It also goes without saying that the World Wide Web offers the best next-step option for most new Internet explorers. But in some ways, its sheer size makes using it a daunting proposition.

The first concept you need to come to grips with when using the World Wide Web is the fact that as soon as someone creates something, there is someone else waiting in the wings ready to step in and replace it with something better. In this sense, the World Wide Web is like a continually and rapidly evolving animal that continues to change, often while you are using it.

To keep ahead of this changing technology, you not only need to learn how to use the Web, but also how to surf it. In the past this meant spending hours logging on to new computers using Telnet and retrieving the latest copies of FAQs and Requests for Comment documents using FTP, but now this has all changed. With the introduction of the World Wide Web, the art of Netsurfing can now be learned by anyone with a little bit of time to spare and the desire to find out about the world around them.

Unlike environments such as America Online, whose menu system is designed primarily for interaction with a fixed set of resources, the World Wide Web is the ideal environment for exploration. Because there is technically no limitation to the number and diversity of pages that can be placed on the World Wide Web, it is an ever-changing world whose boundaries are limited only by your time and ability to explore them.

The art of Netsurfing, unlike ocean surfing, is relatively easy to pick up. Basically, you pick a point on the World Wide Web and then follow the pages and links like a surfer riding a wave. When you read a page on the World Wide Web, there will usually be at least one link to some other page of information; if not, you can always skip back a few pages and follow another link to see where it leads. In addition, if you do manage to get yourself totally lost, a simple click on the home icon takes you quickly back to familiar ground.

But where do you start? This actually doesn't really matter, because you can start just about anywhere and still eventually wind up at a page that points you to many other sources of information. However, to recap some of the more popular World Wide Web directory listings mentioned in Chapter 13, "World Wide Web Productivity," here is a short list to get you started:

The Yahoo directory: `http://www.yahoo.com/`

TradeWave Galaxy home page: `http://galaxy.einet.net/`

The Global Network Navigator: `http://gnn.com/gnn/gnn.html`

Mirsky's Worst of the Web: `http://mirsky.turnpike.net/wow/Worst.html`

Glenn Davis' Cool Site of the Day: `http://cool.infi.net/`

Infinet's Explore the Net Page: `http://www.infi.net/explore.html`

The Virtual Tourist: `http://wings.buffalo.edu/world/`

Matthew Gray's comprehensive list of Web sites: `http://www.netgen.com/cgi/comprehensive`

The OFFWORLD Metaplex: `http://tribble.com/index7.html`

Online Help and FAQs

Other good sources of useful information are the online help screens provided by both AOL and GNNWorks. If you find yourself in a situation that does not make sense or are facing a dialog box whose contents you are not familiar with, clicking on the Help button will always bring up a screen load of information to help you better understand where you are.

You shouldn't be afraid to ask for help when using any Internet service, although you should always make sure that you have read any relevant Frequently Asked Questions (FAQ) documents to make sure that you are not asking a question that has been answered many times before. In fact, I cannot overemphasize the importance of reading every FAQ you come across. These documents have been created by people who want to help new users to better understand the Internet, but at the same time they may be very busy people who probably won't appreciate seeing messages asking questions they have sorted into FAQs. Although there are many people who will be only too happy to assist a new user, the Internet also relies heavily on the concept of self-help. Basically, if you are willing to put forth a little bit of effort to help yourself, others will be glad to guide you further.

What's New Announcements

With the number of changes America Online is currently implementing, the AOL Spotlight pages should also be a top priority on your list of regular places to go.

Similar services are also available at a number of World Wide Web sites, but instead of listing new happenings on America Online, these sites contain lists of new happenings on the World Wide Web.

One of the most popular of these services is operated by the NCSA in association with the Global Network Navigator. To access this site, use the following http address: `http://www.ncsa.uiuc.edu/SDG/Software/Mosaic/Docs/whats-new.html`.

For a slightly different list, take a look at the What's New page operated by Netscape at `http://home.netscape.com/escapes/whats_new.html`.

Summary

In the immortal words of one of the world's great orators, "B'd, b'd, b'dee, that's all, folks!"

Well, not quite. In the pages that follow, you will find five appendixes and a glossary of popularly used Internet terms. The appendixes cover the following topics:

Appendix A	Explores some of the options available to those who are interested in exploring the use of other Internet service providers
Appendix B	Looks at how people with an existing Internet service provider can take advantage of TCP/IP to log on to America Online using the Internet instead of the AOLnet dial-up network
Appendix C	Contains a list outlining the various Winsock-based applications that can be used in conjunction with the new AOL Winsock and with GNNWorks MegaWeb dial-up PPP connections
Appendix D	Examines some of the popular encoding and encryption programs and discusses their use
Appendix E	Takes a look at the major differences between the Macintosh and Windows versions of AOL

In closing, I hope this book has been of assistance to you as you begin your exploration of the Internet. For many people, the Internet is now a place where they can both work and play. It offers opportunities that were unimagined only a few short years ago, and allows you to communicate with people and exchange ideas, dreams, thoughts, and expectations. In addition, it offers people many opportunities for involvement, whether it's as a programmer, a World Wide Web publisher, or simply a lurker who enjoys what others have created. It is rapidly becoming a service that can be all things to all people.

However, at the same time it is a world that won't come to you. There is an entire world of information, entertainment, and interaction waiting for you on the Internet. All you need to do is reach out and grab it.

Good luck, and see you on the Net.

—Wes Tatters (wtatters@world.net)

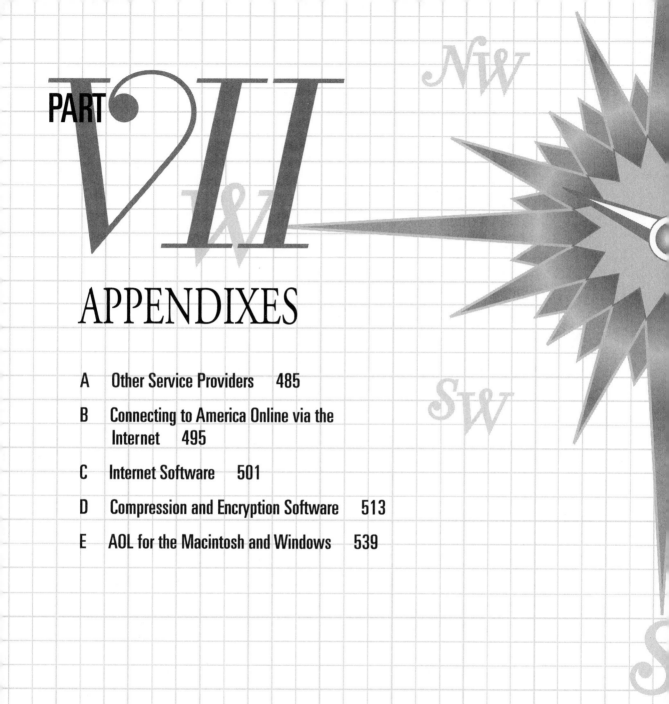

PART VII

APPENDIXES

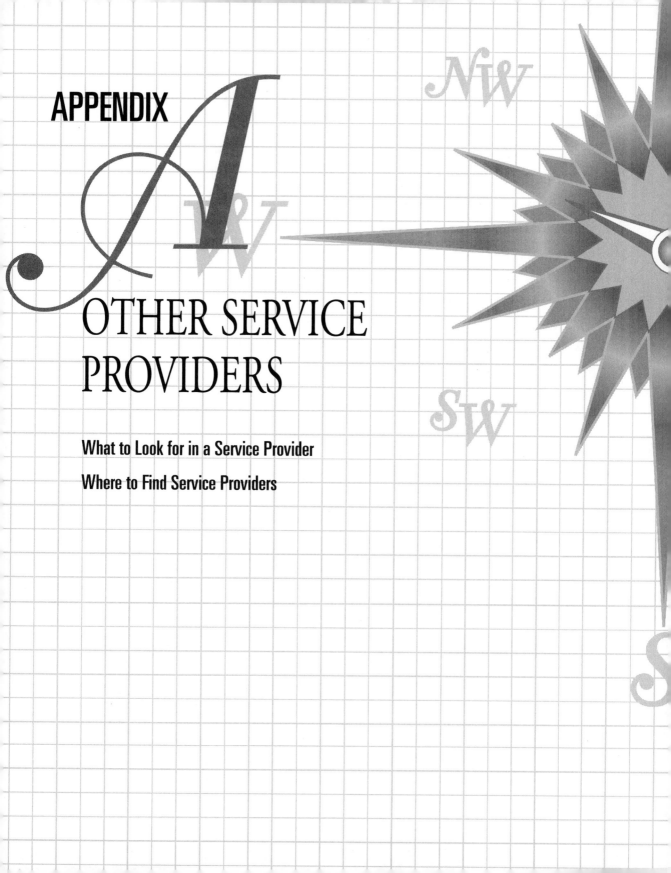

APPENDIX A

OTHER SERVICE PROVIDERS

What to Look for in a Service Provider

Where to Find Service Providers

Although in many parts of the country America Online now offers access to the Internet, its pricing structure may not be suited to the needs of every user. For people living outside the major cities who use the AOLnet 1-800-716-0023 number, where network access fees are charged in addition to AOL's standard rates, there may be a local Internet service provider (ISP) who can offer you more attractive pricing.

> To find out more information about your local AOL pricing, use Keyword: `billing`.

This appendix shows you what you should look for in an ISP and discusses ways to locate Internet connections in your part of the world.

What to Look for in a Service Provider

There are six important aspects that you need to consider when choosing an Internet service provider.

◆ Pricing
◆ Connection options
◆ Performance
◆ Customer support
◆ Value-added services
◆ Connectivity software

Pricing

If you thought trying to make sense of AOL's pricing plan was difficult, you'd better take a seat. There are a multitude of options available in the Internet market.

Almost every ISP has come up with a different sort of pricing structure designed to give its members the best possible deal. The problem is, what may be the best possible deal for one user is usually not the best deal for everyone else. As a result, when you are shopping around for an ISP you need to pay careful attention to the fees it charges and exactly how and when they are calculated.

Flat-Rate Services

The flat-rate service, as its name implies, charges you a fixed rate for every hour you are online. Depending on the ISP and your location, the rates for these services can vary from as little as $0.50 an hour to as high as $10 or $15 an hour. But on average you can probably expect to pay around $2.00 to $4 an hour for flat rate services.

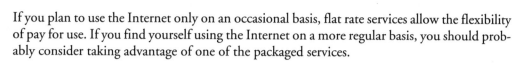

If you plan to use the Internet only on an occasional basis, flat rate services allow the flexibility of pay for use. If you find yourself using the Internet on a more regular basis, you should probably consider taking advantage of one of the packaged services.

Flat Rate with After Hours

Another type of flat-rate service that is becoming more popular is the *after hours* service. These services offer reduced connection rates for people who use the service outside of business hours. By taking advantage of these discount rates you can often save up to 50% on your Internet usage bill. However, you do need to be careful when using such services as many of them charge much higher rates during business hours than a standard flat rate service.

If you don't mind the inconvenience of not being able to connect whenever you want and you're an infrequent Internet user, after hours rates offer good value for the money.

Packaged Services

Many ISPs now offer special pre-paid connection packages. By taking advantage of these packages, you can often gain considerable savings over flat rate services.

There are two main types of packages offered at the moment. The first allows you to purchase a fixed number of hours a month that you can use whenever you choose. The second variety allows you to purchase a fixed number of hours each day for a month. Of these two packages, the first offers the best freedom and value for the money. With the second option, if you don't take advantage of the service every day, there is no way to recover the lost hours.

At first glance, pre-paid packages offer the best value for the money, but there is a nasty "gotcha" with most packaged services. If you exceed your daily or monthly limit, any additional hours you use in excess of those purchased in your prepaid package, are often charged at the highest rate a service charges. This can sometimes amount to as much as $10 or $15 an hour.

> The best services to look out for are those that offer unlimited connection packages. With these services you pay a monthly fee for unlimited connection time.

Note

Metered Usage

There is one other form of online charge used by some ISPs that needs to be used with some care, although it is being phased out by most sites.

This fee is calculated by metering the amount of data you send and receive while connected to the Internet. This includes file transfers, e-mail, WWW use, and Telnet connections. Under this structure you are charged a fee for every 1,024 characters of data transmitted at what appear to be very low rates of between half a cent and one cent.

Before the introduction of high-speed modems and services like the World Wide Web, using this sort of pricing structure was a very good way of keeping prices down. However, when you start to use 28,800 bps modems to browse WWW pages, downloading a single page can cost up to 50 cents to load. As a result, this sort of service can start to become very expensive.

In today's climate, metered usage is simply not practical for most users and should be avoided unless you fully understand how the charges will affect you. That said, for certain types of usage—Telnet in particular—metered charges can offer considerable savings over other pricing methods.

Connection Options

Price is not the only factor you need to consider when looking at Internet service providers. There are a number of different connection options available that can greatly affect the type of service you obtain, and in some cases even the performance.

Connection Speeds

When you connect to the Internet, the connection speed is determined by your modem's capabilities and those of the ISP. As a result, to get the best value from your Internet connection, you should make sure that the ISP allows you to connect at 14,400 or 28,800 bps. On your end, you will also need to obtain as fast a modem as your budget allows.

If you plan to use the WWW with your Internet connection (and who doesn't?), you should make sure that the ISP selected offers 28,800 bps connections even if your current modem does not support it. You should also check to make sure that there are no additional fees and charges for higher connection speeds. When you connect at higher speeds you get more done in your allotted time. As a result, some ISPs choose to add on additional charges to compensate them for the reduced time you spend online.

One of the ways they do this is by setting limits to the amount of data you can transfer to or from your computer. This includes screen displays, file transfers, WWW pages, and even e-mail. When you connect at higher speeds, you are much more likely to exceed these limits and as a result attract additional charges.

Shell or Terminal Sessions

Some ISPs, and even some bulletin boards, offer shell- or terminal-based connections to the Internet.

To use these services, you use a communications program to dial into the service and from there connect to the Internet. In recent years, this type of service has begun to lessen in popularity in favor of direct Internet connections. This, for the most part, is because with a shell account it is difficult, if not impossible, to take advantage of tools such as graphical World Wide Web navigators and other Winsock client-based services.

On the plus side, a number of these sites offer access at rates far below those available from commercial service providers. To find out more about these sites, check out the public Internet service providers listing topic later in this Appendix.

SLIP and PPP Connections

By far the most popular method of connecting to the Internet is through the use of a TCP/IP connection. When you use TCP/IP, your computer actually becomes a physical part of the Internet instead of a fancy terminal emulator.

There are currently two ways of doing this using a dial-up connection: SLIP and PPP. *SLIP* is the older of the two methods, and should be avoided where possible due to the lack of built-in error checking and data compression. In addition, *PPP* is an official Internet communications protocol for dial-up TCP/IP connections, and SLIP is not. As a result, ISPs that offer PPP connections should, as a rule, be considered over those that offer only SLIP.

> *SLIP* is an acronym for *Serial Line Internet Protocol*, while *PPP* stands for *Point-to-Point Protocol.*

Occasionally you will also hear mention of a third dial-up protocol called CSLIP. This is an improved version of SLIP that offers more reliable connections and improved performance. Depending on who you talk to, this protocol is still not as good as PPP, but it should definitely be considered over services that only offer SLIP.

Performance

Even if you have the fastest modem ever made and your ISP has a matching one, it will be of little use if the ISP cannot feed it information fast enough.

Of all the criteria you should consider when selecting an ISP, the performance issue is by far the hardest to resolve. Obviously, every ISP is going to tell you that their service is the fastest and most reliable around. Your best bet in these situations is to talk with other people who are already using the service and see what they think of it. For starters, some astute queries posted to the Internet message boards and online chat areas at America Online may give you some guidance, or maybe you can ask the ISP for some reference clients who you can talk to.

Most important, don't be baffled by the barrage of facts and figures that some ISPs will give you to explain just how great their service is. In all cases it comes down to usage. If you can, try to wrangle a look at a computer that is connected to the service before you make your final decision.

Customer Support

For AOL users who have come to expect good quality customer support and simple-to-use navigation tools, getting connected to the Internet can be quite a culture shock.

It is important to check out the customer support offered by ISPs before you take the plunge. Because many of the cheaper services are often operated by only one or two people, sometimes out of garages or their basements, getting help can sometimes be a difficult task.

If you are fairly technically competent, you can probably afford to opt for reduced online charges over customer support. On the other hand, if you are not a hacker you can expect to make at least one call to customer service while setting up your Internet connection. As a result, good customer support should be considered a must.

Value-Added Services

When comparing some of the major ISPs, eventually the choice comes down to a comparison of the value-added products and services they offer.

Newsgroup Servers

In the past, people have often been cheated when subscribing to very cheap ISPs that seem to offer unbelievable prices. To achieve these low prices, many cheaper services cut corners by operating low-speed connections to the Internet or by leaving out access to some Internet features.

For example, operating a Usenet connection requires a considerable investment of time and money, not to mention a large hard drive. To cut costs some smaller ISPs simply don't operate a Usenet connection. As a result, even though they provide you with an Internet connection, you will not be able to use your account to read newsgroups.

Therefore, it's important to check what services are provided by the ISP, and in some cases what additional fees and charges are associated with using them.

Private Directories and FTP Access

Some ISPs allow you to store files on their host machine in your own private directory. Depending on the ISP, you may also be able to use this area as your own private FTP site and allow other people to access it via anonymous FTP.

If an ISP permits this type of activity, you should also check on any usage limitations and extra charges that might be incurred if you use more space than your designated allowance.

Home Page Links and the World Wide Web

With the growth in popularity of the World Wide Web, some ISPs are now beginning to allow their customers to create their own home pages and link them to the ISP's WWW server and customer pages.

Like sites offering FTP access, most of these sites will set parameters that determine how much space you can use for your pages and images, while others also set limits to the level of access you have to things such as forms and other special WWW services. Given this, these sites offer their customers very affordable access to WWW publishing.

Connectivity Software

Some of the more organized ISPs are now offering special software packages similar to GNNWorks to help get you over the initial connection teething problems encountered by many people.

Depending on your skill level, services offering one of these packages can take a lot of the heartache out of getting an Internet connection up and running. For this reason, when you're talking to ISPs it is a good idea to see if they offer one of these packages and more importantly to try to find out if they are willing to bundle it with your connection fees.

Where to Find Service Providers

There are a number of sources that you can turn to for information about Internet service providers, but the best source of information is obviously the Internet itself.

In the past, this has resulted in a crazy "chicken and the egg" scenario. To find out about connecting to the Internet, you needed to be connected to it already. Nowadays, with services like America Online providing you with the initial means of connecting to the Internet, this problem has pretty much disappeared.

The Internet Society

As a service to the Internet, a gentleman named Barry Raveendran Greene, in association with the Internet Society, operates a collection of pages containing a list of network service providers around the world. (See Figure A.1.) These pages are stored on the Internet Society WWW server at the following http address: `http://www.isoc.org/~bgreene/nsp-index.html`.

FIGURE A.1.

Network Service Providers Around the World.

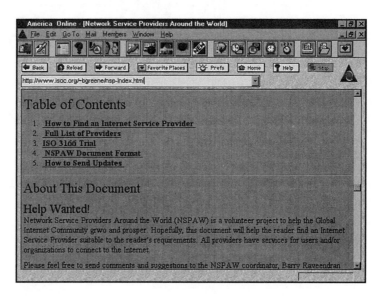

To complement this listing, he has also compiled a do-it-yourself guide to finding an Internet service provider. If you are looking for an Internet service provider, you should definitely take a look at this page before you proceed any further.

The Commercial Internet Exchange

If wading through lists of ISPs seems like a lot of hard work, maybe the novel approach offered by the Commercial Internet eXchange (CIX) will be more suited to your needs.

Instead of listing its member ISPs page by page, CIX has created a Map of the World page (Figure A.2) that allows you to simply click on the part of the world in which you live. When you click on the map, CIX shows you a list of all the Internet service providers offering Internet connections in that part of the world.

To take advantage of this map use `http://www.cix.org/Maps/CIXmap.html`.

FIGURE A.2.

CIX membership by geographic location.

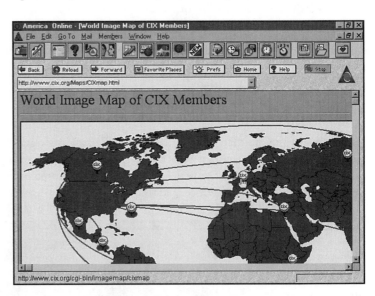

Tip

> Because all CIX members must agree to abide by the exchange's rules, using one of these service providers tends to ensure that your service will not disappear the day after you become a subscriber.
>
> This in itself is sufficient incentive for many people to consider only CIX-recognized commercial ISPs.

> There is also another very good ISP list maintained by the Commerce Net site discussed previously. The URL for this list is `http://www.commerce.net/directories/products/isp/`

Public Internet Service Providers Listing

To cater to the growing number of public ISPs, Bux Technical Services maintains a listing of all known public sites.

You can obtain a copy of this listing by sending an e-mail message to `mail-server@bts.com`. In the body of the message, enter either **get PUB nixpub.long** or **get PUB nixpub.short**.

They also operate a mailing list for those people who want to be kept up to date with regard to all the latest Public Internet Service Providers. To subscribe to this list, send an e-mail message to `mail-server@bts.com` with the following entry in the body of the message:

```
subscribe NIXPUB-LIST 'First Name' 'Second Name'
```

Universities and Research Institutions

The last type of Internet service provider is one that not everyone has access to, but that at the same time offers a number of potential connection opportunities. If you haven't guessed already, these are educational service providers.

Every major university and research institution the world over has access to the Internet and in many cases offers its students and employees access either through dial-up connections or in-house terminals. If you are a student, you should contact your campus computer center to find out about what types of Internet access they offer.

Non-profit organizations and grade schools should also consider these sites as a possible alternative, because many institutions offer special rates and sometimes even free connections for worthy causes.

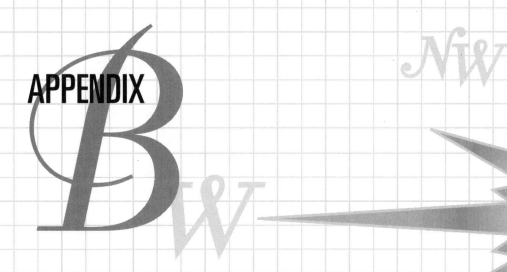

APPENDIX B

CONNECTING TO AMERICA ONLINE VIA THE INTERNET

AOL for Windows and TCP/IP

AOL for the Macintosh and TCP/IP

Connection Issues

For people who have access to the Internet through an Internet service provider, America Online now offers the option of a direct connection via the Internet. This enables you to log on to America Online via the Internet instead of a more common dial-up connection using AOLnet, Tymnet, or Sprintnet.

Even though for most people a dial-up connection is the simplest and most efficient method of connecting to America Online, for some users there are advantages to using an Internet-based connection. There are a number or reasons why people choose to do this, but for many of them the main controlling factor is price.

If, like myself, you don't live in an area that has a local America Online phone number, the additional costs associated with long distance telephone charges or network connection surcharges can easily make the cost of connecting to America Online prohibitive.

By making use of an Internet service provider, it is possible to reduce the cost of connecting to America Online under these circumstances by at least $3.00 a hour. For example, if you use the AOLnet 1-800-716-0023 number, you are charged an additional 8 cents a minute or $4.80 an hour on top of your standard usage fees. As a result, if you were charged $1.50 an hour—a fairly average rate—by your local Internet service provider, you would save $3.30 by using the Internet to connect to AOL instead of AOLnet.

There is another advantage to using an Internet connection that is often overlooked by most people. When you connect via the Internet, the speed of your connection to AOL is limited only by the speed of your Internet connection. Therefore, if you have access to America Online only via a connection that supports 9600bps or 14,400bps modems, but have access to a 28,800bps Internet connection, you will be better off using the Internet connection when logging on to America Online.

For other users who have access to a permanent, high-speed Internet connection, the attraction of an Internet connection to America Online stems from the ability to take advantage of their existing Internet links to connect to America Online without the need for dedicated modems. For large corporate and educational institutions, this can lead to big savings by reducing the need for local phone calls and modem hardware.

AOL for Windows and TCP/IP

Assuming that you have access to an Internet connection already, there a few minimum requirements that you will need to meet, before you can use AOL's built-in TCP/IP connection:

◆ Microsoft Windows version 3.1 or greater.

◆ TCP/IP Winsock version 1.1 or greater.

◆ America Online for Windows version 2.5 or later.

If you have not already done so, now would be an ideal time to upgrade your AOL software to version 2.5. The Keyword: **upgrade,** takes you to a free connection area that allows you to download a copy of the latest version of AOL.

Once you have met these requirements, all you need to do to take advantage of a TCP/IP connection to America Online is follow these steps:

1. Make sure that your Internet connection is up and running.
2. Start your AOL Windows software as you would normally.
3. Click on the Setup button on the Sign On screen.
4. In the Network and Modem Setup dialog box click on the Create Location button.
5. Give the new location the name **Internet**.
6. Set the Modem Speed: option for both the primary and secondary connections to 57600 bps.
7. Set the Network: option for both connections to TCP/IP.
8. Click on the Save button to store this new location.
9. Choose Internet as your new location and click on the OK button.
10. Click on the Sign On button to start your AOL session.

Assuming that everything goes according to plan, in a few seconds you will be connected to America Online using a TCP/IP connection. However, if there appear to be problems, first make sure that you are physically connected to the Internet. To do this run another Winsock-compatible program that you know works.

If you are still encountering problems, the next thing you need to check is that you don't have two copies of the winsock.dll file on your computer. As a rule, you should rename every copy of this file except the one stored in the \windows or \windows\system directory.

If all else fails, try sending a message to AOL customer support or make a visit to the Tech Live online chat area at Keyword: **CSLIVE**.

There are many different versions of the winsock.dll currently available, each of which is specific to the needs of different TCP/IP stacks. When copying, deleting, or renaming the winsock.dll file make sure you make a backup onto a floppy disk before proceeding.

AOL for the Macintosh and TCP/IP

As was the case when using the Windows version, there are a few minimum requirements that you need to meet before you can connect your Macintosh to America Online via the Internet. These are

◆ System 7 or System 6.0.5 (no graphics support).

◆ MacTCP version 2.0.6a or greater.

◆ The Mac Communication Toolbox install.

◆ America Online for the Macintosh version 2.6 or greater.

Once you have met these minimum requirements all you need to do is

1. Connect your Macintosh to the Internet.

2. Start your AOL Macintosh software.

3. Choose TCP Connection from the Locality: pop-up menu on the Sign On screen.

> If the TCP Connection locality is not listed in the pop-up you may need to re-install your AOL software. You should check in your System folder to make sure that TCPack for AOL is installed. If it is, check the Online Files folder in your AOL MAC Software folder for the TCPack and TCP Connection files. If any of these files are missing you will need to reinstall your Macintosh AOL software.

4. Click on the Sign On button to start you AOL session.

If your system was configured properly you should now be connected to the AOL via the Internet.

> The most common problem people encounter when trying to use a Macintosh to connect to AOL via the Internet is using an old version of MacTCP. You must use version 2.0.6 or greater. You can obtain a copy of this version as a part of the Apple System 7.5 update which is available in the Macintosh Operating Systems area. To reach this area use the Keyword: **MOS**.

Connection Issues

If you find yourself using the TCP/IP connection option on a regular basis there are a few issues which you will need to consider.

Security

Because the Internet by its very nature is an open and unrestricted environment, you need to pay careful attention to protecting your screen name and password.

Whenever you log on to AOL using the Internet, your screen name and password are transmitted across the network in an unprotected form that anyone with the right software could technically read. While this sort of activity is less prevalent than some people would have you believe, you should change your password on a regular basis to protect yourself from illegal use of your account.

A good rule of thumb is to change your password once a week if you use the Internet.

Performance

When you use the Internet, you are vying for communications bandwidth with millions of other users, all of whom want to send their information down the same pipeline as you. As a result, system performance when connected to AOL across the Internet can vary dramatically from day to day and even from hour to hour.

As a result, if you find that AOL is taking a long time to respond to your requests, it may be a good time to take a break and try again later. Over time you will no doubt discover those periods of time when your Internet connection is at its worst and learn to avoid them. Not connecting to AOL during these periods makes good sense since you are being charged for the time you use on AOL and not for the amount of data you download.

Lost Connections

On rare occasions, the Internet will lose a packet of information. If this packet happens to be one of yours, AOL displays a message indicating that your TCP/IP connection has been lost.

If this ever happens to you, there is very little you can do about it except try to sign on again. However, when you do try to sign on again, under some circumstances, AOL will indicate that you are already signed on. If you receive such a message, shut down your AOL software and wait for a few minutes. You should then be able to start AOL again and sign on without any difficulties.

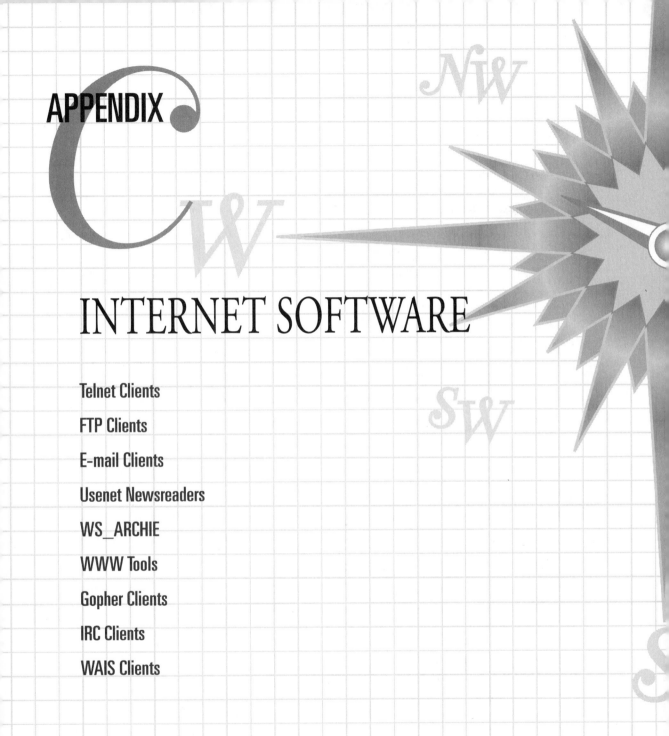

APPENDIX
C

INTERNET SOFTWARE

Telnet Clients

FTP Clients

E-mail Clients

Usenet Newsreaders

WS_ARCHIE

WWW Tools

Gopher Clients

IRC Clients

WAIS Clients

With the recent addition of Winsock support for users of the Windows version of AOL, America Online users now have access to the wide variety of Internet client applications that continue to flood the Internet.

This appendix takes a look at some of the more popular Winsock-compatible programs to give you some idea of what's currently available. It's designed to give you a brief look at what's being offered without any explanations or discussions of the way you use these programs. Such explanations are better left to the many books written specifically for that purpose.

Before looking at the various programs available, let's look at some of the places where you can obtain copies of them for yourself.

The best place to start looking for copies of the latest version of files is in the Internet Connection Software Library. In addition, obviously all the programs are also available on the Internet from many anonymous FTP servers and software archives. To get started, you should take a look at the files available from the CICA archive, which is located at `ftp://ftp.cica.indiana.edu` in the `/pub/pc/winsock` directory.

If you prefer using the World Wide Web, Forrest Stroud's Consummate Winsock Apps List contains links to the most popular Winsock-based applications available on the Internet. The http address for this home page is `http://cwsapps.texas.net/`.

This list contains information about the latest release versions of each product, its status as freeware, shareware, or otherwise, and links to the host sites for each.

> If you are having difficulties connecting to this site, you may like to try the Papa Winsock-L FTP Site (The Papa Site) located at Indiana State University. The Papa Site has formed a partnership with the Consummate Winsock Apps List and maintains an FTP archive of all the files reviewed as apart of the Consummate Winsock Apps List. The URL for the PAPA FTP site is `ftp://papa.indstate.edu/winsock-l`.

Another good list of Winsock applications can be found at the TUCOWS WWW site whose URL is `http://www.tucows.com/`. This site is the home of the "The Ultimate Collection of Winsock Software."

Telnet Clients

There are a number of different Telnet clients available on the Internet, each offering different capabilities. Of the programs available, the two most popular are the Trumpet Telnet program and EWAN, which is by far the most comprehensive, offering a totally configurable interface.

In addition, for Windows 95 users there is a Telnet client supplied as a part of the TCP/IP package.

There is also another type of Telnet program designed specifically for connections to IBM computer systems requiring 3270 terminal emulation, instead of the more common vt100 emulation offered by most Telnet packages. This type of program is referred to as a TN3270 emulator.

Trumpet Telnet

Common file name: TTEL0_07.ZIP

Status: freeware

This Telnet program was developed by Peter Tattam—the man behind the Trumpet Winsock— in part to demonstrate the capabilities of his Winsock program. Although it's not the most configurable Telnet client available, it performs reasonably well and does have the dubious honor of being the smallest Telnet program available.

When you download a copy, don't expect any fancy installation scripts or online help files. It's pretty much a what-you-see-is-what-you-get affair, but it will get you online if your Telnet needs are limited.

EWAN Telnet

Common Filename: EWAN1052.ZIP

Status: freeware

EWAN is far and away the most powerful freeware Telnet application currently available. It offers vt100, vt52, and ANSI terminal emulation, which can be configured independently for each Telnet site stored in its configuration list. You can also define keyboard maps, input filters for each site, and tailor the emulation in every way imaginable.

Support for the program is very good, with a comprehensive online help system built in and regular updates from the author. The current version of EWAN—version 1.052—or the most recent version, is always available from the EWAN home page at `http://www.lysator.liu.se/ ~zander/ewan.html`.

IBM 3270 Terminal Emulation

Common Filename: QWS3270.ZIP

Status: Freeware

Not all Telnet connections support the use of the standard VT100 terminal emulation. Principal among these sites are some of the older IBM-based services. To connect to any of these sites, you need to use an IBM3270 terminal emulator such as the Winsock 3270 emulation program. Like the Trumpet Telnet program, QWS3270 seems to be unsupported these days, although the Readme file included with the program indicates that the developer still has further plans for it.

It is a what-you-see-is-what-you-get affair, with neither online help nor anything approaching what could be called a user's manual. But then again, apart from selecting Connect and entering a domain name, what else would you expect a Telnet program to do?

FTP Clients

When it comes to FTP, there is only one option you need to consider as a Windows user. Windows 95 does bundle a terminal-based FTP client as a part of its TCP/IP package, but the only time you would even consider using it would be to download a copy of a real FTP client like WS_FTP.

WS_FTP

Common Filename: WS_FTP.ZIP—16-bit

Common Filename: WS_FTP32.ZIP—32-bit

Status: Freeware

WS_FTP is a Windows-based FTP client that allows you to log on to FTP sites using a graphical interface. Once connected, you can send and retrieve files by selecting them from the lists provided, in much the same way as you did when using the America Online FTP client.

There are two versions of WS_FTP currently available, one of which is designed for the older 16-bit Windows environment, the other for 32-bit platforms such as Windows 95 and Windows NT. If you own a copy of Windows 95 or Windows NT, you should consider using the 32-bit version, although the 16-bit version will work. This is because the newer 32-bit version has been designed so that it takes advantage of the improved multitasking features available in both Windows 95 and Windows NT.

Note

The latest version of WS_FTP can always be found at `http://www.csra.net/junodj/`.

E-mail Clients

At this stage, America Online does not technically support the use the use of e-mail clients. However the following section briefly discusses some of the more popular e-mail clients.

> An e-mail client is a program that lets you read e-mail messages stored in an Internet mailbox. For example: GNNWorks contains a built-in e-mail client to send and receive mail.

Eudora

Common Filename: EUDORA.EXE

Status: Freeware/Commercial

There are two versions of Eudora, a freeware version and a more capable commercial version. Most users find that the freeware version is well suited to their needs, however, and for them there is no need to ever purchase the commercial version.

Eudora supports built-in MIME and BinHex encoding for file attachments and a nickname list for all your commonly used e-mail addresses. The only reason that many people would ever consider purchasing the commercial version would be to gain access to the intelligent mailbox features. They enable you to define parameters that tell Eudora how to sort your incoming mail. Because Eudora supports multiple mailboxes, it is possible to have mail from certain people, or mail containing certain words, automatically sorted into its own mailbox.

There is one downside to the freeware version of Eudora. It contains no help file and only limited usage instructions. That said, the layout and simple configuration options mean that Eudora is very easy to use.

Pegasus Mail for Windows

Common Filename: WINPM.ZIP

Status: Freeware

Like Eudora, Pegasus offers users a wide variety of features that make it very much a personal preference issue when you're determining which one you prefer.

All the features available in Eudora—including many of the commercial-only features—can also be found in Pegasus, although I personally find the Pegasus layout is slightly less intuitive. There are some major advantages that give Pegasus the edge in some situations, however.

The first of these is the inclusion of a comprehensive built-in help system. There is also extensive support for the creation of mail distribution lists and a more powerful address book. In addition, the incoming mail filtering features that were available only in the commercial version of Eudora are all available in the freeware version of Pegasus.

Usenet Newsreaders

You cannot currently use a separate Usenet newsreader with AOL, but you can use one with GNNWorks.

Although the newsreader built into GNNWorks is full featured, you may discover that another newsreader is better suited to your needs. This section takes a look at all the popular Winsock-based newsreaders.

Trumpet News Reader

Common Filename: WTWSK1.ZIP

Status: Shareware

The Trumpet News Reader is yet another program from the stables of Peter Tattam. However, unlike the Trumpet Telnet application, this program comes compete with online help and detailed installation and configuration instructions. There does not appear to be much support in the way of ongoing development with this program despite the fact that it is a shareware product. As a result, it is starting to show its age in the face of some stiff competition.

As a news reader, it allows you to subscribe to newsgroups and read the messages they contain. You can also reply to these messages either via e-mail or as a response to the original message. There is also built-in support for the decoding of UUENCODED messages and the ability to attach files to messages you send. Trumpet can also double as a simple e-mail client through its built-in e-mail utilities.

WINVN

Common Filename: WINVN16.ZIP—16-bit for Windows 3.xx

Common Filename: WINVN32.ZIP—32-bit for Windows 95

Status: Freeware

WINVN is a highly Windows-integrated newsgroup reader that supports such features as multiple message areas, built-in encoding/decoding of MIME and UU/XX formats, extensive thread management, and full multitasking, including background operations while downloading messages. In addition, the developers of WINVN have put a lot of effort into its visual appearance, taking full advantage of all the capabilities offered by the Windows environment.

For Windows 95 users, the 32-bit version is not simply a recompile in 32-bit mode, but an extensive rebuild that adds support for the new Windows Explorer-style dialog boxes and MAPI32 mail capabilities. About the only thing that it can't do is retrieve mail from your mailbox like an e-mail client.

This program is also well-supported by its developers, all of whom donate many hours of their free time to its maintenance and support. As a result, regular updates for both the 32-bit and

16-bit versions have been appearing regularly over the last 12 months. Although the version available on CompuServe will usually be fairly recent, to obtain a copy of the very latest version you need to use the official FTP site at `ftp://ftp.ksc.nasa.gov/pub/winvn/`.

News Xpress

Common Filename: NX10B2.ZIP

Status: Beta Freeware

News Xpress is a relatively new entrant into the newsgroup reader fraternity. Its main claim to fame seems to be the fact that it is the first Windows MDI-compliant program of this type. This allows it to multitask very well under Windows and handle more than one open newsgroup at a time.

It also supports thread-based access to newsgroup messages and background processing capabilities for message retrieval and thread sorting. For a program that is still in its early beta-testing stages, it is quite feature-packed and surprisingly stable.

Free Agent

Common Filename: AGENT99a.ZIP

Status: Freeware/Commercial

All the newsgroup readers you have looked at so far have one thing in common. To use them effectively, you need to be online the entire time you are reading newsgroups and sending messages. Because you are usually being charged for the time you are connected, it would appear that some sort of offline newsgroup reader would be a useful tool.

Until recently, no such tool was available for use with Usenet, which effectively forced people to waste a considerable amount of connection time. To remedy this inadequacy, a new program is currently being developed that can act both as an online and an offline newsgroup reader. To give people a sample of what's in store, the developers have released a freeware version to the general public called Free Agent. You can obtain a copy of this program at `http://www.forteinc.com/forte/` or place an online order for a copy of the enhanced commercial version.

With Free Agent or Agent—the commercial version—you can choose a group of newsgroups that you are interested in and then have Free Agent log on to your Usenet server and retrieve either a list of article headings or all the messages currently stored in each newsgroup. If you have retrieved a list of headings, you can scan through the headings while offline and select the ones in which you are interested. Then when you are ready, reconnect to the server and have Free Agent retrieve a copy of all the messages associated with the headers you selected.

Free Agent uses a concept similar to the FlashSession concept available via AOL, but provides you with far more control over the articles that are received. However, you should be warned that some newsgroups can generate literally thousands of messages each day. As a result, you need to be somewhat selective about the number of newsgroups you choose to watch.

WS_ARCHIE

Common Filename: WSARCH08.ZIP

Status: Beta Freeware

WS_ARCHIE is currently the only Archie client available for Windows. It allows you to log on to any of the Archie servers around the world and request information about the location of files stored on FTP sites.

When you generate a request using WS_ARCHIE, it attempts to retrieve a list of all the sites containing files meeting your requirements. You can then select from the files listed and have WS_ARCHIE automatically open WS_FTP to retrieve a copy of the file for you.

WWW Tools

Apart from GNNWorks and AOL's built-in WWW browser, there are a number of different World Wide Web navigators currently available, all of which offer different features and capabilities. To mention them all here, however, would be a waste of time, because it seems that as fast as one group brings out a new capability in their browser, someone else releases something different on theirs.

As a result, your best bet is to take a look at the latest list of WWW browsers in the Consummate Winsock Apps List. With this information in hand, download one or two and try them out. Choosing a WWW browser is a bit like buying a car—we all want one with at least four wheels, but apart from that, everyone has their eye on something different.

That said, the next sections mention two particular WWW browsers that between them offer the most features and are by far the most popular.

NCSA Mosaic

Common Filename: MOS20FB.EXE

Status: Beta Freeware

No discussion of World Wide Web navigators could ever be complete without mention of NCSA Mosaic, the WWW browser that all the others are based on.

In its latest incarnation, NCSA Mosaic is available only as a 32-bit application, but that does not mean that Windows 3.xx users cannot use it. Microsoft has released a special set of libraries called WIN32s that allow many 32-bit programs to operate on the older Windows operating system. A copy of this set of libraries can be downloaded from the Microsoft FTP site at `ftp://ftp.microsoft.com/` or from the Consummate Winsock Applications List.

The latest version of Mosaic, version 2.0 final beta, includes a number of new features including support for tables and embedded OLE integration. To find out what's happening on the leading edge of WWW technology, this browser is a good place to start.

A copy of the latest version of Mosaic can always be obtained from `http://www.ncsa.uiuc.edu/SDG/Software/Mosaic/NCSAMosaicHome.html`.

Netscape

Common Filename: N32E12N.EXE 32bit for Windows 95 & NT

Common Filename: N162E12N.EXE 16bit for Windows 3.11

Status: Freeware/Commercial

If NCSA Mosaic is the granddaddy of all Web browsers, Netscape is its upwardly mobile younger son. This is due, in no small part, to the fact that many of the developers who were originally responsible for the creation of Mosaic are now employed by Netscape. As far as features go, Netscape has them all—including many not provided by any other WWW browser. Like Mosaic, there is built-in support for tables and inline JPEG images, as well as background images and textures, dynamically updating pages, and even rudimentary animation capabilities.

For many people there is no other Web browser, and because its 16-bit version doesn't require the installation of the Microsoft WIN32s library, it's also the easiest program to set up. There is also a 32-bit version for Windows 95 and NT users.

To obtain a copy of Netscape, you should use the download page provided on the Netscape WWW server, which is located at `http://www.netscape.com/`.

Gopher Clients

With the rapid development of WWW browsers, the need for dedicated Gopher clients is currently on the downturn, because all the features provided by even the most capable Gopher clients are now included as a part of every WWW browser.

For those of you who would still like to take a look at a Gopher client, there is at least one available in the Internet Connection Software Library. Alternatively, the Consummate Winsock Apps List also contains links to BCGopher, HGopher, and WSGopher, each of which offers slightly different capabilities. In Chapter 11, "Gopher & WAIS," there is a discussion of each of the major gopher clients.

IRC Clients

If you want to participate in IRC conversations using the Internet, you will need to obtain a copy of one of the IRC clients, because America Online does not currently support access to IRC via AOL.

WSIRC

Common Filename: WSIRC20.EXE

Status: Freeware/Shareware/Registered

There are a number of different versions of WSIRC currently available, each of which offers slightly different capabilities. Both the freeware and shareware versions offer a limited number of concurrent connections, reduced support for DCC chat, and no CTCP services. The help file for both of these versions is also limited to basic information and setup guidelines.

The shareware version also includes a timed usage limitation that locks you out of the program after 21 days. The registered version allows you to open up to 255 concurrent public and private sessions, adds full DCC and CTCP support for file transfers and IRC games, and includes a detailed help file.

mIRC

Common Filename: MIRC351.ZIP

Status: freeware

According to its developers, this program has been released as unsupported software. It is not quite as full-featured as the registered version of WSIRC, but it compares favorably with both the freeware and shareware versions.

If you are looking for a good IRC client that does not overload you with millions of unnecessary options and that allows you to get up and running with a limited knowledge of IRC, this is the program for you.

WAIS Clients

Although AOL's built-in WAIS client provides you with an easy method of accessing some WAIS databases, to explore the full potential of WAIS you need to consider the use of a dedicated WAIS client. Using a dedicated WAIS client also has a number of advantages over the WWW-based gateways discussed in Chapter 13, "WWW Productivity." Among these, the ability to store search queries and results for later use is without a doubt the most popular.

WAIS for Windows

Common Filename: WWAIS24.EXE

Status: Freeware

A number of the different WAIS clients currently available are based on the freely distributed source code for WAIS for Windows. This program has been through a number of different incarnations to arrive at the most recent version known as WWAIS24.EXE. To obtain a copy of this version, which was released by Tim Gauslin of the U.S. Geological Survey, Information

Systems Division, log on to their FTP server at `ftp://ridgisd.er.usgs.gov` and open the `/software/wais/` directory.

WAIS Inc's FTP Archive

Common Filename: wwais22a.zip

Status: Freeware

Common Filename: EIWAIS155.zip

Status: Shareware

WAIS Inc, the company that brought you WAISgate, maintains an archive of popular WAIS clients including versions for Windows, the Apple Macintosh, and SUN computers. The URL for this archive is `ftp://ftp.wais.com/pub/freeware/windows/`. You will find two major WAIS clients in this archive. The first is `WWAIS22A.ZIP` and the second `EIWAIS155.zip`.

`WWAIS22A.ZIP` is regarded as the WAIS client of choice. What has made it so popular, is that the source code for this version was released into the public domain. There are many similarities between this version and the WWAIS24.EXE discussed previously.

`EIWAIS155.ZIP` is also similar to WAIS for Windows, and demonstrates its obvious shared heritage both in its layout and usage. This version does add a number of new features, including better support for multimedia-based information and the ability to save existing queries.

It is not a freeware program, however, and as such you must register it if you choose to continue to use it after the 30-day trial period. However, the exact status of EIWAIS is somewhat up in the air these days because EINET—now TradeWave—no longer appears to be supporting the program.

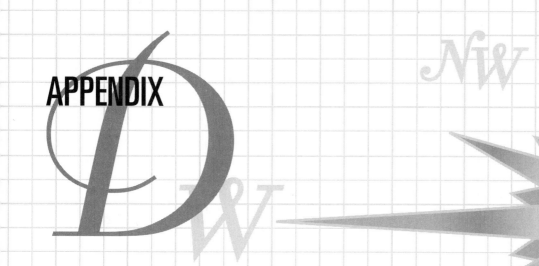

APPENDIX D

COMPRESSION AND ENCRYPTION SOFTWARE

WinZip

Wincode

WinPack

Internet Privacy

Encryption Software for the Apple Macintosh

Throughout this book I've mentioned a number of utilities that enable you to compress or encrypt files before you transmit them across the Internet. I've also discussed the complements of these tools that can unpack and decrypt such files.

By taking advantage of such programs, you can considerably reduce the amount of time required to send or retrieve large files. When you consider that many of the files available on the Internet are over a megabyte in size, reducing their size by up to 80% before transmission can add up to considerable savings in connection time. For the security-conscious, those tools that allow you to encrypt files provide the additional benefit of creating files that only the person they are intended for can read.

Some of these tools can also encode and decode files so that they can be transmitted via e-mail and Usenet. Because e-mail messages can consist only of ASCII text, files distributed this way need to be converted into a special format that is ASCII text-compatible.

This appendix looks at some of the programs that perform one or more of these tasks and discusses places to obtain a copy of the latest version.

Note

> AOL includes built-in support for decompressing ZIP and ARC files and can unpack MIME encoded files sent as e-mail messages. The Macintosh version can also unpack Stuffit files as well.

WinZip

Without a doubt, PKZIP is by far the best-known file compression utility available today. Developed and distributed by a company called PKWare, during the past six years this program has become the standard compression system used by bulletin boards and commercial operations like America Online.

However, although PKZIP is an extremely popular compression tool, its command-line interface is not the most user-friendly. To get around this difficulty, a number of shell and graphical user interfaces (GUIs) have been developed that make using PKZIP less complicated. For Windows users, the most popular of these is WinZip. (See Figure D.1.)

Instead of using a command line, with WinZip you can create compressed or *zipped* files using a simple point-and-click interface. It also allows you to decompress existing zip files using the same environment.

FIGURE D.1.

WinZip is the first zip utility to include features designed specifically for Windows 95.

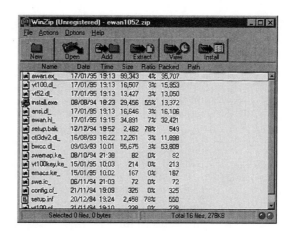

Decompressing a Zipped File

To decompress a zipped file that you have downloaded from the Internet or America Online, open WinZip and follow these steps:

1. Click on the Open button in the WinZip toolbar. This opens a file dialog box similar to the one shown in Figure D.2. (This is the Windows 95 dialog box. Under Windows 3.11 you may see a slightly different one.)

2. Using this dialog box, locate the file you wish to decompress and click on the Open Button. As a rule, files created with PKZIP or WinZip are given a .zip file extension to indicate that their contents have been compressed. The file selected in Figure D.2 was ewan1052.zip which is in fact a copy of the EWAN Telnet client discussed in Chapter 10, "AOL and Winsock."

> Depending on how you have configured WinZip, it can also decompress files created with a number of other compression utilities. These include ARJ, LZH, LHA, and ARC. In addition, as of version 5.6a, you can also decompress files stored in many Internet-specific formats that have file extensions such as TAR, GZ, Z, TAZ, and TGZ.

3. When you click on the Open button, WinZip scans the archive file you have selected and displays a list of all the files it contains. Figure D.1 discussed previously shows the contents of ewan1052.zip.

FIGURE D.2.

Under Windows 95,
WinZip uses the standard
File Open dialog box.

Apart from being useful as a compression tool, using WinZip makes it easy to distribute many files at the same time. This is because it can store any number of files and even entire directories in a single file. This is why zip files are often referred to as *archives*.

4. Once WinZip has opened the zip archive, you can perform a number of tasks to manipulate it. These include extracting the files it contains, viewing the contents of a single entry, or in some cases even installing the archive's contents using the standard Windows SETUP.EXE program.

5. In this case, you want to simply extract the contents of ewan1052.zip and place them on your hard drive. To do this, click on the Extract button located in the WinZip toolbar. You should now be presented with a dialog box similar to the one shown in Figure D.3. This is the Extract dialog box. Using it, select the location for WinZip to place the files you are extracting. You can instruct WinZip to store the files in any existing directory or create a new directory by clicking on the Create Dir… button.

FIGURE D.3.

The Extract dialog box lets
you select the directory in
which the archive's contents
will be stored.

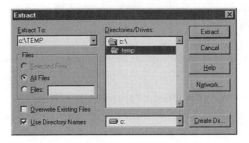

6. Once you have located the directory where you want to store the extracted files, click on the Extract button to start the decompression. In Figure D.3 the \TEMP directory of the C: drive is selected.

Compressing a File with WinZip

Like decompressing a zip archive, compressing files and storing them in an archive using WinZip is a relatively straightforward process. Just follow these steps:

1. Click on the New Button in the WinZip toolbar to open a New Archive dialog box, like the one shown in Figure D.4.

FIGURE D.4.

Using the New Archive dialog box, select the location for your new zip file.

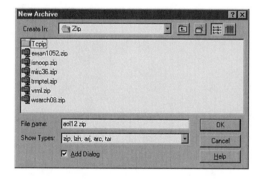

2. Select the directory in which to store your new zip archive.
3. Enter the name for the new zip archive in the File Name field.

> You can also use WinZip to create compressed archives in ARJ and LZH format provided that WinZip has been configured to use these programs. To use one of these programs, replace the `.zip` file extension with `.arj` or `.lzh`. However, you can't use WinZip to create ARC, TAR, or GZ files, even though you can use it to extract files stored in these archives.

4. Select the Add Dialog check box to tell WinZip that you want to open the Add dialog box once the new archive is created.
5. Finally, click on the OK button to create your new archive. When you do this, WinZip opens the Add dialog box shown in Figure D.5.
6. This dialog box offers you a wide variety of options, allowing you to select the files you want to compress. If you want to compress all the files in a directory, all you need to do is click on the Add button.

> To find out more about the various options provided by the Add dialog box, click on the Help button or hit the F1 key to bring up WinZip's online help system.

FIGURE D.5

The Add dialog box allows you to select the files you want to compress.

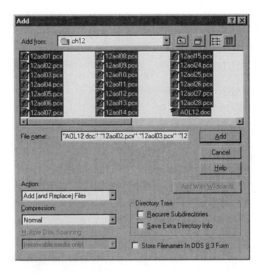

7. When WinZip finishes adding these files to the new archive, it returns you to the main WinZip window and displays the contents of your new archive. (See Figure D.6.) From here, you can click on the Add button again to include more files.

FIGURE D.6.

WinZip instantly displays a list of the files you have added to your zip archive.

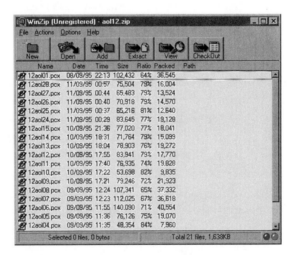

8. When you have finished working with your new archive, open the **F**ile menu and select the **C**lose Archive option.

Downloading WinZip

To obtain a demonstration copy of the latest version of WinZip, you can either go to the WinZip WWW home page at `http://www.winzip.com/winzip` or do a search of America Online's Software Library.

> WinZip is not a free program. If you continue to use WinZip after the 21-day trial period is over, you must pay a registration fee to Niko Mac Computing, WinZip's developer. At the time of this writing, this fee was $29 U.S.

Wincode

To transmit a file using e-mail or Usenet, you must first convert it into an acceptable format. On the Internet, there are currently two main formats that achieve this goal: UUENCODE and MIME. Creating a file in one of these formats requires a special utility designed to perform this type of conversion. Under Windows, one of the more popular programs of this sort is called Wincode. (See Figure D.7.)

FIGURE D.7.

Wincode allows you to manipulate files in UUENCODE and MIME format.

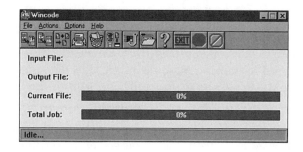

Wincode has developed a large following due to its ability to manipulate files stored in both UUENCODE and MIME format. For many people, this has made Wincode the only tool they need for e-mail file conversions.

Another reason for the popularity of this program is its status as a *freeware* program, although it should probably be called *figure-it-out for-yourself-ware* for reasons that will become obvious. When you download a copy of Wincode from either America Online or the Internet, you receive a *free,* fully working version of Wincode—there are no registration requirements. However, what you do not receive is a copy of the manual or the online help file. As the program's author puts it:

> The HELP file is NOT required for Wincode to function properly. If you can figure out all of Wincode's features on your own, then by all means enjoy the FREE program. If you would like assistance and/or the HELP file to discover Wincode's FULL potential (that is, network support, limited auto-line correction, and so on) then order the HELP and support…
>
> —*George Silva–Snappy_Inc.*

Wincode Features

In deference to George Silva, how you use Wincode is not described here. Instead, some of its features and capabilities are discussed to give you some idea of what Wincode can do.

Supported Formats

Wincode can convert any 8-bit binary file into 7-bit UUENCODE format and convert it back. It fully supports both the UU and XX encoding specifications for UUENCODED files and allows you to create custom encoding specifications. For mail systems that set limits on message size, Wincode can also automatically split large files into small UUENCODED segments and recombine received messages containing split files.

> Once you convert a file into UUENCODE format, you can then transmit it using e-mail. For more information about sending e-mail messages, take a look at Chapter 6, "The Internet E-Mail Gateway."

Wincode also fully supports the MIME 1.0 standard that uses Base64 encoding. This format was designed for the distribution of multimedia files using e-mail. Wincode can also handle multipart MIME files and automatically launch image viewers, MPEG players, and audio players when decoding multimedia components.

When you are encoding files, Wincode can also be configured to compress the files with PKZIP before they are converted to reduce the size of the resulting ASCII encoded files.

> Currently, there are plans to add an additional format, known as BinHex, to Wincode. This format was made popular by the Apple Macintosh and has since been adopted by the developers of a number of e-mail packages as an alternate encoding format.

Downloading Wincode

A copy of the latest version of Wincode can usually be found at the CICA archive located at `ftp://ftp.cica.indiana.edu`. However, Wincode's author recommends Archie as the best method for finding copies of Wincode stored on the Internet.

WinPack

Another program has just arrived on the scene that promises to combine the best features of WinZip and Wincode into a single program with some other bells and whistles thrown in for good measure. This new program in called WinPack. (See Figure D.8.) According to the WinPack press release, its developers aim to create a program that is easy to use and that can also encode and decode every mainstream archive format currently available.

FIGURE D.8.

WinPack lets you create many different types of archives using one consistent interface.

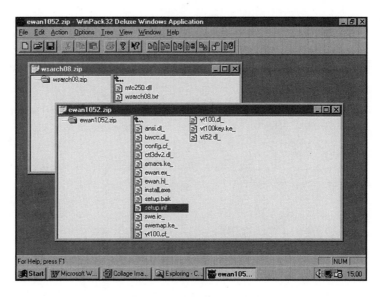

When this appendix was being written, WinPack was still in beta testing. As such, the exact makeup of the final release version is still unknown. However, due to the nature of this program, its content is significant enough to include here—if only as a prelude for things to come.

Pre-Release Information

In many ways, using WinPack is a lot like using WinZip, although WinPack lets you work with a wider variety of archive formats, including

- ◆ ZIP archives
- ◆ ARC archives
- ◆ Freeze archives
- ◆ GNU ZIP (UNIX) archives
- ◆ UNIX compressed archives
- ◆ UNIX Tar archives
- ◆ UUENCODE/UUDECODE
- ◆ BinHex encode/decode
- ◆ Stuffit archives
- ◆ Packit archives
- ◆ ARJ archives
- ◆ MIME encode/decode

Downloading WinPack

When WinPack is released, there will be two separate versions available: a shareware version that provides support for zip archives only, and WinPack Deluxe, a commercial version including all the archive modules.

Copies of the shareware version will be available on America Online and the Internet following the official release. The commercial version, on the other hand, will be available only from RetroSpect (WinPack's distributors) and should retail for around $20.00.

To find out more information about WinPack, please contact Randy Snow at RetroSpect—`snow@retrospect.com`.

Internet Privacy

The biggest problems facing the Internet today are privacy and security. Due to the unrestricted nature of the Internet, it is far from what anyone would call a secure system.

From the time a message leaves your computer to the time it arrives at its destination, it may pass through hundreds of different computer systems. At any stage during this journey, any unethical person with a little bit of knowledge and access to one of these systems could read your private message and even take a copy of it for their own use.

> If you connect to America Online via the Internet, make sure you change your password on a regular basis, to protect this information from prying eyes.

Although this may sound a bit like the story of the boy who cried wolf or someone's idea of Internet scare tactics, this unfortunate fact of life remains. In the past, and possibly still today, there were people who use systems like the Internet for activities that are not altogether legal. There are numerous stories that circulate on the Internet telling of credit card information and other private details being stolen from e-mail messages. For this reason, there is a silent rule on the Internet that says, "Thou shalt not use the Internet to send private or confidential information."

The problem is, the Internet is simply too convenient a method of communicating with people for such a rule to have any practical value. As a communications tool, many people want to use the Internet to send and receive confidential information. Yet at the same time, they also want their information to be secure.

Encryption

Because of the nature of the Internet, about the only reliable way of securing your information is to encrypt it before you send it. By encrypting your files you are preventing prying eyes from viewing the contents of your private messages. Even though they may still have access to the contents of your transmissions, unless they have a suitable decoder, the information will be of little use to them.

There are two main types of encryption services you can use on the Internet, or anywhere for that matter: private key encryption and public key encryption.

Private Key Encryption

Private key encryption is a relatively straightforward process. You create a file that you want to send securely to another person. When you have created the file, a special program uses an encryption key to create an encrypted version of your original file. If you look at this new file, it appears to be a jumble of letters and numbers that make no sense.

You can now send this file to your destination without any fear of a security breach. When the file arrives at its destination, the person receiving it must run the file through an encryption program identical to the one you used. They must also be able to tell the program exactly what encryption key you used when you created the file. Without knowledge of this key, it is impossible to decode the file.

As long as the contents of your encryption key remain a secret between you and the person you are communicating with, your security is guaranteed. This is the reason for the name "private key encryption"—you need to keep your key private to protect it.

Public Key Encryption

Although private key encryption may be suitable for communications with people you know, this reliability breaks down if you need to give the key out to many people. This type of key is also of little use for conducting activities such as online shopping, because it is not practical or viable for everyone you deal with to have a copy of your private encryption key.

This is where the concept of public key encryption comes into its own. Unlike private key encryption, which uses a single key to both encrypt and decrypt a file, public key encryption requires a pair of keys: one to encrypt the information, and a different one to decrypt it. The advantage of this approach is simple. Because the key used for the encryption process can't also be used to decrypt the file, you can freely give a copy of it to anyone who wants one. You can even publish it on Usenet or in WWW pages. This key is called your *public* key. By using this key with an encryption program, anyone can create an encrypted file for you. Even the person who created the encrypted file for you using your public key cannot decode it. The file they created can be decoded only by you, because only you have the second part of the key—your secret key.

Like a private key, you need to keep this secret key's contents to yourself, but unlike a private key, no one else ever needs to know its contents. In this sense, public key encryption is actually a more secure method of encryption. There is no way for anyone to find out the contents of the key that decodes files encrypted by your public key—unless, of course, you leave it lying around.

Pretty Good Privacy

The most popular public key encryption system available today was developed by Philip R. Zimmerman in 1990. His aim was to create a public key encryption system that would provide a means of secure data transmission for all members of the Internet community. This program is called *PGP (Pretty Good Privacy)* and is distributed as freeware, provided that it isn't used for commercial purposes.

MIT also distributes a version of PGP. This version contains a different encryption module called the RSA public key cryptosystem. Although the program code for the encryption system in each version of PGP was written independently, both versions are sufficiently compatible to permit the exchange of encrypted files between the two systems.

PGP is also currently at the center of potential criminal proceedings between Philip Zimmerman and the U.S. Customs Department. This is because the government views the distribution of encryption software in much the same way as it views the sale of arms to foreign governments. Basically, the United States government contends that the distribution of encryption software by electronic means is a breach of ITAR restrictions (the restrictions controlling the export of munitions and cryptographic technology from the U.S. and Canada).

This is why there are currently two separate versions of PGP: one that can be used in the United States and Canada, and one that can be used only outside the United States. The version that can be used in the United States uses the RSA cryptosystem developed by MIT, while the international version is based on the algorithms designed independently by Philip Zimmerman. This second version, although based on an illegally exported version of PGP, can be used legally anywhere else in the world because it falls outside the restrictions of the RSA License and U.S. Customs limitations.

That said, the use of PGP may be illegal in different parts of the world, depending on local governments' views of encryption systems. For example, in the United Kingdom it is illegal to transmit encrypted data over the radio.

To confuse matters even further, there is also a commercial version of PGP that was licensed from Philip Zimmerman by ViaCrypt. This version cannot be used outside the United States for the reasons previously discussed, and because ViaCrypt also owns a license for the RSA cryptosystem.

Downloading a Copy of PGP

As a result of all these legal wranglings, depending on where you live, you need to obtain either the international version of PGP or the U.S. version. For most America Online users the U.S. version is the one you should use.

North American Version

MIT operates a PGP home page containing the latest version of PGP (currently 2.6.2) for people in the United States and Canada. (See Figure D.9.) This home page also has a number of discussion pages on encryption technology and links to other PGP-related home pages.

FIGURE D.9.

For people in the United States and Canada, the MIT PGP home page always contains a copy of the latest version.

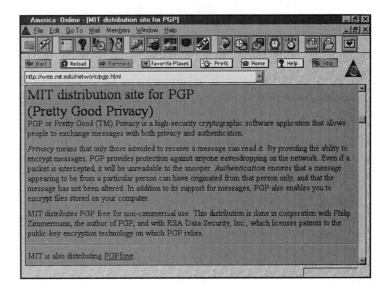

To obtain a copy of PGP from this site, you are first required to fill out a declaration form. This form asks you to acknowledge that you agree to abide by the RSA and MIT licenses and certify that you are a resident of the United States or Canada. To access this home page, use the following URL: `http://web.mit.edu/network/pgp.html`.

Alternatively you can download a copy from America Online's Software Library by doing a search for PGP in the Software Search window.

For Macintosh users, the only version currently available is the restricted U.S. version, which is available from the site listed above or from the Macintosh Software Library at America Online.

At the same time, Macintosh users might also like to take a look at PGPfone (see Figure D.10), a program that uses PGP security for secure voice-based communications via modem.

FIGURE D.10.

PGPfone brings secure, voice-based communications to the masses.

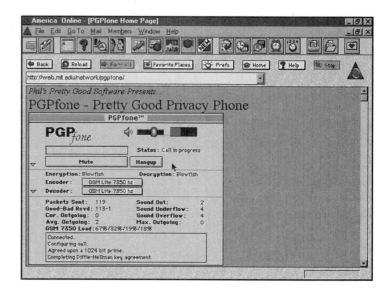

International Version

People outside the United States can obtain information about the latest international version from the International PGP Home Page (see Figure D.11) located at `http://www.ifi.uio.no/~staalesc/PGP/home.html`.

The current international version of PGP is 2.6.2i, although for legal reasons it is not an "official version." In addition to housing a copy of the latest international version, this site also contains a wealth of information about the various versions of PGP and discussions of the technical and legal ramifications of PGP usage.

FIGURE D.11.

The International PGP Home Page contains links to all the well-known PGP sites.

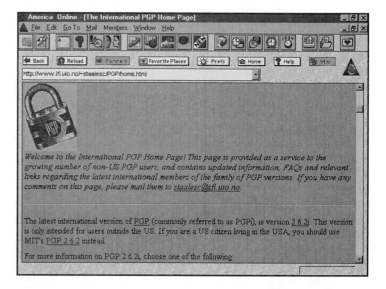

> People living in the U.S. and Canada should not use a copy of the international version, because it may be illegal to do so. You should obtain either a copy of MIT's version or the commercial version distributed by ViaCrypt.

Warning

Using PGP

PGP, like PKZIP, is a command line-based program. To work with PGP, you type strings of switches and names at the DOS prompt. For example, to create your own personal public and secret keys, enter the following command: **pgp.exe -kg**

> Macintosh users will find some differences in the use of MACPGP but the concepts behind the encryption process remain the same.

Note

The PGP program then prompts you for some information that it uses during the key creation process. You are first asked to give your name and possibly your e-mail address as a means of identifying your public key. I use Wes Tatters <wtatters@world.net> for my public key name, but it can be anything you choose.

The most important piece of information you are asked to provide is a *pass phrase.* This is the phrase you'll need to enter to unlock files encoded using your public key. It should be something you can easily remember but can never be guessed by anyone else.

When PGP finishes creating your keys, you are returned to the DOS prompt. If you now look in the directory where you installed PGP, you'll find two new files: PUBRING.PGP and SECRING.PGP.

Stored in these two files, or *keyrings* as they are known, are your secret and public keys. PGP uses the keyring analogy for all its encryption information. This is also true for any public keys that you are given by other people. When you receive a public key, you need to place it on your public keyring before you can use it to encrypt files.

Signature Files

Apart from being an encryption system, PGP also provides you with an electronic method of signing documents to signify that their contents are yours.

For many people, this validation tool alone makes PGP a valuable addition to their software collection. Although a discussion of the actions required to use PGP as an electronic signature are beyond the scope of this book, it is important that you at least understand that the capability is there.

The best place to find out about using this capability and all the features included in PGP is the *PGP Users' Guide,* written by Philip Zimmerman. Regardless of which version of PGP you obtain, a copy of the two files that constitute this guide are included. In most cases they are installed in a DOC subdirectory in the main PGP directory. The files you need to look for are PGPDOC1.TXT and PGPDOC2.TXT.

PGP WinFront

As you begin to work with PGP, it probably won't take long before you become frustrated with the command line interface. To reduce the hassles associated with using PGP, a number of shells and front ends have been designed that allow you to replace the command line with a more user-friendly Windows interface.

> *Note*
>
> All the current PGP front ends and shells still require you to have a copy of PGP installed. You need to do this because each one actually uses PGP to perform encryption tasks. This avoids all the complex licensing and export restrictions discussed earlier.

FIGURE D.12.

WinFront brings point-and-click simplicity to PGP.

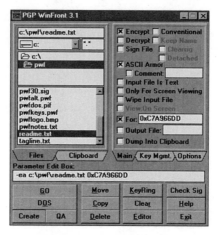

One of the more popular contenders in the PGP shell stakes is WinFront. (See Figure D.12.) This shell provides you with point-and-click access to all of PGP's functions. You can encrypt and decrypt files using public and secret keys and manage the contents of your public keyring, including any public keys that you have been given.

Encrypting a File with WinFront

To encrypt a file using a WinFront, follow these steps:

1. After opening WinFront, select the options shown in Figure D.12. Click on the checkbox next to the Encrypt option because you want to encrypt a file. In this case, the ASCII Armor option is selected so that you can send the file using e-mail. If you don't select this option, the encoded file is stored in binary format, not ASCII format.

2. Click on the **K**eyring button to select the people that can decode the file. This will open the Key Ring window, shown in Figure D.13. Using this window, you can select any of the people stored in your public key ring. In this example, Philip Zimmerman and Wes Tatters are the only people who will be able to decode the encrypted file.

Once you have selected the recipients, click on the **H**ide Keyring button to return to the main WinFront window.

FIGURE D.13.

Select the people who can decode your message using the Key Ring window.

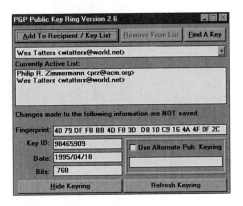

> In the next version of WinFront, the author plans to add the capability of automatically sending the encrypted file as an e-mail message to each of the people you select.

3. When you return to the main window, select the file you want to encrypt. In Figure D.12, the file readme.txt was selected. Once you are happy with your selection, click on the **G**O button to begin the conversion.

> As you select from the various options available, WinFront displays the parameters it is going to send to PGP in the Parameter edit box. By studying these entries, you can learn a lot about the way PGP operates.

4. When you hit the **G**O button, WinFront launches PGP in a DOS window and performs the requested actions. (See Figure D.14.) As these occur, they are displayed one at a time down the screen.

5. When PGP completes the encryption process, it creates a new file with the same name as the original file. This new file has an .asc extension. You can now send this file to its intended recipients, confident that no one else can decode its contents.

Decrypting a File with WinFront

The process involved in decrypting a file is much the same as the encryption process. Naturally, you can only decode a file that has been encoded with your public key, but apart from that, the process is relatively straightforward.

FIGURE D.14.

WinFront launches PGP in a DOS window to perform the requested actions.

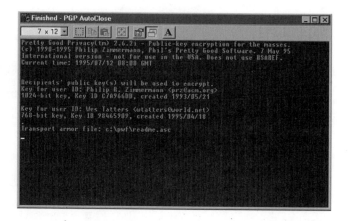

To decrypt a file using a WinFront, follow these steps:

1. After opening WinFront, select the Decrypt option, as shown in Figure D.14. Also select the Keep Name option to force PGP to store the decrypted file using the original file's name. If you don't select this option, PGP stores the decrypted file without a file extension. (See Figure D.15.)

FIGURE D.15.

If you don't select the Keep Name option, PGP saves the decrypted file without an extension.

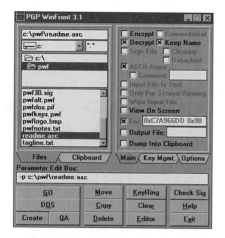

2. Select the file you want to decrypt. Files encrypted using PGP usually have either a .pgp or .asc extension. In this case, you want to decode the readme.asc file you created earlier. Once you have selected the file, click on the **G**O button to launch PGP.

3. WinFront opens PGP in an MS-DOS window similar to the one shown in Figure D.16. If PGP finds that the file is valid and you have a secret key corresponding to one of the public keys used to encrypt the file, PGP asks you to enter the pass phrase for your secret key. Once you enter a valid pass phrase, PGP decrypts the file and saves it using the file's original name. In this case, PGP recreated the file called readme.txt.

FIGURE D.16.

Before PGP can decrypt a file, you must enter the pass phrase needed to unlock your secret key.

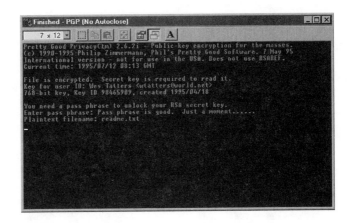

Downloading a Copy of WinFront

The best place to obtain a copy of WinFront is from the CICA anonymous FTP archive. The file you are looking for is located in the /win3/util directory, and its name is PWF31.ZIP. To obtain a copy of this file from the SUNET CICA mirror, use the following FTP address and directory: ftp://ftp.sunet.se/pub/pc/windows/mirror-cica/win3/util/.

WinPGP

If the up-front approach of WinFront seems a bit too complex for your needs, maybe WinPGP would be more to your liking. Instead of trying to give you everything at once, WinPGP uses the "big, friendly buttons" approach to guide you step by step through PGP's available options. (See Figure D.17.) This user-friendliness comes at a price, however. WinPGP is not a freeware program, but is instead released as shareware. If you continue to use WinPGP after the 30-day trial period, you must pay the author a licensing fee.

FIGURE D.17.

WinPGP uses big, friendly buttons.

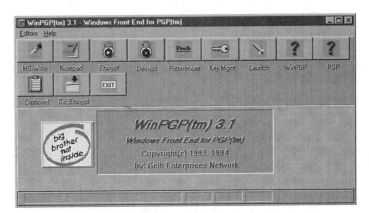

Encrypting a File with WinPGP

To encrypt a file using WinPGP, you should follow these steps:

1. Open WinPGP and click on the Prefs button to open the PGP Preferences window, shown in Figure D.18. This window allows you to configure a number of default settings for PGP. For this example, select the ASCII Armor option to let PGP know that you want to create an e-mail-compatible file. Leave the Recover File Name on Decrypt option set to the default to force PGP to recover the original file name when decrypting files. After making these changes, click on the OK button to return to the main WinPGP window.

FIGURE D.18.

The Preferences window allows you to customize the way WinPGP operates.

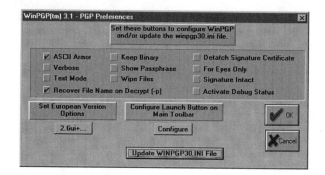

2. To encode a file, click on the Encrypt button (it looks like a combination padlock). Doing this opens a window similar to the one shown in Figure D.19. This window allows you to select from one of four different encryption types: signed encryption, unsigned encryption, idea encryption, and signing of a text file. For this example, let's look at unsigned encryption, which is what you actually did previously in the WinFront example. To do this, click on the Unsigned button.

FIGURE D.19.

PGP lets you choose from four different encryption options.

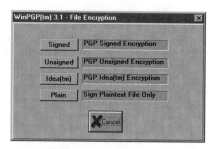

3. When you do this, WinPGP opens the Unsigned Encryption window, shown in Figure D.20. Into the first field, enter the name of the file you want to encrypt, or click on the Browse button to open a file dialog box that allows you to select the file you want. (See Figure D.21.) WinPGP requires you to enter an ID code from one of the public keys stored on your public keyring in the second field. To obtain the ID

code that corresponds to the person you want to send the encoded file to, click on the ListNames button. This opens a Listing window which lets you make your selection from any of the keys currently stored on your public keyring. (See Figure D.22.)

FIGURE D.20.

The WinPGP Unsigned Encryption window.

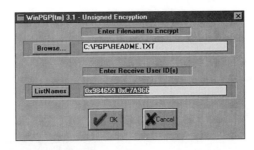

FIGURE D.21.

The Get File Name To Encrypt dialog box allows you to choose the file you want to encrypt.

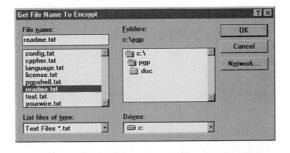

FIGURE D.22.

To locate a public key ID, use the View Key Names List.

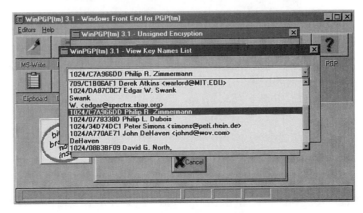

The current version of WinPGP does not allow you select more than one recipient with the Listing window. However, if you know the ID codes of each person, you can enter them all into the ID field one after the other, separated by spaces, as was done in Figure D.20.

Note

4. When you are satisfied that the correct information has been entered, click on the OK button to launch PGP. Like WinFront, WinPGP calls PGP with the appropriate codes and switches turned on. PGP then encrypts the file and stores the result in a file called readme.asc.

Decrypting a File Using WinPGP

To reverse the process and decrypt a file using WinPGP, follow these steps:

1. Click on the Decrypt button in the WinPGP main window to open the File Decryption window. (See Figure D.23.) The Decrypt button looks like an open combination padlock.

FIGURE D.23.

The File Decryption window is used to select the file you want to decrypt.

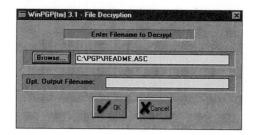

2. Either enter the name of the file you want to decrypt or click on the Browse button to open a dialog box similar to the one mentioned during the encryption process. (See Figure D.21.) If you did not select the Recover File Name on Decrypt option, as discussed previously in Figure D.18, you also need to enter the name that PGP is to use for the decrypted file. Otherwise, PGP creates a new file without an extension.

3. After you have selected the file, click on the OK button to begin the decryption process. Like WinFront, once PGP starts, you are asked to enter the pass phrase for your secret key. (See Figure D.24.) When you enter this phrase, PGP decodes the file and attempts to save a copy in the current directory. If a file with the same name already exists, as is the case in Figure D.24, you are given the opportunity to overwrite it or enter a new name for the file.

Downloading a Copy of WinPGP

Depending on the version, the file you are looking for will be called something like PGPW31.ZIP. To get you started, all the SimTel mirror sites have a copy stored in the .../win3/security directory. This includes the UK Hensa FTP site, whose copy is stored at ftp://micros.hensa.ac.uk/mirrors/SimTel/win3/security.

You might also like to try the WWW server operated by the Electronic Frontier Foundation, which contains a considerable amount of information dealing with encryption and security issues in general. This server is located at http://www.eff.org/.

FIGURE D.24.

If the file already exists, you are given the opportunity of either overwriting it or selecting a new name.

Encryption Software for the Apple Macintosh

On the Internet there is a rapidly expanding collection of Macintosh software that allows you to decode and encode files stored in a variety of different encoding formats. Apart from the PGP utility discussed earlier in this appendix, these utilities fall into two main categories: compression utilities and ASCII file encoders/decoders.

In the following sections of this appendix you will find a brief discussion of some of the more outstanding utilities currently available, all of which can be downloaded from the University of Texas Macintosh archive. The URL for the Mac Compression page shown in Figure D.25 is: `http://wwwhost.ots.utexas.edu/mac/pub-mac-compression.html`.

FIGURE D.25.

You will find a brief description, explaining the use of each utility listed on the Mac Compression page, at the University of Texas Mac Archive site.

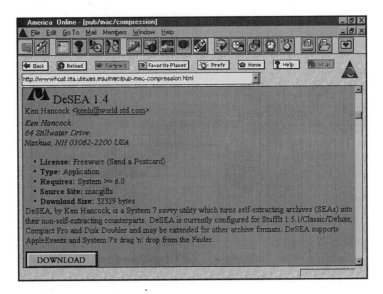

Compression Utilities

To allow large files and programs to be transferred as quickly as possible across the Internet and other online services, most people compress files before sending them. By doing this, a 1MB file that would have take 10 to 20 minutes to transfer in a uncompressed format can often be sent in a matter of minutes when compressed.

On the Macintosh there are a number of popular compression utilities that allow you to compress files and also decompress files you receive from other people.

Stuffit

Stuffit, is by far the most popular compression program available for the Macintosh, which places it on a par with PKWare's PKZIP program for DOS users. Because Stuffit was first released as a shareware program there have been a number of releases and enhancements, with Stuffit Lite being the latest incarnation.

Stuffit Lite lets you create compressed archive files similar to those created by PKZIP. However, the two file formats are not directly compatible, meaning that an archive created by Stuffit, cannot be unpacked by PKZIP and vice versa. In addition to being able to create compressed files, Stuffit Lite can also encode and decode BinHex files, which are the Macintosh equivalent of UUENCODE.

The latest version of Stuffit Lite is version 3.5 and costs $30 to register. To download a copy of Stuffit Lite click on the Download button accompanying its description in the University of Texas archive, or alternatively do a Software Search of the Macintosh Software Library on America Online.

Stuffit Expander

If you don't need a full-blown compression utility, but still want to be able to decompress Stuffit files, then Stuffit Expander is a good choice.

> Stuffit Expander can not compress or create new archives. It can only decompress archives created by other compression utilities.

Stuffit Expander is capable of decompressing archives created by any version of Stuffit and can also decode files compressed by another popular Macintosh program called Compact Pro. BinHex support is also provided in this package, including a number of special features for decoding multipart files, sent as a series of messages via the USENET.

You can download a copy of the latest version either from the University of Texas site or from its home page at `ftp://ftp.netcom.com/pub/leonardr/Aladdin`.

Drop Stuff

Drop Stuff is an add-on program for Stuffit Expander that lets you decompress files by dropping them on the Drop Stuff icon. While being useful, on its own this feature would not be worth mentioning, but it is the additional capabilities that Drop Stuff brings to Stuffit Expander that make it a valuable tool for your collection.

When you add Drop Stuff to Stuffit Expander, you gain the ability to decode a number of additional compression formats including: ZIP archives created on a PC by PKZIP or WinZip, UNIX archives compressed using either the .Z or .gz format, ARC archives, AppleLink packages, and also UUENCODE format text files.

> For Power Mac users, Drop Stuff also includes native PowerPC code for all decompression routines.

Compact Pro

Like Stuffit, Compact Pro creates compressed files and archives. The format that these files are stored in, however, is different from the format used by Stuffit.

So why would anyone want to use two different compression tools if they both do the same job? The answer to this question lies in the routines both programs use to compress file. Depending on the types of files you are compressing, you will often find that one of the programs creates a file that is significantly smaller that the other.

As a result, if you are trying to copy a large file to a floppy disk, for example, and it won't quite fit, compressing it with a different program might just do the trick. Unfortunately, there is no clear cut way to know which program will work better for you, so the best option available is to experiment with both and get a feeling for the types of files each utility favors.

BinHex and UUENCODE

There are three main ASCII encoding formats available today: UUENCODE, which is based on the original UNIX encoding specification, BinHex, which is predominantly used by Apple Macintosh users, and MIME, the more recent Multipurpose Internet Mail Extension format.

Apart from the programs already mentioned, which support the BinHex and UUENCODE formats, there are a few programs currently available that have been designed solely for the support of ASCII encoded files.

MPack

MPack is one of the only programs currently available on the Apple Macintosh that can decode and encode files using the MIME format. If you find yourself receiving encoded files via e-mail, chances are that they will have been sent using MIME. You can recognize a MIME encoded message by the text in the first part of the message which describes the type of MIME format used to encode the file.

You can obtain a copy of the latest release of MPack from the MPack host site at `ftp://ftp.andrew.cmu.edu/pub/mpack`. Unlike most of the other programs discussed so far, MPack is available as freeware.

> You will occasionally encounter files encoded in a format called BASE64. This is effectively the same format as MIME, and as a result, most programs that support MIME will decode BASE64 encoded files as well.

UULite

The easiest way to decode UUENCODE format files on a Macintosh is using a program called UULite. One of the main reasons for this, is the level of intelligence built into UULite when it comes to dealing with the complexities of multipart files.

UULite oversees all the actions required to collect, sort, and decode a set of ASCII files back into its original binary format. You can also encode binary files into either a single UUENCODE ASCII file or into a set of files suitable for posting to either newsgroups or via e-mail.

The best place to obtain a copy of UULite is via the University of Texas archive.

UMCP Tools

In addition to providing UUENCODE and UUDECODE support, UMCP Tools also deals with another important UNIX to Macintosh conversion issue. Text files stored on a UNIX computer are saved in a slightly different format from those sorted on a Macintosh.

As a result, if you attempt to use a UNIX computer to read an ASCII text file created on a Macintosh, or vice versa, you will often notice some strange codes buried in the text. To solve this problem, UMCP Tools contains a small utility that can strip out the unwanted characters from a text file and also reinsert them when converting a file in the opposite direction.

Like most of the other programs listed in this section, you can download a copy of the UMCP Tools from the University of Texas Macintosh Archive.

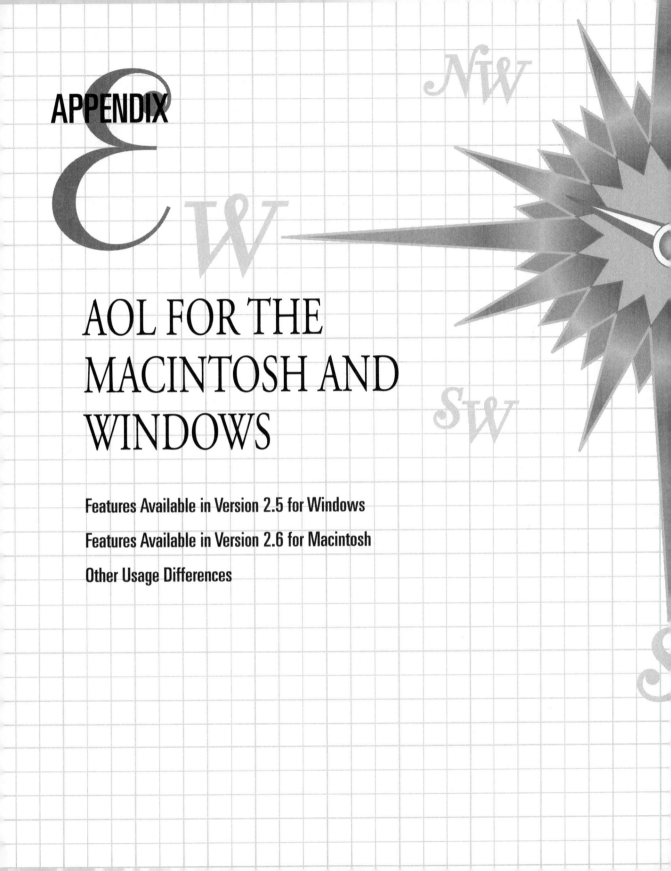

AOL FOR THE MACINTOSH AND WINDOWS

Features Available in Version 2.5 for Windows

Features Available in Version 2.6 for Macintosh

Other Usage Differences

Because the two versions of AOL—one for the Macintosh and the other for Microsoft Windows—are currently at different stages of their development, this appendix has been included to give you a better idea of the major features currently included in each version.

The current version for Windows users is 2.5 and the current version for Macintosh users is 2.6. Despite what these release numbers may seem to indicate, the Windows version is, in fact, the more recent release.

Features Available in Version 2.5 for Windows

The features listed and described in the following section are only available in the Windows version of AOL.

The Toolbar or Flashbar

To help you quickly locate many of AOL's most used features, AOL for Windows includes a toolbar across the top of the screen. Clicking on any of the icons in this toolbar causes AOL to open the service or feature it represents.

Personal Filing Cabinet

Instead of saving copies of e-mail messages you want to keep as individual files, the Personal Filing Cabinet lets you store them all as a part of AOL itself. Messages received via FlashSessions are also stored in this Filing Cabinet, and you can even ask AOL to automatically save a copy of every message you send to other people.

Your Filing Cabinet is organized into folders, some of which are defined automatically by AOL and others which you create yourself. AOL also makes use of drag-and-drop to let you easily move messages and files from folder to folder.

Note

The term folder, when used in the context of AOL's Filing Cabinet, relates to the storage area maintained by AOL. These folders should not be confused with the directories/folders used by the Macintosh and Windows 95, which store information in an entirely different format.

Favorite Places

If you discover a WWW page or AOL service that you really like and want to keep a record of it for future use, you can tell AOL to list it in your Favorite Places window by selecting the Add to Favorite Places option from the Window drop-down menu.

From then on all you need to do to return to the WWW page or service again is open the Favorite Places window and double-click on the service's menu entry. AOL takes care of the rest by opening the appropriate service or forum, or by starting the WWW browser and retrieving the desired page.

Technically, the Favorite Places feature is a part of your Personal Filing Cabinet, and as such you can edit your favorite places and even create subcategories using the tools provided by the Personal Filing Cabinet.

Integrated World Wide Web Browsing

When you open a WWW page using the Windows version of AOL, a WWW browser that is built into AOL is used. This allows AOL to interact more closely with the World Wide Web and share features such as the Compose Mail and Favorite Places windows.

Offline Newsgroup Reading

Another feature that owes its existence, in part, to the Personal Filing Cabinet, is the ability to read newsgroup articles offline. In this version of AOL you can configure your FlashSession to retrieve copies of articles in selected newsgroups and store them in your Personal Filing Cabinet.

After you have signed off, you can read the articles by opening the appropriate folder. While reading these articles, you can also create new articles and reply to those you have read. The contents of your responses will be uploaded during AOL's next FlashSession.

Graphics Editing Tools

When you open a graphics image in AOL for Windows, you can make some minor alterations to the image by selecting the **S**how Tools option from the **E**dit menu.

Doing this opens a small toolbox that allows you to rotate the image in 90-degree increments, flip and reverse the image, alter the contrast and color saturation, or remove all color from the image.

Locate Text in AOL Windows

Selecting the Find in Top Window…option from the **E**dit menu enables you to search pages of text for a specific word or words.

Multimedia Features

Provided that your computer has a sound card, AOL is capable of playing WAV and MIDI files automatically for you. In addition, if you're using Windows 95 or have installed AVI drivers, AOL can play AVI movies for you.

Features Available in Version 2.6 for Macintosh

The features in this section are only available in the Macintosh version of AOL.

Separate World Wide Web Browser

When you request a WWW page using this version of AOL, a separate program is started to display the page. As a result, there are some operational differences between this and the Windows version. (See Chapter 12, "The World Wide Web," for more details.)

FTP Upload Support via the World Wide Web Browser

The World Wide Web program included with this version includes an FTP client program that allows you to upload files to an anonymous FTP site.

> The FTP client built into AOL only allows you to download files, however, it has been suggested that upload support may become available in the future. Windows users who want to upload files to an FTP site will need to use a dedicated Winsock FTP client.

Alter Fonts and Styles in Messages

You can alter the appearance of messages you send to other Macintosh users by adding different fonts and text styles. You can include any number of font and style changes in a message, but unless the person who receives the message has all the same fonts installed, your typographical extravaganza will be displayed using the default font.

> If you send a message to someone on the Internet or to anyone using the Windows version, all your text formatting will be lost.

Text-to-Speech via Apple Plain Talk

For Power Macintosh and Macintosh AV users, AOL now includes a text-to-speech tool that "reads"—as in speaks—the contents of text files to you. You can also listen to chat sessions and instant messages using this feature.

In addition, you can also define different sounding voices for different areas and even for different screen names in an online chat area.

Multimedia Features

AOL is capable of playing MIDI sound files and System 7 sounds automatically for you. In addition, if you have installed the Apple QuickTime System extension you can play QuickTime movies using AOL.

Other Usage Differences

Because America Online tailors itself to accommodate which version of AOL you are using, you will often notice some differences in forums and other services.

For example, when you select the Search Software Library option AOL determines which version you are using and displays either the Macintosh or Windows Software Library search window. You can still visit the other software library if you want by selecting the appropriate entry in the Computing Channel or by using the correct keyword—Keyword: **Mac Software** or Keyword: **PC Software**.

By now you should also be aware that PCs use the Control (Ctrl) key while Macintoshes use the ⌘ key. Apart from this, however, each service uses the same letters and numbers to represent like features.

GLOSSARY

This glossary contains a short description of many terms that you will find mentioned in Request for Comment documents, World Wide Web pages, Internet-related magazines, and trade and public newspapers or journals. Although this list is reasonably comprehensive, the Internet has a propensity for creating new words and jargon faster than any other area of interest.

As a result, if you come across a term or piece of Internet jargon not covered here, there are a number of resources on the World Wide Web that may be able to offer you further assistance. These include:

> Collaborative Virtual HyperGlossary
> `http://www.cryst.bbk.ac.uk/glossary/index.html`
>
> WorldCom Network Services—Telecommunications Glossary
> `http://www.wiltel.com/glossary/glossary.html`
>
> The Glossary of Internet Terms
> `http://www.matisse.net/files/glossary.html`
>
> The Definitions and Acronyms Glossary
> `http://www.itsi.disa.mil/cfs/glossary.html`
>
> A Glossary of World Wide Web Terms and Acronyms
> `http://www.ncsa.uiuc.edu/SDG/Software/Mosaic/Glossary/index.html`

You may also want to obtain a copy of the FYI18—the Internet Users' Glossary from the InterNIC. This document is maintained by the User Glossary Working Group of the User Services Area of the Internet Engineering Task Force (IFTF) and is the basis on which parts of the glossary that follows was based. Where a definition is based on this FYI or other sources, the reference appears after the definition, such as [FYI18], which stands for "For Your Information" document 18.

A

acceptable use policy	Many transit networks have policies restricting the ways in which the network is used. A well-known example is NSFNET's AUP, which does not allow commercial data on the NSFNET backbone. [FYI18]
address	There are many types of addresses to be found on the Internet: e-mail addresses, IP addresses, domain names, and URLs.
address resolution	When you type a domain name into an address field, it needs to be converted to an IP address before it can be used by programs communicating via the Internet. This process is called address resolution. *See also* domain name system.
alias	Many e-mail clients allow you to define aliases or single words that represent much longer e-mail addresses. The Eudora e-mail client refers to these aliases as *nicknames*.

anonymous FTP	Using anonymous FTP, a person can retrieve files from an FTP server without the need for an account at the site that operates it.
ANSI	The American National Standard Institute is responsible for approving all U.S. standards for computer communications, software, and hardware.
application	Any computer program that can be run locally on a user's system or remotely using Telnet.
Archie	A client/server application that allows you to search FTP sites for specific files.
archive	A single file which usually contains one or more other files in a compressed format (that is, ZIP, ARC, .Z).
archive site	Any machine that permits access to its files through the use of anonymous FTP.
article	Any message sent to a Usenet newsgroup.
ARPANET	Advanced Research Projects Agency Network—A pioneering long-haul packet network funded by ARPA (now DARPA). ARPANET served as the basis for early networking research, as well as a central backbone during the development of the Internet. The ARPANET consisted of individual packet-switching computers interconnected by leased lines. [FYI4]
AUP	*See* acceptable use policy.

B

backbone	The highest level in the Internet network. NSFNET is an example of a backbone, as are AARNET and JANET.
bandwidth	Technically, the difference in Hertz (Hz) between the highest and lowest frequencies of a transmission channel. As typically used, the amount of data that can be sent through a given communications circuit. [FYI18]
BBS	*See* bulletin board system.
BFN	Bye for now.
binary	The base 2 numbering system that is the foundation for all computer operations.
binary file	Any file containing data stored in machine readable format. *See also* text file.
BinHex	The Macintosh-based program that converts binary files into ASCI text files. Once a file is encoded into this

format, you can send it using e-mail. BinHex is similar to MIME and UUENCODE, but is not directly compatible with either system.

BITNET	The network responsible for the distribution of LISTSERV mailing lists, among other things. It is operated by academic institutions to allow for the exchange of information dealing with educational pursuits. *See also* CREN.
bounce	When you send e-mail to an address that doesn't exist, the message is bounced back to you.
BRB	Be right back.
BTW	By the way.
bulletin board system	Any computer system operated for the purpose of the public exchange of electronic messages and files. BBS systems are as a rule not directly connected to the Internet, but instead use the FIDOnet network.

C

CCITT	Comite Consultatif International de Telegraphique et Telephonique—An organization that is a part of the United Nations International Telecommunication Union. It makes technical recommendations about telephone and data communications standards and acts as the regulatory body for the distribution of the standards it approves.
Channel (AOL)	At America Online, each of its main service areas are referred to as channels.
Channel (IRC)	When using IRC, each of the discussion areas or rooms are called channels.
CIX	Commercial Internet Exchange—The organization responsible for the administration of the commercial Internet backbone.
client	A computer system or process that requests a service of another computer system or process. A workstation requesting the contents of a file from a file server is a client of the file server. [RFC18]
client/server	The term used to describe the process used by many Internet services. FTP, Usenet, and WWW are all examples of client/server systems.

CREN	Corporation for Research and Education Networking—This organization is the result of the merger between CSNET and BITNET in 1989. Technically, it is now responsible for the operational oversight of BITNET.
CSNET	Computer and Science Network—When education institutions found that they were being denied access to ARPANET, they set up their own private network. CSNET no longer exists, following the creation of NSFNET and CREN.
CU Later	See you later.
cyberspace	A term coined by the novelist William Gibson to describe the electronic world he created for his series of cyberpunk novels—*Neuromancer, Count Zero,* and *Mona Lisa Overdrive.* The name has also become a popular method of describing the Internet to newbies.

D

decoding	*See* UUDECODE.
decryption	The process of converting an encrypted file back into a readable format. To do this, you need to know either the original key that the file was encrypted with or its secret key (if the file was encrypted using a public key system).
dial-up network	Any network that allows access using dial-up modems. To connect to the Internet using a dial-up network, you usually need access to either a PPP or SLIP terminal server.
distributed database	A collection of several different data repositories that looks like a single database to the user. A prime example in the Internet is the domain name system. [FYI18]
domain name system	This system provides the mechanism that allows domain names to be converted into IP addresses.

E

EEF	The Electronic Frontier Foundation was formed to address the many legal issues facing people when dealing with electronic communications using computers.
e-mail	Electronic mail—The term used to describe the electronic exchange of messages via computers and typically across the Internet.

e-mail address	The address used to describe the location of the intended recipient of an e-mail message. This address takes the form `userid@domain.name`.
encoding	*See* UUENCODE.
encryption	The process that converts a file into a seemingly scrambled format to ensure its secure transmission across the Internet. The file must then be decrypted before it can be read by anyone at the receiving end.

F

FAQ	Frequently Asked Questions—Documents published on many sites and servers that contain a list of questions and answers relating to the service on which they are contained.
finger	A small program used to display information about a person logged onto the Internet.
flame	A strongly worded message sent in response to an article posted on an Usenet newsgroup or in a mailing list.
flame war	What happens when a flame triggers a stream of responses and counter-flames.
file://	A URL protocol that defines a file which can be downloaded via FTP.
fragmentation	The IP process in which a packet is broken into smaller pieces to fit the requirements of a physical network over which the packet must pass. [FYI18]
FTP	File Transfer Protocol or File Transfer Program. A system that allows files to be transferred from one computer to another via the Internet.
FWIW	For what it's worth.
FYI	For Your Information—Documents maintained by the InterNIC that contain useful information about the Internet and its operation.

G

<G>	A grin emoticon. Also <g>, <grin>, <bg> (big grin), and <vbg> (very big grin).
gateway	A communications tool used to exchange information between different networks. America Online uses a gateway to exchange information between itself and the Internet.

GD&RFC	Grinning, ducking, and running for cover.
GIF	Graphics Interchange Format—A graphics format used to store photographic quality images. Due to legal issues surrounding the use of this image format, it is rapidly being replaced by JPEG as the format of choice.
gopher	A text-based predecessor to the World Wide Web that is still in use on many systems.
gopher://	The URL header that defines a link to a gopher site.

H

hacker	Any person who has a detailed understanding of computer systems and networks. In recent years this term has also come to refer to people who attempt to break into computer systems, although the term "cracker" more correctly applies to such people.
hardware	Any physical components of a computer system, including CPUs, keyboards, hard drives, monitors, and printers.
hierarchical routing	The complex problem of routing on large networks can be simplified by reducing the size of the networks. This is accomplished by breaking a network into a hierarchy of networks where each level is responsible for its own routing. The Internet has basically three levels: the backbones, the mid-levels, and the stub networks. The backbones know how to route between the mid-levels, the mid-levels know how to route between the sites, and each site (being an autonomous system) knows how to route internally. [FYI18]
host	A term used to refer to any computer that allows people to connect to the Internet. The new GNN Internet service is a form of host computer system.
host name	The domain name of a host computer system. America Online's host name is `aol.com`.
HTML	Hypertext Markup Language—The language used to define pages that can be displayed by World Wide Web navigators.
http://	The URL protocol entry that identifies a document as a WWW page.

I

IAB	The Internet Architecture Board oversees the Internet Engineering Task Force and the Internet Research Task Force.
IETF	The Internet Engineering Task Force is the technical body formed by the IAB to develop protocols and design strategies for the Internet.
IMHO	In my humble opinion.
Internet protocol	The Internet Protocol is defined in RFC 791 as the network layer for the TCP/IP protocol suite.
Internet registry	The registry operated by InterNIC that is responsible for the allocation of IP addresses and the registration of domain names.
IP address	The individual address assigned to every computer connected to the Internet that distinguishes it from every other machine. This address is usually represented as a dotted quad—four numbers separated by a dot, as in 192.190.215.5, which represented the IP address of my Internet host at `world.net`.
IRC	Internet Relay Chat—The CB radio of the Internet world.
IRTF	The Internet Research Task Force is charted by the IAB to examine the future of the Internet and discuss the long-term implications of services such as Internet radio and the possibility of video on demand.
ISDN	Integrated Services Digital Network—An emerging technology that is beginning to be offered by the telephone carriers of the world. ISDN combines voice and digital network services in a single medium, making it possible to offer customers digital data services as well as voice connections through a single "wire." The standards that define ISDN are specified by CCITT. [RFC1208]
ISOC	The Internet Society is a nonprofit, professional membership organization that facilitates and supports the technical evolution of the Internet, stimulates interest in and educates the scientific and academic communities, industry, and the public about the technology, uses, and applications of the Internet, and promotes the development of new applications for the system. The Society provides a forum for discussion and collaboration in the

operation and use of the global Internet infrastructure. The Internet Society publishes a quarterly newsletter, the *Internet Society News*, and holds an annual conference, INET. The development of Internet technical standards takes place under the auspices of the Internet Society with substantial support from the Corporation for National Research Initiatives under a cooperative agreement with the U.S. Federal Government. [FYI18—V. Cerf]

J

JPEG	A graphics image format developed by the Joint Photographics Experts Group. JPEG is rapidly replacing the older GIF format because of its ability to store pictures in a highly compressed format.
JPG	The file extension used by JPEG format files.
Jughead	Jonzy's Universal Gopher Hierarchy Excavation and Display—Jughead is a Gopher search tool similar to Veronica.

K

K12	A collection of newsgroups, IRC channels, and WWW pages devoted to discussions by students and educators. There are topics in these areas ranging from Kindergarten to Grade 12.
Kermit	An early file transfer protocol that is still in use on some systems. Unlike FTP, Kermit isn't a network transfer protocol but is instead a computer-to-computer protocol.

L

LAN	Local Area Network—A popular method of connecting computers in a network that are situated in the same physical location.
LISTSERV	The mailing list management software supported by BITNET.
layer	Communication networks for computers may be organized as a set of more or less independent protocols, each in a different layer (also called a *level*). The lowest layer governs direct host-to-host communication between the hardware at different hosts; the highest

consists of user applications. Each layer builds on the layer beneath it. For each layer, programs at different hosts use protocols appropriate to the layer to communicate with each other. TCP/IP has five layers of protocols; OSI has seven. The advantages of different layers of protocols is that the methods of passing information from one layer to another are specified clearly as part of the protocol suite, and changes within a protocol layer are prevented from affecting the other layers. This greatly simplifies the task of designing and maintaining communication programs. [FYI18]

lurkers

Any person who reads messages posted to newsgroups, mailing lists, or AOL message boards but does not post any responses. As a rule, newbies are encouraged to lurk for a while before participating to get the feel of the style of messages and the nature of the conversations.

M

mail gateway

A gateway that permits two separate networks to exchange electronic mail. America Online uses such a gateway to exchange messages with the Internet.

mailing list

A form of distributed messaging system that forwards a copy of every message it receives to all participants in the mailing lists. The two most common mailing list managers are LISTSERV and Majordomo.

mail server

An Internet site that acts as a post office for a number of users by collecting and distributing their electronic mail.

mailto:

The WWW URL header that defines an e-mail address.

majordomo

The mailing list manager designed for UNIX-based computer systems that is based on the popular PERL scripting language.

Martin packets

A humorous term applied to packets that turn up unexpectedly on the wrong network because of bogus routing entries. Also used as a name for a packet that has an altogether bogus (non-registered or ill-formed) Internet address. [RFC1208]

message board

Term used by America Online to describe its internal newsgroups.

MIME

Multipurpose Internet Mail Extension is regarded by many as the replacement for the tiring UUENCODE format, which sometimes cannot properly encode files

	relating to multimedia-based activities like compressed video and audio.
moderator	The term used to refer to the person who moderates or determines which messages are distributed to all the recipients of a mailing list or newsgroup.
MOO	*See* MUD.
MUD	Multi-User Dungeon—Interactive, text-based role playing games that can be played across the Internet.

N

Netiquette	A pun on "etiquette," referring to proper behavior on a network [FYI18].
network	Any collection of computers connected for the purpose of real-time data transfers. The Internet is considered to be a network of networks.
newbie	A term used to describe new Internet users.
newsfeed	In the Internet world, this refers to sites that provide access to USENET traffic, while in the commercial world it refers to services that provide access to news from organizations like Associated Press and CNN.
newsreader	A client program that can access articles stored in newsgroups on a Usenet server.
NIC	A Network Information Center—The most well known of which is the InterNIC site at `ds.internic.net`.
NNTP	Network News Transfer Protocol—This protocol allows Usenet servers to exchange newsgroup articles using the Internet instead of the older UUCP process.
NSF	National Science Foundation—The government agencies that administer the NSFNET, which for a long time was regarded as the primary backbone of the Internet.

O

OCLC	Online Computer Library Catalog—A nonprofit membership organization offering computer-based services to libraries, educational organizations, and their users. The OCLC library information network connects more than 10,000 libraries worldwide. Libraries use the OCLC system for cataloging, interlibrary loan, collection development, bibliographic verification, and reference searching. [OCLC]

P

packet	The smallest unit of data sent across a network. A generic term used to describe a unit of data at all levels of the protocol stack, but it is most correctly used to describe application data units. [FYI18]
PING	A small program used to test your Internet host's ability to reach another point on the Internet. Usually, it also reports the amount of time taken for a message to traverse the Internet as well.
POP3	The standard e-mail post office protocol that allows users to retrieve messages from their mailbox on an Internet mail server.
PPP	Point-to-Point Protocol—The common method of connecting a computer to the Internet via a dial-up connection using a serial line.

Q

QuickTime	QuickTime is a movie file format developed by Apple Computer for playing realtime multimedia movies on a desktop computer. Versions of QuickTime are available for both Macintosh and Windows-based computer systems.
Quotes	A symbol such as '>' is used in newsgroup articles and e-mail messages, to indicate a quote from a previously received message.

R

reassembly	The IP process in which a previously fragmented packet is reassembled before being passed to the transport layer. [FYI18]
remote login	The process of logging on to a computer using the Internet. *See also* Telnet.
RFC	Request for Comment Documents are an integral part of life on the Internet. Now numbering in the thousands, these documents describe all the protocols used by the Internet and discuss all natures of Internet usage. The informational RFCs are also known as FYIs, and those that contain published standards are STDs.
ROTFL	Rolling on the floor laughing.

route	The path that a packet of information takes as it travels from one host to another.
RTFM	Read the *[censored]* manual. (I'll let you work out what the F stands for. Some people say it could be "fabulous," but somehow I doubt it <G>.)

S

screen name	An America Online account name.
server	Any computer that provides services to the Internet community. FTP sites, WWW hosts, and Usenet providers are all examples of servers. To access the information contained on a server, you need to have a complementary client program running on your local system.
signature	The tag line that is appended to the end of messages by e-mail clients and Usenet newsreaders. These lines often contain quotes and information about the message's sender.
SLIP	The original serial line IP process, which allows a computer to become a part of the Internet via a dial-up connection. On most hosts, SLIP is being phased out in favor of the more reliable PPP method.
smileys	:-) and all his friends.
SMTP	Simple Mail Transfer Protocol—A protocol defined in STD 10, RFC 821, used to transfer electronic mail between computers. It is a server-to-server protocol, so other protocols are used to access the messages. [FYI18]
snail mail	A derogatory term used for mail sent through the postal service that reflects the amount of time taken for the mail to be delivered.
sneaker mail	The process of delivering mail by hand. Computer programs distributed this way are often said to have used sneakernet.
SNMP	Simple Network Management Protocol—The Internet standard protocol defined in STD 15, RFC 1157, developed to manage nodes on an IP network. It is currently possible to manage wiring hubs, toasters, jukeboxes, and so on. [FYI18]

STD	The Request for Comments documents containing official Internet standards.
Stuffit	A file compression and archive format used by Macintosh computers.

T

T1	A high-speed digital connection that can transmit data at speeds up to 1.544 megabits per second.
T3	A high-speed digital connection that can transmit data at speeds up to 44.746 megabits per second.
TCP	Transmission Control Protocol—An Internet standard transport layer protocol defined in STD 7, RFC 793. It is connection-oriented and stream-oriented, as opposed to UDP. [FYI18]
TCP/IP	The suite of protocols that allows computers to communicate with each other using the Internet.
Telnet	The standard communications protocol used for remote terminal logins across the Internet.
terminal emulator	Any computer program that emulates a terminal.
text file	A file containing only the characters that can be read by a text editor. They are often referred to as ASCII text files.
TN3270	Another version of the Telnet program that lets you log on to IBM mainframe computers by making the mainframe think that it is connected to a 3270 terminal.
TTFN	Ta ta for now—A common way to sign off services such as IRC.

U

UDP	User Datagram Protocol—An Internet standard transport layer protocol defined in STD 6, RFC 768. It is a connectionless protocol that adds a level of reliability and multiplexing to IP. [FYI18]
UNIX	The operating system developed by AT&T Bell Labs. Most Internet servers are UNIX-based. One of the main features of the UNIX operating system is its ability to handle many tasks at once. This is called multitasking.
URL	Uniform Resource Locator—This is the common method used by the World Wide Web to describe the

	location of a document by defining its type, site, and directory path, along with its name.
Usenet	A collection of thousands of topically named newsgroups, the computers that run the protocols, and the people who read and submit Usenet news. Not all Internet hosts subscribe to Usenet, and not all Usenet hosts are on the Internet. [FYI18]
UUCP	UNIX-to-UNIX Copy—This program was originally the primary method of distributing articles published in Usenet newsgroups. It has now been replaced for the most part by NNTP.
UUDECODE	The UNIX program used to convert binary files encoded as ASCII text files back to binary files.
UUENCODE	The UNIX program that converts binary files into ASCII text files. Once a file is encoded into this format, you can send it using e-mail.

V

virus	A small program that is capable of replicating itself on computer after computer in much the same way as a virus infects humans. Some computer viruses are harmless, but others are more malicious and have been known to destroy hard drives and wipe files.
virtual reality	VR is the latest catch phrase of the computer industry. It refers to computer programs that create virtual worlds where people can interact in a variety of ways. MUDs, and their counterparts, MOOs, are often referred to as text-based virtual reality environments.
VRML	A new markup language that lets people navigate around the Internet as if it were a 3D world. When used in conjunction with a WWW browser, VRML turns the WWW into a visual cyberspace.

W

W3	*See* World Wide Web.
WAIS	Wide Area Information Servers let you search thousands of documents stored on computers all over the Internet.
Web, The	A common method of referring to the World Wide Web.

worm	A lot like a computer virus. The main difference is that worms are designed primarily to work in network environments like the Internet. Not all worms are malicious—some often perform useful tasks such as roaming the World Wide Web looking for new home pages to add to indexes.
WWW	*See* World Wide Web.
World Wide Web	The Internet equivalent of AOL that allows you to navigate the Internet using a graphical point-and-click interface based on the popular hypertext system.

X

X Windows	A UNIX-based Windows environment popular with users of Sun workstations that fully supports the TCP/IP protocol as an integral part of its working environment.
X.500	A directory standard that one day may result in the creation of the ultimate white pages for the Internet.

Y

Yahoo	By far the most well-known WWW directory. It can be found at `http://www.yahoo.com/`.
YFNSA	An acronym for Your Friendly Neighborhood System Administrator.
YMMV	Your Mileage May Vary—A popular automotive term that is now used on the Internet with reference to Internet bandwidth and the performance of a TCP/IP connection.

Z

ZIP	ZIP is a file compression format developed by PKWARE. ZIP is by far the most popular compression format used by PC-based computer systems.
ZOO	Like ZIP, ZOO is also a file compression and archive system. You most often encounter files compressed into a ZOO archive, on UNIX-based computer systems.

INDEX

Add to Your Sams.net Library Today
with the Best Books for Internet Technologies

ISBN	Quantity	Description of Item	Unit Cost	Total Cost
0-672-30737-5		The World Wide Web Unleashed, Second Edition	$39.99	
0-672-30714-6		The Internet Unleashed, Second Edition	$45.00	
0-672-30667-0		Teach Yourself Web Publishing with HTML in a Week	$25.00	
1-57521-005-3		Teach Yourself More Web Publishing with HTML in a Week	$29.99	
0-672-30764-2		Teach Yourself Web Publishing with Microsoft Word in a Week	$29.99	
1-57521-039-8		Presenting Java	$25.00	
0-672-30735-9		Teach Yourself the Internet in a Week, Second Edition	$25.00	
1-57521-004-5		The Internet Business Guide, Second Edition	$25.00	
0-672-30595-X		Education on the Internet	$25.00	
0-672-30718-9		Navigating the Internet, Third Edition	$22.00	
0-672-30669-7		Plug-n-Play Internet for Windows	$35.00	
1-57521-010-X		Plug-n-Play Netscape for Windows	$29.99	
0-672-30723-5		Secrets of the MUD Wizards	$25.00	
		Shipping and Handling: See information below.		
		TOTAL		

Shipping and Handling: $4.00 for the first book, and $1.75 for each additional book. If you need to have it NOW, we can ship product to you in 24 hours for an additional charge of approximately $18.00, and you will receive your item overnight or in two days. Overseas shipping and handling adds $2.00. Prices subject to change. Call between 9:00 a.m. and 5:00 p.m. EST for availability and pricing information on latest editions.

201 W. 103rd Street, Indianapolis, Indiana 46290

1-800-428-5331 — Orders   1-800-835-3202 — FAX   1-800-858-7674 — Customer Service

Book ISBN 0-672-30763-4

What's on the Disc

The companion CD-ROM contains AOL software mentioned in the book and other useful third-party tools and utilities.

Windows 3.1 Installation Instructions

1. Insert the CD-ROM disc into your CD-ROM drive.
2. From File Manager or Program Manager, choose Run from the File menu.
3. Type `<drive>INSTALL` and press Enter, where *<drive>* corresponds to the drive letter of your CD-ROM. For example, if your CD-ROM is drive D:, type `D:INSTALL` and press Enter.
4. Follow the on-screen instructions in the installation program. Files will be installed to a directory named \AOL, unless you choose a different directory during installation.

INSTALL creates a Windows Program Manager group called AOL. This group contains icons for exploring the CD-ROM. The Guide to the CD-ROM program starts automatically once installation has been completed.

Windows 95 Installation Instructions

If Windows 95 is installed on your computer, and you have the AutoPlay feature enabled, the Guide to the CD-ROM program starts automatically whenever you insert the disc into your CD-ROM drive.

The Guide to the CD-ROM program requires at least 256 colors. For best results, set your monitor to display between 256 and 64,000 colors. A screen resolution of 640×480 pixels is also recommended. If necessary, adjust your monitor settings before using the CD-ROM.

To learn how to use the Guide to the CD-ROM program, press F1 from any screen in the program.

Macintosh Installation Instructions

1. Insert the CD-ROM disc into your CD-ROM drive.
2. When an icon for the CD appears on your desktop, open the disc by double-clicking on its icon.
3. Double-click on the icon named Guide to the CD-ROM, and follow the directions that appear.